Global
Borderlands

SERIES EDITORS: IGNACIO MARTINEZ, LESLIE WATERS, AND SAMUEL BRUNK

Also in the series:

Mexican Americans in West Texas: The Borderlands of the Edwards Plateau and the Trans-Pecos, by Arnoldo De León

Indigenous Autonomy at La Junta de los Rios

Traders, Allies, and Migrants on New Spain's Northern Frontier

Robert Wright

TEXAS TECH UNIVERSITY PRESS

This book is typeset in EB Garamond. The paper used in this book meets the minimum requirements of ANSI/NISO Z39.48-1992 (R1997). ♾

Designed by Hannah Gaskamp
Cover designed by Hannah Gaskamp

Library of Congress Cataloging-in-Publication Data

Names: Wright, Robert, 1946– author. Title: Indigenous Autonomy at La Junta de Los Rios: Traders, Allies, and Migrants on New Spain's Northern Frontier / Robert Wright. Other titles: Traders, Allies, and Migrants on New Spain's Northern Frontier | Global Borderlands.
Description: Lubbock: Texas Tech University Press, [2023] | Series: Global Borderlands | Includes bibliographical references and index. | Summary: "A detailed research study exploring the unique history of Indigenous nations in the valley of the Rio Grande that is now Ojinaga and Chihuahua, Mexico, and Presidio, Texas—the La Junta valley in the colonial period—and their dealings with Hispanic military personnel and civilians and Franciscan missionaries"—Provided by publisher.
Identifiers: LCCN 2023024267 (print) | LCCN 2023024268 (ebook) |
ISBN 978-1-68283-191-5 (cloth) | ISBN 978-1-68283-192-2 (ebook)
Subjects: LCSH: Indians of North America—Texas—La Junta de los Ríos—Government relations. | Indians of North America—Texas—La Junta de los Ríos—Economic conditions—18th century. | Indians of North America—Colonization—Texas—La Junta de los Ríos. | Indians of North America—Cultural assimilation—Texas—La Junta de los Ríos. | Indians of North America—Missions—Texas—La Junta de los Ríos. | La Junta de los Ríos (Tex.)—History.
Classification: LCC F392.L33 W75 2023 (print) | LCC F392.L33 (ebook) |
DDC 976.4933—dc23/eng/20230530
LC record available at https://lccn.loc.gov/2023024267
LC ebook record available at https://lccn.loc.gov/2023024268

Printed in the United States of America
23 24 25 26 27 28 29 30 31 / 9 8 7 6 5 4 3 2 1

Texas Tech University Press
Box 41037
Lubbock, Texas 79409-1037 USA
800.832.4042
ttup@ttu.edu
www.ttupress.org

To the people of the Rio Grande country in Texas who have befriended and taught me since 1973, and to the Missionary Oblates of Mary Immaculate, my religious family, who first entered the Rio Grande country in 1849 and have dedicated their lives to the people there ever since. *¡Que Dios les cuide a todos!*

Contents

Illustrations

Acknowledgments

Two colleagues, both since departed from this life, drew me into writing a book that I had not originally intended. Twenty years ago, Eva Maria Flores asked me to be part of a panel at a West Texas Historical Association conference. I had not researched anything on Trans-Pecos Texas, but I had a continuing interest in religion and society in the Rio Grande borderlands. So I decided to write an essay on the early church and society in the Trans-Pecos region between 1848 and 1900. That resolution led me to the discovery that the first clergy upon whom the people of the Trans-Pecos depended were from Presidio del Norte (now Ojinaga) on the Mexican side of the Rio Grande. This piqued my interest in the history of settlement at that place, known as La Junta de los Rios during most of the Spanish colonial period. Local historian Enrique Madrid graciously welcomed me into his home and introduced me to the history and archaeology of the area, and the priest at the Ojinaga parish of Jesús Nazareno allowed me to study the church records dating back to the later 1700s. When Jefferson Morgenthaler asked at the 2011 meeting of the Texas State Historical Association (TSHA) for someone to share a panel on La Junta with him the following year, I promptly volunteered. I did not realize at the time that he had privately published a book on La Junta in 2007. At the 2012 TSHA meeting, I was surprised that his presentation of the mission history at La Junta was very negative, in contrast to my positive presentation. That set me to research the history more thoroughly whenever I could find the time and wherever I could. What I discovered became more and more fascinating and called for many revisions in the previous historical accounts.

The research materials included many archival collections, in person and online, as well as primary and secondary literature published in the United States and Mexico. As any historian is well aware, scholarly work is built upon the research and leads provided by many others. Archivists are unfailingly generous in going out of their way to help locate resources. I am indebted to all, but in a special way to Nancy Brown Martinez at the Center for Southwest Research and Special Collections in the Zimmerman Library at the University of New Mexico; Dennis Daily at New Mexico State University who gave me access to the closed collections there during the Covid shutdown; Marisa Jefferson at the Briscoe Center for American History at the University of Texas at Austin who tracked down items in other collections; and Donna Guerra at the Sisters of Charity of the Incarnate Word Archives in San Antonio. A special thanks to Carmen Rodriguez at the O'Shaughnessy Library at Oblate School of Theology in San Antonio, who did an amazing job of obtaining interlibrary loan material. A special thanks also to Bradley Folsom and the anonymous readers of successive manuscripts of this book, who made valuable suggestions to improve the text, and to the editor of the university press who first agreed to consider the initial manuscript for publication. That press ultimately decided not to publish, prompting me to further research and revisions that have greatly improved (and augmented!) the text. Finally, I am most grateful to Travis Snyder and his colleagues at Texas Tech University Press for enthusiastically accepting this work and for all the effort they have put into it this past year.

Indigenous Autonomy at La Junta de los Rios

Introduction

U nknown to most, a remote river valley along what is now the international border between West Texas and the Mexican state of Chihuahua is "one of the oldest continuously inhabited places in the vast Chihuahuan Desert, ranking in age and dignity with the Anasazi pueblos of New Mexico." Several Native American groups who maintained self-ruling permanent towns there formed "a more or less homogeneous cultural unit" for centuries.[1] The principal towns in this valley today are Ojinaga on the Mexican side and Presidio on the Texas side. When Spanish explorers arrived in the 1500s, they called the place La Junta de los Rios, "the junction of the rivers," since it is there that the Rio Conchos, flowing northward through the state of Chihuahua, replenishes the Rio Grande flowing southeasterly from El Paso. In colonial times the Rio Grande in this region was called the Rio del Norte, due to its origins far to the north in upper New Mexico.[2] That is the name used in this study. The valley is enclosed on all sides by mountains beyond which stretch semi-arid lands. Even today it is a journey of more than 130 miles in every direction to reach a town that has a population of over 10,000. Such distances were even greater in colonial times.[3] From the river junction the augmented Rio del Norte proceeds to the southeast to enter the canyons that form the great bowl-shaped curve known as the Big Bend, the name now given to the major national park in that area of West Texas.

Contrary to what several historians have concluded, all but one of the core Native[4] groups settled at La Junta remained there at mostly permanent locations from the time of the first Spanish expeditions in the 1580s until the dramatic events of the 1760s.[5] Each of these groups had its colonial name, mostly Native in origin. Colonial writers and modern historians have used various collective titles for all the groups taken together—Jumanos, Patarabueyes, Julimes, Norteños, Cholomes—but those names are either incorrect or inadequate if not properly delimited. I have chosen the simple solution of using the Spanish place name to indicate all the permanent villagers in the valley, thus "the Juntans." Whenever the sources permit, I give the specific name of each group.

This narrative recounts the history of the Juntans prior to the first probable Spanish contact by the castaway party of Álvar Núñez Cabeza de Vaca in 1535, the various Spanish expeditions in the next century and a half, the resultant occupations of many

Figure 1: North Central New Spain along the Rio del Norte / Rio Grande. (By Robert E. Wright)

Juntans as seasonal migrant laborers and military auxiliaries among Hispanics[6] in Nueva Vizcaya, the sporadic establishment of Franciscan missions beginning in the 1680s, and the major crises of the 1760s that led to the flight or removal of the Juntans from their ancestral valley and their voluntary resettlement in Coahuila up through the 1780s.

The Juntans, the La Junta District, and the Coyame Valley

It is very important to recognize that what Hispanics called the La Junta district included more than the La Junta valley. The people in a village immediately across the steep mountain ridge that the Spaniards named the Cuesta Grande, that formed the southwest barrier to the valley, were physically and ethnically related to the Juntans. Therefore, the Spaniards considered that village to be part of the larger La Junta district. The Spaniards called their village Cuchillo Parado (upright knife), presumably due to its lying at the foot of the Cuesta Grande. When Franciscan missions were finally formally established in the district by the colonial government in 1715, two settlements of the Cholomes not too distant from Cuchillo Parado were also assigned to these Franciscans' care. Since the La Junta valley towns and these three trans-mountain villages were one single Franciscan mission district with its core in the La Junta valley, Hispanics of those times generally referred to the entire area as the "La Junta district."

To distinguish this trans-mountain section from the La Junta valley, I call it the Coyame valley. This takes account of the fact that the small stream named the Arroyo Coyame that empties into the Rio Conchos just below Cuchillo Parado flows down

4

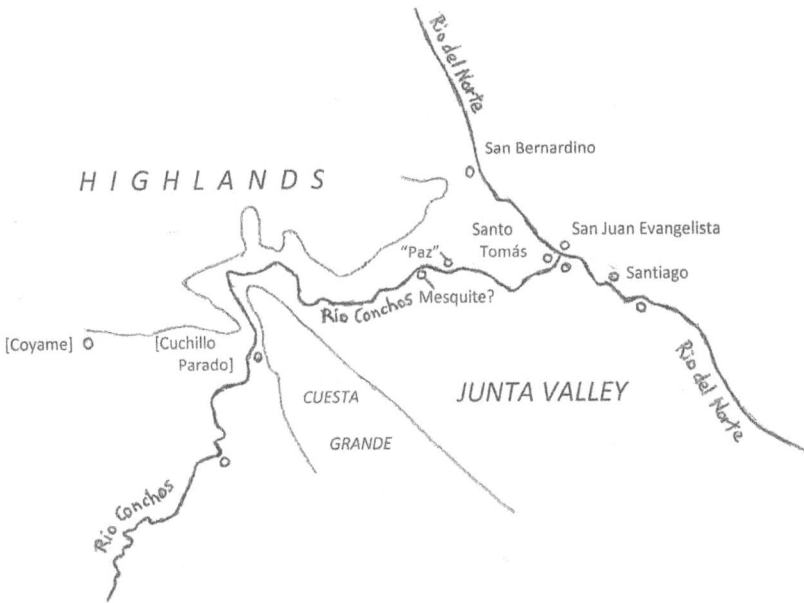

Figure 2: La Junta district in 1583. (By Robert E. Wright)

from the former Cholome town of Coyame to the west. It also has the advantage that the present-day municipio (Mexican county) of Coyame includes not only Cuchillo Parado but also the other colonial Cholome village named San Pedro, on the Rio Conchos just across some ridges to the south of Cuchillo Parado. Thus, although the La Junta valley is the core part of the La Junta district, that district in colonial times included both the La Junta and the Coyame valleys.[7] In the 1700s the Hispanics of central Nueva Vizcaya referred to the nations of the La Junta valley or even the entire La Junta district as the Norteños. By the 1720s this was typically "a generic reference to the La Junta peoples" within the La Junta valley, but by midcentury it referred to "all peoples from the general La Junta area" or district. However, it was also still used sometimes to denote only those in the La Junta valley itself.[8]

As stated above, I employ the name "Juntans" as a shorthand way to refer only to the permanently resident nations in the La Junta valley itself. I do this to distinguish them not only from other Native groups who only resided temporarily in the La Junta valley but also from the people in the Coyame valley. The historical record reveals an important difference in relations with Hispanics by most of the permanently settled Natives of the La Junta valley—the Juntans—in contrast to many of the Natives in the Coyame valley, the Cholomes in particular. The failure to clearly make this necessary distinction has led some authors to several gross overgeneralizations and to an unjustifiably negative history of the relations between Hispanics and the permanent residents of the La Junta valley.

The Juntans and the Hispanic world

Although the Native settlements of the La Junta district were always far beyond the Spanish frontier, their migrant labor in the agricultural fields of central Nueva Vizcaya, especially in the valley of San Bartolomé and later in the greater Chihuahua district, requires that an explanation of their history include the territory extending to the south and southwest of La Junta for over 200 miles—that is, the eastern half of today's Mexican state of Chihuahua that was the northeastern part of the earlier colonial province of Nueva Vizcaya.

Up until 1760, there were only two Hispanic settlers, and no military, who are known to have briefly resided anywhere near La Junta, and they were quickly gone. That was how the Juntans, determined to retain their autonomy like all nations, wanted it.[9] They did welcome one group of Hispanic residents, however. Those were Franciscan missionaries, unaccompanied by military or civilians, at irregular intervals from the 1680s through the 1750s. This situation was practically unique in the history of the northern frontier of New Spain. The typical account of Native encounters with Hispanics is full of stories about Hispanic soldiers, missionaries, and civilians all moving within a relatively brief time into Native lands. This is not one of those stories.

It was only after hostile Native raids began ravaging the zone between Chihuahua and the Rio del Norte from El Paso to La Junta in the 1750s that the Hispanic military treacherously installed themselves in the heart of the La Junta valley on Christmas Eve of 1759. That action, followed only seven years later by the removal of the presidio and all the Native town-dwellers, drove many of the Juntans to seek out a situation beyond Nueva Vizcaya where they could still maintain at least a relative autonomy as a people within the encroaching Spanish empire. Even though a presidio was reestablished in the La Junta valley in 1773, indeed probably because of the presidio, the Juntans never returned to their ancestral valley. La Junta would no longer have its original townspeople. The story of the La Junta valley itself after 1773, that of a Hispanic frontier outpost with no Juntans and no missions, is a very different history, to be told by others.[10]

In her impressive study of central Nueva Vizcaya up through the early decades of the 1700s, Chantal Cramaussel's unfamiliarity with the La Junta district allowed her to unduly generalize her conclusions to apply to all of Nueva Vizcaya throughout the colonial period:

> [The Spaniards] did not recognize the original towns of the Natives nor even their persons of authority other than the offices given them in the missions by the Spaniards. . . . In the colonial period the only "towns of Indians" were the mission towns. For this reason we do not see in the north what happened in the center of the viceroyalty, the development of a strong Indian stratum capable of defending its interests or, at least, those of its local oligarchy. In Nueva Vizcaya the Indians never had

their own voice, rather they were always subordinated to "intermediaries" whether the protector of Indians, the secular priest, or the Jesuit or Franciscan missionary upon whom they were dependent.[11]

None of these statements are true of La Junta. In fact, any situations comparable to that at La Junta are extremely rare along the entire northern frontier. Nowhere else can there be demonstrated to have been a long-term residence of missionaries without accompanying Hispanic military and civilians within hundreds of miles. The Zuñi and Hopi districts in New Mexico–Arizona that had Franciscan missionaries from 1629 to 1680 were also very distant from Hispanic settlements, but they had an at least intermittent presence of non-missionary Hispanic residents, even if very few at a time. The same held true for the Zuñi mission in the 1700s. And yet, due to the long-distance labor of Juntans within Hispanic colonial farms, they assimilated much more of the Hispanic culture than the Zuñis and the Hopis did. The only other district on the northern frontier that was more comparable to La Junta was that of the Yaquis and the Jesuit missionaries on the Sinaloa coast from 1617 to about the year 1675, when Hispanics began to move much closer to them. The Yaquis also engaged in long-distance work among Hispanics. But almost nothing is known about the situation in their homeland between 1633 and the decade of the 1680s. As Jefferson Morgenthaler wrote: "La Junta provides a vivid example of Spanish frontier activity, an example entirely distinct from experiences elsewhere."[12]

At the outset this study of the interrelations of Juntans with Hispanics had in mind only the period when they were living within their traditional homeland—that is, up to 1766—assuming that after that they disappeared fairly rapidly as a distinctive group through absorption into the Hispanic world.[13] But the research took a surprising and yet, in hindsight, very predictable turn in discovering and tracing their voluntary relocation beyond Nueva Vizcaya from 1760 to 1786. That discovery also required a closer look at the nearest Native settlements in Nueva Vizcaya south of the La Junta district during that period, those near the junction of the San Pedro River with the Rio Conchos.

The Historical Record

Documentation discovered so far for life within the La Junta valley is relatively rare, unlike that for other frontier districts like upper New Mexico, central Chihuahua, central Texas, and California that have been the habitual haunt of historians of the Spanish colonial period. There are no known extant church registers from the missions that existed within the La Junta valley for six decades. Correspondence or reports from the missionaries are extremely limited. Most of our information comes from rare military expeditions. Even then, since the documentation is from Hispanic sources, the vision obtained is necessarily from a Hispanic perspective. Yet Hispanics themselves often differed in their perceptions, at times dramatically. Every effort has been made to raise the voices of the Natives of the La Junta district whenever possible. And, since indeed "actions speak louder than words," the actions of the Natives, themselves not always in agreement with each other, go a long way in revealing their own perspectives.

The perennial geographic remoteness of the La Junta district even to this day and its marginal location on the edge of every successive human empire or political territory has resulted in its people and their history being unknown by the general public and hardly noted even in state histories. Its dedicated scholars have been few and far between, and their work has hardly made a dent in general historical surveys.[14] This study is an effort to substantially broaden and deepen the story of the Juntans and their relations with Hispanics as well as with other Native groups, hopefully bringing about more deserved recognition of these remarkable people. While the focus is upon the La Junta district, the larger context of the history of northern New Spain, particularly what are today the Mexican state of Chihuahua and the western section of Texas, are necessarily considered. Multiple issues intersect that are common to the northern frontier, although often realized in a distinctive way in the La Junta district: intercultural encounters, Native autonomy and subordination, labor arrangements, evangelization processes, and hostilities and alliances among Native groups and with Hispanics. The very uniqueness of the La Junta district helps to shed greater light on these broader issues.

As in all historical research, this account is built upon the previous studies of others, several of whom have already been noted. I have endeavored as much as possible to go back to the original sources while discovering new ones, in the process making many corrections to the record. The story of the La Junta valley and the Juntans in particular is too unusual, too fascinating, too deeply reflective of human aspirations and interactions, to leave in oblivion. The Juntans were a peaceable yet powerful people who were initially strongly admired and relied upon by Spaniards and Hispanics as allies for seven decades. And yet they were for the most part treated as enemies when frontier conditions fell into turmoil and unsubstantiated suspicions were allowed to dictate colonial policy. So goes the story of fearful empires—a lesson still unheeded by many today. Yet, through it all, the people of the La Junta district refused to surrender their autonomy to missionary or governor.

Long-Distance Encounters, 1535–1583

It was a permanent settlement and the people were very clean, handsome, and war-like, the best featured we had encountered thus far. . . . We asked them if any men like us had passed that way, and they replied that a long time ago four Christians had passed through there. By the descriptions they gave, we realized clearly that the leader must have been Álvar Núñez Cabeza de Vaca.

—Hernán Gallegos, 1581

In all these pueblos the visitors were received with much rejoicing, and music similar to that of the flute but made with the mouth. The Indians of this community are all farmers; even though they live in pueblos, they have flat-roofed houses in their fields. Besides these three cities there are many others and many rancherías.

—Diego Pérez de Luján, 1582

In the Christian calendar, it was the year 1535. The Natives of a town in a river valley that most scholars conclude was La Junta were told by two Native women sent to them as messengers that a very unusual party was approaching them. The two women returned to the wandering strangers to tell them that they had found at the Native town "very few people, since all had gone buffalo hunting."[1] It would be another four decades before the first definitely recorded visit of Spaniards to the La Junta valley. By then Spanish frontier outposts had leapfrogged from central Mexico to within 300 miles of La Junta. That brought far-ranging slave hunters, poisoning relations that had to be remedied by the first Spanish *entradas* (formal exploratory expeditions) passing through the district in the early 1580s. From those expeditions would come the first demonstrable as well as most detailed descriptions of the Juntans and their way of life at first contact.

First Encounter

The four lost travelers, three Spaniards including Álvar Núñez Cabeza de Vaca and the Moorish African Estevanico, had every reason to be delighted with their encounter with the Juntans. It was the most encouraging moment so far in their years-long odyssey. As the last-known survivors of the ill-fated Panfilo de Narváez exploration of Florida in 1528, barely seven years after the Spanish conquest of the Aztec capital of central Mexico, they had become totally destitute castaways enslaved for years by Natives along the Texas coast in their attempt to get back to those other Spaniards.[2] When they finally managed to escape in 1534, their relations with other Natives in their long trek across the continent vastly improved when they began to heal the ill among them by praying and blowing upon them while making the sign of the cross.[3] Treated thereafter with great reverence and indeed fear, they were escorted from one Native band to another and showered with gifts as they sought to find their way overland. Immediately preceding their arrival in what was presumably the La Junta valley, they had been guided across one of the continent's most daunting features: the Bolson de Mapimí, more than 125 miles of extremely rough and arid mountains with no human habitation, before crossing a large river (probably the Rio del Norte) and entering some plains.[4]

What a phenomenal spectacle the "Old World" strangers with their never-before-seen physical features must have been to the Juntans. In the passage of Cabeza de Vaca's travel account that most commentators interpret as about the La Junta valley, he wrote of "a river flowing between some mountains" where there was a town that had "the first houses that we saw that looked like real houses" permanently established (*de asiento*). They found the land to be well populated (*muy poblada*), as they went upriver to "other permanent houses (*otras casas de asiento*) the next day."[5] "The people were of the best physique that we saw, and of a greater acuity and ability, and understood and responded better to our questions." The males went about "completely naked," while the women and a few men not useful for war, particularly old ones, were clothed in deerskins.

Cabeza de Vaca reported that the people ate beans and calabashes, as well as corn brought from the west. Asked why they themselves were not sowing corn, they responded that they did not want to lose the crop as they had the previous two years, due to the great drought they were experiencing. Not having cooking pots, they filled half of a large gourd with water and threw heated stones into it to obtain boiling water with which to cook. The travelers were given buffalo robes and deerskins. The Spaniards named these people the people of the cows, since that was the closest species they knew to the buffalo of the Great Plains, "the greater part of [which] are killed close to here, and for more than 125 miles upriver they kill many of them." They were told that although upriver the people spoke the same language as those in this valley, the two were enemies. They were also told that those people upriver would give these fearsome travelers many cotton blankets and deerskins, but there would be nothing to eat for many days. And so it was, although what the travelers received were buffalo robes, not cotton blankets.[6]

This description has many striking similarities to the accounts of the first Spanish explorers passing through the La Junta valley decades later. Indeed, it probably influenced those later reports, since the story of Cabeza de Vaca and his companions, promptly published upon their return to the fledgling colony of New Spain, spread like wildfire among ambitious Spaniards. That was due not only to its incredible novelty. Cabeza de Vaca wrote that some Natives he encountered told him that the emeralds they treasured came from towns in some very high mountains to the north with many people and very large houses. In a time when fables about the New World were given high credence, that was enough incentive for adventurous spirits to set out in search of a wealthy "New" Mexico City, a *Nueva México.*[7]

The Land and the Juntans

The vast Chihuahuan desert that surrounds the La Junta valley for hundreds of miles extends from what is now the southern edge of New Mexico deep into north central Mexico. The winters are cool and the summers very hot. Given such characteristics, "the environment is hostile to people and can support only small populations." In the midst of this vast stretch of high semi-arid flatlands punctuated by rugged ridges and mountains, the La Junta valley was and is an oasis.[8] It differs from the other valleys along the Rio del Norte below El Paso in that it has a major river flowing into it, the Rio Conchos. In fact, in historical times the Rio Conchos has always been by far the larger of the two streams at that point, replenishing the flow of the Rio del Norte. Otherwise, the valley terrain is the same all along the river:

> The Rio Grande [del Norte], from southern New Mexico to the Big Bend Region of Texas, occupies a narrow alluvial valley restricted on both sides by mountain ranges or barren gravel pediments and terraces. Stretches of open valley land up to five miles in width and tens of miles in length alternate with gorges or canyons throughout this stretch of the river. . . . The valley alluvium is sandy and uncompacted, and in the wider valleys the course of the river channel changes often, leaving many sloughs and marshy areas after the periodic floods. Climactically, this region is arid. . . . [It] has a frequency of 10 desert years out of every 20 years. The region, therefore, cannot support agriculture except through temporal or riverine irrigation, or as at present, by river diversion irrigation.

When Native agriculture developed in the La Junta valley, then, it would be principally through riverine irrigation—that is, by growing crops on the lowlands along the river when high water spread out over them without totally inundating them.[9]

Various nations of hunter-gatherers and intertribal traders traversed the vast expanses of the Chihuahuan desert by relying upon scattered water sources. As a rare larger oasis in the middle of such lands, the La Junta valley served as an important destination for Native traders spread across the 500-mile southern edge of the vast semi-arid Great Plains region, from today's northwestern Chihuahua to the present San Antonio vicinity (see figure 1). It was along such a trade route that the Cabeza de Vaca party was guided by Natives in 1535.[10] But this oasis was so remote and unattractive economically—with cyclical droughts, no mineral deposits, and accessible only through lands often frequented by hostile Natives—that among Europeans not even missionaries attempted to reside there until the 1680s, a century after the first expeditions in the 1580s and eight decades after the colonization of New Mexico much further north.

Thus, the La Junta valley was nowhere close to being a Nueva México. But it contained the final, even if less advanced, extension of the Southwest agricultural town culture that originated among the Mogollon and Anasazi peoples of New Mexico and Arizona. Archaeologists estimate that this culture reached the La Junta valley as early as AD 1200. Certain local peculiarities suggest that these traits may not have been due to the migration of a new people into the La Junta area but rather to cultural elements diffused through trade relations into preexisting mobile hunter-gatherer populations dating back several thousand years. In any event, there is universal agreement that the culture of the valley people was "an admixture of Southwestern and [Texas] Plains elements, and the more recent phases were less Southwestern and more nearly Plains in affiliation."[11] From the vantage point of more recent yet still nonconclusive archaeological research, Mallouf hypothesized that the people of the La Junta valley "never fully made the transition to a sedentary, agricultural-based existence. Instead, their material assemblages reflect semi-sedentary lifeways with continued strong reliance on hunting and gathering as a means of supplementing their agricultural stores."[12] This remains a hypothesis that I find expressed too strongly, as explained below.

All the known agricultural town-dwelling sites in the La Junta district were established before 1400, including at least forty miles up the Rio Conchos from its junction with the Rio del Norte. The permanent housing was typically rectangular, with interior wooden posts supporting a probably flat multilayered roof through which one entered the room. The architectural influence and much of the earlier pottery have recently been attributed to the Tularosa Basin in northeastern New Mexico, with some pottery also coming from Casas Grandes in northwestern Chihuahua. Mescal-processing pits were scattered along the river.

Shortly after 1400 the number of villages became reduced to those encountered by Spaniards in the 1580s, possibly due to sustained drought conditions, nomadic pressure, and the breakup of the Casas Grandes–El Paso interaction sphere. Very few ceramics have been discovered dating to this period, leading to the dual hypotheses that either the sedentary agriculturalists abandoned the area (Kelley) or all the local people reverted to a largely hunter-gatherer economy (Mallouf) for more than a century. When agriculture and pottery finally reemerged around 1550, there was an absolute break from the previous imported pottery style, now replaced by plain red-and-brown vessels in simple forms like that of the Río Conchos culture to the southwest and the Plains culture to the northeast. The many side-by-side rectangular houses excavated at the Juntan town of San Cristóbal from this period were four times larger than before 1400. Jacal walls and very thick interior posts, often over a foot and a half in diameter, supported the flat roofs with wood beams. Several fire locations were evident inside each house. This all suggests that each of these large rooms housed several family units, possibly an extended family.[13]

Archaeologists hypothesize that the effort that had to be invested in different house forms indicates the degree of the mobility of the inhabitants.[14] The evidence that the rooms in the principal La Junta towns after 1550 were much larger, lined up side-by-side, and undoubtedly contained more people within them, and that the support posts were much thicker all points to an even greater energy investment than previously. By itself, therefore, the archaeological record supports a great degree of commitment to a sedentary lifestyle after 1550, without negating the continuing strong presence of arrow points and stone tools necessary for a hunting dimension within the settlements.[15]

Archaeological indications of non-Christian religious practice at La Junta are almost nonexistent. Limited archaeological investigations in the entire eastern Trans-Pecos region have turned up some evidence of the religious-ceremonial lives of non-sedentary groups outside the La Junta valley. Highly abstract and stylized petroglyphs may be impossible to decipher, but their mere existence along with the use of mountain-top sites and non-practical objects such as beaded rattles and prayer sticks along with the careful preparation of the dead for burial all substantiate the practice of ritualism among these non-sedentary groups.[16] But only one item of plausible Indigenous religious significance, a probable fetish figure found at the lower extreme of the valley, has been noted in the published reports about the La Junta settlements during the prehistoric period.[17]

The earliest Spanish chroniclers described the people of the La Junta valley as attractive, welcoming, joyful, highly intelligent, in a well-ordered society and very capable of defending their settlements.[18] Chroniclers and archaeologists have described the town layouts and dwellings in the entire La Junta district, the people's instruments, and their means of sustenance. But little else is known about their culture and social structure.[19] The earliest chroniclers noted that there were two principal languages spoken in the La Junta valley and probably two others in the Coyame valley. Much later we learn that each village had its own lands, within which property was privately owned. We hear of chiefs, captains, and occasionally caciques. But even though missionaries worked among the people for seven decades and researchers have sifted through archaeological sites, there is very little known about their Native religion. Other than certain described gestures of reverence and celebration, "notably lacking are references to shamans, priests, medicine bundles, fetishes, maize pollen, prayer sticks, and ceremonial houses."[20] This is due in great part to the scant extant correspondence from missionaries, but even that correspondence never explicitly mentions Native religious leaders nor items. Nor do such items clearly appear in the archaeological record. In this respect also, La Junta was no Nueva México.

The Spanish Colonial Advance to the North

The report of large cities and precious gems far to the north in the accounts of Cabeza de Vaca and his companions prompted the Coronado expedition in the early 1540s. Francisco Vázquez de Coronado's army approached today's US Southwest using the route hundreds of miles to the west of the La Junta valley by which Cabeza de Vaca had descended toward Culiacán along the Pacific coast. Coronado's expensive *entrada*, carried out in completely different terms of engagement than that of the totally Native-dependent Cabeza de Vaca party, was nevertheless an abject failure for the Spaniards. Among the Pueblo Natives of upper New Mexico it left a bitter taste and very negative memories. To disappointed Spaniards it demonstrated that *la Nueva México* was much less than a new Mexico City.[21]

When silver discoveries began to be made much closer to central New Spain along the eastern edge of the Sierra Madre Occidental, interest in thousand-mile adventures beyond the northern frontier like that of Coronado quickly faded. The rich mines of Zacatecas were opened in 1546, and prospectors feverishly worked their way northward. In 1567 the mining town of Santa Barbara was founded almost 300 miles below the river junction at La Junta (see figure 1). The newcomers began developing farm lands in the Valle de San Bartolomé (today's Valle de Allende), somewhat closer to La Junta, that became the major agricultural center to feed the miners and merchants of all of central Nueva Vizcaya. Nueva Vizcaya had only been organized as a colonial province in 1563, with Durango, 270 miles south of Santa Barbara, as its capital.[22]

Such rapid developments, jumping forward hundreds of miles, manifest the eagerness with which Spaniards were seeking their fortunes in the heady first century of conquest in New Spain. The mining, farming, and ranching operations around Santa Barbara needed laborers, and many Spaniards had no qualms about enslaving Indigenous people to add to their workers recruited from further south in New Spain. Even though Spain's New Laws of 1542 abolished wholesale Indian slavery, "rebellious" groups could still be legally enslaved when captured by punitive expeditions. This legal pretext was continually abused, with Spanish raiders and military commanders throughout the northern frontier capturing "hostile" Natives for profit. In the Santa Barbara–San Bartolomé district, some slaves were put to work in the nearby mines or used for household labor, while others were taken to central Mexico.[23]

The Chamuscado Expedition, 1581–1582

In the summer of 1581, the people of the La Junta district apprehensively awaited a slowly approaching small caravan led by armed Iberians from the distant Santa Barbara district. By that time the saga of Coronado's stinging disappointment in New Mexico forty years earlier had practically disappeared from the memory of frontiersmen. Rumors resurfaced of a great Nueva México beyond the northern frontier, and Cabeza de Vaca's *Naufragios y comentarios* seemed to have been read by or told to every prospector in Nueva Vizcaya. Eight Spaniards and one Portuguese mounted on horses were accompanied by three Franciscans and nineteen Native servants including two women. They were herding 600 stock animals and ninety saddle and pack horses. Indigenous nations in their path probably hoped that their slow progress with plodding herds and pack animals loaded with trade items signaled non-hostile intentions. Indeed, Native messengers sent ahead by the expedition leaders announced that they were coming in peace.[24]

Nevertheless, Natives had reason to be guarded. By the early 1570s Spanish slaving parties ordered by Francisco and Diego de Ibarra, the founders of the province of Nueva Vizcaya, had reached as far as the Coyame valley. Since Francisco, the younger Ibarra, died in 1575, these incursions must have taken place by that year.[25] During those same years a child subsequently named Pedro by his Spanish masters was among those carried off from a village just inside the La Junta valley, by raiders led by Mateo González, chief of Juan de Zubia, captain from the mines of Santa Barbara. It was this raiding party that gave the name of Patarabueyes to the valley people—a nickname that did not last.[26] In 1578 a Franciscan visitor was scandalized by the Spaniards from the Santa Barbara region who regularly pillaged and enslaved the Natives. He was shocked to see "a great multitude of Indians chained to each other" in the San Bartolomé Valley, guarded by about forty Spaniards.[27]

The Spanish expedition in 1581 was ostensibly led by a Franciscan Religious, Agustín Rodríguez, as favored by the revised royal policy of 1573 precisely in order to prevent slaving expeditions. Fray Agustín was accompanied by two other friars, Francisco López and Juan de Santa María. But the real leader was the hopeful prospector Francisco Sánchez, nicknamed Chamuscado, the "singed" or red-bearded one. Descending the Rio Conchos toward La Junta, they first passed through territory frequented by Conchos Natives whom they reported as receiving them hospitably.[28] Beyond the Concho nation they were accompanied by a group for whom the expedition chronicler, Hernán Gallegos, had no kind words: non-agricultural Natives who called themselves the Yoslli and apparently spoke a different language. According to Gallegos they were "naked like savages," "very ill-featured" (*muy mal agestada*), "lazy," and "dirty." Those characterizations are probably why the contemporary writer Obregón classified them under the more generic Spanish name of *chichimecos*. They survived on squash, ground mesquite beans, prickly pear fruit, *mixcale*, and fish from the river. Proceeding further down the river the Spaniards met a people whom they called Cabris, at the base of the rough mountainous ridges that included the Cuesta Grande beyond which lay the La Junta valley. Thus they had traversed the Rio Conchos or eastern section of the Coyame valley to arrive at the place later named Cuchillo Parado (see figure 2).[29]

These people differed dramatically from those encountered previously. Although they also went about "naked" and spoke a different language than the Conchos, they were described as "very handsome, spirited, and much more active and intelligent," indeed "very well built." They were "cleaner and more modest" than the Conchos. The men had short-cropped hair like a skullcap, and their faces, arms, and bodies were painted with neat stripes. They grew squash and beans in season, but otherwise survived on ground mesquite beans, prickly pear fruit, and *mixcal*.[30] The people in the La Junta valley on the upper reaches of the Conchos and Norte Rivers would be described in several similar ways. Hence these Cabris would come to be seen by the Spanish as part of the larger La Junta district.

Told by Native messengers from Chamuscado's group that these Spaniards were going to be their friends and reconcile them with their enemies, these people came out in great numbers, offering large amounts of their food stores in the traditional Native gesture of hospitality. They told the Spaniards that other Natives in the area had fled into the mountains, out of fear caused by the earlier slaving raids ordered by the Ibarras. Through an interpreter Chamuscado assured them that from then on Spaniards would be their friends and allies. They were startled when he then had his men fire "quite a few harquebus shots" and told them that they would all be killed if they misbehaved. Faced with this threatening style of introduction, the Cabris replied that they would be happy not to offend the Spaniards in any way—and that the Spaniards should conduct themselves likewise.[31] The Spaniards then established a peace sign:

> We told the Indians, in order that they might know that the Spaniards were their friends and would not harm them further or steal any more of their people, that they should place crosses in their rancherías, so that in case any Spaniards did come with the intention of doing harm they would refrain, on seeing the crosses. The Indians were very much pleased by this and showed their appreciation by embracing us and promising not to remove the crosses from their towns and rancherías. When we placed them in the latter, they were delighted, and raised their hands toward the sun, because they had been told we were children of the sun.[32]

The "children of the sun" reference brings to mind the Cabeza de Vaca account, with which these Spanish soldier-prospectors were familiar. Obregón's secondhand account stated that for the people of the La Junta valley "the many faces and signs toward the sky" that they made were gestures of worship of the sun. In this way they confirmed the peace pact on their part.[33]

Messengers relaying the same assurances were sent ahead across the Cuesta Grande that blocked the way into the La Junta valley to the east. The expedition had to take the same very difficult route, since it was impossible to follow the Rio Conchos as it looped through a steep-walled canyon to enter the valley. After laboring over the mountain ridge, the explorers came again to the river and halted a few miles downstream. They were soon met by many "very handsome men and beautiful women" who came out to greet them. Obregón called them brave, noble, well disposed, and good hunters and fishers. There was the usual mutual gift-giving between the parties, but initially the Natives were apprehensive, "fearful of the Spaniards on account of what they had heard." In fact, it was in this vicinity that the boy Pedro had been seized several years previously. After the Spaniards through interpreters gave assurances of peaceful intentions, the natives allegedly became quite cheerful. They spoke a different language (Amotomanco) than the Cabris, but the two groups understood one another. Here too the men were "naked" and painted themselves with stripes (thus Obregón called them *rayados*). They had fine "Turkish" bows and buffalo-hide shields, and they indicated that people of their nation extended for more than a hundred leagues. They lived in houses of paling plastered with mud, and had the same food items as the Cabris, but "very little corn."[34]

The next day the Spaniards did not go all the way down the Rio Conchos to its junction with the Rio del Norte to the east. Rather, following Native directions, they headed north to a Native settlement on the latter river about twelve miles upstream from the junction. The Espejo expedition the following year christened this town San Bernardino. Thus the Chamuscado party saw none of the towns clustered near the river junction itself, nor any of those on the Rio del Norte below that junction.[35] One of the awaiting Natives in San Bernardino was already quite familiar with Spaniards from the Santa Barbara district. An uncle of the boy Pedro, he had been captured either at the same time as his nephew or on some other occasion. He must have enjoyed singing, since the Spaniards named him Juan Cantor, Juan the singer. Laboring among the Spaniards, he had learned the *mexicana* idiom, an altered form of Nahuatl. That language was employed by the Spaniards as a common idiom among the mixed Native laborers in the Santa Barbara district. Cantor had evidently gained his freedom in an amicable fashion, since now he would accompany the Chamuscado expedition as an interpreter for Father Agustín Rodríguez.[36]

Cantor must have helped mediate the group's entry into San Bernardino. What else would explain that this town was the first place where Gallegos reported that the Spaniards were received with great pleasure and friendliness, with no reported reticence? If true, this might even indicate that a slaving party had never reached this town, with Cantor having been captured elsewhere, perhaps in the same village where his nephew was captured. The people were standing on the rooftops, as one views a parade, to better see the expedition's arrival. This settlement was the first to be described as a permanent town (*pueblo fundado*), containing more than 300 persons in eight large square houses. "The houses resemble those of the Mexicans, except that they are made of paling. The natives build them square. They put up forked posts and upon these they place rounded timbers the thickness of a man's thigh. Then they add stakes and plaster them with mud." Close by their houses they had granaries built of willow, again in the manner of the Mexicans. Gallegos gratefully reported that here the valley vegetation was vigorous in comparison to the dry and sterile country through which they had traveled. To gather information about what lay ahead, and undoubtedly to benefit from this welcoming rest stop, the expedition spent "almost a whole day" here.[37]

The townspeople spoke the same language and cultivated the same crops as those whom the Spaniards had met the day before on the Rio Conchos upstream from the river junction. As Gallegos told it, the people were of even better appearance. Again he described them as "naked," and also very clean and warlike. They had Turkish bows and many buffalo hides. Obregón wrote that they obtained the hides through trade. Gallegos reported that the people of this town had heard about the Pueblo Indians far to the north long ago from "the people (*la gente*) who killed the buffalo." Thus neither chronicler portrayed the people of San Bernardino as those who themselves went out long distances to hunt buffalo. They treated their own leader with signs of special respect: "[he] was obeyed by the others to such an extent that they carried a seat for him, consisting of a very large tanned buffalo skin."

To instill reverence toward the missionaries and thus also assert the Spaniards' connection to divine power, the expedition members kissed the hands of the friars in order to prompt the people to do the same. The Juntans did so, while adding their own religious gestures:

> The natives then kissed the hands of the missionaries and raised their own to heaven, blowing toward the sky, because we informed them that the friars we brought with us were children of the sun, that they had come down from heaven, and that we were their children, all of which the Indians believed. . . . In their settlement we placed a cross.[38]

The Spaniards knew they could claim a deeper respect by not only brandishing military arms but also asserting a spiritual power explained in terms of Native belief—that is, a reverence for the powers found in nature. The Juntan gestures of reverence were like those in the origin myth of the Ácoma group among the Puebloans in upper New

Mexico, in the broad Mogollon-Anasazi cultural tradition that had helped form the Juntan culture:

> Every morning as the Sun rose, they would thank him for bringing them to the light by offering with outstretched hands sacred cornmeal and pollen. To the tones of the creation song, they would blow the offering to the sky, asking for long life, happiness, and success in all their endeavors.[39]

One may certainly question whether the Juntans believed the Spaniards' religious claims as promptly as the chronicler asserted, but a peace agreement was thus expressed through an intercultural exchange of symbolism: handkissing, raising hands and blowing toward the sun, and planting a cross.

The Spaniards found San Bernardino and its inhabitants to be very similar to a place described in the narrative of Cabeza de Vaca. There were certainly striking similarities. Cabeza de Vaca had written of a river flowing between mountains, a permanent town with real houses, the consumption of beans and squash and corn, trade items of buffalo hides and deerskins, and people of good physique and mental ability, with the males "naked." Consequently, Chamuscado's men, hoping to discover the riches to the north cited by Cabeza de Vaca, asked "if any men like us had passed that way." From the people's replies describing four Christians "a long time ago," the Spaniards "realized clearly that the leader must have been Alvar Núñez Cabeza de Vaca, because, according to his narrative, he had come by way of these people."[40]

After the day's rest the expedition headed up the Rio del Norte accompanied by more than 300 people. The horses that the Spaniards rode, previously unknown to Native cultures, were taken as a manifestation of desired extraordinary power: "[They] approached our horses and rubbed their bodies against the animals' haunches, raising their hands to heaven and blowing toward the sky." After about eleven days the Juntans turned back, since the expedition had arrived at the border of enemy people with a different language. At night during this journey the people had danced:

> Their nation has a *tone* in its dances resembling that of the Negroes, *using some skins attached to a gourd to serve as a small drum*. After doing this, the dancers rise and execute their movements *to the sound like matachines*. They raise their hands toward the sun and *say* in their language with the cadence of the dance, *"ayoa canima."* This they do with *great rhythm and order*, in such a way that though there are 300 *adult men (gandules)* in a dance, it seems as if it were being sung and danced by one man only, due to the fine harmony and *tone* of their performance.[41]

Juan "the Singer" was surely among those dancing and singing. What he experienced during the eight months in upper New Mexico between August 1581 and March

1582 must have given him an even deeper insight into these domineering and yet amazingly daring Spaniards, with the prospector-soldiers hell-bent on finding mineral discoveries and the friars heaven-bent on conversions to Christianity. The expedition's presence among the Pueblo nations became ever more threatened as those people suffered the Spaniards' impositions. Fortunately for Juan Cantor, he did not stay with Father Rodríguez when that friar and his Franciscan companion insisted upon remaining when the Chamuscado party retreated back toward Nueva Vizcaya. He returned to San Bernardino, where seven months later he would facilitate the entrance of a new Spanish expedition into his town. But it is highly unlikely that he joined it again. He probably had seen and experienced more than enough the first time.[42]

The Espejo Expedition, 1582–1583

The Chamuscado party arrived back at Santa Barbara in mid-April 1582, but without its leader. Chamuscado died near the end of the return trip, along the Rio Conchos south of the La Junta district. In Santa Barbara there were conflicting reports about the fate of the two friars who had remained. Their Franciscan colleagues were anxious to come to their rescue if they might still be alive, and Spanish frontiersmen were excited about the signs of mineral wealth reported to be in New Mexico by the Chamuscado returnees. While proposals for a major armed *entrada* were awaiting time-consuming royal approval, an expedition was organized in Nueva Vizcaya by Antonio de Espejo, who had fled from Mexico City the previous year to avoid paying a fine. Claiming that they had permission from a provincial authority, an authorization that was disputed upon their return, Espejo and his colleagues set out from the San Bartolomé Valley, heading for the Rio Conchos.[43]

There were fifteen Iberians, among them the expedition chronicler Diego Pérez de Luján. That was almost twice as many as in Chamuscado's group. None of them had been on that previous expedition. There were also "some servants," 115 horses and mules, and one Franciscan, Bernardino Beltrán. No other livestock were noted.[44] This group was thus intent on moving more rapidly, living off the land—that is, off of the Natives they encountered. On November 24 they encamped two leagues north of the junction of the San Pedro and Conchos Rivers, where Chamuscado had been temporarily buried upon his death the previous spring. Pérez de Luján noted that Captain Lope de Aristi of Santa Barbara had previously taken captives at this place who were brought to Santa Barbara. On December 4, unable to continue along the Rio Conchos at one point where it was swollen by high water, Espejo's group was guided inland for four leagues along a native trail to a spring-fed marsh that they named La Ciénega Llana.[45]

The next day they went another four leagues to get back to the river. In doing so they crossed the boundary between the Conchos nation and the land of the "warlike Pasaguates." Luján's only description of these people was that they were "naked like the

Conchos," who had been described as "naked" people covered in rabbit or deerskins but with the men's private parts and the women's breasts exposed. Besides their own language, the Pasaguates spoke those of the Conchos and of the Patarabueyes in the La Junta valley. Luján made no other comment about them or their dwellings. Espejo's own much briefer account described the rancherías of the Pasaguates as consisting of huts like those of the Conchos, and their food as also like that of the Conchos. All the similarities noted were with the Conchos, with no differences given.

These so-called Pasaguates were probably the Yoslli who had accompanied the Chamuscado expedition after they left the Concho territory. In fact, Luján named the place where the Espejo expedition spent the night with these people the Puerto de la Raya de los Conchos—the entry point on the border of the Concho territory. That was the same location at which the Chamuscado expedition had met the Yoslli. The Native interpreters with the Espejo expedition were Conchos, as well as a Pasaguate boy named Juan "belonging to Gregorio Hernández" and Pedro (Juan Cantor's nephew), identified as a Patarabuey boy "belonging to Diego Pérez de Luján." Thanks to the Native interpreters, the Pasaguates who came to see the Spaniards did so peacefully, and even warned that farther ahead the Patarabueyes were waiting to fight.[46]

For the next stage of the journey before entering the La Junta valley, Espejo's report is the more credible. He stated that the expedition was accompanied by the Pasaguates for four days covering fourteen leagues—around thirty-five miles. Then, the day that they departed from the Pasaguates, the expedition came across people called Tobosos who ran away from their huts, since they had experienced previous slaving raids. The Tobosos ate the same type of food as the Pasaguates and were similarly "unclothed" (*sin bestiduras*). Reassuring them that they would not be harmed, the Spaniards set up crosses among them and gave them some religious instruction. Several of the Tobosos accompanied the Espejo expedition for eleven leagues over two or three days to the limits of their sparsely inhabited territory.[47]

In Luján's account, there was no mention of Tobosos on the journey toward the La Junta valley, but he did note their presence on the expedition's return trip. Eight leagues beyond the river junction on their way back toward central Nueva Vizcaya, and thus presumably right around the Cuesta Grande, they encountered an old Toboso man. The rest of his people had fled, "wary due to the captures that had been done there." Nine leagues further, during the night some Tobosos stealthily shot with arrows two mules and a war horse of Pérez de Luján, even though earlier that evening two Tobosos had professed peaceful intentions. Luján's men wanted to seize the occasion to take prisoners, but he insisted that "even if the Indians should kill all of his horses, there would be no captives taken on his account."[48] Thus, although the Espejo and Luján accounts differ significantly in what transpired before entering the La Junta valley, both have Tobosos in a territory of nine to eleven leagues south of the Cuesta Grande. In both cases, the Tobosos had previously experienced slave raiding. This presence of the Tobosos in the Coyame valley merits notice, in view of future events that would occur in that valley to a much greater degree than in the La Junta valley.⁴⁹

Neither Luján nor Espejo mentioned a group like the Cabris on the south side of the Cuesta Grande. They did not even note the imposing Cuesta Grande itself. Espejo simply stated that after leaving the Tobosos the expedition entered "the territory of another [nation], known as the Jumanos, whom the Spaniards call also by a different name, 'Patarabueyes.'" Mostly mirrored by Obregón, Espejo only gave a very summary account of the people and settlements in the La Junta valley as a whole, reserving his more detailed description for New Mexico. The territory that Espejo ascribed to the Jumanos or Patarabueyes consisted of the La Junta valley and twelve days' journey above the river junction along the Rio del Norte. He reported that in the valley he saw five settlements (three more than Chamuscado), all with flat-roofed houses, allegedly containing more than ten thousand Natives. He also stated that they were of large physique and had striped faces. The only place to which Espejo gave specific attention was the "small pueblo" on the Rio Conchos near where their expedition camped the first night upon entering the La Junta valley. His account of the disturbance that occurred there conforms very closely to that of Luján that follows.⁵⁰

Thankfully, Luján's account of what transpired in the La Junta valley is much more detailed, giving the first descriptions of the towns at the river junction itself. In fact, he distinguished between the people there and those in the valley on the upper reaches of the Conchos and Norte Rivers. He said that the first village that they encountered coming down the Rio Conchos was a *ranchería* of the Otomoacos. This nation, he wrote, had been named Patarabueyes several years earlier by the slaving expedition that took captives there. Those captives included Pedro, a thirteen-year-old now serving as his interpreter, whom he had taken into his household. This village may have been the place identified in later years as El Mezquite. Unlike the reportedly peaceful if apprehensive welcome given the previous year to Chamuscado's group in this vicinity, the people of this ranchería attacked the expedition's horse herd at midnight and then fled into the mountains.⁵¹

Why they surreptitiously attacked Espejo's party may have been due to the different aspect of the two expeditions. Chamuscado had arrived with fewer men and a slow-moving stock caravan, Espejo with a light-traveling and more numerous military squad that could be easily perceived as slavers. In fact, a slaving party led by Gaspar de Luján, brother of Diego Pérez de Luján, had passed through the La Junta valley "a year before (*abia un año*)," that is, while the Chamuscado expedition was in New Mexico. Perhaps they had once again taken captives in this small pueblo. Gaspar was a member of the Espejo expedition, and he certainly would have been noticed by the watchful Natives as the Espejo party drew near them.⁵²

Another reason may have been that they recognized the young boy Pedro in this group. The Natives who attacked the horse herd included Pedro's father and relatives.

Perhaps they were hoping to give him a chance to escape, or at the very least they were angered by seeing him in the expedition. Now the Spaniards used Pedro to coax their leaders into a parlay, and many finally came back to their ranchería. "We erected crosses for them and left *written statements that they were left at peace*, but that any passersby should nevertheless be cautious." To dispose these Otomoacos favorably toward the friar, they were told that their lives had been spared only because he had pleaded on their behalf. The Otomoacos in turn tried to shift the blame for the horse killings to the people living at the junction of the Conchos and Norte Rivers. This in itself signifies an ethnic difference between those two groups.[53]

Luján observed that the Otomoaco men were "naked" in that they had no undergarments, but they wore well-tanned and softened buffalo skins. They were buffalo hunters who ranged as far as eighty miles away with strong "Turkish" bows. The women were clothed in scapular-like deerskins to cover their breasts, deerskin skirts, and tanned buffalo hides for shawls, and had long hair tied up on their heads. The men's small "cap" (*pequeña gorra*) of hair was described like the year before among the Cabris on the other side of the Cuesta Grande, but in more detail: at the center was a long lock of hair to which was fastened large bird feathers. The people cultivated "corn, beans, and calabashes, although very little in this ranchería." There were large numbers of this nation, farming together, all along the Rio Conchos.[54]

That same day the expedition traveled two and a half leagues down the Rio Conchos and then halted. While at this place, they were approached by two leaders from the Abriache people who lived at the river junction. They came to find out if the Spaniards were approaching in war or peace. Their people had fled to the hills, since the Otomoacos had previously warned them of the Spaniards' approach. The Abriaches spoke a different language than the Otomoacos, but the two groups were interrelated and understood one another. Due to that cultural and linguistic relationship, the whole valley was called that of the Patarabueyes by the Spaniards of that time. Espejo's party was able to assure the Abriache emissaries of the Spaniards' peaceful intentions through the interpreter Pedro. The Abriaches recognized the boy from his having been in the valley with Luján's brother Gaspar a year before. In recognition of the successful outcome of this parlay with the Abriache emissaries, the Spaniards named this place La Paz.[55]

Espejo, just as had Chamuscado the previous year, did not proceed from there to the river junction but rather due north to the place on the Rio del Norte that his group called San Bernardino, the name of their friar chaplain. Many of the town's residents fled upon the news of the expedition's approach—another strong contrast from the reported happy reception of Chamuscado's group the previous year, and another strong indication that slaving had indeed occurred since then among the Otomoacos on the upper Río Conchos. Juan Cantor went out to meet the Espejo party. Undoubtedly his fellow townspeople considered him their best interlocutor, given his service in the previous Spanish expedition and his linguistic ability. The Spaniards were relieved to see him—he "was known by all" of them—and he was happy that they were happy. He and his nephew Pedro immediately coaxed the people to return. As they did so, the people approached "making musical sounds with their mouths similar to those of the flute," and kissed the hand of Fray Bernardino, as they had been prompted to do the previous year. "The ranchería resembled a pueblo, as it was composed of flat-roofed [de terrado] houses, half under and half above the ground." The Natives offered corn, beans, mascales, dried calabazas, gourd vessels, buffalo hides, and Turkish bows and arrows to the Spaniards. Upon their arrival the Spaniards repaired the cross left by Chamuscado and Rodríguez a year and a half earlier. They spent a full eight days at this place to rest the animals.[56]

Some members of the expedition, "accompanied by many Natives singing and dancing," went five leagues (about twelve miles) down to the river junction. Their purpose was "to *establish peace with* those pueblos, especially some that were known by the interpreter [the Otomoacan Pedro] and by Gaspar de Luján, who the year before had been there by commission of Juan de la Parra, captain of Indehé, to take captives, and had left them in peace [de paz]." This statement when carefully considered demonstrates that Gaspar de Luján's party had not included the river junction in its slave-taking activity the previous year. In fact, the crosses that he had left in these towns were still in place when Espejo's group visited.[57] At the southwest corner of the river junction the Espejo explorers gave the name of Santo Tomás to an Abriache town (pueblo) of 600 inhabitants with its leader Baysibiye (see figure 2). A century later Hispanics were calling it San Francisco. Its people offered them corn and beans and other vegetables and a few native mantas (cloaks) and arrows. The natives had "*in their* houses and garments *bows* like the other Otomoacos [sic]." A written notice of peace was left here also.[58]

Crossing the Rio del Norte, the Spaniards visited a town a mile or two away upriver that they called San Juan Evangelista. Its leader was Casica Moya. The town had flat-roofed houses built above and below a ridge. The next day the visitors traveled an unspecified distance to the largest town (pueblo) of all, a farming community that they called Santiago (the later San Cristóbal). Besides the houses in the town, its inhabitants also had flat-roofed houses in their fields where they resided during harvest time. This town's leader, named G. bisite or J.brisite, was the most respected of all those in the valley.[59] Luján reported that the Spaniards were received "with much rejoicing and music made with the mouth" in all the towns, and the people kissed Father Bernardino's hand. In all of these places the Natives related that Cabeza de Vaca and his two companions and a Negro had been there. Luján noted that "apart from these three cities (tres ciudades) there are many others and many rancherías (ay otras munchas e munchas rancherías) both upriver and downriver on the Rio del Norte.[60] But his party apparently did not visit the right bank of the Rio del Norte downstream from the river junction, and thus said nothing specific about towns such as Guadalupe and Púliques noted there a century later.

In his chronicle Espejo noted the same Native religious gestures reported by Gallegos and Luján, but now, at least in his mind, more explicitly influenced by Christianity:

> Apparently these Indians have already received some enlightenment regarding our holy Catholic faith: for they point to God our Lord while looking up to the heavens [*porque señalan a Dios nuestro señor mirando al* çielo], calling him "Apalito" in their language and saying that He is the One they acknowledge as their Lord and Who provides them with everything they have. Many men, women, and children came to have the sign of the cross made over them by the friar and the other Spaniards, showing great pleasure at this gesture. They told us, or explained through interpreters, that three Christians and a Negro had passed through their land.[61]

The belief expressed may have been as Native as it was Christian, but the Christian gesture of the sign of the cross was a new addition to the Native repertoire. The Juntans' memory of the Cabeza de Vaca party had undoubtedly been sharpened by their conversations with the Chamuscado group the previous year.

The expedition left San Bernardino on December 17, heading up the Rio del Norte. At this point there were thirty-nine of them, including Father Beltrán and the servants. Thus, as in the previous Chamuscado expedition, the servants outnumbered the soldiers and friars. For the next two weeks and forty leagues (about 100 miles) Luján called the "naked" people whom they encountered Otomoacos, since they were of the same language and dress as those so named in the La Junta valley. They lived on mesquite beans and *maxcales*. On New Year's Eve, their second-to-last day among these people, Espejo's group was given deerskins and trade items from the west: *mantillas* (shawls) and feathered headdresses.

That night the Natives danced as they had for the Chamuscado expedition. This time the rhythm was set by the Natives' clapping their hands together while sitting around a bonfire. "They sing, and in time with the singing they dance, a few rising from one side and others from *another*, with two, four, or eight persons performing the movements to the rhythm of the song." On January 2 the expedition entered the territory of the Caguates, whom Hammond and Rey identified as Sumas. The first Caguate cacique they met was the grandfather of the boy Pedro. Luján reported that the Caguates were "*related* with the Otomoacos and *thus of the same* language."[62] Espejo, however, reported that upon meeting the people who gave them feathered objects and *mantillas* "we did not know to what nation they belonged due to a lack of interpreters." This would mean that they were not of the same culture as the Juntans, since the boy interpreter Pedro was still with the Spaniards. This leaves the status of the people between La Junta and the El Paso district uncertain.[63]

The boy Pedro accompanied Espejo and Luján throughout New Mexico. Thanks to him they were able to understand some Jumanos who were hunting near the lower Pecos River as the expedition was passing through the buffalo plains of what is now West Texas, trying to find their way back to Nueva Vizcaya. The Jumanos guided them to the Rio del Norte at some settlements about twenty-two miles above San Bernardino. Luján commented that these Jumanos, in the area above the Davis Mountains of West Texas, were "in their appearance, *except in the houses*, similar to [*en el traje de manera, eseto en las casas, como*] the Paratragueyes." Significantly, this part of the journey was Luján's only use of the name Jumanos in his chronicle.

By this time it was August 1583. Traveling down the Rio del Norte, the Espejo party was welcomed by the people with dances and festivities. At San Bernardino, where they were met by the caciques of all the towns, "our feeling of security was so great that we went about almost in shirt sleeves"—that is, without their usual protective chain-mail and/or leather vests and jackets. After resting at San Bernardino for a day, they continued twelve miles downriver to Santo Tomás. All along the Rio del Norte down to Santo Tomás, they were fed abundant ears of corn, beans, roasted and raw calabashes, catfish, and a fish called *matalotes*. Prevented for three days from crossing the Rio Conchos because it was too high, they traded blankets *they were carrying* for many buffalo skins and strong Turkish bows from the "fine, bright" natives.[64]

With the passing of these expeditions Juan Cantor, his nephew Pedro, and the rest of the Juntans disappear again into the mists of history. At least one Juntan did not fare very well thereafter. When the Espejo party finally arrived back in the Santa Barbara district in September 1583, the *alcalde mayor* there arrested them for not having received permits in Santa Barbara for the expedition. Espejo had instead obtained permits from the powerful Ibarra family in Durango. The *alcalde mayor* also "appropriated the Indians that they brought as guides and another Indian, a Xumana, who had come with them." This "Xumana" was "a native of the same place as the Indian Pedro of the Jumana nation whom they had taken along as interpreter."[65] Juan Cantor?!

The Emerging Picture

From these earliest accounts in the 1500s three very important things stand out. The first is the detailed physical description of the people and their clothing, weapons, dwellings, food, and some religious gestures. The second, building upon the first, is the clarification of distinctive groups within both the La Junta valley and the Coyame valley. The third is the fact that, contrary to the scholarly consensus, these first expeditions established a "peace regime" between the Spanish and the people of the La Junta district.

Without these earliest accounts, ethnographers would have very little to work on. The expeditions' chroniclers gave disparate information about the people and settlements of the Coyame valley. But an analysis of the extant manuscripts strongly suggests a corrected geography of Yoslli/Pasaguates, Tobosos, and Cabris as one approached the Cuesta Grande. The dwellings of the first two groups in their rancherías as well as those along the Rio del Norte above San Bernardino were more modest huts. The dwellings of the Cabris were not described and were thus presumably of no particular notice either. Neither expedition visited the entire La Junta valley. But all the major towns were described except for those on the right bank of the Rio del Norte below its junction with the Rio Conchos. Although the first settlement on the upper Rio Conchos in the valley was called a small pueblo, all five towns that were visited by Espejo were reported to have flat-roofed houses with walls made of palings plastered with mud. Those at San Bernardino were half underground and squared off with thick corner posts. At the major farming community of Santiago, the people also had houses out in their fields for use during the harvesting season. There were granaries made of willow at San Bernardino.

The people of the La Junta valley as well as Gallegos' Cabris at the foot of the Cuesta Grande in the Coyame valley were described much more favorably than the Conchos, Yoslli/Pasaguates, and Tobosos. The Cabris and the Otomoacos were depicted as very handsome, spirited, and intelligent. Clean and modest, the men painted their bodies with stripes and wore only buffalo skins, while the women dressed in tanned deerskins with buffalo wraps. The men had short hair cropped to form a skullcap with a tuft into which feathers were inserted; the women had long hair tied into a bun. The Jumanos in the Davis Mountains area were vaguely described as similar in appearance. The Abriaches at the river junction were not described as to physical type nor clothing, presumably since they were similar to the Otomoacos as implied by Espejo.

The people of the La Junta valley and the Cabris grew squash and beans in season, although very little by those in the first small Otomoaco village since they were primarily hunters and ate all kinds of fish and game. Throughout the La Junta valley the people had strong Turkish bows and buffalo-hide shields and also grew corn. All possessed buffalo hides and deerskins that they received in trade. In their celebrations they danced like the Africans known to the Spaniards, to the beat of a tambourine-like drum, singing in great harmony. Their gestures of reverence were to raise their arms and blow toward the sky, singing with voices sounding like flutes. Only the first Otomoaco group was explicitly said to be buffalo hunters who traveled long distances, while the people at Santiago were apparently the strongest agriculturalists among those met by the Spaniards.

The second important point invites a careful analysis of the distinctions made among the various Native groups in the district, particularly in regard to language. Morgenthaler helpfully categorized people in the La Junta district into three basic civilizational types: those settled more or less permanently in the district in sturdy houses; "transient" groups whose "sedentism was more intermittent than progressive" including Jumanos and Cíbolos; and nomadic visitors or raiders including Conchos,

Chisos, and Apaches.[66] One could add Tobosos to this last group. Events will demonstrate that when uprisings were contemplated or actually occurred in the district, they were usually favored by groups in the Coyame valley whose degree of sedentism is unclear (Morgenthaler's first or second groups), aided and often instigated by outside agitators (some of his third group). The Natives who tended to be more protective of the missionaries were from among those who permanently resided close by the river junction in the La Junta valley (some of his first group).[67]

The expedition narratives of the early 1580s provide a basis for these distinctions. There were two kinds of people across the mountain ridge from the Rio del Norte in or near the Coyame valley. One kind were the Yoslli and Tobosos who were apparently not permanently settled, with at least some considered very unattractive by the Spaniards. On the other hand, Gallegos described the Cabris near the Cuesta Grande as very handsome and intelligent, similar to the people in the La Junta valley but with a different Native language, although understanding the upriver groups (Luján's Otomoacos) in the La Junta valley. Due to the very differing locations assigned to the Pasaguates and the minimal descriptions of them, they are less clearly classifiable although most probably the same as the Yoslli.

According to Gallegos, there were two principal interrelated groups in the La Junta valley itself, the Otomoacos who spoke Amotomanco and resided on the upper reaches of the two rivers, and the Abriaches at the river junction itself. Otomoacos or people very similar to them also frequented the banks of the Rio del Norte in rancherías for many miles upriver. Although they spoke different languages, the Otomoacos and the Abriaches understood each other. The largest settlements were those of the Abriaches at the river junction, and that is where the head cacique resided. The Abriaches also had the strongest agricultural community (Santiago), while the Otomoacos had the clearest buffalo-hunting one (the small pueblo or ranchería on the upper Rio Conchos, possibly the later El Mezquite). Both groups were usually on friendly terms with each other but were not beyond blaming the other for their own actions.

As for the much-discussed question of the use of the generic ethnic terms of Patarabuey and Jumano,[68] no distinction can be drawn from these accounts in regard to the La Junta valley itself. One or both terms are applied to all the people of the entire La Junta valley, and even upriver on the Rio del Norte. For his part, Luján identified as Jumanos only the people he met outside the valley between the middle Pecos River and the Rio del Norte. The Spanish *entradas* in the early 1580s passed through La Junta too quickly, with their thoughts set on lands further north. They were not intent upon more precise ethnic distinctions other than language in the district. The name Patarabuey itself was coined by the Spanish raiding parties in the 1570s and promptly fell out of use in later documents.[69]

However, a Franciscan who ministered in the La Junta district almost a century and a half later, in the early 1720s, provided a remarkable correlation to the 1580s chronicles. In a report he wrote in 1749, Andrés Varo made the only known comment about languages since those earliest accounts. He stated that the people at the town of San Cristóbal (Luján's Santiago) spoke the same Pozalme language as the people of that name at the town of San Francisco (Luján's Santo Tomás). Those were the two surviving towns of the three described by Luján as Abriache. And in an astounding echo from the deep past, Varo wrote that the people living on the upper reaches of the Conchos and Norte Rivers within the La Junta valley spoke "Patragueye"! These were the upriver locations of Luján's Otomoacos as he initially distinguished them from the Abriaches. With these comments, Varo confirmed the abiding geographical distribution of two languages and connected the extinct ethnic terms of the 1580s with the terms in use ever since the 1660s.[70]

That still leaves the question of the Jumanos and La Junta. Espejo was the only one of the chroniclers who actually took part in either of these earliest expeditions who called the people in the La Junta valley Jumanos. A century later Jumanos would be key diplomatic brokers in Texas and New Mexico. Kelley devoted his doctoral thesis to demonstrating that the Jumanos were not the core residents of the La Junta valley but rather a Plains-type hunting people who traveled throughout the South Plains. They "enjoyed an intimate trade and friendship relationship with the La Junta peoples and perhaps should even be included with them. However, the Jumano were plains hunters who at best only spent the cold winter months at La Junta, returning to the bison plains to hunt and trade when spring came each year." These Jumanos may have been a local development out of the much earlier hunting culture in the region, or they may have been the advance wave of Athapascan migration into the area that would eventuate in the Apaches.[71]

The third important consideration, in view of what has usually been written about the La Junta settlements, is that these expeditions established a "peace regime" between the Spanish and the people of the La Junta district.[72] That was not something offered to all groups at this time. It was probably in 1575–1585, the period of the Chamuscado and Espejo expeditions, that slave raiding reached its peak in Nueva Vizcaya. "By the 1580s it was such an important business that the soldiers started wars in order to get slaves."[73] But the only villages within the La Junta district that were clearly reported to have been victims of slave raids were in the Coyame valley and just inside the La Junta valley on the upper Rio Conchos. The towns at the river junction itself apparently never experienced Spanish raiding, and it is possible that neither did San Bernardino upriver on the Rio del Norte. It was probably the size and proximity to each other of La Junta's core established settlements, more than their great distance from Hispanic outposts, that protected them. Also, the Juntans' physical and intellectual attributes and military prowess at a key frontier location most probably made them more desired as allies than as captive labor pools.

That is how the two Nueva Vizcayan expeditions in the early 1580s dealt with the La Junta district—brandishing their weapons, yes, but also distributing gifts and blessings and erecting crosses in the towns and leaving notes as pledges of protection. For their part, the Juntans reciprocated with gifts and even festivities while learning to recognize some basic signs and content of Christian faith.

Entering the Colonial Labor System, 1600s

These Polagnes have come to serve with much punctuality due to the good treatment that I gave them, their work being paid very well so that they returned to their lands very content and thus attracted many other non-civilized people (*bozales*) to come out from their lands.

—Francisco Martínez Orejón, Hacienda of San Diego del Corralejo, 1655

Although the Juntans probably experienced at least one more expedition passing through their valley in late 1590, those Spaniards left no record of that event.[1] Juan de Oñate, the leader of the Spanish occupation of upper New Mexico in 1598, took a more direct route from Santa Barbara to that territory through the El Paso district. That became the Camino Real that bypassed La Junta by a rugged 140 miles.[2] As the Spanish province of New Mexico slowly developed in the 1600s among the Pueblo Indians to the far north of Nueva Vizcaya and a few decades later in the El Paso district, the people of the La Junta district remained way beyond the frontier of New Spain.

But they were no longer beyond contact with Hispanics. As the latter's presence expanded in central Nueva Vizcaya, especially after 1630 due to new mining discoveries in the Parral district and the development of more agriculture in the San Bartolomé Valley, people of the La Junta district were gradually drawn into the colonial labor system. This occurred even earlier and to a greater extent for the Native groups below them along the middle Rio Conchos and its tributaries such as the San Pedro River, who lay closer to the Hispanic centers and experienced more involuntary cooption. Earlier scholars judged the participation in this labor system by the people of the La Junta district after the initial slaving raids of the 1570s as mostly voluntary. Some recent scholars have supposed it to have continued to be the result of slaving raids. Here one enters the complex colonial field of Native labor: slaving, *encomiendas*, *repartimientos*, and seasonal migration.

During the seventeenth century the Juntans and the Indigenous nations around them come more visibly into the light of history. Toward the end of that century an experienced Franciscan in the region wrote that approaching La Junta from the Santa Barbara district to the south one encountered the Conchos, Julimes [Yoslli/Pasaguates?], and Tobosos, in that order.[3] By that time the Conchos and Julimes were being rapidly absorbed into the Hispanic system. Tobosos sallied forth from the rugged desert country, broken by mountains and canyons, to the southeast of La Junta to attack the frontier Hispanic settlements and sometimes the missions in Nueva Vizcaya. To the northwest of La Junta the non-sedentary Sumas and, below them, the Sumanas/Jumanas frequented the lands descending the Rio del Norte from the El Paso vicinity down toward La Junta. During this century the Jumanos and other more mobile nations that traveled the vast uncharted Southern Plains north and east of the La Junta district were being pressured more and more by the Apaches.[4]

This report by the Franciscan leader probably came from the first known visits by Franciscans to the very distant La Junta valley since the initial *entradas* a century earlier. The missionaries came from almost opposite directions, having been invited by the Juntan laborers in the Parral district and by Jumanos visiting El Paso. Before relating those invitations, the colonial labor system in Nueva Vizcaya that drew Juntan laborers must first be described.

Native Labor for Hispanics in Northeastern Nueva Vizcaya

William Griffen described the cultural relations between Hispanics and most of the Indigenous nations on the northeastern frontier of Nueva Vizcaya as exhibiting Native autonomy:

> Because Spaniards could not maintain themselves permanently in this region, they had little direct control over the native population. The culture contact, then, was nondirected, since the Indians maintained "free choice" regarding the cultural elements they would incorporate into their own social systems—albeit while often coping with situations that the Spaniards, wittingly or not, had obliged them to meet. . . . A number of individuals and groups from time to time did have more or less direct contact with Spanish civilization at both missions and haciendas, where they learned of new items and ideas that they later took back to their own territories.[5]

The way of relationship followed by groups the Hispanics called Tobosos was that of attacking Hispanic travelers and raiding their settlements, often in response to Hispanic offenses, in an ongoing or sporadic (depending on the group) exchange of violence.[6] Toboso raiders were increasingly noted throughout Nueva Vizcaya in the 1600s. Luján's encounter with Toboso raiders in 1582 has already been noted. There were repeated Hispanic military expeditions against Toboso groups as well as efforts to missionize them as early as 1611 in the vicinity of the San Bartolomé Valley. In 1621 some Toboso bands indicated that they were ready to work in the harvests in that area, but Tobosos were a major component of the great 1644–1645 uprising across a wide swath of that province.[7]

But there were other choices of relationship. Particularly in regard to the lower Rio Conchos and the Rio del Norte areas that included La Junta, most scholars have concluded that relations were generally peaceful, although with occasional outbreaks of rebellion.[8] While slave labor had been and continued to be employed to some extent in Nueva Vizcaya, this was soon paralleled by a "more or less voluntary" labor system throughout the region. Jack Forbes gave an early summary of this view:

> The Spaniards needed laborers to work in the mines and the *estancias de labor* ("farms and ranches") which developed to supply the miners with food. Mexicans, Tlaxcalans, and other conquered Indians came north in large numbers, but local labor was also needed. Since at first the seminomadic northerners were not inclined to such work and were hostile anyway, the slave-raiding system developed. . . . The slave-labor system seems to have been partially replaced by a more or less voluntary labor system, whereby natives were recruited to work in the *estancias* and were remunerated for their services. In this way Indians from as far away as southern Texas came to work in the area of Santa Bárbara and Parral in Chihuahua.[9]

In the La Junta valley the "peace regime" established by the 1580s expeditions would supposedly provide a basis for such labor arrangements. Once the Parral district was established in the 1630s, some people on the outer edges of the La Junta district (not the core river junction area) may have been initially brought there by force, while others began migrating there for seasonal labor. To understand how this came about, one must understand the modified form of the *encomienda* system that developed in Nueva Vizcaya.

The new Hispanic outposts in central Nueva Vizcaya stood way beyond the existing military garrisons of New Spain. For fifty years there were no presidios (Crown-financed military forts) on the great northern plateau between Durango and Santa Barbara.[10] For these new territorial conquests, as in Nuevo León to the east and New Mexico to the north, the Spanish Crown relied initially upon private enterprise to provide the finances and military arms to found and defend new Hispanic settlements. The royal government financed the missions that were established to bring the Indigenous nations into the Spanish orbit. But Hispanic colonists had to commit themselves and their people to provide arms when needed for their defense and the service of the colonial authorities.

Those colonists who were deemed more meritorious—or more favored by the viceroy or the governor—were awarded with an *encomienda*, an "entrusting" to them of a portion or all of an Indigenous community or communities. Those Natives were thereby obliged to provide the *encomienda* holders (*encomenderos*) unpaid labor levies and annual tribute from their local products. Abuses of Natives in this system became rampant, and in an effort to curb them the 1573 royal colonization laws declared that such grants could not include the use of these Natives' land nor their unpaid labor, only the reception of their tribute. But that did not prevent such labor requisitions as well as sometimes onerous tribute demands from being made. The *encomendero* was also required to see to the Natives' Christianization and Hispanicization, but in practice that also was often not observed. In fact, it might even be obstructed.[11]

Encomiendas were granted in Nueva Vizcaya, but in its northern region (the future state of Chihuahua) the smaller and more scattered Native settlements, often of a semi-migratory nature with little farming, precluded any regular gathering of tribute in Native produce. Thus *encomenderos*, with royal approval by 1582, required labor levies for their mining, farming, and ranching operations rather than tribute from their allocated Native communities. These levies were supposedly limited to three weeks annually. Many Natives were brought once or twice a year for the sowing and harvesting seasons, but some actually became permanent workers on haciendas to take care of the regular daily needs.[12] In the San Bartolomé Valley, wheat fields were prepared for planting in the late fall, sowing was done in early December, and harvesting began in early June just before the rains started. Maize fields, on the other hand, were planted in early June and harvested in late September and early October.[13]

In the second quarter of the 1600s, while *encomiendas* continued to exist, Nueva Vizcayan governors began the practice of assigning seasonal Indian labor in *repartimiento* (distributing Native laborers) without granting an *encomienda*. This practice allowed the governors to have more direct control over labor provisions. After 1670 by royal decree *encomiendas* were no longer granted in Nueva Vizcaya, leaving the *repartimiento* as a supposedly remunerated arrangement for alternating labor levies without explicitly requiring their assigned employer to see to their Christianization and Hispanicization.[14]

Chantal Cramaussel has made the important observation that many of the *encomiendas* in the 1600s for Native groups north of central Nueva Vizcaya, such as along the Rio del Norte near the El Paso district, were granted decades before any missions were established among those groups. She also cited the policy (if not always the practice) that "the Indians are not to be granted in *encomienda* until they have been baptized for five years" while employed by the landowner.[15] Cramaussel has attempted to demonstrate that in these cases "the still unconverted Natives knew no other Spaniards than the slave hunters," who were the ones who brought them into forced labor.[16] Taking this even further, she has asserted as a major thesis in all her writings that Native labor was always coerced in Nueva Vizcaya up until around the 1750s, whether through slaving, *encomiendas*, *repartimientos*, or debt peonage. Thus, she challenges the earlier conclusions of Forbes and Griffen. Griffen claimed that along the Rio Conchos that eventually joins the Rio del Norte at La Junta these labor arrangements were generally voluntary: "All along the Conchos River the Indians seem to have been rather satisfied with the arrangement of working on Spanish haciendas and occasionally they even requested permission from the Spanish governor to do so."[17]

Writing specifically about the *encomiendas* of Natives from the Rio Conchos and Rio del Norte in the 1600s, Cramaussel asserts that they were "probably war *encomiendas*, and Spaniards had already integrated these Indians into their haciendas as well as others that no longer had their Rancherias." By war *encomiendas* she meant the "relocating [of] unbaptized Indians by force."[18] This may well have been true for some of the earliest *encomiendas* along the lower Rio Conchos south of the La Junta district, such as the Julimes, those at La Chorrera or Chorreras, the Ochanes, and the Mamites. These will all be discussed below. However, the reality probably lay somewhere in between the apparently contrasting theses of Forbes and Griffen and that of Cramaussel.

Neither Forbes nor Griffen generalized his descriptions to apply universally. And Cramaussel in her concluding thoughts to this part of her thesis made a very rare concession:

> It is not preposterous to think that with time, especially when the [Native] harvests had been bad, epidemics devastating, or war permanent, the Indians presented themselves voluntarily in the haciendas; the colonial society permitted them to feed themselves and to obtain goods like knives and woolen and other cloths that ended up forming part of the indispensable objects of their daily life. The distance of their native place and the hunger that sometimes afflicted the Indigenous towns, after years of drought or of excessive rains or after the destruction of their crops by invaders, obliged many Indians to establish themselves next to the Spaniards with the risk of never returning to their native land nor recovering their freedom.[19]

A few pages earlier she noted that missionaries in the 1630s reported that Natives liked to come to the San Bartolomé fields to obtain clothing. She also shared how the Parral miners in 1684 offered the Natives advance pay to persuade them to stay in the spring and summer, whereas during the winter season they would sometimes come on their own. Otherwise, however, when she reported a voluntary Native presence, as in the case of the Yaqui barrios in the towns of Parral and Chihuahua, this was in the 1700s and with an accompanying thesis of debt peonage. By 1748, she asserted, *repartimientos* were becoming less and less frequent since the majority of the Natives in the haciendas had become assimilated—and, according to her, indebted laborers. A stronger point she made is that they could not move from one owner to another without permission.[20]

Paul Conrad has noted that between 1648 and 1679 there were repeated orders to emancipate Natives illegally enslaved in Parral, such as Apaches from New Mexico, and that these efforts "did have an impact" despite the persistence of enslavement. At least some of the "freed" Apaches remained in the labor system, being paid wages. Some working on ranches were paid the same as mestizos. Some even became recognized as *vecinos*, citizens of the town. Conrad also noted, however, that actual life conditions remained about the same for some and perhaps many. On the other hand, applying the seminal study of James Brooks to the Parral district, Conrad discussed how a Hispanic becoming the godparent of a Native at baptism might on occasion bring about a true sense of kinship.[21]

The lieutenant governor of Nueva Vizcaya did not see *repartimientos* becoming less frequent in 1744. Temporarily acting as governor, he complained to the viceroy that the owners of the haciendas and mines gave the governors such continuous orders (*mandamientos*) for laborers that too many Natives were absent from their own towns during the growing season. That left those Native communities insufficient manpower for their own agriculture, with the result that many Natives in order to provide for themselves either chose to remain laboring for Hispanics or went on frequent hunting forays away from their towns. Both these circumstances frustrated the efforts of missionaries in those towns to "properly" educate—more bluntly, culturally and religiously subordinate—their inhabitants. The governor had just forced several Tarahumara groups back to their missions and even sent 200 Native families in the Chihuahua vicinity back to their towns. Not only were too many Natives absent for too long from their own towns, but also their days of travel to the haciendas or mines were often not being counted as part of their work contract even though that requirement was stipulated by royal decree. Furthermore, according to the governor, when they were finally paid it was only with vouchers for obtaining goods from merchants, mostly from Chihuahua, who gave the Natives items for which they had no need and to which they had to travel many leagues from the haciendas and mines where they had been working.

Among his various recommendations, the governor proposed that no one from a Native town work for any Hispanic for more than a month, but that each labor levy be for a third of a Native community's work force. He stated that the royal regulation was for only 4 percent, but that stipulation was regularly disregarded. He also recommended that each levy be given as its captain an old Native affectively tied to his home town whose only job would be to see that all returned to that town. Those presidial captains who also had the title of protector of Indians, as well as the *alcaldes mayores* (officials in charge of Hispanic districts), should be forbidden to make labor assignments of Natives as they had been doing up to the present.[22]

The acting governor's observations are revealing. For one thing, requiring that the Native captain be an old person affectively tied to his home town to make sure that everyone returned home does not support a thesis of the general forced retention of laborers, at least not by this time. But his proposal, as well intentioned as it may have been, seems too unrealistic given the actual situation and the desires of both Hispanics and Natives. Nevertheless, it may have had an impact. Cramaussel cited a viceroyal document for all of New Spain issued two years later that appears to have been in response to these recommendations. The work period was reduced from two months to a month and a half, the laborers were only men, their number was increased to a third of the group, and—most surprisingly—laborers could not be brought from more than ten leagues' distance. Cramaussel duly noted that governmental decrees were one thing, actual practice another.[23] Thus what actually occurred in the case of the people of the La Junta district needs to be determined by documented research, not predetermined by governmental decrees or scholars' inclinations.

Even if voluntary, labor for Hispanics did not preclude discontent when Natives viewed impositions as unjust or too onerous. In 1644–1645 there was a spreading uprising across all of central Nueva Vizcaya. One of the leaders was "Bautista," by his Spanish name a supposed convert. He preached a strong nativistic anti-Spanish message, including outlawing anything Christian—very similar to what would happen in New Mexico 35 years later. Christian symbols were ridiculed: a Native given the title "bishop" performed a burlesque of the Mass and married and divorced persons at will. On March 25, 1645, Concho Natives along with a large number of "gentile" (non-missionized) nations from a wide swath of the country up to the Rio del Norte destroyed the missions of San Francisco de Conchos (where two missionaries were killed) and San Pedro de Conchos. Those were the northernmost missions in that direction. Hispanic forces went after the attackers, pursuing them to the north in the direction of the Rio del Norte.[24]

Along the Lower Rio Conchos

Three of the groups named in this uprising were associated with the La Junta district. The Oposmes and Tapacolmes are identified decades later as having towns in the La Junta valley. The Cholomes are later known to be living in the Coyame valley within the larger La Junta district, although they could also be found upriver toward the Suma territory below the El Paso district.[25] Also listed were the Julimes and Mamites, located along the Rio Conchos south of the La Junta district.

The Julimes are associated at various times with the history of the Juntans; they have even been mistakenly identified with them. As early as 1658 they were apparently visited by a missionary from the Franciscans' Zacatecas Province, the group in charge of Franciscan missions in Nueva Vizcaya. In 1684 the Domínguez expedition, related below, passed through their village on the Rio Conchos, by then named San Antonio de Julimes, slightly downriver from where it is joined by the San Pedro River, about 100 miles upriver from La Junta. Domínguez described the inhabitants by that time

NUEVA VIZCAYA
1590-1720

▲ MISSIONS
■ PRESIDIOS
● OTHER SETTLEMENTS
♀ SPRINGS

MOUNTAINS
— — POLITICAL BOUNDARIES

0   20   40   60
MILES

Figure 3: Northern Nueva Vizcaya. (From William B. Griffen, *Culture Change and Shifting Populations in Central Northern Mexico*, Tucson: University of Arizona Press, 1969)

as Christians, fluent in the Mexican language, and very hospitable. They already had an adobe church, but still no resident priest.[26] "Mamites" was an early Native-group name that soon disappeared. Since they were often mentioned in relation with the Julimes, Griffen conjectured that they lived close to the junction of the Conchos and San Pedro Rivers, somewhat upriver from Julimes.[27] Another possibility, however, is that they were downriver from Julimes, closer to the La Junta district.

The key battle of the uprising in 1645 took place in July, "some 10 leagues from the Rio Grande, and almost certainly on or very near the Conchos River." That places it within the Coyame valley. The Mamite chief was the first to surrender, followed by Simón Guajacole, "the son of the chief of the La Junta pueblos." The Julimes, who with the Mamites had been the prime movers of the rebellion in the north, were among the last to surrender by the beginning of September. Around 400 captives, including women and children, were "settled" at the San Francisco and San Pedro missions and other Native pueblos, and more than 200 Native workers were returned to the San Bartolomé Valley. Griffen singled out the Mamites as having two chiefs killed.[28]

"The nation Mamites and Gorretas with the two caciques" had already been given in *encomienda* for three generations around 1621 to the father of Pedro Vázquez Cortés of the Valley of San Bartolomé.[29] This one "nation" grant of the two groups together might indicate that the Mamites were somewhat close to Cuchillo Parado, since the name

Gorretas (little caps) is the descriptive term that was given to the distinctive hair style of the men in the Cuchillo Parado and Mezquite locations of the La Junta district by the Hispanic expeditions of 1581 and 1582. Those were the same places that had previously experienced slave raids in the 1570s. If these were the people called Gorretas in the Cortés grant, this would place the Mamites nearer to the La Junta district. It also would have some of the "Gorretas" from the Cuchillo Parado or Mezquite locations in the La Junta district apportioned to an *encomendero* as early as the 1620s. Two other Native groups known to have been along the Rio Conchos between Julimes and Cuchillo Parado that were assigned in *encomienda* in these earlier decades were people from La Chorrera in 1584, as a result of the Chamuscado expedition, and the Ochanes ("Oclames") in 1621.[30]

The 1645 uprising clearly demonstrates great Native discontent with the colonial system by many of the groups along the lower stretch of the Rio Conchos. Those non-missionized groups had already experienced slaving in the 1570s. Since the 1580s, *encomenderos* were being given authority to engage some of them as laborers, whether involuntarily or voluntarily. The 1645 uprising speaks to the anger of many of them. In the quelling of that uprising many experienced their men being killed or executed and members of their families, especially women and children, led as captives to be settled further south within the Hispanic colonial enterprise. Thus by 1645 one should expect to find at least some people from the greater La Junta district laboring within the Hispanic realm in central Nueva Vizcaya. And so one does.

Juntans in the Colonial Labor System

The first clear record so far discovered of people from the La Junta district engaged in the colonial labor system is from the 1640s, a decade after the important silver-mining center of Parral was founded in 1631 near Santa Barbara and the San Bartolomé Valley (see figure 1). That event increased the demand for needed laborers, both for the mines and for the greater agricultural and ranching production that these new enterprises required. The need was probably sharpened even more by the outbreak of death-dealing epidemics among the laborers in central Nueva Vizcaya in the 1630s and 1640s.[31] Reaching out for new workers, the Nueva Vizcayans turned to the Juntans among others. In the 1640s and 1650s some Polacmes, a nation identified with La Junta in documents from the 1680s onward, were laboring for Francisco Martínez Orejón in his hacienda of San Diego del Corralejo. He stated that these people's own name for themselves was "Polagnes," whereas others called them Conejos (another group found at La Junta). Martínez Orejón described them as "having come to serve with much punctuality due to the good treatment that I gave them, their work being paid very well so that they returned to their lands very content and thus attracted many other non-civilized people (*bozales*) to come out from their lands."[32]

Either Martínez Orejón was a big liar, or some Juntans were coming voluntarily as seasonal migrants. The Polacme town at the river junction in the La Junta valley would be named after Nuestra Señora de Guadalupe in 1715. It is the site of today's Ojinaga. When the labor of the Polacmes was assigned in *encomienda* to Bernardo Gómez by a different governor in 1653, an act that Martínez Orejón protested, the grant specified in typical *encomienda* fashion that it would be the responsibility of Gómez to have them instructed in the Catholic faith and that he had to always be ready to do his part in battles with hostile Natives and pay the *media anata* to the Durango treasury.[33] Gómez was certainly not against coercion. In 1652 he had brought 180 captives from Toboso territory, killing another 300 in the process.[34]

Some indication of other groups from the general La Junta district laboring in the San Bartolomé Valley can be obtained from the sacramental registers of the Franciscan convent that was established there to take care of the Natives and initially the Hispanics. In a Hispanic dispute over Native laborers that occurred in 1715, the local priest was asked to review the sacramental records to ascertain the entries about *norteños*, that is, the Natives in the La Junta district. After explaining that the registers did not identify the nations of those receiving sacraments before 1656, he reported that the first entry that he found for a Norteño nation was the baptism of a Tapacolme female in 1657. The first marriage was again of Tapacolmes, in 1663, with the witnesses being Conchos. The only other information that he gave was that there were also "Oposmes, Cacalotes, Pusalmes [Pocsalmes], Batlaboylas and others" in the records.[35] The Tapacolmes, Oposmes, Cacalotes, and Pocsalmes are all known to have had towns in the La Junta valley.

Griffen provides a closer look at these records. Unsurprisingly, the vast majority of the extant baptismal entries for 1663–1686 were among the Conchos. There was a Julime baptism almost every year and a Mamite every once in a while. Most notably in regard to Juntans, eighteen Tapacolmes were baptized in 1663–1664, followed by nine more in the next three years. But after that only two more were recorded up through 1686, in 1672–1673. During that period there was only one Oposme baptism, in 1670, and no Cacalotes, Pocsalmes, or Polacmes.[36] Cramaussel presented a good argument that these baptismal records demonstrate that violent seizures of Natives did continue. Twenty-three percent of the entries for Natives in the second half of the 1600s gave no father or mother but indicated the Native group: "concho, julime, tapacolme, etc." Cramaussel argued that these were young children torn from their families—thus their parents were unknown—in order to be *criados* (raised) in Hispanic homes or otherwise incorporated in Hispanic haciendas. This rate reached as high as 40 percent in 1666 and 50 percent in 1670, years in which there were known sorties against Natives who sheltered in the rugged mountains across the plains to the east and north.[37] It should be remembered, however, that the only baptisms registered at Valle de San Bartolomé for people possibly from the La Junta district up through 1686 were for Tapacolmes and one Oposme.

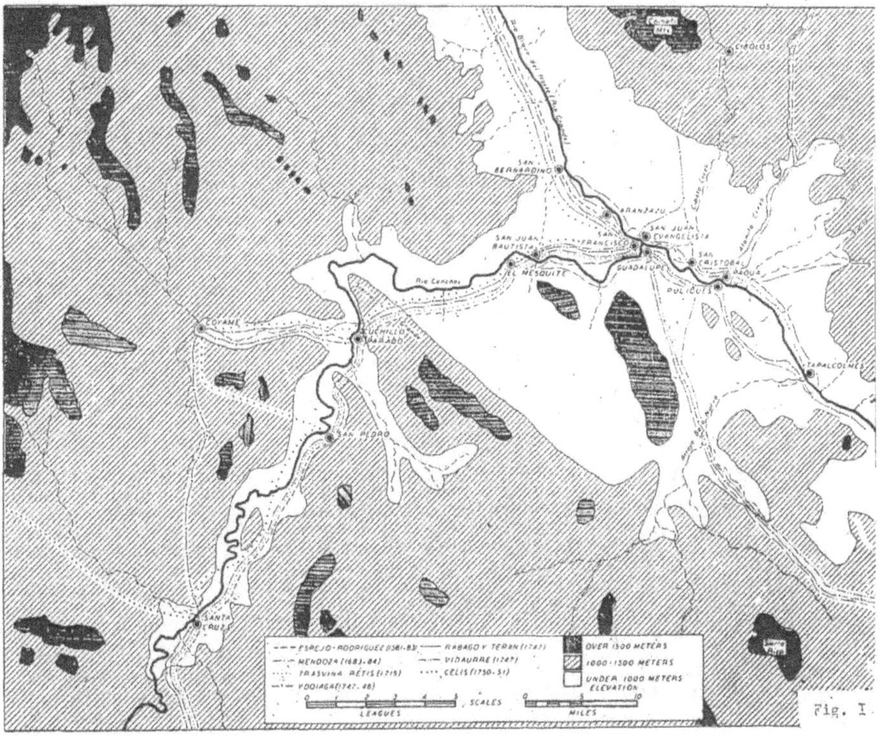

Figure 4: La Junta district with Tapacolmes at the eastern edge. (From J. Charles Kelley, "The Historic Indian Pueblos of La Junta de los Rios," *New Mexico Historical Review* 27, no. 4 (1952))

The Case of the Tapacolmes

These sacramental details from the San Bartolomé Valley are particularly intriguing as regards the Tapacolmes. Scholars generally assume that there was a Tapacolme village before the 1690s at the far lower end of the La Junta valley, but long abandoned by the 1740s. At the same time, a town named Santa Cruz de Tapacolmes (today's Villa de Rosales) is known to have existed in the 1700s far south of the La Junta district, to the southwest of Julimes. In fact, a 1763 report by the Franciscan provincial gave the much earlier year of 1649 as the date of the founding of "the town of Santa Cruz de Tapacolmes along the San Pedro River with 25 families of the Tapacolme nation."[38]

The provincial's information is so specific that one would be inclined to accept it, except for the fact that, as Griffen noted, there is almost no documentation on Santa Cruz in the 1600s. Griffen concluded that Santa Cruz was not identified with the Tapacolmes until the 1700s, when they began to be in greater number there. Two pre-1700 manuscripts that mention the village, in 1678 and 1693, do not add the designation "de Tapacolmes."[39] What is demonstrable, as discussed above, is that the Tapacolmes were among the groups "from the North" combating the Hispanics in 1645. Some of them may have been taken captive and resettled by the Hispanics at that time. This possible forced relocation would certainly help explain that when the Franciscans in San Bartolomé began indicating the ethnicity of Natives in their sacramental registers in 1657, the Tapacolmes were practically the only Northern group to be noted in the baptismal records, and in significant numbers, with the possibility that some had no parents listed.

The same year of the first noted Tapacolme baptism in the San Bartolomé records, the year 1657, is when that nation was assigned in *encomienda* to the Hierro family in that valley. As noted previously, baptisms were part of the legal requirement to obtain and maintain an *encomienda*. Some Tapacolme laborers remained with the Hierro family until 1715. At that point they became part of the massive transfer of La Juntan laborers from the San Bartolomé Valley to the newly developing district of San Felipe el Real de Chihuahua that will be described at that later date.[40] Thus, while some Tapacolmes may have been taken as captives to the San Pedro River and other places as a result of the 1645 uprising, it is certainly known that by 1657 some were laboring in the San Bartolomé Valley under the *encomienda* obtained by the Hierro family that year. At some point in the future the village of those who remained at the eastern extreme of the La Junta valley would be left vacant as they moved elsewhere.

La Junta in the Eastern Conchería Governorship

The reported absence or scarcity in the San Bartolomé church records of several other nations later known to be at La Junta does not necessarily mean that they were not among the Natives working in the area. Almost all the Natives in the San Bartolomé Valley lived on the haciendas where they worked, rather than being congregated together into a mission community at the town itself.[41] So none of them were under the direct supervision of a priest, and some were much farther from the town than others. How much they were encouraged or even allowed by the landowners to take time to receive the sacraments is an open question. Furthermore, some of the Juntan groups may have been working on haciendas outside the San Bartolomé mission jurisdiction, somewhere else in the Parral area. Apart from the Sonorans and Sinaloans and Mexicans also noted in the baptismal register, who clearly were very long-distance migrants, the other groups that appear in the San Bartolomé records during this period are those whom one would expect, coming from within an extended radius of the San Bartolomé Valley. The Conchos lived in a large district to the immediate north of that valley, and the Julimes came from above them in the middle Rio Conchos district.

In 1653 Hernando Obregón, "Indian Captain of the Julimes and Mamites," was appointed by the governor of Nueva Vizcaya as Native governor of the Eastern Conchería, newly divided from the larger Conchería district. The Eastern Conchería was described as "of all the Concho nation on all this side of the Río del Norte up to the land of the Tobosos, and of the Mamites, Julimes, Chisos, Oposmes, Conejos,

Tapacolmes, and of all the other nations that reside in said part." Obregón continued to be confirmed in the office of Native governor by successive Spanish governors through at least 1684.[42] The last three named groups in the list—Oposmes, Conejos (Polacmes?), and Tapacolmes—were all identified as in the La Junta valley in the 1680s. As already noted, at least some Conejos/Polacmes and Tapacolmes were assigned to *encomenderos* by mid-century and clearly had members laboring in central Nueva Vizcaya, and an Oposme appeared in the San Bartolomé records in 1670.

The Spanish designation of the Eastern Conchería thus seems to have included the La Junta valley during these decades, even if the future San Cristóbal was not "this side of the Río del Norte." The Native governorship of an entire region like the Eastern Conchería was a salaried position, and it carried serious responsibilities. The governor was to visit his communities, defend them, and not consent that they be mistreated. That was to the Natives' benefit. But there were even more important reasons for the Spanish governor to give a Native this paid position of prestige. Obregón was obliged to raise Indigenous forces to help defend the province when so ordered by the Spanish governor or his lieutenant. He was also to see that the Natives complied faithfully with *encomienda* orders, bringing them out of their settlements to their designated work assignments. Natives were not to be allowed to contract their labor outside of Nueva Vizcaya. The Native governor was even supposed to see that in their villages they cultivated crops, attended religious instruction, and built sturdy dwellings. In sum, he was to see to the good functioning of the Nueva Vizcayan system of relations with Native communities.[43] The same expectations, non-salaried but apparently rewarded, were held more locally with the Native governors or captains of each village or town allied with the Hispanics:

> By the second half of the seventeenth century, the task of recruiting Indians for this type of work fell to the Indian governor of each mission or the Indian captain of a *ranchería*, who were themselves exempt from tribute and furthermore received a reward in exchange for turning over *repartimiento* Indians to *hacendados* that needed their labor. . . . Governors and captains of *rancherías* were not always willing to cooperate with the colonizers, but if they refused to join the military expeditions, they were considered outlaws and threatened with death.[44]

Unlike the Native governors, one for the Western part of Nueva Vizcaya and the other for the Eastern Conchería, the Hispanic protector of Natives was appointed for all "the Tarahumara and Concha nations" throughout the province. But his role was much more restricted and dealt only with Natives already under Hispanic jurisdiction, to serve as their attorney in legal disputes. Thus the list of Native towns to be served by the protector who was appointed in early 1678 included Santa Cruz, San Pedro de Conchos, and San Antonio (Julimes)—the closest places of missionary activity below the La Junta district—but no town in the La Junta district itself.[45]

Missionary Outreach to the La Junta Valley

While groups from the northern frontier were being drawn into the migrant or per-manent labor system of central Nueva Vizcaya far to the south, the mission frontier was only inching northward toward La Junta. At this time San Pedro de Conchos on the San Pedro River was still the frontier salient of resident missionaries of the Franciscan Zacatecan province in northeastern Nueva Vizcaya. That was still 135 miles southwest of the river junction in the La Junta valley. To the far northwest of La Junta, the Franciscans of the older Santo Evangelio (Holy Gospel) Province, that had given birth to the Zacatecas Province, began a permanent mission center in 1659 in El Paso (today's Ciudad Juárez, Chihuahua). El Paso served as a very important way station to their missions in upper New Mexico. Six years later they built another mission, San Francisco de los Sumas, thirty miles down the Rio del Norte below the El Paso one.[46] Although that was still 220 miles from the La Junta river junction, it placed the Holy Gospel Franciscans amidst the Suma nation, who roamed the territory upriver from La Junta and were possibly even distant relatives of some Juntans.[47]

That makes it less of a surprise that the first reported visit of a missionary to La Junta after the expeditions in the 1580s was by Francisco García de San Francisco. García was a member of the Discalced Franciscans or Alcantarines in New Spain, called the Diegeños since San Diego was the name of their religious province. In 1628 he and a Discalced companion had volunteered for the New Mexico missions of the Holy Gospel Province of the Observant Franciscans. García founded the first El Paso mission, Nuestra Señora de Guadalupe, in 1659. The Juntans themselves testified to Father García's visit among them, as well as to a subsequent visit by a Father Sumesta, when questioned in 1684 about previous visitors:

> They only knew, since they saw it happen, that Reverend Father Fray Garcia de San Francisco had arrived at their towns, said Mass, and left having set a date for another visit. After that date had passed, another Religious arrived named Fray Juan de Sumesta from the same order of our father San Francisco. He only arrived at the first town before turning back. Since then they have not seen Spaniards nor more Religious.[48]

Father García's visit was in January 1671, eight months before his last entry in the El Paso sacramental registers (thus his non-return to La Junta). According to Father Colina, a missionary at La Junta in 1687–1688, García was accompanied in his visit to La Junta by Juan Álvarez, a member of the Holy Gospel Province. Father Sumesta, on the other hand, was from the mission district of central Nueva Vizcaya, and thus a member of the Franciscan Zacatecas Province that directed the San Pedro de Conchos mission.[49]

The La Junta district had finally come within the field of vision of the missionaries, but still only marginally. A century before, Franciscans had merely passed through there with eyes focused on a much bigger kingdom, that of New Mexico. Thereafter the conversion of the Pueblos of New Mexico and Arizona had demanded all the energy of the friars of the Santo Evangelio Province. During that same time the Franciscans of the Zacatecas Province were intent on the conversion of the nations in newly developing Nueva Vizcaya. Various groups of Juntans through their time as laborers in central Nueva Vizcaya, voluntary or otherwise, had become more familiar with Hispanic culture—crops, clothing, language, religion, priests. They had experienced the missionaries' care for the Natives, as culturally deaf as the friars may have been in certain respects. They had undoubtedly also noticed the material development of certain Indigenous villages as missions, the consequent work demands, and how Natives in those missions had responded in various ways.

Some Hispanic cultural elements had to have filtered back into La Junta with the returning laborers. Many Juntans must have wanted to have a stronger connection to some of those elements, including items for the Native trade network, and some possibly desired the ministrations of missionaries in their own valley. On the other hand, the great majority of Juntans would clearly demonstrate over time that they wanted those Hispanic cultural benefits on their own terms. As Morgenthaler wrote, "La Juntans did not embrace Christianity only for itself, but also for the promise of a larger social relationship."[50] In the aftermath of the Pueblo Revolt in upper New Mexico in 1680, the Juntans and their allies the Jumanos saw a golden opportunity.

Forging an Alliance, 1680–1712

These captains of La Junta, with this witness Juan Sabeata . . . resolved in a junta which they convoked that this witness should come to this pueblo of El Paso to ask for a minister so that when they were sick he might comfort them, and those who would die he might bury as Christians and the rest of the people he might baptize. . . . At the same time, he says that he was sent by said people to seek favour of the Spaniards in order that they may defend them from their enemies, the Apaches.

—Petition of Juan Sabeata, El Paso, 20 October 1683

In remote lands and without any aid, one cannot apply pressure since we were without any Spanish official. And, Sir, even though the Natives there are of the most docile nature, they are surrounded by many enemy nations and they more easily unite with each other than with their missionaries. . . . The departure of the people for work in the haciendas without the arrangements desired by our Lord King for the protection of the poor Indians keeps most of them absent, with the missionary not knowing how to keep them under regular instruction.

—Fray Agustín de Colina to Governor Pardiñas, 18 November 1688

The last two decades of the 1600s and the first decade of the 1700s saw major realignments in the Indigenous and European societies throughout the northern frontier of Spain's American colonies. The Apache establishment of dominance in the South Plains led a group of harried Jumanos in the early 1680s to join Juntans in asking for missions and a military alliance with Hispanics. The New Mexico Hispanics, reduced to a struggling presence in the El Paso district due to the successful Pueblo Revolt in upper New Mexico in 1680, were eager to investigate this promised new field of expansion. But the missions[1] begun in the La Junta valley failed to gain the support of the viceroyal authorities, as those officials quickly became preoccupied with the new major incursions of the English and the French along their northeastern frontiers from Texas to Florida. Reactions to the missionaries were mixed among the Juntans themselves and definitely hostile from neighboring Native groups. The Franciscans ceased their perilous efforts at La Junta after 1689, not to be renewed until the French threat drew much closer after 1710. The frustrated mission efforts revealed the basic issues that would define the history of the La Junta district for the next century. Yet the migrant labor of Juntans increased and their military alliance with Hispanics remained firm.

A Native Request and the First Missions

Juan Sabeata knew his way around. As a Jumano leader, he was familiar with the vast Southern Plains in which they operated as international traders between nations like the Caddo in East Texas and the Pueblo Indians and Hispanics in New Mexico. And as would any good trader, he knew his way around people. As an adult he had been baptized in Parral. There and elsewhere, he learned what appealed to Hispanics and what would attract their cooperation. And as a savvy diplomat, he knew when a great opportunity presented itself.[2]

In "the year '80"—the year 1680—the major revolt of the Pueblo Indians throughout upper New Mexico expelled all the Hispanics from that territory, causing them to seek refuge in the El Paso district. Most of the Pueblos had taken up arms after more than a decade of drought, pestilence, Apache attacks, and renewed religious persecution had further exacerbated a half-century of simmering tension over religious imposition, labor and tribute demands, and periodic acrimonious relations between Hispanic governors and Franciscan missionaries.[3] Some Jumanos who had up until recently been living in the Eastern Pueblos also retreated to the El Paso district, as it became the new (and only) western trading destination for the Plains Jumanos. Around this time, the Jumanos who customarily hunted along the Pecos and Concho[4] Rivers in West Texas, 160 miles or more northeast of La Junta, were being forced out of that area by the Apaches and taking refuge along the Rio del Norte, especially near the La Junta valley.[5] At the same time a feeble attempt by the Hispanics and their Native allies in 1681 to reconquer New Mexico failed. So everyone set about forming a more permanent presence in the El Paso district, establishing there in 1682–1683 the first presidio north of Parral and several villages for Hispanics and Natives respectively.[6] This sudden expansion of the El Paso district caused Nueva Vizcaya to try to claim it as part of its territory, but El Paso's new status as the multi-settlement linchpin of any future Hispanic New Mexico promptly led to the El Paso district being declared a part of New Mexico in 1685.[7]

Hearing of this concentration of refugee missionaries and poverty-stricken Hispanics and Pueblo Natives at El Paso del Norte, Sabeata and his Jumano colleagues seized the opportunity to offer the Hispanics renewed trade goods, food supplies, and a major new field of expansion including mission establishments. Up to this time there were no Hispanic foundations in what is today's Texas other than the new El Paso settlements. For their part, the Jumanos who had taken refuge near La Junta were greatly in need of military help against the Apaches on the South Plains. So in August 1683 a small delegation led by Sabeata came to El Paso to ask New Mexico governor Antonio de Otermín to authorize resumed visits to their lands for trading purposes and to aid them in resisting the Apaches. The envoys said that they lived close by the people at La Junta, who raised various food crops and were their friends.[8]

But the delay involved in sending a new Hispanic governor impeded a response, and so in October 1683 Sabeata and six companions again traveled to El Paso to petition the new governor, Domingo Gironza Petris de Cruzate. Cruzate probably had the Franciscan superior, Nicolás López, at his side. The Jumano leader lined up his arguments accordingly, at least as Cruzate reported it. He began with spiritual pleas. Introducing himself as a baptized Christian, he said that many of the Jumanos, including himself, were presently at La Junta, where the six Christian captains—Don Juan, Alonso, Bartolomé, Luis, Don Francisco, and Joseph—and himself were "disconsolate because, being Christians, they do not have a minister to teach them the things of God." The effect of over a century of Juntan relations with Nueva Vizcayans was evident in the Spanish personal names of the six captains and the claim of being Christian. Sabeata said that these leaders sent him to ask for missionaries to baptize their people, console them, and give them Christian burial. Cruzate reported that Sabeata stated that there were "more than ten thousand souls who are asking for baptism, and these are the Julimes and Humanas." Sabeata then turned to what was assuredly his most urgent request: help against the Apaches. To bolster his appeal, he added that there were many tribes to the east, all the way to the vaunted kingdom of the Natives whom the Spaniards called "the Tejas" (the Hasinai in today's East Texas) and the fabled Gran Quivira, who would welcome trade and missionaries. Indeed, he reported, some messengers from the Hasinai had told him that "Spaniards are entering by water in wooden houses" to barter with them.[9]

Presumably Governor Cruzate recognized as exaggerated propaganda the claim of ten thousand persons asking for baptism. The news that really jolted the governor and others was that ships bearing "Spaniards" were trading with Natives to their east. No Spaniards were known to be along the future Texas–Louisiana coast of the Gulf of Mexico. But Spanish officials were aware of proposals being made in France for incursions there. This was the first notice to reach Hispanic ears anywhere that the French were actually entering into the lands along the Gulf Coast. Unknown to them, the French explorer La Salle had sailed down the Mississippi River in 1682, passing from the mouth of the Arkansas River on March 4 to the mouth of the Mississippi on April 9. La Salle had visited with Natives who told him that there were rich mines across the plains to the west. Thus it is quite possible that the Hasinai nations had heard of, if not actually seen, Frenchmen using sailing ships before Sabeata's trip to El Paso in the summer of 1683. Another possibility is that the reported traders on boats were French pirates operating in the Gulf of Mexico.[10]

Sabeata ended his presentation with an extended avowal of the divine hand in all of this. About four years previously, he claimed, a large cross floated down from the sky to the Jumano settlement just as enemies were entering their lands. Using the cross as a battle standard, they had a great victory, and the cross continued to protect them. The Hispanics would be able to come and see it.[11] Cruzate reported Sabeata's declaration to the viceroy, pointing out the French danger. But the Hispanics cooped up in El Paso had plenty of other reasons to act on Sabeata's petition. Citizens and soldiers were still captivated by alleged rich kingdoms to the east and despondent if not despairing of their current situation. For his part, Father Nicolás López, the new acting *custos* (leader) of the New Mexico Franciscans, must have been hardly able to contain his excitement. A criollo (born in New Spain of Spanish parentage), in 1654 he had professed religious vows as a member of the austere order of Discalced Franciscans or Alcantarines, the same group to which Father García de San Francisco had belonged. Probably around the age of fifty, López was looking for new spiritual and physical challenges.

Since the Discalced Franciscans in New Spain generally preached only among Hispanics, López had volunteered for the New Mexico missions conducted by the Observant Franciscans of the Holy Gospel Province among the Pueblo nations. He must have been terribly disappointed when upon his arrival in El Paso with Father Ayeta's supply caravan in the summer of 1680 he learned that all the missions above El Paso had just been destroyed. López accompanied Ayeta during Governor Otermín's failed attempt to reconquer New Mexico in late 1681 and early 1682.[12] Sent to Mexico City in late 1682 to report on the situation on the frontier, he was appointed by the Franciscan authorities there as the *procurador* (supply master) and vice-custos for those missions.[13]

On one of his journeys from or to Mexico City, Father Lopéz had already been told by a priest in Parral that many of the nations from the La Junta district had come there and asked repeatedly for ministers but had been denied due to their great distance from the Hispanic outposts in Nueva Vizcaya. As delighted as he must have been at Sabeata's proposal, López was a seasoned minister, not a reckless enthusiast. He decided to test the good faith of the emissaries, who said that their people were serving the king in the mines and fields of the Parral district, by demanding that churches be built at La Junta to receive the missionaries when they arrived. Immediately Sabeata's group took measurements of the El Paso altars and dispatched Native messengers. Within twenty days, more than sixty persons—men and women—arrived in El Paso to proclaim that two churches were being built.

Accompanied and guided by a large group of the petitioners, Father López set out for La Junta through the Suma territory, walking and barefoot in keeping with his Discalced Franciscan austerity. With him went two other Franciscan priests, Antonio Acevedo and Juan Zavaleta, and some Tigua aides. The Tiguas had either voluntarily or involuntarily come to the El Paso district with the Hispanics after the 1680 rebellion in upper New Mexico. A standard missionary practice, whenever possible, was to bring along some Christian Natives to serve as aides and even more importantly as "models" of behavior in new mission efforts.[14] It was the beginning of December. Two weeks later, on December 15, Captain Juan Domínguez de Mendoza, the governor's second-in-command and an experienced frontiersman on the Southern Plains, and his twenty volunteers set out for La Junta from San Lorenzo, the site of the Spanish headquarters about thirty miles downriver from El Paso del Norte. They were all intent on a major expedition into the Southern Plains and the nations beyond.[15]

The Spanish officials at El Paso—Otermín, Cruzate, and Domínguez—called the people at La Junta "Julimes," an error echoed by several historians ever since.[16] Father López never identified the Juntans as such; rather he referred to them generically as "Indian nations." As noted in the previous chapter, in 1686 Alonso de Posada, cognizant of the reports by his fellow Franciscans, located the "Sublimes" between the Concho and Toboso nations, where one would expect the Julimes to be as one descended the Rio Conchos toward La Junta. At La Junta itself he specifically identified, besides the "Jumanos rayados," the Oposmes, Boloaques/Poloaques [Polacmes], and Polulamas/Colutames/Polumas [probably Pocsalmes]. Later information would identify these three nations as those nearest the river junction, where the first missionaries established their residence. Posada also reported that these people "go during their times (*por sus tiempos*) to work in the fields of the Real de Parral and in its mines."[17]

The Franciscans undertaking this first effort to establish missions at La Junta in 1683 were acting from within the religious jurisdiction of their Holy Gospel (*Santo Evangelio*) Province headquartered in Mexico City. This was the mother province of all the Observant Franciscans in New Spain, first established in 1534. At the end of that century they began their missionary work in upper New Mexico and, as previously noted, opened the El Paso district in 1659, as the gateway into that territory. Early on these missions had been constituted as a regional unit of the Holy Gospel Province and given the title of the Custody of the Conversion of St. Paul (*la Custodia de la Conversión de San Pablo*)—for shorthand, the San Pablo Custody. In that way a local Franciscan in New Mexico appointed as the custos of the custody could provide more immediate direction for the local missionary efforts than could be done from the great distance geographically and temporally of Mexico City.[18]

One of López's companions on this expedition, the criollo Fray Juan Zavaleta, had been serving in Isleta in central New Mexico before the Pueblo Revolt. A veteran missionary, having professed vows as a Franciscan in 1645 in Puebla, he was one of the fortunate few to escape the violence in 1680. As a refugee in the El Paso district, he helped organize the Tiguas who had also come down from Isleta into the new El Paso mission of Corpus Christi de Ysleta in 1682. It must have been Zavaleta who brought along the Tiguas to help found the La Junta missions. He was surely selected for the expedition at least in part because he knew the Jumano language. Although not fully proficient, he had dealt with the Jumanos during those people's visits to Isleta prior to the Pueblo Revolt.[19] The third Franciscan in this expedition, Antonio Acevedo, a criollo native of Veracruz, made his religious vows in Puebla in 1674, almost thirty years after Zavaleta. Considering that he still had to complete several years of study of philosophy and theology before being ordained, he may have been entering his first missionary assignment when he arrived in El Paso by May 1682.[20]

Captain Domínguez caught up with the missionaries at the river junction on December 29. As he had traveled down the Rio del Norte from San Lorenzo, the people in the scattered rancherías of the Suma nation, many of whom were already Christian—that is, baptized—had asked him for help against the Apaches. Upon arriving at La Junta, Domínguez did not tarry, spending only one full day there. He was in a hurry to reach the alleged great kingdoms across the Southern Plains. Nevertheless, he waxed eloquent about the abundance of wood and the suitability of the lands along the river. Later observers would moderate those statements. Domínguez named the river junction La Navidad en las Cruces due to it being the days of Christmas (*la Navidad*) and "the crosses possessed by the rancherías which are settled on both sides of the Rio del Norte." So the peace crosses planted a century earlier had remained or been replaced by newer ones. The El Paso captain noted that the people were versed in the Mexican (Nahuatl) language. He reported that over one hundred persons were baptized by the time his expedition left the river junction.[21]

With the benefit of having spent two weeks at La Junta, Father López gave more detail from a missionary perspective. He found "a great many Christian Indians" in the valley who had been baptized in the Parral district. López approvingly noted that they had carefully constructed, as promised, a very large church and a house for the friars at the river junction. Another large church with its altar built to specifications had been built of reeds at the first town the missionaries had reached about fourteen miles upriver, probably the 1580s' San Bernardino. The people were cultivating a mixture of native and imported crops: native corn, beans, and squash, and Spanish-introduced wheat, melons, watermelons, and even tobacco (tobacco was a New World crop, but not previously among the Juntans). Thus Juntan society was already manifesting elements of Spanish-colonial cultural influence in crops, language, and religion obtained through their migrant-labor experience.

López reported that the missionaries "began to catechize and baptize many children because their parents requested it so insistently." He counted more than 500 baptisms, of whom "many were children saved (*logrados*) who died during this time." This is the first notice of what must have been an epidemic at La Junta. The Franciscan wrote Governor Cruzate in El Paso asking that sixty men be sent to settle at La Junta at their own expense, attracted by the richness of the country, to help safeguard the

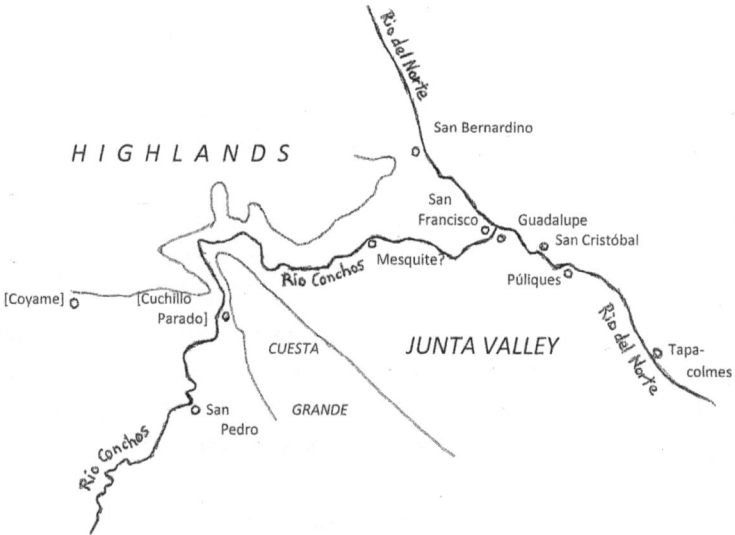

Figure 5: La Junta district in the 1680s. (By Robert E. Wright)

inhabitants so that they would not abandon the valley. The governor, worried enough about keeping able Hispanics from deserting El Paso, refused the request, that probably would not have sat well with the Juntans anyway. Four other chapels were begun at La Junta, making a total of six for the nine nations whom the friars were attending.[22]

This was probably one chapel for each of six towns. From events already recounted and those to be discussed, it is clear that five of those towns were the ones that Hispanics sooner or later named San Bernardino, San Francisco, San Cristóbal, Guadalupe, and Púliques—all along the Rio del Norte. The sixth was either at Tapacolmes at the lower end of the La Junta valley (see the discussion below) or El Mezquite along the Conchos River near the base of the Cuesta Grande. Both of the 1580s expeditions as well as Domínguez on his return journey to El Paso in 1684 (see below) noted a settlement at a location like El Mezquite, but not at the future site of San Juan, on the Conchos River closer to its junction with the Rio del Norte.[23] Since the town organization in the La Junta valley, including homes and property management, was already established before the arrival of the missionaries, the churches built there were not the center of a missionary-designed and managed town as in Texas and California. They were most probably like the situation in New Mexico, where churches were usually additions on the edge of town and land management remained under Native control.[24]

On December 31 Captain Domínguez accompanied by Fathers López and Zavaleta left the river junction to march out toward the Southern Plains. The much younger Father Acevedo, a relative novice at missionary work among Natives, was left alone to carry on the ministry in the La Junta valley. When the travelers passed back through

La Junta six months later on their return journey, Zavaleta remained to assist Acevedo. López went back to the Hispanic settlements to begin petitioning for the official founding of missions at La Junta and beyond. By that time the six churches were all made of wood (*madera*) and straw, to be built of adobe later. On this return passage through La Junta, Domínguez counted more than 500 natives from seven nations assembled to pledge allegiance to Spain in a formal act of possession that he carried out. At the alleged request of the native governors and captains, Domínguez named four of them as officially recognized captains "to better come to the service of both majesties" (God and King), and he handed them the coveted staffs of authority. With this official act of possession, the recognized Native intermediaries, and the resident missionaries, La Junta henceforth was considered a part of the Spanish realm.[25]

The missionary part of the strategy of Sabeata and his allies had worked well: there were now Franciscans residing at La Junta, and official colonial approval would be sought for these foundations. The second part of the strategy, and undoubtedly the major one for the Jumanos and their Plains companions, was engaged when the expedition marched out onto the Southern Plains. The Jumanos anticipated that the expedition would push back the Apaches who were driving them from their customary territory.[26] When the joint expedition reached the Pecos River, Sabeata and the other Indigenous captains convinced Captain Domínguez to go after the Apaches who were reportedly nearby. Directed by frequent reports from Jumano scouts about Apaches ahead as they advanced, the Hispanics were repeatedly advised to pitch camp for a day or more to verify the situation. During these halts everyone actually spent their days killing buffalo. They reached the Concho River without Domínguez's men ever sighting Apaches, although one night a few of their animals were stolen.

Domínguez decided that the scouts' reports were all a ruse designed by Sabeata, and on February 19 he banished Sabeata and the Jumano scouts from his expedition. Two Piros departed with them. Domínguez even charged later that Sabeata tried to incite some Natives to kill him and his men, but those Natives did not cooperate in the plot. In his report the Spanish captain guessed that Natives had killed Sabeata (*que le habran muerto*) due to his bad actions. Actually, the Jumano leader remained very much alive and would reappear at La Junta in late 1688. Captain Domínguez tarried for the next two months on the Colorado River, allegedly waiting for forty-eight nations whom he was expecting, including the "Tejas." During this time, thousands more buffalo were slaughtered, not even counting those with carcasses left on the plains. On May 1 the expedition turned back toward La Junta, after Apaches finally appeared and along with some Salineros from Nueva Vizcaya attacked them three times in a row.[27]

When he reached La Junta again, Domínguez was warned of uprisings by the Sumas and other nations upriver along the Rio del Norte toward El Paso. Those nations were reacting to the disturbed situation of their district due to the greatly increased settlement by Hispanic refugees from upper New Mexico, and they were encouraged by the success of the Pueblo Revolt along with instigators from the north. So, leaving Fathers Acevedo and Zavaleta to continue the mission work at La Junta, on June 14 Captain Domínguez, Father López, and the rest of the expedition departed to the southwest, taking a long detour back to El Paso by way of the Conchos and Sacramento Rivers. Eight leagues from the La Junta river junction they passed through "a place with a lot of people" before halting at the foot of a mountain ridge, undoubtedly the Cuesta Grande at the western limits of the La Junta valley. Eight leagues further on they came across a "very numerous ranchería," and about eleven leagues beyond that "other rancherias that are very close to each other." These distances correspond in a very approximate way to places later known as El Mezquite, Boca del Rio de Conchos, and either San Pedro or Coyame. Domínguez made no further comment about any of these populations.[28]

Divided Indigenous Responses

Fathers Zavaleta and Acevedo lasted at La Junta only two months after the departure of the Domínguez expedition in mid-1684.[29] By that time the uprisings against the Spanish that had caused the Domínguez expedition to detour to the south on their return to El Paso reached La Junta. The first hostilities on the Nueva Vizcayan frontier had broken out in early May much farther west, undoubtedly with some inspiration from the still unquelled Pueblo Revolt, but also due to more local factors. The Janos and western Sumas in the far northwest area of Nueva Vizcaya attacked the new Janos mission and the older Casas Grandes settlement below it. Then the Mansos at El Paso, who had been restless since 1681, rebelled with the Sumas in their area. By late May the laborers in the Parral district who were from the Rio Conchos and La Junta were leaving to join the uprising to their north. The hostilities thus stretched across the entire northern belt of Nueva Vizcaya.

What prompted these various uprisings is not entirely clear. One factor in the northwest and in the El Paso district had to have been the tensions accompanying the very recent settling of Hispanic refugees from New Mexico in those places: at Casas Grandes, along the Santa María River to the east of that place among the western Concho natives above the Tarahumara country, and in the El Paso district itself. But that does not explain what happened in the Rio Conchos drainage, where Hispanic settlement was already well established, nor at La Junta where there were no Hispanic immigrants. A Concho leader later testified that the hacienda workers were reacting to recent imprisonments of some of their people.[30]

In July word reached Parral that rebels coming from a wide region were gathering at La Junta at the ranchería of Don Juan de Salaíces with its church of San Cristóbal. The name of the Native leader of the ranchería indicates an earlier connection, either of godparenthood or esteem, with the brothers Juan and Antonio Salaíces, who arrived in the Parral district in the 1640s. Neither is known to have been an *encomendero*.

But when Juan died in 1676, he had thirty to forty slaves and "many free and salaried workers." His brother Antonio who inherited his estate already had several haciendas, including a farming estate with 4,000 cattle in the San Bartolomé Valley that was named, wouldn't you know, San Cristóbal.[31]

The reports of a rebel gathering at La Junta are the first to identify all the nations there with the names by which they were known ever since. Twenty years later, in 1715, the names of all the towns where these nations lived and the location of those towns were provided by another expedition. Adding that later information enables a much more informative analysis of the events in 1684 (see figure 5).[32] The mention of San Cristóbal as the rebel gathering point makes it the first La Junta town to be noted with its permanent colonial name. In 1715 it was inhabited by Pocsalmes and located on the left-hand (east or future Texas) side of the Rio del Norte a few miles below the river junction. A town already called San Francisco by 1715 and inhabited by the Oposmes was in the southwest corner of the river junction. That is where in December 1683 the Natives had received the Franciscans with a church and a residence prepared for them (Dominguez's La Navidad en las Cruces). It was therefore at San Francisco where Father Juan Zavaleta joined Father Antonio Acevedo upon the former's return from the trip into the Southern Plains. From this mission center the two priests visited the other La Junta valley towns.

It is worthy of note that these two places, San Cristóbal and San Francisco, were the towns named Santiago and Santo Tomás at the river junction by the Espejo expedition a century earlier. That they would be the only ones that already had Christian names known by the 1715 expedition before it arrived is a further indication of the local prominence of these two towns in the century between 1580 and 1680, and supports the earlier conclusion that Espejo's Santiago, the most important town then, was the place named San Cristóbal a century later. Whatever names the missionaries in 1683–1684 gave to the chapels in the other towns at this time did not last, since the 1715 expedition gave new names to them.

Griffen discovered the story of the nativistic Concho religious leader Taagua, who made the church at San Cristóbal his ceremonial center during this revolt. That San Cristóbal was the staging center for the uprising makes sense: it was probably still the largest town, missionaries were not residing there, and even more important it was on the other side of the Rio del Norte and thus better protected from any approaching Hispanic forces. Taagua would sit in front of the altar and address the assembly through another man standing close by him (mimicking a Hispanic with his interpreter?), assuring the Natives of the supernatural power he had been given and exhorting them to attack the Hispanics. The Native witnesses to these events later told the Hispanic authorities that all the Indians feared him and thus followed him—statements that were perhaps too self-exculpatory. Taagua had the people express obedience to him in the Spanish manner—coming before him one by one, kneeling three times, and kissing his hand—before giving them a priest-like blessing. One witness stated that Taagua had been joined by the "Pusalmes [Pocsalmes], Polalmes [Polacmes], Cacalotes, Conejos, Cholomes, and Conchos, and a number of other groups that he [the witness] was 'unfamiliar with.' Other nations—such as the Oposmes, Púlicas, Auchanes, and Tapacolmes—had claimed that they were not angry with the Europeans." Infuriated, Taagua had threatened them.[33]

The report of this witness, who was evidently himself from the La Junta district given the groups with which he was familiar, is the first of several between 1685 and 1693 that establish the Native names of almost all the Indigenous groups in the La Junta district. The first four rebel-allied groups that he named were identified in 1715 as those in the valley towns of San Cristóbal (Pocsalmes), Guadalupe (Polacmes) in the southeast corner of the river junction (today's Ojinaga) across the Conchos River from San Francisco, San Juan Bautista (Cacalotes) along the Conchos River above San Francisco, and Aranzazu (Conejos) north of San Francisco along the Rio del Norte. The nation of the Cholomes was from across the Cuesta Grande in the Coyame valley and upriver along the Rio del Norte. Even though there were Conchos in the town of San Antonio in the La Junta valley in 1715, that nation was not named in any of the other listings of people at La Junta in this earlier 1683–1693 period. The Conchos noted as part of the 1684 uprising, therefore, were from their own territory below that of the Julimes south of the Coyame valley. Those groups resistant to the revolt were from San Francisco (Oposmes) at the river junction; the Púliques and Tapacolmes both below the junction along the Rio del Norte; and the Auchanes who lived between the Cholomes and the Julimes south of the Cuesta Grande.[34]

Table 1: Pueblos / "Nations" Noted along the Rio del Norte, 1582, 1684*

	upriver west side	NW river junction	SW river junction	SE river junction	near NE river junction	down-river	south end of valley
1582	San Bernardino	San Juan Evangelista	Santo Tomás		Santiago		
1684	San Bernardino (unnamed) (1715 Conejos at Aranzazu)	presumably abandoned	La Navidad (mission residence) (Oposmes) (1715 San Francisco)	(Polacmes) (1715 Guadalupe)	San Cristóbal (Pocsalmes)	(Púliques)	(Tapacolmes)

* Besides these places/groups along the Rio del Norte, in 1684 the Mezquites and Cacalotes were noted (in 1715 their location is given as along the Rio Conchos within the La Junta valley).

Father Agustín de Colina, who ministered at La Junta in 1687–1689, later listed the nations there as "mezquites, conejos, cacalotes, polagmes, pusalames, oposmes, pulicas, y tepacolomes." This list faithfully followed the order of the three zones of population in the La Junta valley in 1715. The first three nations listed were those above the river junction, at El Mezquite, Aranzazu, and San Juan along the Conchos and Norte Rivers. The next three were at the river junction itself, at Guadalupe, San Francisco, and San Cristóbal. The final two were below the river junction along the Rio del Norte at Púliques and Tapacolmes. This confirms that some Tapacolmes were still in the La Junta valley at this time and points to their being at its lower end. The nations listed by Colina are the same as those given by the revolt witness in 1685, but with the addition of the Mezquites, actually named for the first time. The Cholomes, Conchos, and Auchanes in the 1685 witness list were not named by Colina because they were outside the La Junta valley, across the Cuesta Grande and thus not within the initial mission district.[35]

Colina wrote that the rebels in 1684 attacked the missions at La Junta and took everything (*lo que tenian*) from the friars. The two missionaries would have been killed, he asserted, if some Polacmes and Oposmes had not come to their aid: "they gave some assistance to go out (*dieron algun favor para salir*) toward Julimes." In their flight the Franciscans became separated, yet, "stressed by hunger and nakedness," they providentially encountered General Retana who was in pursuit of the Julimes and other rebel nations. Retana brought the friars safely to his presidio of Conchos.[36] A much later source asserted that the Julimes were the principal instigators of the uprising in this area. It also reported that the Tigua aides of the friars were not as fortunate as the Franciscans, since the Tigua were executed.[37]

The uprising in the more settled districts of northeastern Nueva Vizcaya ended about six months after it began, with natives returning to their work on haciendas and ranches and in mines.[38] Griffen concluded that "Taagua's message had only momentary attraction, and not even this for all of the people congregated at La Junta. . . . These riverine pueblos by this time were rather adjusted to a relationship with the Spanish Empire which supplemented the local economy."[39] If the 1685 witness account is reliable, in the La Junta valley the settled communities had more or less split in their response to the uprising, taking into consideration that the Polacmes of the town later named Guadalupe were divided, with some protecting the missionaries according to Father Colina. On the other hand, the Cholomes from across the Cuesta Grande in the Coyame valley, as well as the Conchos to their south and west, opted for the rebel alliance.

By 1715 the people on both sides of the mountain ridge would be known as agriculturalists and migrant laborers. Perhaps the difference was that those in the Coyame valley were more exposed to possible hostilities from other groups, and thus more apt to join with them for self-preservation, than those in the more sheltered La Junta valley. The towns at the river junction were also the more concentrated and populous settlements, and as a result better able to fend for themselves. Finally, the Cholomes were not as linguistically or culturally associated with those in the La Junta valley as the latter were among themselves. This difference between the valley Juntans and the Cholomes across the western ridge would repeat itself in subsequent flare-ups.

Missionary Visions and Viceroyal Priorities

Back in El Paso after the expedition into Texas, Father López was initially unaware of the flight of the missionaries from La Junta. With visions of many nations awaiting conversion, he held a meeting of all the Franciscans in the El Paso district in September to discuss the discouraging situation in El Paso and New Mexico and what he thought was the promising situation in La Junta and Texas. They agreed that he should go to Mexico City to petition, among other things, that the viceroy send missionaries and settlers to the nations encountered by the Domínguez expedition. After his arrival at the capital, López petitioned the viceroyal authorities in May 1685 to authorize sending twenty missionaries. At the same time, he obtained permission from the friar in charge of all the Franciscan work in Nueva España to send out an appeal for missionaries to all the Franciscan provinces of the viceroyalty. The missionary ardor of the Franciscans was still strong in New Spain: forty-six friars volunteered. But Pedro de la Bastida, the *fiscal* (legal counselor) of the Audiencia (high court) in Mexico City, did not support the proposal and the Junta General (High Council) in Mexico City refused his request. López repeated his petition with a more formal memorial and documentation in early August but was again rejected.[40]

Father López was determined. Still in Mexico City, he finally learned in the first few months of 1686 of the royal decree of August 2 the previous year, in which the king asked for information about any possible sightings of Frenchmen and the advisability of settling the Gulf Coast between Florida and Tampico. López seized the opportunity to resubmit his petition to the viceroy in March. Predictably refused once more, he wrote directly to Madrid. Given the usual slowness of transoceanic communications, his April letter did not arrive at the royal court until November 11.[41] It took almost another year, after the habitual involved consultations and deliberations in such matters, for the king on September 26, 1687, to direct the viceroy to "send 20 missionaries to assist in the *conversiones* of the Río del Norte." The king also charged the viceroy "to heed the proposals made by Father Fray Nicolás López concerning the conversions of New Mexico, and to give a full and detailed report of that which he [the viceroy] is doing."[42]

In the meantime, however, realizing that communications with Madrid would take many months, López had announced that he would depart Mexico City for the El Paso district at the end of May 1686. He declared himself ready to reenter the lands to the northeast of La Junta, having already made a manual of the Jumano language that he intended to have printed.[43] Now appointed as the custos of the San Pablo Custody and reappointed as its supply master, he was determined to at least reoccupy La Junta with missionaries. Once back at El Paso, he soon arranged to send Fathers Agustín de Colina and Joaquín de Hinojosa, whom he had probably brought with him from central New Spain, and Brother Diego de San Miguel.[44]

Father Colina was from the same province of San Diego of the Discalced Franciscans as Father García de San Francisco and Father López. He must have been one of the zealous Franciscans who responded to López's appeal from Mexico City in 1685 for missionaries.[45] Father Hinojosa was a criollo, born in Puebla. He entered the Holy Gospel Province of the Franciscans in 1677 at the young age of 16 or 17, a decade before he went to La Junta. Considering that he still had to study philosophy and theology for several years, La Junta may have been his first missionary assignment.[46] He was evidently held in high regard from the beginning, since he was initially designated as the leader (*presidente*) of the Franciscan trio. They would minister at La Junta from February 1687 to October 1688.[47]

In the La Junta context of baptized and unbaptized Natives, the inexperienced Hinojosa immediately had his youthful idealism and lessons in sacramental theology put to the test. According to Catholic teaching, baptism into the Christian community requires faith on the part of an adult or, in the case of children, on the part of their parents. Hinojosa therefore had qualms about baptizing Natives too quickly. He wrote that he would not do it, being unconvinced by the argument given by some missionaries that, by baptizing many, at least a few would be saved, presumably through their actual good faith or by dying promptly after having been baptized (as in the case of small children). A fairly universal missionary practice also gave him pause: the well-known axiom of attracting people's adhesion through filling their stomachs or by other gifts.

Suspecting that the Juntans probably thought that such gestures were only being done in order to convert them and not out of true charity, Hinojosa consulted Father Martin del Castillo, a Franciscan elder back in Mexico City. Castillo wrote back that a missionary should avoid giving any type of gift that could be interpreted wrongly. Hinojosa put this advice into practice, alluding to the biblical passage of Romans 10:17, "because I know that it is not through the mouth but rather through hearing that faith enters." If others argued that one should offer all sorts of things to new people being brought into mission life, Hinojosa asserted that those of that opinion should go and live among the people and they would experience the failure of material gifts to bring about real conversion. "We experienced this quite well in the two Fathers Juan de Zavaleta and Antonio de Acevedo [previously at La Junta]. With all their love and good example (that indeed matter a lot in efforts at conversion), we see what they experienced."[48]

Who knows if Father Colina, Hinojosa's more experienced elder, agreed with him. If he did, there may have been very few baptisms during their time at La Junta. As for gifts, whatever the missionaries managed to spare in terms of food supplies must have been very gratefully accepted. Colina stated that there had been a drought for several years and the people were lacking grain. The three Franciscans maintained themselves with supplies sent at times from El Paso. Later missionaries would learn that a continual problem at La Junta was the alternating periods of several years of drought interspersed with times of crop-destroying floods, providing an important stimulus for Juntans to engage in migrant labor for Hispanics.

In October 1688 the El Paso supply line for the Franciscans at La Junta was cut off when the Sumas upriver toward El Paso revolted again. The Juntans were invited by the Sumas to join in attacking El Paso, but they refused to take part. In fact, they promptly warned their missionaries and promised to defend them to the death before they would allow any harm to come to them. Governor Posada in El Paso sent ten soldiers to La Junta, who brought an order from the Franciscan vice-custos Diego de Mendoza for the missionaries to leave for Parral on account of the disturbances. Custos López must have been away, probably on another supply trip. Would he have reacted in the same way? By now Colina was president of the La Junta missions, and to hear him tell it, the parting between the Juntans and the missionaries was heartfelt and tearful on both sides.[49]

Writing to the governor of Nueva Vizcaya after arriving safely at the Zacatecan mission center of San Pedro de Conchos, the closest Franciscan residence to La Junta, Colina encapsulated the challenges that would face both Natives and missionaries at La Junta throughout the decades. Predominant were the remoteness of the place, the lack of any Hispanic authority, and the hostilities by outside nations:

> [We feel] compassion and regret for those poor Natives who were growing in affection for our teaching, even though there are many obstacles to its success which are not in our power to remove. In remote lands and without any aid, one cannot apply pressure since we were without any Spanish official. And, Sir, even though the Natives there are of the most docile nature, they are surrounded by many enemy nations and they more easily unite with each other than with their missionaries.... Our Superior was obliged to remove us since the Suma nation is in revolt and it would not have been easy to come to our aid.

Not only did the missionaries have to tread lightly with the Juntans, the Juntans had to tread lightly with the surrounding Native nations.

But Colina asserted that another obstacle was the Juntans' migrant labor situation. He found fault with the Juntan leaders, but even more so with their Hispanic employers:

> Besides, even if there were not a revolt, the departure of the people for work in the haciendas without the arrangements desired by our Lord King for the protection of

the poor Indians keeps most of them absent, with the missionary not knowing how to keep them under regular instruction [*reducirlos a la doctrina*]. This situation is due solely to the Native lieutenants and governors, whose only goal is to send the necessary number of workers. Some remain absent a long time trying to obtain the pay for their work. For this reason I have written to your Lordship a letter that Don Nicolás the [Native] lieutenant will give to you, begging that you make [their employers] pay, so that our injustice not scandalize the Natives, since it is very important that we be who we ought to be in order to make them what they should be. . . . [W]ithout remedying these things the [obstacles to] ministry are insurmountable.[50]

Colina's assertions underline the strong migrant-labor system already in place among the Juntans and indeed the role of the Native governors in providing the "necessary number" of workers. If the migrant-labor system at La Junta were indeed a *repartimiento* system in the full sense, the Juntans through their governors would be constrained by the colonial authorities to provide laborers seasonally to their Hispanic employers. If this labor were not forthcoming, the *repartimiento* system would call for an armed body from the Parral district to travel all the way to La Junta to enforce the labor levee.[51] No records of such compulsion have been found; the documentation actually indicates the opposite.

These events and statements manifest the complex and difficult intercultural realities faced by the Juntans who welcomed the Franciscans into their river junction towns. One option was to go along with those immediately surrounding Native groups who were hostile to the Hispanics by not protecting the missionaries nor even inviting them. The opposite was to stoutly defend the missionaries even though there was no Hispanic military support within hundreds of miles. A middle path was to protect the missionaries in minor situations but in major ones to quietly warn them and help them to escape from the violence of the neighboring groups. The latter option, protective of the missionaries but also of the Juntan towns that harbored the Franciscans, seems to have been chosen most of the time.

Shifting Borders

In the last two decades of the 1600s much larger problems were on the minds of Spanish officials in Mexico City and Spain. The Pueblo Revolt of 1680 was only one of several major regional and international events that made the next thirty-five years a time of trying to hold on to what had been gained—or at least claimed—in North America during the previous century and a half of rapid northward expansion.[52] After the Pueblo Revolt and the Great Northwestern uprising that followed it, viceroyal officials knew that they had to retake New Mexico to remove its potent demonstration of native autonomy. The uprisings brought about the establishment of a new line of presidios along the northern borders of Nueva Vizcaya and Sonora, stretching from

San Francisco de Conchos and El Paso westward through Janos to Fronteras.[53] In the following decades it became increasingly clear to Spanish officials that a major gap in that defensive line was La Junta, but it would take them half a century to fill it.

Further east, French penetration along the northern coast of the Gulf of Mexico threatened to establish a huge territorial menace between northern New Spain to the west and Spanish Florida to the east. Fearing especially the danger to New Spain's mining country of Nueva Vizcaya and Sonora and to Florida's Atlantic trade routes, Spanish officials in Mexico City and Havana focused their attention upon the pre-emptive establishing of forts and missions in East Texas in 1690 and Pensacola in 1698. But the Texas effort fizzled in 1693, removing any western impediment to the founding of French settlements at Biloxi and the mouth of the Mississippi in 1699 that signaled the beginnings of French Louisiana. Even further east the Spanish were unable to prevent the massive destruction of the missions all across northern Florida by raiding English Carolinians and their Native allies between 1680 and 1706, reducing Spanish Florida to three very isolated coastal forts. From then on Spain faced a daunting inter-European competition along most of the northern frontier of its colonies. In Europe itself Spain was absorbed in the War of Spanish Succession between 1701 and 1713, pitting the new Bourbon monarchy of Spain supported by France against the other European powers of England, Holland, and Austria.[54]

The news of Frenchmen in Texas was brought to the authorities in northwestern New Spain by the Natives who accompanied the three Franciscans who were ordered to leave La Junta for their safety in 1688. When word reached General Fernández de Retana, commander of the Conchos presidio to the south of the San Pedro mission, he alerted Governor Pardiñas in Parral. On November 2 the governor ordered Retana to organize a large expedition of ninety soldiers with additional Native allies to proceed to La Junta, wage all-out war against all the hostile nations in that direction below and beyond the Rio del Norte, and try to determine the location of the reported strangers. Retana was to treat the peaceful nations he encountered with the utmost urbanity in order to draw them into alliance with the Spaniards, and he was to erect crosses claiming possession of those lands for the Spanish empire in order to preempt any French claims. To make the same claims in the name of the Church, Retana was to take along Father Juan Sumesta, still the Zacatecan missionary in the Valley of San Bartolomé and "conversant in the languages of the Rio del Norte" area. The governor realized that such an expedition would require more than 100 days.[55]

Governor Pardiñas also wrote directly to Father Colina at the San Pedro mission on November 13, urging the Franciscans to return to the La Junta valley with Retana's expedition. Colina replied with expressions of consummate Diegeño unworthiness, assuring the governor that he was most willing, but stating that the decision rested with the custos (the newly appointed Francisco de Vargas) who at that very time was in Parral.[56] To gather more information, Retana summoned to his presidio some of the Natives who had accompanied the friars to the San Pedro mission. They were Don Nicolás, Juan de Salaises, and Salvador. Don Nicolás, around forty years old, was called lieutenant of La Junta at this time, indicating that he held an important Native position in the Spanish system. In his deposition on November 21, he declared through an interpreter that friendly Cíbolos living on the Rio del Norte were told by messengers from a Cíbolo leader further downriver that he and his people were coming with a "Spaniard" who had fled from his companions. They were also bringing letters from those "Spaniards" for the priests on the Rio del Norte. Thirty-six-year-old *ladino* Don Juan de Salaises and twenty-eight-year-old Salvador confirmed this information. They both belonged to the "people who are in the charge" of Don Nicolás (*su gente que es de su cargo*).[57]

The mention of Salaises is certainly interesting, as is the fact that he was *ladino*—that is, knew Spanish,[58] since it was at his town of San Cristóbal, with his name reported as Salaíces, that the rebels had gathered in 1684, only four years previously. Now he and his companions were protecting the missionaries. Salaises was the leader or former leader of San Cristóbal, and Don Nicolás was the primary agent of the Hispanics for the Juntans who were "in his charge." Actually, he was the governor of San Antonio de Julimes, the village on the Rio Conchos visited by Zacatecan missionaries from the San Pedro mission. So by this time, and probably much earlier, Spanish authorities had incorporated the La Junta district into their governing structure. Don Nicolás probably escorted the three Franciscans withdrawing from La Junta once they passed through his village of Julimes. By 1691 he was "governor of the nations of the north," a new jurisdiction separate from that of the Eastern Conchería, the older one actually disappearing around this time. Not only would Don Nicolás be the Hispanics' Native agent among the Juntans, he would also be the agent through whom nations beyond the Rio del Norte could approach the Hispanics.[59]

After these interviews Retana sent two other Juntans, Pedro and Alonso, back to their people to announce to them that their missionaries were returning with him to instruct and comfort them once more. They were also to tell the captains of the peaceful nations downriver from La Junta on the Rio del Norte that Retana would be entering there to punish the ones committing hostilities and that the captains should come to meet him. The Cíbolos were to be instructed to go to meet their Native captain approaching from downriver and bring back the "Spaniard" and the letters he was said to have.

The next day Retana's force moved to the San Pedro de Conchos mission, and Father Colina was formally interviewed. Colina declared that the previous year the Cíbolos and Jumanos had asked him for a letter to give to the "Spaniards" who were visiting among the Texas Indians, and that he told them that they should first bring him a letter from those Spaniards and he would answer it. The past September (1688) five Cíbolos had come to La Junta and told him through interpreters that a "Moro" clothed in armor with a helmet was with the nation next to the Texas Indians. Afterwards other Cíbolos had arrived and reported strangers who lived on the water in wooden houses. They declared that one of those houses had sunk. They also reported that those strangers told the people of that land as well as the "Cíbolos Jumanas" that the Spaniards of Parral were not good and that they [the French] were going to enter all of the country with their wagons. Father Hinojosa was also interviewed and reported the same news from the "Cíbolos and Jumanas."[60]

The End of the First Franciscan Period and of Jumano Diplomacy

Thus the Franciscans returned to La Junta after an absence of only a month. While Retana ventured into Texas, the friars continued to receive news from visiting Natives. Four days' journey beyond La Junta, Retana encountered Juan Sabeata, who had been dismissed by Captain Domínguez in 1684 and presumed executed. Far from it. He was now declared to be the principal leader of the Cíbolo and Jumana nations. Sabeata was reportedly happy to see Hispanic military beyond the Rio del Norte again and asked Retana for the purpose of the latter's expedition. When he was told about the concern with the French, he replied that they had been killed. In fact, he carried with him some items from the spoils of that incident that he had been given: some papers and a drawing of a ship with French writing. Never one to miss an opportunity, Sabeata declared that he himself would now take those to Governor Pardiñas. Some other Natives with Sabeata said that there were four or five Frenchmen who took refuge among the Texas Indians. In mid-April 1689 the Sabeata party arrived in Parral and were formally interviewed by the governor. One of them was Miguel, leader of the Cíbolos who visited La Junta, who had been baptized by Father Colina. Several of Miguel's people had been in the Valley of San Bartolomé during the harvest season.[61]

Although Sabeata's party in Parral spoke of the Franciscans as still in the La Junta valley, the friars apparently left those missions again around this time. Hinojosa's name appears in the El Paso records in March 1689, and Colina's in April of that year.[62] During the friars' few months back at La Junta, an outside nation, the Hediondos, had again posed a threat. This time it was an immediate one. They had planned to kill Father Hinojosa and Brother San Miguel at the Púliques village. But once again the missionaries were protected by the valley Juntans. Colina explained:

> The ones there [at Púliques] secured the Fathers safely and promptly alerted me. And the matter was so resolved with the captains of that people [the Hediondos? the Juntans?] that they themselves corrected the Native who had incited the others. The people there were so attentive [*finos*] that they did not allow the Fathers to leave, assuring them with their own lives.[63]

Perhaps it was this new incident that prompted the friars' departure. In doing so they avoided more peril the following year. In 1690 some Sumas, Conchos, Apaches, and even Janos gathered at La Junta while awaiting the departure of Gironza Cruzate, once more governor in El Paso, for another military campaign into upper New Mexico. Their plan was to attack El Paso in his absence. But a native in the Socorro mission warned Cruzate, and so he instead marched his men to La Junta. The plotters were alerted to his coming, and by the time he arrived in the valley they had dispersed.[64]

The resolute promoter of the La Junta missions, Father López, must have been deeply disappointed at the turn of events. He died in the El Paso convent before March 1692. In that same year Juan Sabeata paid his last known visit to Governor Pardiñas in Parral. Bringing a letter written almost two years earlier by the first Spanish missionaries in Texas who came from Coahuila, Sabeata mentioned that formerly there had been priests at La Junta. The Jumano leader admitted openly that he had finally brought the letter of the Texas missionaries to Nueva Vizcaya because he had been battling with other nations across the Rio del Norte, including Satagolillas and Sisimbles, who "had killed a good number of his people because they would not join with those nations against the Spaniards." He came to the Rio Conchos to ask the governor of the Julimes at the town of San Antonio (de Julimes) to go to La Junta and come to his aid with 400 or 500 of "his people"—that is, the Julimes and the Juntans.[65]

Sabeata's Jumanos were not the only nation being attacked by Sisimbles and other Chiso groups, who frequented the country within and south of the Big Bend of today's West Texas. In mid-1693 the leaders of the Suninoligla nation, itself a Chiso group, offered to ally with the Spanish against the hostile Chisos to the southeast of La Junta. A military expedition was formed with most of the Native auxiliaries gathering at La Junta. Among these allies were "those of the Cibola and Jumana nation with their governor Don Juan Fabiana [Sabeata] and his lieutenant Don Nicolás." This and a subsequent less garbled statement are the last known mentions of this tireless diplomat for his Jumano people.[66] Sabeata and his Jumanos, by now closely associated with some Cíbolos, never succeeded in making either the Hispanics or the French their strong military allies. Their final solution, rather than submitting themselves to sedentary subordination among either European group, is generally concluded to have been to blend into the more familiar semi-sedentary life of the Apaches, their previous mortal enemies, and disappear as an autonomous Native nation.[67]

The same 1693 Retana expedition had as its chaplain the last Franciscan who can be verified to have been in the La Junta valley for the next two decades. During the troops' presence there in July 17–22, Fray Gabriel de Montes de Oca from the mission of San Francisco de Conchos baptized 249 infant children of the "Christian" natives who lived there. Noting the lack of resident missionaries, Captain Retana had Governor Castillo petition the viceroy in November to have the Franciscan Zacatecas Province, whose mission territory lay below the La Junta district, send at least four priests for all the nations in the La Junta valley. In view of this petition the treasury officials in Durango and Zacatecas were asked to determine if missionary positions in the La Junta valley had ever been financed by the Crown. The viceroy's legal advisor, Juan de Escalante y Mendoza, may have been aware of the earlier strong exchange between the Mexico court's legal advisor and Father López of the Holy Gospel Province when he wrote that, once the treasury information was obtained, "one may determine whether to proceed to place and name missionaries from the Province to which these places pertain."[68]

The answer from the treasury officials in Durango in February 1694 was that no payment had ever been made for the La Junta district, and the matter was apparently dropped.[69] Even though at this time the Santo Evangelio Province in Mexico City with its San Pablo Custody was absorbed with the refounding of the New Mexico missions, they may have protested extending any invitation to the Zacatecas Province to take over the mission field in the La Junta valley. There was no mention of La Junta in a mission-by-mission report on the San Pablo Custody by Fray Juan Álvarez on 12 January 1706.[70]

Military Allies and Migrant Laborers

The major continental events at this time go a long way toward explaining why there was no enthusiasm in Mexico City for Father López's proposed major missionary movement at La Junta as a staging ground for conquests farther east. The French threat demanded a response much closer to its source along the Gulf Coast, and many other concerns had also arisen to preoccupy the Spanish authorities in Madrid, Mexico City, and even El Paso and Parral. Regionally, in the 1690s the Hispanic military were absorbed in putting down the Tarahumara rebellions and in the reconquest of upper New Mexico. The drawing off of Nueva Vizcayan resources to those areas made the Juntans all the more important as military allies of the Hispanics against local hostile groups. So did a major decrease in the population of Natives who could serve as allies. Due to "severe epidemics of smallpox and measles in 1692 and 1693 . . . an estimated one-third of Nueva Vizcaya's Indian population succumbed. When drought and famine followed in 1693–1694, Spanish mining operations in the Tarahumara were severely threatened."[71] There are no statistics on Juntan population numbers during the late 1600s, but an apparent epidemic has already been noted during the first missionary arrival in December 1683.

In 1691 some Norteños were part of a multi-nation coalition of auxiliary fighters from northeastern Nueva Vizcaya operating under Hispanic direction against the uprisings in the upper Tarahumara region.[72] In mid-1693 Captain Retana at the Conchos presidio organized the previously mentioned military campaign against the Chisos. The first step was to travel to the La Junta valley to meet the promised Native auxiliaries led by Governor Don Nicolás of Julimes. On July 16 Retana arrived at "the first settlement of friends, of the Mezquite nation," three leagues inside the valley along the Rio Conchos. Thus the named location of the Mezquites settlement appears for the first time in the known literature. The captain was warned to wait until night to proceed to the "Posalmes" settlement [San Cristóbal] at the river junction, since "the enemy Chisos are accustomed to approach to rob animals and so that we would not be discovered."[73]

Sending for some Cholomes from further up the Rio del Norte, Retana also ordered Governor Nicolás to bring the Suninoligla captain who had previously offered to make peace with the Spanish and to aid them in subduing the hostile Chisos groups. At this time the Suninoligla people were reported to be a day's journey from the easternmost La Junta settlement, gathering prickly-pear fruit to sustain themselves. When their captain appeared, he said that his people were happy to "live pacifically and attached to [agregado] the friends of this place." On July 22 the allied forces left for the Chisos territory. Retana listed each member. From the "nations of the North" came Governor Don Nicolás "de nacion Topacalme" and sixteen others, fifteen Púlicas, seven Cacalotes, thirteen Oposmes, seventeen Posalmes, nineteen Polacmes, eight Mezquites including Captain Juan de Salaises, and ten Conejos—in all, 106 warriors. Among the others, there were thirty Cíbolos-Jumanos, but only four Suninoliglas.[74]

The listing of the Tapacolmes among the nations of the North merits special notice, since when Captain Retana met with three Suninoligla captains and one Batayoligla captain upon the return of this expedition to La Junta, he invited them to live "at the place where the Tapacolmes had lived on this side of the canyon entrance" that marked the eastern end of the La Junta valley. So the Tapacolmes were no longer there, yet they were still being included among the nations of the North. The fact that Governor Don Nicolás, whose primary residence was Julimes, was numbered among the Tapacolme nation as their leader suggests that they had moved to the lower San Pedro River district by now, but only very recently. On the other hand, when asking for missionaries Retana had the Tapacolmes as well as the Jumanos among the nine Christian "friendly nations settled in said Junta de los rios." Perhaps this was a loose way of speaking. For their part, there is no evidence that the Suninoliglas ever settled in the La Junta valley. Although expected to be allies in a second campaign against the Chisos in November, none showed up. The Juntans, who did join Retana's forces again, told him that the Suninoliglas and the Cíbolos "had gone to the buffalo country to get meat."[75]

Retana's notice of the Tapacolmes no longer living at their former La Junta site is probably why Griffen stated that "some" Tapacolmes had moved into the already existing Santa Cruz pueblo south of the La Junta district "by 1693 or soon after." Even though a document in 1710 called Santa Cruz a Concho town, in 1724 the governor was a Tapacolme and he testified that the principal nation there was Tapacolme.[76] Another possible indication of an approximate date in the early 1790s for the major Tapacolme move is the statement of Don Marcos, the Santa Cruz governor in 1723, about the town having been "founded more than twenty-five years ago." That would be somewhat before 1698.[77] Since Santa Cruz is known to have existed long before that, this may have been a reference to a major Tapacolme arrival. That some people of this nation had already made their home before 1715 in the Rio Conchos area below La Junta, probably at Santa Cruz, is known from testimony in that latter year that eight Tapacolmes and four Julimes working in the San Bartolomé Valley were from "the rancherías of the Rio Conchos," explicitly distinguished from "the towns of the Rio del Norte."[78]

Hostilities were apparently frequent in the environs of the La Junta district in the 1690s, as Hispanics and Juntans battled alongside each other. The Chisos were reported to have been raiding the La Junta towns from campsites on both sides of the Rio del Norte below the La Junta valley. The Suninoliglas and Batayoliglas who made peace with Retana were Chisos bands, and some of their members continued to join others in raiding in the following decades.[79] Apparently, therefore, there were both Chisos raiders and Chisos allies with Hispanics at this time. "Del Norte" natives were also Hispanic allies in campaigns in 1697, 1704, and 1715.[80] Around 1712 a band of Cholomes, including at least some from Coyame, raided the environs of San Antonio de Julimes and nearby San Pablo, after having spent more than a month in Julimes trading and selling deerskins. This is the first definite mention of the place-name of Coyame given to the site inhabited by Cholomes at the head of the Coyame valley in the La Junta district, and of a group resident there. No raids were noted as the work of people from the La Junta valley itself.[81]

The Juntans also became more significant in the migrant labor system. Captain Retana noted their military and labor value when asking for missionaries in 1793. He held that establishing missions was important not only due to the great spiritual benefit they would provide to the already "Christian" nations in the La Junta valley but also for peace and security: "Those nations are on the frontiers of the Apaches and other enemy nations and also many from said nine Christian nations go to work in the haciendas of the Valley of San Bartholome, and the four new nations will do the same."[82] Another indication of their increasing importance as Christianized laborers is the marriages recorded at the Valle de San Bartolomé between 1686 and 1704. Marriages indicate a stronger commitment to Catholicism than baptism, since marriages are usually voluntary adult decisions and moreover involved higher church fees.[83]

Since there were no longer priests resident at La Junta after early 1689, any sacraments received by Juntans after that had to be at other places such as the Valle de San Bartolomé. During the 1686–1704 period there was a much more diversified presence of Juntans among the marriages there than there had been among the baptisms in the earlier period. There were two marriages for Cacalotes in the 1690s, one for Conejos in 1700–1701, ten for "del Norte" in 1702–1704, one for Oposmes in 1702–1704, nine for Polacmes in 1691–1704, nine for Púliques during the same period, and two for Pocsalmes in 1691–1696. The preponderance of Polacmes and Púliques is noticeable.

Figure 6: The Rio del Norte in French perspective, 1703. (Guillaume Delisle, *Carte du Mexique et de la Floride, 1703*. Courtesy of the Yana and Marty Davis Map Collection at the Museum of the Big Bend, Sul Ross State University, Alpine, Texas)

Only the Sonorans with a total of thirty-eight had more, and they most probably came from a much broader area. That the Polacmes and Púliques were two of the groups with the highest number of Christian marriages correlates well with the Polacmes' protection of the missionaries in 1684 and the Púliques' protection of them in 1689.[84] It also needs to be remembered that other Juntan migrant workers were certainly present in other places, and that even sacramental records for the Valle de San Bartolomé would not include all the Juntans in that valley.

The French Threat Reappears

The Juntans were demonstrating their importance to Nueva Vizcayans as faithful regional military allies and seasonal laborers. The continued absence of Hispanics, even missionaries, in the La Junta district itself might have remained for decades longer, had it not been for developments to the east after 1699. In that year the French began establishing posts along the coast of the Gulf of Mexico near the mouth of the Mississippi River. Their plan to make trade connections with the mining and ranching establishments of northern New Spain led to a warning sent to the viceroy in 1707 from the Spanish governor in Pensacola.[85] Witness to this interest are French maps in 1701–1703, the first ones known to indicate Christian-named settlements at La Junta, six towns in fact.[86] The consequent state of alert probably contributed to the inquiry of the new viceroy, the Duke of Linares, in 1712 to the Commissary General of the Franciscans in Mexico City as to how many missionaries would be necessary for the new conversions in the "provinces" of New Mexico. When the Commissary General passed the request on to the provincial of the Holy Gospel Province, the latter responded that up until 1708 there were twenty-one ministers in New Mexico (including the El Paso district) and that in 1708 thirteen more were authorized and were sent. That made a total of thirty-four, all of whom the provincial declared as necessary for the custody's present commitments in upper New Mexico and the El Paso district. He added that the province was willing to take on other new missions if missionaries were requested.[87] Thus all that was needed for the return of Franciscans to La Junta was a strong political reason. The French promptly provided it.

CHAPTER 4

Migrant Labor, Missions, and Neighbors, 1713–1722

Today more than ever the experience is that for all the other orders for labor that Your Lordship gave for the wheat harvest, the designated number of Indians did not come, in many cases not even half and in other cases none. And even if said Tarahumaras came promptly in the number needed by each grower, they could not make up for the lack of the Juntan labor. That is because these latter, as raised in those fields and many born in them, are already skillful in all the needed tasks.

—San Bartolomé growers to Governor San Juan, August 1715

More and more disorders had been growing among the missionized Christian Indians, as had the depredations of the neighboring barbarians. . . . The Christians loved the freedom of the heathens, and both groups were led by the desire for plunder. They attacked the missions in the year 1720. . . . We owed the saving of our lives, and the fact that not all of the vestments and sacred vessels were lost, to a few Indians who faithfully protected us and took us out to the Villa of Chihuahua.

—Fray Andrés Varo, Mexico City, 1749

Franciscan missionaries returned to the La Junta valley in 1715 and established themselves for the first time in the Coyame valley. Their return, but now by way of Nueva Vizcaya rather than El Paso, was the result of a combination of factors: the repeated requests of the Juntans, the French advance on Texas, and the sudden development of Chihuahua and its greater environs as the new magnet for migration in Nueva Vizcaya. Juntan labor was redirected to this new Hispanic district, at the same time that a more extensive missionary presence in the La Junta district renewed or exacerbated tensions among the nations along the Rio del Norte. The missionaries soon appealed for military protection, but none was forthcoming.

The Return of Missionaries

In 1704 spectacular silver deposits were discovered at a hilly location christened Santa Eulalia, about 150 miles north of Parral. But the locale was confined in a narrow canyon and lacked a reliable water supply. Within five years a more hospitable site fourteen miles to the west was chosen as the administrative and family-dwelling center for the mine owners, merchants, pack-train managers, and everyone else who rushed into the area. Initially named the Real of San Francisco de Cuellar, the town was soon elevated in status and renamed the Villa de San Felipe El Real de Chihuahua—abbreviated here to simply Chihuahua. This new boom district shifted the political and economic emphasis of the province of Nueva Vizcaya, as well as its frontier problems, from its southern half to this northern region.[1] The founding of the Chihuahua–Santa Eulalia district brought Hispanic settlement thirty-five miles closer to La Junta than the Conchos presidio and with much larger numbers and trade goods. On modern highways La Junta is 150 miles from Chihuahua, while the Juntans' traditional migrant commitments near Parral lay at twice that distance (see figure 3).

At least some of the Juntans persisted in wanting to have missionaries back among them. By mid-1713 Fray Andrés Ramírez of the Franciscan Province of Zacatecas had traveled three times up to La Junta from the nearest missionary residence, now Santa Cruz on the San Pedro River, where some Juntans, especially Tapacolmes, resided. Each time the people had asked him to have priests sent to reside among them. They had even sent a delegation to Chihuahua to make the same request to Coronel Juan Joseph Masoni, the visiting agent of the viceroy. Masoni sent Father Ramírez to visit them (his third visit) to verify their firm intent, upon which he formally presented their request to the viceroy on May 30, 1713.[2] The viceroy was the Duke of Linares, the same one who had inquired the previous year about the need for missionaries in this part of the northern frontier.

Why did Juntans keep making this request? Subsequent events would make it very clear that it was not to draw Hispanic military or civilians to their lands. They did not want such a large and distinct presence among them. Rather they had been the ones helping Hispanics combat hostile groups in distant places. The Apaches were drawing closer, but at this time they usually approached La Junta as traders, not raiders. The Juntans' requests for missionaries had to have been for other benefits. They already had an at least minimally satisfactory arrangement of migrant work with the landowners in the far distant Parral region, although they might indeed have welcomed a closer destination. What they did not have was year-round Hispanic benefits in their own valley.

One of those benefits sincerely desired by a number of them, although certainly not universally, was to have their own resident ministers of the Catholic faith. Over the past half-century at least some Juntans had clearly come to value the Franciscan missionaries and even the religion that they taught. In the 1680s some of them had sworn to protect the missionaries at La Junta with their lives, and had done so, escorting them to safety. By the 1690s the Franciscans in the San Bartolomé Valley were witnessing the marriages of dozens of migrant Juntans in the church, a greater sign of personal commitment than baptism. Writing decades later, Father Menchero reported that some baptized and catechized Juntans who had accompanied the friars in their retreat in the 1680s had remained in the San Bartolomé Valley. One of them, Francisco, returned to La Junta after missionaries came back in 1715 and was reported to have very piously and scrupulously made his confession there as he neared death in the 1720s. The next day, after requesting and receiving the rites of the Church for the dying, he made an impressive act of Christian faith that attested at the same time to the persistence of Native religion among other Juntans:

> Taking an image of the holy Christ in his hand, he called his wife and children and exhorted them, saying that the law that the Fathers preached to them was the true one, that they should not believe in the fables of the old men and women which were all lies, and that there was but one God, creator of the universe, whom they ought to serve and keep his holy commandments. Having said this, he continued with these words and acts of love of God: "I believe in God, I love God, I trust in God who will save me, and may God's will be done in all," and expired.[3]

Yet there was probably another reason that missionaries were invited time and again to La Junta, since one may legitimately wonder how many Juntans were as devoted as Francisco. The Franciscans brought with them, and could call upon, outside supplies. That was something not to be regarded lightly in a district that often experienced alternating drought and floods. This also meant a more continuous connection to Hispanic trade goods. Not all Juntans were migrants, and even the migrants spent only a few weeks, perhaps months, away from La Junta. The La Junta valley had always been a Native trade center. When conditions were difficult, all could use supply-connected Franciscans.

Nevertheless, as events would also demonstrate, there were others in the larger La Junta district, particularly some Cholomes in the Coyame valley, who did not want the missionaries' presence to interfere in any way with their own lives, and certainly not to make them the target of other Native groups hostile to Hispanics. This would become especially true after Cholomes and Juntans alike experienced the changes in lifestyle and in their relations with non-converted nations that missionaries always sought to bring about.

The requests of the Juntans for missionaries might well have continued to go unanswered if not for news that reached the Duke of Linares a few months after he received their petition. In late August 1713 the Spanish governor at Pensacola wrote to the viceroy to warn him about the expedition of the Frenchman St. Denis, slated to depart from Mobile to establish trade with the frontier outposts of New Spain.[4] Shades of the La Salle expedition a quarter century earlier! With this renewed challenge to the northern reach of the viceroyalty, attention was once more directed to the large gaps in its frontier defense. By October 1714 the Duke of Linares had concluded the usual lengthy consultations. The last week of that month he dispatched orders to organize a new expedition to La Junta that would bring the missionaries that the Juntans had been requesting.

The friars were to "check out (*reconocer*) and visit the Indians." The viceroy ordered the governor of Nueva Vizcaya to provide the missionaries with a sufficient escort for their safety and to appoint a very capable official to lead the troops. A rich co-founder of Chihuahua, Sergeant Major Juan Antonio Trasviña Retes, was to provide the supplies. A separate letter to Trasviña Retes ordered him to join the expedition and provide a report about the Juntans as well as their lands, so that the viceroy could take the measures that he deemed appropriate.[5] This was the first time that the La Junta district itself was the goal of such an expedition and that a thorough inspection of the entire district would take place. The resulting reports disclosed settlements hitherto unnoted, and for the first time all the Native groups were identified with specific towns.[6]

This visit would result in the more permanent foundation of missions, due to the fact that they would now be officially recognized and supported by the Spanish regime. But that was not a foregone conclusion. It would all depend upon the results of the visit. The missionary presence at La Junta in the 1680s had been undertaken solely under the authority of the Franciscan leadership and never obtained approval nor support from the viceroyal administration. Support for founding and maintaining missions at great distances from major colonial markets was an expensive enterprise. The Spanish Crown was willing to enter into such an alliance with the missionary groups when it was determined that trying to establish peaceful relations with the Indigenous groups of northern New Spain was done more effectively by putting the missionaries in charge rather than trying to subdue them through military campaigns, often accompanied by slaving practices. Part of this approach was also establishing a *paz y guerra* (peace and war) fund that provided governors with designated amounts to be used for gifts to peaceful Natives not gathered into missions and for recruiting Indian auxiliaries.[7]

When it was an official institution of the colonial regime, a mission was a place where missionaries were entrusted with the supervision and instruction of Indigenous communities in an effort to incorporate them into the Spanish colonial empire, its Catholic religion, and certain aspects of Hispanic culture, with the support of and ultimate control by the Spanish state. The state authorities decided "where and when missions would be founded or closed, what administrative policies would be observed, who could be missionaries," how many missionaries would receive state financial support, "and how many soldiers if any would be stationed at a mission. In turn, the state paid for the missionaries' overseas travel, the founding costs of a mission, and the missionaries' annual salary. The state also usually provided military protection and enforcement." The missionary ideal was to develop Native Christian towns that when fully matured religiously and politically could be incorporated into ordinary colonial society, albeit with all its racial and class distinctions. In order to accomplish this, the missionaries sought to exercise minute control over every aspect of Native life and to insulate the people from the possible negative influences of other Native groups and of Hispanics themselves. "Daily life was to follow a highly organized routine of prayer, work, training, meals, and relaxation, punctuated by frequent religious holidays and celebrations."[8]

That was the ideal, but it was never closely approximated at La Junta. The Juntans were willing to be migrant laborers and military auxiliaries with the Hispanics but never to be subordinated in their own homeland. Their fierce insistence on autonomy was countered after 1715 by the missionaries' repeated appeals for local military protection and support. The fact that such support was never given for almost half a century, nor any Hispanic settlement even attempted, left the Juntans in charge, not the missionaries. And yet at the periodic requests of the Juntans, missionaries did remain, off and on at times, during those years. All these factors are what make the story of Native-Hispanic relations at La Junta practically unique on the northern frontier of New Spain.

Missionary work on the northern frontier was divided into territories assigned to various groups of Franciscans and Jesuits. The Franciscan Province of Zacatecas and the Jesuits divided up Nueva Vizcaya, with the Zacatecan friars in charge of most of the northeastern portion.[9] Even so, and even though Father Ramírez of the Zacatecan Province had been visiting La Junta most recently, the viceroy called upon the Holy Gospel Province with its Custody of San Pablo in New Mexico to missionize the La Junta valley. That was probably due to the latter province's prior "claim" on missions at La Junta dating back to their ministry there in the 1680s. It may have also been due to the very recent offer of the Holy Gospel provincial to provide more missionaries for new conversions.

Thus the procurator (supply agent) for the New Mexico missions, Father Joseph Arranegui, made the proper arrangements in Mexico City and joined a caravan heading north. He departed with sealed letters from the viceroy containing the orders for the Governor of Nueva Vizcaya and for Sergeant Major Trasviña Retes of Chihuahua. Arranegui and the friars he brought with him reached Parral by March 15, 1715, on which date he handed the viceroy's instructions to the new governor, Manuel de San Juan y Santa Cruz. Arranegui's own note to the governor asked that the military escort for the La Junta expedition consist of twenty men and that it be led by the captain of the Conchos presidio, the closest one to La Junta.

Remarkably, he also asked that once the missionaries entered La Junta the escort return to their presidio. Oftentimes missionaries viewed other Hispanics as bad examples for Natives or as contesting the friars' role among them. Therefore they sometimes idealistically counted upon their own self-perceived benevolence and the Natives' peaceful declarations, foregoing any military protection. That hope was probably at work here, as the Franciscans relied upon the Juntans' repeated desire for missionaries. Hardly ever would any other Hispanic presence be so absent and distant as it would be here. On April 1 Governor San Juan's dispatch implementing Arranegui's requests was sent to Joseph de Beasoain, captain of the Conchos presidio.[10]

Arranegui himself proceeded up to Chihuahua, where he delivered the viceroy's orders to Sergeant Major Trasviña Retes on April 12.[11] Not only was the 53-year-old sergeant major the chief military officer in Chihuahua, he was also a person with extensive military experience on the frontier and a sizeable fortune that could finance such an undertaking. Following a typical pattern for ambitious Spaniards, upon first arriving in Nueva Vizcaya he had helped in battles with Natives, settled in Parral, and married the daughter of one of that area's first successful miners. After a mining boom developed in Cusiguiraichic in the Tarahumara country to the far northwest of Parral in the 1680s, Trasviña Retes had moved there, where he amassed a fortune in silver mining, helped suppress the Tarahumara revolt in 1694, and served briefly as chief political officer (*alcalde mayor*). This had given him the means to be one of the first developers of the rich mining veins discovered at Santa Eulalia.[12]

The arrangements that had been made in Mexico City included a detailed list of the supplies to be provided by the government for the founding of each mission. There were all the things necessary for religious services, carpentry tools and metal items, farming and ranching supplies and animals, and various things to be distributed among the natives: tools, clothing, blankets, tobacco, and religious medals and rosaries.[13] Most of these items were not allocated immediately, since this initial expedition was one of assessing the reality and the needs, including how many missions should be founded. Rather, the viceroy's orders instructed the sergeant major to supply the missionaries with whatever they needed—presumably to be reimbursed later by the government.

In order to make Trasviña Retes the chief commander of the expedition, the governor sent him the title of acting lieutenant captain general of Nueva Vizcaya. On his own initiative, Trasviña Retes recruited an additional thirty armed Hispanics, twenty Native auxiliaries, and ten muleteers for fifty pack animals, all in view of the territory through which they would have to travel, exposed to hostile groups such as Sisimbles, Chisos, Chinarras, Cocoyames, and Acocolames. The Juntans would describe most of these groups as usually to be found in the rugged country to the southeast of the La Junta valley, at the edge of the Bolson de Mapimí, but the Chinarras were along the Rio del Norte above La Junta, along with the Sumas and Cholomes. This shows both how dangerous a journey to La Junta was considered to be and the great expense that the sergeant major was shouldering. The Native auxiliaries were drawn from Julimes and the lower San Pedro River villages, led by Don Antonio de la Cruz, governor of Julimes and Spanish-designated general of all those places. Don Antonio was said to be extremely loyal to the Hispanics and to have a "great following among the Indians of La Junta, of which he is a native."[14] Trasviña Retes was not making such a large financial commitment out of pure disinterested patriotism. As will be seen, he hoped to redirect the Juntans' significant migrant labor to his own rapidly developing Chihuahua district. How better to accomplish that objective than by his own gift-bearing visit among the Juntans and his crafting of the official report and recommendations to the viceroy?

Father Arranegui and Father Ramírez, the Zacatecan missionary, were among the contingent led by Trasviña Retes when it departed from Chihuahua on May 23. Arranegui was acting as the Santo Evangelio Province's official in charge; Ramírez came along as the missionary already familiar with La Junta and the Juntans. Captain Beasoian and his troops brought with them two of the three Franciscans destined for La Junta, Gregorio Osorio and Juan Antonio García, who had been conducted to the Conchos presidio from Parral. The third, Raymundo Gras, had fallen ill and was recuperating at the hacienda of Don Juan Cortés del Rey near the presidio.[15]

Native Societies in the La Junta District

When this military expedition entered the La Junta district, they encountered people who, besides their own local farming, hunting, and trading, were thoroughly engaged as kinship-based groups in long-distance seasonal migrant work among Hispanics. Just as Mexican American seasonal workers today, they traveled and labored as families.[16] The new missionaries would promptly discover, as Father Colina already had three decades previously, that the Natives' involvement in this labor system had become paramount to them, given the unreliability of their own agricultural means and their acquired appreciation for certain Hispanic goods. This migrant arrangement, along with men serving at times as military auxiliaries with Hispanic troops, had familiarized many of the people with Hispanic ways, and often Catholic ritual. There were a number of *ladinos* (Spanish speakers) among them, especially among their leaders who were the societal brokers with the Hispanic world.

The first people of the La Junta district to receive the expedition as it made its way down the Rio Conchos were the Cholomes, a group named for the first time in clear relation to La Junta. Two decades earlier the captain of the Conchos presidio had described Cholomes as still unconverted but very *domésticos* (well-behaved). He added that they were a widespread nation, bordering on the Sumas who extended down the Rio del Norte from El Paso.[17] The expedition rested at the Cholome settlement of San Pedro on the morning of May 29, and that afternoon continued a few leagues downriver to the town of Cuchillo Parado (so named for the first time in the literature). Thus

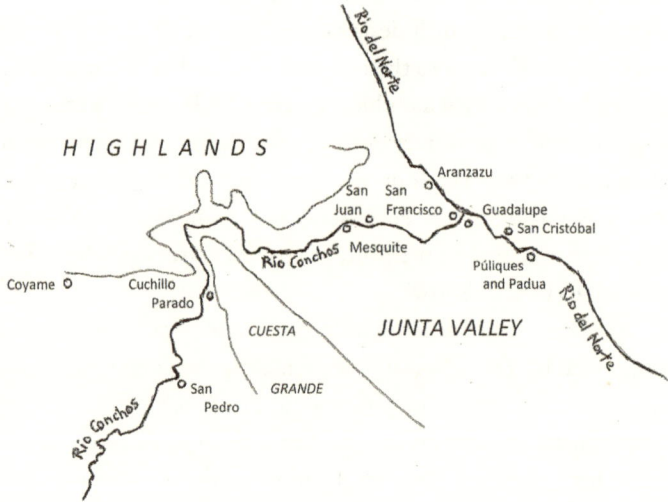

Figure 7: La Junta district in 1715. (By Robert E. Wright)

they had traversed the Rio Conchos section of the Coyame valley, arriving near the base of the Cuesta Grande on the opposite side from the La Junta valley.

Demonstrating their familiarity with Hispanic customs of greeting dignitaries, the people of both these settlements had built welcoming arches at the approach to their towns. In both places they gave Trasviña Retes the oath of obedience. At San Pedro the Native "lieutenant" in charge was Don Santiago, small and stocky in stature if one goes by his nickname El Torito (little bull)—a name to be remembered in light of future events. He said that there were 190 people at San Pedro. In fluent Spanish he informed the expedition leaders that the general of all the Cholomes, Don Andrés Coyame, lived in a *cienega* or wetland two leagues [*sic*] distant. That probably was the origin of the place name Coyame. But Don Andrés was away with many of his people for the seasonal harvest at the house of his master Juan Cortés del Rey. El Torito was himself about to lead a group from San Pedro to join the wheat-harvesting crew.[18]

The Cortés del Rey family that employed the Cholomes as seasonal migrants was reputed to have a good relationship with the unconverted nations on the Hispanic frontier. In fact, they were sometimes accused of being too allied with them. Valerio, Juan's father and the scion of the family, developed his great landholdings in the later 1600s. He was appreciated and obeyed by the Natives called Tobosos due to his power and fearlessness. His haciendas contained "a great number of servants of doubtful condition: vagrants, men without fixed residence, fugitives from the law or deserters." This same situation continued with his descendants in the 1700s. Thus it is not that surprising that in the 1750s these types of people would be found in the Coyame valley.[19]

The Cholomes at San Pedro were described by Trasviña Retes as "mostly Christian" and had several Hispanic-origin food items. They welcomed their guests with string beans and fish. They also had ripe (*en color*) wheat crops, corn with ears in abundance, and other crops not yet ready to gather: plantings of melons, watermelons, and pumpkins. Trasviña Retes reciprocated with some meat and two bundles of tobacco. The Cholome village leaders bore the honorific Spanish title Don. Captain Beasoian added that Father Ramírez said that these people were independent of the eight pueblos of the La Junta valley. Upon learning that this expedition was to bring two priests to the Juntans, Don Santiago said that he would ask Juan Cortés del Rey and Andrés Coyame to have priests sent to the Cholomes also.[20]

The people at Cuchillo Parado, where the expedition spent the night, were ethnically different from the Cholomes. Both Trasviña Retes and Beasoian reported that they were Conejos, although Trasviña Retes initially wrote that Ramírez identified the people as from the eight La Junta valley pueblos and called the latter their "relatives." Other than stating a widespread kinship, this probably did not mean that people from all eight valley towns were in Cuchillo Parado. The expedition would find a small village in the La Junta valley inhabited by Conejos. The ethnic distinctions made here recall the earliest reports in the 1580s, in which the people at the location hypothesized to be Cuchillo Parado were described as similar to some of those in the La Junta valley, while those encountered before Cuchillo Parado were not. That distinction within the La Junta district will loom larger and larger as events unfold.

The very town structure at Cuchillo Parado was notably different by now. There was already a church one hundred paces outside the town, with the town itself formed like a presidio with its houses having covered porches. This is the first notice of any such buildings in the Coyame valley. Trasviña Retes wrote that the village was now called Nuestra Señora de Begoña. Whether it already had that name or it was given by this expedition, the name did not stick. The town continued to be called Cuchillo Parado, as it is to this day. Its defensive arrangement and building style showed clear Hispanic influence. The joyful reception by the people and the defensive layout of the village prompted Trasviña Retes to leave some worn-out horses and mules along with a cache of food supplies in the safekeeping of these people, waiting for his return journey. Only forty-four residents were counted there. If others were absent as migrant workers, it was not noted. The people's wheat crop was ready to be cut and they also had the other crops noted in San Pedro. Here again the people said that they would like to receive a resident priest themselves.[21]

On May 30, Ascension Thursday, the expedition traveled five leagues along the Rio Conchos at the base of the Cuesta Grande before camping. The next day they traveled about twelve winding leagues to reach El Mezquite along the Rio Conchos in the La Junta valley. This required entering a canyon before climbing laboriously over the severe mountain ridge, with the Native auxiliaries splitting boulders or pushing them aside. El Mezquite was given the title of Our Lady of Loreto, "since we carried this most holy image as the guide of our journey and this was the first town" in the La Junta valley. People from all the towns came out to meet them, gave the oath of obedience, and kissed the hands of the missionaries. The expedition rested there for the remainder of the day.

The next morning, June 1, after traveling one league they passed through the Cacalote pueblo with its governor, captains, and caciques. The fact that this and the other towns of La Junta now had their own Spanish-recognized officials—governors and captains—as well as their own traditional leaders, the caciques, is one more demonstration of their increasing relations with the Hispanic officials of Nueva Vizcaya. The expedition christened the Cacalote pueblo San Juan Bautista. In both El Mezquite and San Juan Bautista the houses were constructed of "thin walls plastered inside and outside and some with adobe walls, all with álamo [cottonwood] roof-beams." Continuing another two leagues or so, the travelers arrived at the town at the river junction that they named San Francisco. At all these places the people's decades-old association with Hispanics was evident. Ceremonial arches stood along the road, and the fields on both sides of the river contained much wheat and legumes in addition to corn. A great crowd of people from all the towns came out to meet them at San Francisco, led by their governors and captains in military formation and bearing the by-now-standard peace banners.[22]

San Francisco was the town of the Oposmes, on the left bank of the Conchos where it joins the Rio del Norte. Its governor was Don Pascual de Ortega. The people from all the valley towns were convoked there for the following day, a Sunday. On that day three Masses were celebrated and the people came dressed in their best clothes. The governors, captains, caciques, and other principal people came to the last Mass. The colonial truism that European clothes were the sought-after sign of prestige among the Natives was on full display:

> We were pleased to see Indians with such good reason and *social skill (política)* without having had any education and also to see them so well-dressed, men as well as women, the chiefs and their wives being outstanding with better clothes in the Spanish fashion, with shirts of fine white linen worked in silk. Some had skirts of serge, silk shawls, Cordovan shoes, imported Brussels silk socks. I found men, women and children with good-natured, happy faces, who were very sociable with the Spaniards. . . . In order to buy clothes, they travel more than 130 leagues at the risk of meeting enemies to work on the farm estates of San Bartolomé Valley.[23]

At the end of the third Mass Father Ramírez reminded the people in Spanish how they had asked for priests and told them the Christian obligations that they were accepting in receiving missionaries. When he finished, Governor Don Antonio de la Cruz of

Julimes explained what Ramírez had said in the local idiom for those who did not understand Spanish. Then all moved from the church to the plaza, where Don Antonio translated for Trasviña Retes. The sergeant major also reminded the Juntans that they had come to Chihuahua asking for priests, and how he had given them provisions at that time at the direction of Colonel Masoni. Now he distributed among the Native leaders flour, meat, clothing, and tobacco. All the others received various woolen and cotton garments, knives, tobacco, rosaries, and other items.

Since Fathers Osorio and García decided to initially live together at San Francisco, Trasviña Retes instructed the people to build an adobe friary there and repair the current churches so that their roofs would not leak during the coming rainy season. After the rains had passed they should build churches with sufficient capacity for each town and with the best dignity possible. Beasoian wrote that the churches in all the La Junta towns were thatch-roofed pole structures (*ramadas que tienen hechas con zacate*) and that the people were charged to build new and more capacious ones of adobe. The captain reported that he too exhorted the Juntans about their obligations, and that the priests immediately set about baptizing children and marrying couples. Trasviña Retes wrote that fourteen children were baptized that afternoon, with Captain Beasoain and some of his soldiers serving as godparents. Both expedition leaders noted that about four miles above San Francisco on the same right bank of the Rio del Norte was a smaller town of the Conejo people. They named that village Nuestra Señora de Aranzazu.[24]

According to Trasviña Retes, the people of the valley immediately asked that two more missionaries be sent for the four towns downstream from the river junction for a distance of two leagues. Perhaps so, but the sergeant major was probably putting words in the Natives' mouths when he wrote that they also requested that the Crown provide church vestments, bells, the other church furnishings, and the farming tools that were given for the founding of missions. The two friars, following a missionary strategy implemented since the beginning of the conquest of Mexico, requested that each of the towns "bring to the said priests two boys, ten years of age more or less, who should live with these Fathers so that the latter might teach them Christian doctrine, after which, in the absence of priests in their pueblos, they could teach (the doctrine) to the rest in the meanwhile until the arrival of the necessary priests for said pueblos."[25]

Across the Rio Conchos from San Francisco at the river junction was the pueblo that the expedition named Nuestra Señora de Guadalupe, with two plazas, one for the original Polacmes and the other for the Cíbolos. To reach it Trasviña Retes had the people make a raft (*balsa*) to ferry him, Captain Beasoian, and the missionaries across the river while twenty-five soldiers swam their horses across. By this time Guadalupe was by far the largest town, three times as large as any other. The two nations there are united in order to be able to defend themselves from the enemies that have attacked them occasionally, because [the Juntans] did not want to admit their councils (*tlazoles*) and rise up with them into the mountains. This is verified by the help that on occasion General Don Antonio de la Cruz has brought to them from the Pueblo of Julimes, coming to their aid when notified. By these means they have maintained themselves without admitting the evil councils (*tlazoles*) of the enemies and without help from the Spaniards, which proves their constancy in the Catholic faith.[26]

This comment about resisting pressure from anti-Hispanic Natives might well refer as far back as the disturbances in the 1680s that at least momentarily divided the Juntans.

The same defensive concerns present in the Guadalupe pueblo have already been noted at Cuchillo Parado. They were also evident at El Mezquite and San Juan Bautista. El Mezquite, "with its plaza in the middle, is well *enclosed* with a wall." San Juan Bautista, only two or three miles away, was also enclosed with its plaza in the middle.[27] The pueblo of San Francisco was composed of three wards separated about 300 yards from each other, and the Conejos' pueblo of Aranzazu was only about four miles upriver from it on the Rio del Norte. Along the Rio del Norte below the town of Guadalupe were three pueblos "in the same form as the rest," not too far from one another. The one of the Pocsalmes was already known as San Cristóbal; the village of the Púliques was given the name San José by the expedition; and the one of the Conchos was given the name San Antonio de Padua. Nothing other than their population was noted by either Trasviña Retes or Beasoian, not even which side of the river they were on. And Tapacolmes was not mentioned at all.[28]

Thus the outlying towns and the new nations that settled in the La Junta valley had been drawn closer together in defensive concentrations. There was no longer a town at the old site of San Bernardino farther up the Rio del Norte that had welcomed the expeditions of the 1580s and 1680s, nor at Tapacolmes at the far southern edge of the La Junta valley. Along the Rio Conchos the settlements had also apparently been moved much closer to those at the river junction.

According to the count reported for each town, there were 1,405 Natives present in the La Junta valley, and eighty men and their families who were absent doing migrant work. There is no previous total with which to compare this number. But in 1581, over a century earlier, Gallegos estimated over 300 persons at San Bernardino (that no longer existed in 1715), and the following year Luján estimated 600 people at the future San Francisco and stated that the future San Cristóbal was even larger.[29] Clearly, and not surprisingly, the population had decreased considerably. Without taking into account any other factors, an epidemic had occurred in the valley in 1683. There had undoubtedly been epidemics at other times also, given the Juntans' decades of contacts with Hispanics and others during their migrant work in the Parral district. By that very fact of long contact, however, intermittent epidemics would not take as severe a toll in the 1700s, as the Juntans and surrounding nations acquired immunities.[30]

Table 2: Pueblos / "Nations" Noted along the Rio del Norte, 1582, 1680s, 1715*

	Upriver left side	SW river junction	SE river junction	near NE river junction	down-river	down-river	south end of valley
1582	San Bernardin	Santo Tomás		Santiago			
1680s	present but unnamed	La Navidad: mission residence		San Cristóbal (in 1702 map)			
		(Oposmes)	(Polacmes)	(Pocsalmes)	(Púliques)		(Tapacolmes)
1715	aban-doned (closer): Aranzazu	San Fran-cisco Residence	Guadalupe	San Cristóbal	San José	San Antonio	abandoned
		180	550	180	92	87	
	71 Conejos	Oposmes	Polacmes Cíbolos	Pocsalmes	Púliques	Conchos	

* Besides these places/groups along the Rio del Norte, in the 1680s the Mezquites and Cacalotes were noted, and in 1715 they were located along the Rio Conchos within the La Junta valley, at El Mezquite (80 Mezquites) and San Juan Bautista (165 Cacalotes) respectively.

From these accounts, we learn that only two of the towns in the entire La Junta district had Christian titles already known by the Hispanics who arrived in 1715: San Pedro in the Coyame valley and San Cristóbal in the La Junta valley. Of the names given to the other towns at this time, San Francisco, Nuestra Señora de Guadalupe, and San Juan Bautista would become of common usage among Hispanics. Cuchillo Parado, Mezquite, and Púliques would remain identified mostly by their older topographic or ethnic names.

By this time some Apaches were becoming known at La Junta. The people at the river junction had made friends with an Apache baptized earlier by Father Ramírez. He was named Antonio de la Cruz, a name taken from his godfather, the Native general from Julimes. This Apache had promised that when missionaries came he and his band of about sixty families would come to live immediately downriver or upriver from La Junta, and that they would all be catechized and baptized. But the Juntans were aware that his *ranchería* was experiencing a smallpox outbreak, and so he was not advised of the friars' coming.[31] Captain Beasoian stated that the Juntans told him that they did not know the distance to the nation of the Apaches, who lived "to the east or north . . . up until the territory of the Pananas."[32] In other words, at this time the Apaches were still mostly distant and rare visitors.

Nine years later Hispanics would capture a Christian named Gerónimo who had been sold to a Lipan Apache headman after being captured by Tobosos along the Rio Conchos. This Gerónimo had seen Jumanos bring two missionaries with them to the Apache camp on the Colorado River in West Texas. When this occurred, and who these missionaries were, remain a mystery. Were they from New Mexico or Texas or La Junta? Gerónimo "intimated that the plains Apaches refrained from violence when near La Junta, leaving even the Spanish missionaries who occasionally visited the region alone."[33] In that same year of 1724 some Apaches trading at La Junta had their horses stolen by a tribe from outside the valley.[34] Thus by this time Apache bands had replaced Jumanos as the principal trans-Plains traders at La Junta. This relationship would endure, to the consternation of the Hispanic authorities.

Post-Visit Arrangements

Trasviña Retes wanted the dependable migrant laborers from the La Junta valley for the new Chihuahua district. A very recent decree by the Nueva Vizcaya governor gave him an opening. In early March Governor San Juan had mandated that all Natives in Nueva Vizcaya return to their towns to be counted and to register how many were available for the defense of the province.[35] This would serve to pull the Juntan migrants out of their current employments, as a first step in reallocating their labor. Before leaving the La Junta valley, Trasviña Retes ordered that "when the wheat harvest was finished all those [absent] Indians be brought back to their towns with those who were about to leave [La Junta] for the harvest." Undoubtedly anticipating the uproar that this would cause in the San Bartolomé valley, the sergeant major gave the workers who were about to depart a letter to San Juan asking that official to support this order. He couched his request in a good religious reason: in order that the new mission situation at La Junta could be properly assessed, these migrants should "come to acknowledge (*reconocer*) their towns and see their religious ministers in order that these latter can make the census of the people of each town with the proper distinctions."[36]

On June 5 the entire expedition began their return trip back to their respective bases in Nueva Vizcaya, leaving Fathers Osorio and García at San Francisco. Trasviña Retes left the missionaries with meat, flour, soap, lard, tobacco, powders, paper, a jug of wine for celebrating Mass, and six pounds of wax. When he reached Cuchillo Parado the next day, he was pleased to find the horses, mules, and supplies that he had left there well cared for and rewarded the people with meat and tobacco. There being no livestock whatsoever at La Junta other than horses, when Trasviña Retes reached Julimes he had thirty-five gelded sheep (*carneros capones*) and six goats that had recently delivered kids (*cabras paridas*) sent to the missionaries to supplement their diet. These animals were brought to the missionaries by the Juntans who had accompanied Trasviña Retes for that purpose. The sergeant major arrived back in Chihuahua on June 11, where a few days later a Juntan leader named Captain Pedro passed through the town with forty Juntans on their way to the San Bartolomé Valley for the wheat harvest.[37]

Once back in Hispanic Nueva Vizcaya, Fathers Ramírez and Arranegui wrote their observations to the superior of all the Franciscans in Mexico, the Commissary General. Ramírez heaped praise upon Arranegui for the success of the venture, alleging that "even the new missionaries (with one exception) had so cooled in their ardor that in my presence, in Parral, one came to tell the Father Procurator [Arranegui] that he was without spirit to go to La Junta." Not only did Arranegui strengthen that friar, he also "in Chihuahua and the whole journey encouraged Sergeant Major Don Juan Antonio Trasviña who had more fear than faith." All were happy with the reception given to them by the Juntans. They were pleased by "the good manners [educación] that all knew, their well-ordered civic life, the pleasantness of the valleys, and fertility of the land."[38]

A month later Arranegui, ill in bed ever since his return, indirectly confirmed Ramírez's assessment of Trasviña Retes. Arranegui asked the sergeant major to be the scribe for the friar's own letter. Given that Trasviña Retes was the scribe, the letter stated more generically that there was so much fear of the Indians along the route to La Junta, due to their continual invasions and killings, that Arranegui had to work hard to bring about the expedition. It also reported that "the Kingdom [of Nueva Vizcaya] is in such a calamitous state that neither corn nor wheat can be found at any price."[39] The Commissary General also received a more perfunctory note from Captain Beasoian, who described the Juntans as docile and well organized, and offered to be of whatever help he might be in the future.[40]

Back at the San Francisco mission in La Junta, Father Gregorio Osorio wrote Trasviña Retes on June 17 that "I now have a terrible pain in one shoulder-blade, that is felt also in the chest, which I have had for five or six days, although it lets up at times, because God always sends illness with mercy when there is no medicine." He asked for some medicine and various other small items, including a copy of Castaño's *Doctrinas* for use in catechizing. All was calm, he reported; some adobes had been made and an oven was being built.[41] Father Raymundo Gras, the third missionary destined for La Junta who had stayed behind due to illness to recuperate at the hacienda of Juan Cortés del Rey, was now reportedly healthy and eager to be conducted to La Junta. Trasviña Retes learned this from Cortés when the latter responded to the sergeant major's letter of June 20. In that letter Trasviña Retes had asked Cortés to speak with the Cholome leader Andrés Coyame, who at that time was with his people on Cortés's hacienda of Nuestra Señora del Pilar. Trasviña Retes wanted to know if Coyame and his people would agree to having resident missionaries in the Coyame valley, that served as the strategic gateway to the La Junta valley. The towns in the Coyame valley were twenty leagues closer to Chihuahua than La Junta, while still forty leagues from the Hispanic town by the shorter route to the west of the Rio Conchos. Responding on July 1, Cortés wrote that Andrés Coyame and his people happily consented.[42]

Advised of this, Governor San Juan wrote Cortés to send Father Gras and the Cholome leader to Parral to make the agreement official. The two along with a Native interpreter for Coyame arrived in Parral the next day. In the declaration that he made before the governor, Andrés Coyame was said to be a baptized Christian and the head of all three settlements in the Coyame valley, with that of Coyame having 180 persons. The Native leader declared that he desired to take Father Gras to minister at Coyame and the other two places and was given the title of general of all three. Whether Andrés Coyame was actually recognized as head by those in Cuchillo Parado itself, who were of a different nation than the Cholomes, has no further evidence, but the much greater number of Cholomes in Coyame and San Pedro in comparison to the number of Conejos at Cuchillo Parado certainly must have carried a lot of weight. In this same meeting in Parral the Ciénaga of Coyame was given the religious title of Nuestra Señora de la Redonda y San Andrés—thus explaining the subsequent use by several Franciscans of the Marian title of La Redonda for this mission. The governor ordered that fifty cattle, fifty sheep, and other things be sent immediately for Coyame's women and children.[43]

Having successfully obtained this agreement, Trasviña Retes in his report to the viceroy in July recommended that two missionaries be sent to the Coyame valley to minister to the three settlements there. Unaware of the religious title bestowed in Parral to the Ciénaga of Coyame, Trasviña Retes named it Santiago, thus giving rise to a title confusion that would endure for decades, probably contributing to its eventually being called simply Coyame. He also proposed two similar mission clusters, each also served by two priests, in the La Junta valley itself: one for the four settlements including San Francisco and San Juan in the northwest section of the river junction, and the other for the four settlements including Guadalupe and San Cristóbal below the river junction.[44]

Trasviña Retes made the important observation that the La Junta valley would probably remain without Hispanic settlers, since the absence of timber made mining impossible, and mining was what attracted Hispanics to the semi-arid region of northern Nueva Vizcaya:

> From what I have seen, it seems to me that said missions will probably be maintained without Spanish settlers, because the territory is suitable only for farming and cattle raising, as there is no forest or woods between this Real [Chihuahua] and La Junta and for many leagues beyond and on either side. . . . Lacking in timber, it is not possible to establish mining towns, which are the villages that support this kingdom, but these new missions can remain and maintain themselves very well with *all kinds of produce* and the fish of the rivers and with them be of great assistance to this Real.[45]

Undoubtedly, Hispanics would also be deterred by the fact that the closest Spanish military protection was 200 miles away at the nascent Chihuahua, a journey of about four days for those traveling at a good pace. The route was regularly threatened by hostile bands, and the soldiers had gone back home, as Arranegui had requested at the beginning.[46] For the time being, and as they mutually desired, the Natives and the Franciscans once again remained alone in the La Junta district. Soon events would make the Franciscans change their minds—but not the Juntans.

Shifting Juntan Labor to the Chihuahua District

Sergeant Major Juan Antonio Trasviña Retes was not only one of the founders of the settlement soon known as Chihuahua, he was also its primary booster. And he hoped to be rewarded on both accounts. At the end of his letter to the viceroy that accompanied his detailed journal of the expedition to La Junta, he magnanimously asserted that he was happy to donate without expectation of being reimbursed the 6,000 pesos with which he had subsidized the undertaking. He took the occasion to add his "service of settling and founding this Real [Chihuahua]" that had grown already in eight years to be one of the best and richest of New Spain. He had built the parish church at his own expense and provided all its furnishings, in total costing him 1,800 pesos. He tithed annually from the silver his mines produced. When such a person made a request, a governor, even a viceroy, paid close attention.[47]

In his letter to Governor San Juan on June 20, Trasviña Retes reported that the Juntans would soon be in the San Bartolomé Valley for the wheat harvest, as well as to aid in a military campaign as the governor had requested. He silently shifted the initiative for recalling all the Juntans to their home towns from himself to the Juntan leaders: "The governors of the towns" had asked that all the people return for a census except those slated for the military campaign. "This seems reasonable to me and thus I am notifying you."[48] His underlying motive was finally expressed in his report to the viceroy in early July. In that report he sought to redirect the Juntan labor to the district of his own Real de San Francisco de Cuellar (Chihuahua). But he had the political astuteness to not alienate the powerful Juan Cortés del Rey, the hacienda owner who had the use of the Cholome labor:

> It seems to me that the Juntans should be relieved of going to work in the fields of the San Bartolomé Valley, by the Governor of Vizcaya giving to those landowners people to do the cultivation from the towns close by them. Let those of La Junta de los Ríos come out to work at this Real, where they will be saved half of the journey and the greater risk of enemies . . . but leaving undisturbed the Cholomes who come out to the estate of General Juan Cortés that is closer than those of the Valley [of San Bartolomé].[49]

The Cortés del Rey hacienda of Nuestra Señora del Pilar was his cereal-raising center along the upper Río Conchos to the west of the San Francisco de Conchos mission and presidio.[50] As such, it was actually not that far northwest of the Valle de San Bartolomé, but Trasviña Retes could use that somewhat lesser distance as a pretext for not interfering with the powerful Cortés del Rey clan. He did not want to get at cross purposes with them, even if they were having some financial troubles at the time.[51]

Given the background and history of Governor San Juan, his response to Trasviña Retes was practically preordained. San Juan was a perfect exemplar of the stereotypical image of Spaniards as coming to New Spain to get rich quickly through family connections and corruption. In his case the stereotype fits. He was a newcomer in Nueva Vizcaya whose governorship had been bought at a large price by his older brother, who held the important and lucrative post of royal treasurer in the port city of Veracruz. San Juan was a young thirty-five-year-old when he was installed as governor in early 1715. Following a frequent pattern among governors in the northern provinces of New Spain, he was intent on making his family's major investment in the governorship pay off handsomely through means that were officially illegal—such as engaging in commerce while in office—but unofficially expected and left unpunished. His position as governor, initially residing at Parral where his family already had some investments, allowed him to assume a commercial importance throughout Nueva Vizcaya that he would continue to exploit afterwards.[52]

By 1715 the focus of the mining that was the basis of fortunes in the province had definitely shifted from the Parral district to those further north at Cusiguiriachic and Chihuahua. Any enterprising governor would want to establish favorable relationships with the elite in those places, and San Juan was nothing if not enterprising:

> By 1719 his lavishly stocked *tiendas* in Chihuahua, Parral, and Cusiguiriachic had made him, in the words of one local resident, "the absolute lord of all the commerce" in Nueva Vizcaya. Troops assigned to the Conchos presidio worked his silver refinery, while generous grants of repartimiento Indians labored at his hacienda of San Pedro de Alcántara, near San Felipe el Real.[53]

Governor San Juan's economic interests, including his future hacienda near Chihuahua, called for assuring the new Chihuahua district of dependable laborers. In August he decreed that the Juntan migrant laborers in the San Bartolomé Valley return to La Junta and be replaced at San Bartolomé by Natives living closer by, as Traviña Retes had recommended. That resolution cleared the path for diverting the Juntan labor to the Chihuahua vicinity.[54]

Perhaps the Juntans themselves appreciated the much shorter distance they would have to travel. On the other hand, they may have wanted to maintain their long-standing and apparently satisfactory ties with the Parral district. Hispanics on either side declared that the Juntans wanted what those Hispanics wanted. The growers in the San Bartolomé Valley protested energetically. Twenty-three of them, including a Bartholomé de Porraz,[55] sent a letter demanding that the governor's order be rescinded and that those Juntans who might have already left be newly restored to the haciendas where they had been laboring. They gave five reasons. One was that they had not been consulted about this decision. The second was that previous efforts to bring Tarahumaras had not resulted well, whereas the Juntans had been very reliable and skilled:

> These [Tarahumaras] come against their will, and only for twenty-four days, and many flee even before that. To this is added the great effort and expense involved in obtaining them, and the full allotment never comes. Today more than ever the experience is that for all the other orders for labor that Your Lordship gave for the wheat harvest, the designated number of Indians did not come, in many cases not even half and in other cases none. And even if said Tarahumaras came promptly in the number needed by each grower, they could not make up for the lack of the Juntan labor. That is because these latter, as raised in those fields and many born in them, are already skillful in all the needed tasks.

These declarations speak volumes about the Juntan practice of migrant labor. By implication, in contrast with that of the Tarahumaras, it was voluntary, promptly fulfilled, extending for periods beyond twenty-four days, and already long established, since some of those now laboring were born or raised in the San Bartolomé haciendas. The other reasons given by the growers for retaining the Juntans were that without them the haciendas and thus also the mines would be depopulated; the Juntans were receiving the Gospel and sacraments in the San Bartolomé Valley from the priest at that town (Trasviña Retes had declared that this was not happening adequately); and they helped in the defense of the valley. The growers closed their petition by bluntly stating, "with all due respect," that if the governor did not withdraw his order they would appeal to higher authorities.[56]

In view of their threatened appeal, the governor directed that a file be started to collect and keep the relevant documents, noting that he had written his removal order in response to "the verbal petition made to me by the natives of the Pueblos of Las Juntas [*sic*] de los Rios" and the June 20 petition of Trasviña Retes. Thus the governor, just as Trasviña Retes previously, was careful to attribute this move to the desire of the Juntans themselves. Perhaps the Juntans who had delivered the letter of Trasviña Retes to Governor San Juan made this request, but the file contains no affidavit to that effect. It does contain a copy of Governor San Juan's interview with Andrés Coyame, · but the Cholome leader only spoke for his own people, and their labor was not to be transferred to Chihuahua.

Both the governor and the sergeant major knew that according to royal regulations the proposed labor transfer had to be agreed upon by the Juntans themselves. On that basis the governor named Alonso de Cervantes Villaseñor as allegedly their attorney. In the legal brief that Cervantes submitted, he concentrated upon the Juntans who were still in the San Bartolomé Valley, whose departure the growers were trying to hinder. Citing first the freedoms and privileges guaranteed to Native people, Cervantes went on to address each of the growers' contentions. To the first he responded that the growers had no legal basis to interfere in the Natives' rights which pertained solely to the King, and therefore the growers did not have to be consulted. Second, there were several advantages to the Juntans being in their own lands, while the Tarahumaras were sufficiently skilled laborers. Third—jumping to a different level of discourse—"above all the providence of God would procure the amount" of laborers needed by the growers. Fourth, the Juntans were not receiving any religious instruction since the haciendas were miles apart from each other and from the town where the priest resided—after which Cervantes launched into a pious exhortation about Christian life. Finally, he asserted that the San Bartolomé Valley was well patrolled by the military company.[57]

In response to the charge about lack of religious instruction, the growers had Fray Pedro de Ortega, the priest in their valley for the past fifteen years, write a document attesting to the long-time reception of the sacraments at that place by the *norteños*. As discussed previously in the chapter on early Juntan migration, he noted the appearance of Tapacolmes and other nations in those records since 1657.[58] This affidavit by Father Ortega was actually a very weak argument for the hacienda owners. Being baptized, or even married in the church, was not a demonstration of regular or consistent religious instruction.

The growers' attorney, Joseph de Miguelena, had testimony taken at San Bartolomé from one of the Juntans who knew Spanish. Francisco Cupula, described as the lieutenant governor of the new conversion of the Rio del Norte, declared that

> his governor, who is Don Pasqual in the Rio del Norte, sent him to this valley to see the Indians who are from the Rio del Norte who are helping in the farming haciendas of this valley, and to take back with him those who had worked there before the wheat harvests and leave in those haciendas those who were necessary, as has always been the custom, and that the Missionary Fathers who entered and are now present in the Rio del Norte did not tell him anything.[59]

This could be understood as essentially the same instructions as those given by Trasviña Retes before leaving La Junta. But the expression "leave in those haciendas those who were necessary" could also be interpreted as allowing for a permanent or at least undetermined stay there, which would go against what Trasviña Retes and Governor San Juan were trying to engineer.

Miguelena dealt scornfully with Cervantes's brief for the governor, belittling it as "metaphysical and scholastic arguments" from someone of "little intelligence."

He stated that the royal regulations prohibiting that Natives be forced into labor did not prevent them from laboring voluntarily outside their own lands as long as they were paid what was customary. They did not want to leave, he declared. He also argued that their absence from La Junta was not harmful to developing missions there, since only ten persons at most from each town were in the San Bartolomé Valley, and they came and went.[60] He was only counting adult men, not their families that accompanied them, since earlier on September 4, in itemizing the presence of the Juntan laborers, he specified that he was not including women and children. In this itemized account he provided a unique glimpse of these migrant laborers' town origins and destinations. Those from each town worked for the same landowner, as one would expect in the *encomienda* and *repartimiento* systems as well as from the Natives' kinship-based society.

Hacienda owner Bartolomé de Porras had ten Cacalotes (San Juan), Ana Moreno nine Mezquites (Mezquite), Andrés Delgado ten Pocsalmes (San Cristóbal), Simón Cordero nine Oposmes (San Francisco), Joseph del Yerro three Cíbolos (Guadalupe), and Diego Moreno five Polacmes (Guadalupe). Besides these forty-six men, there were thirty-six more who had been taken from these haciendas for a military campaign, a total of eighty-two men and their families from the Rio del Norte. For this number to conform to Miguelena's assertion of no more than ten men from each town, almost all the fighting men would have had to have been taken from Púliques, San Antonio, and Aranzazu, homes of the three Juntan groups not mentioned, with two additional men over the limit of eighty for the eight towns. It is highly unlikely that almost all the fighting men came from three of the smallest towns, so Miguelena's numbers are suspect here. He wrote that the remaining haciendas of the San Bartolomé area either had no Natives from the Rio del Norte or very few. Miguelena also noted that from the Río Conchos came four Julimes working for Manuel de Ascue y Armendáriz and eight Tapacolmes on the hacienda of Francisco de Navarette. This is confirmation of the permanent location of Tapacolmes in the area of the junction of the Conchos and San Pedro Rivers by this time.[61]

Miguelena's statistics show how widespread migrant labor was among the villages in the La Junta valley, while apparently not substantially emptying any of them. Of the smaller towns of Mezquite, Aranzazu, Púliques, and San Antonio, only Mezquite had persons in Miguelena's hacienda list, and it still had eighty persons back in the La Junta valley. In regard to the Tapacolmes, as previously noted there were still some laboring for the Hierro family in the San Bartolomé valley, but they were not listed in Miguelena's survey, apparently indicating that they were very few.

Governor and Missionaries versus the Old-Generation *Hacendados*

What was actually transpiring with the Juntans during this legal battle between the Hispanic elite in 1715 is revealed by a letter written by Fathers Osorio and García on

September 28. By that time the two friars had been in the La Junta valley for almost four months. Curiously, they made no mention of Father Gras, who by now was supposedly across the Cuesta Grande at Coyame. Osorio and García had experienced what it meant to be on their own, without any Hispanic soldiers or civilians. Writing to the governor from Chihuahua, to which they had gone temporarily, they complained that the hacienda owners had countermanded the official orders. Lieutenant Francisco Velasques had brought only a few women and six or eight men back from the San Bartolomé Valley. So the friars themselves, undoubtedly encouraged by Trasviña Retes, now petitioned the governor to order that all the families return to La Junta to acknowledge their towns and their ministers.

Osorio and García pleaded for this move especially in view of the danger they had experienced surrounding them in the La Junta valley, with few able Juntans at hand to provide a defense. Presumably, the stronger and younger men were most of the male migrant laborers and military auxiliaries. The two friars even declared that this situation could make them desist from the entire endeavor. To demonstrate the danger they cited a recent incident:

> Not too many days ago three Indian enemies attacked a small hut so close to the pueblo where we are stationed [San Francisco] that, if the owner had yelled, we would have heard him without difficulty. He escaped from death because he was out tending to his small garden. . . . Only eight men were able to pursue them, since no more were to be had, and they desisted after a short distance. . . . For the enemy's strategy is to send three or four to do the damage so that those attacked will follow them, and have many remaining in hiding to do greater damage. This has already happened not too long ago, according to what the locals say, with eight trackers killed on a similar occasion.

The two friars argued that an even more important reason to have the people return to La Junta was that otherwise all would remain without knowing their obligations as Christians, not even those duties necessary for salvation: "For they all, even the most *ladinos*, ignore such an important thing." When the priests reproached the Juntans that the latter had learned Spanish perfectly but had not done the same in regard to the Christian faith, the people responded that the growers were only concerned that they work, and nothing else.

The missionaries took these protestations as mere excuses. They asserted that the people needed to have someone continually urging them. In fact, even with that their hopes were not great: "Yet after much work little will be accomplished with them." Since persuasion was not effective, they recommended restricting the Juntans' migrant work. Besides ordering the Juntans back to their towns, the governor should decree that people could only leave La Junta by his express order, in alternating shifts of a determined number. Osorio and García concluded their message by noting that they left other matters to discuss with their Father Procurator (still Father Arranegui?) whose arrival bringing supplies for them they were awaiting in Chihuahua.[62]

Once again, just as with the previous request of Trasviña Retes, this petition of Fathers Osorio and García that the governor order the Juntan laborers to leave La Junta only in shifts and by his direct order was not their own invention. It was San Juan's new policy for all Natives. In May of that year he had received complaints from the Franciscan missionary of the Nombre de Dios mission just north of Chihuahua and from several Native governors about the people from their towns who were at the nearby hacienda of Tabalaopa. They asserted that their people were neither going to Mass at the hacienda nor tending the crops in their home towns, thus leaving those crops to be eaten by the livestock. San Juan promptly ordered that the Natives return to their missions and not leave them for labor except in shifts and only with his explicit order.[63]

No one was fooled: San Juan thus could exercise control over the labor pool from the missions. Through her lawyer, the heiress owner of the Tabalaopa hacienda, María de Apressa Ybarra, appealed to the Real Audiencia in Guadalajara on November 14, stating that the haciendas in Nueva Vizcaya were being threatened with ruin due to San Juan acting "with absolute power" with the sole motive that "everyone come to him for dispatches to bring out those Indians." Her lawyer asserted that the distances to Parral to obtain permission made this measure unreasonable, adding, just as the landowners of the San Bartolomé Valley were arguing, that the Natives should be left free to labor as they were voluntarily doing. The Audiencia granted Apressa Ybarra's petition, ordering San Juan to "act in accordance with what has been customary in that Kingdom until now." By the time the governor received formal notice of this decree on March 27, 1716, he had already had to reassert his original order, since just eighteen days before that the Santo Nombre missionary had written that everyone had promptly ignored San Juan's first decree. San Juan replied to the Audiencia that Apressa Ybarra's statements were not truthful, sending testimonies of his actions that included the Santo Nombre missionary's complaints of the negative effect on his mission and the lack of evangelization taking place in the haciendas.[64]

The dispute reached King Philip himself, but the governor's file on this case is incomplete, since it only contains copies of the correspondence already cited. However, the final document in Governor San Juan's other file about the protests of the growers of the San Bartolomé Valley, described above, is the record of his acceding in June 1716 to the petition of none other than María de Apressa Ybarra that she be given copies of all the previous proceedings in the San Bartolomé Valley case, since she had since signed on to it as having a hacienda also in the Parral–San Bartolomé district.[65] So her lawyers were evidently still pursuing the issue. Future notices point to the conclusion that the San Bartolomé owners had to cede the labor of the Juntans to the new provincial economic elite in the greater Chihuahua district, including the lower San Pedro River. Chief among these nouveau elite were the colluding Sergeant Major Trasviña Retes and Governor San Juan de Santa Cruz.

Juntan Life in 1715

Together, all the descriptions in 1715 portray in greater detail the major elements and patterns of ethnic interrelations in the La Junta district as a new missionary effort was just beginning. The major economic elements were local farming and fishing (only hunting was not noted, probably a Hispanic blind spot), trading with other Natives, and especially seasonal migrant labor. The major political factors were outside Native groups as both traders and hostiles, and La Junta district people as reliable laborers and military auxiliaries for Hispanics. The indications going back to the mid-1600s are strongly confirmed: after a few decades at most of possible involuntary participation by outlying groups in the district, Natives from the La Junta district were not involved in a compulsory migrant-labor arrangement against their will. The growers in the Valley of San Bartolomé highly valued the Juntans' labor as skillful and reliable, extending over generations, in contrast to the forced labor of the Tarahumaras. Juntan leaders were in charge of managing the labor allotments, and the new missionaries actually had to ask that the Juntans be constrained in their labor movements by the Spanish governor. Furthermore, forced laborers would not have made very good conscripted military auxiliaries.[66]

The previous assumption that the migrants traveled as families is confirmed. Many had migrated regularly enough and long enough to be said to have been raised on the Hispanic haciendas, or even born there. Most of the towns in the La Junta district are shown to have been involved in this migrant system, each attached to a different landowner or landowners. The provincial government still had a determining hand in labor distribution, or at least sought to exert that control. Voluntary seasonal migration and availability as military auxiliaries were clearly a major element of life in the La Junta district, as Father Colina had already noted decades previously.

The reports serve not only to finally place the various ethnic groups in their specific locations but also to make clear the cultural distinction between, on the one hand, the Natives at Cuchillo Parado with their "relatives" in the La Junta valley and, on the other hand, the Cholomes and others in the rest of the Coyame valley. The Hispanic influence was evident everywhere, but much more strongly beginning at the town of Cuchillo Parado. The Tapacolmes are confirmed to be resident in the lower San Pedro River area, near its junction with the Rio Conchos, and no longer in the La Junta valley. La Junta remained a Native trading destination but was also subject to hostile raids by other Native groups. This last point is made clear by the contraction and consolidation of the settlements in the valley, their defensive town plans, the incidents of raiding, and the precautions of the approaching Hispanic expedition.

This is the context, not that much different from that of the 1680s, into which the new band of Franciscans entered. They were invited as nonthreatening cultural links to Hispanic society, hopefully economic providers, and also for religious motives by at least some. The Juntans were clearly quite familiar with Catholic ritual and symbols, many were baptized, probably quite a few married by the church. Their level of understanding of Christian faith and of devotion to its practices is another matter. The missionaries did not ask for protection by Hispanic soldiers initially; in fact, they specified that the military withdraw. After all, they had been invited—implored even—and gladly welcomed. But they quickly saw the need for a stronger Juntan presence to protect them. As for evangelizing, they turned to their traditional methods: teaching prayers and doctrine from a catechism manual; asking that young boys be sent to live with them and hopefully take on their ways; and looking for ways to exert more control over the people's lives.

Missionary Expansion and Divided Native Reactions

In a report written by Father Andrés Varo three decades later, he confirmed that the first two missions founded in the La Junta district were San Francisco and Santiago de la Ciénega (Coyame). In that same report Varo wrote that it was not until the year 1719, four years later, that "I entered with other Religious to populate (*poblar*) and found the missions of Guadalupe, San Christoval, San Juan, and San Pedro Apostol" (below Cuchillo Parado). This missionary reinforcement, along the lines proposed by Trasviña Retes back in 1715, was sent at the request made in 1718 by the Franciscans already in the district, who urged that "the harvest of gentiles who were continuously coming under instruction was plentiful." That certainly sounded more hopeful than the note by Fathers Osorio and García in 1715.[67]

Had their experience improved? Or was it simply a matter of obtaining for the very isolated and vulnerable missionaries some companions who might possibly exert more influence at La Junta? Indeed, by that time Father García was gone, since in November 1718 the Franciscan custos, beginning his visitation of the San Pablo Custody at La Junta, recorded that there were only two missionaries, Gregorio Osorio and Raymundo Gras. From Father Varo's statements, one may infer that the two were isolated even from each other on opposite sides of the Cuesta Grande, Osorio at San Francisco and Gras at Coyame. The custos made no other observations about the situation at La Junta, merely leaving the same pro forma instructions there as he would in the New Mexico missions: learn the native languages, make proper registers for recordkeeping, and teach the Christian doctrine at regular times.[68]

The new friars, besides Varo at San Cristóbal, were Antonio Aparicio at San Pedro, Francisco Lepiane at Nuestra Señora de Guadalupe, and Luis Martínez Clemente at San Juan Bautista.[69] Father Varo became a key figure in the history of the Franciscans in the Custody of San Pablo in the eighteenth century, serving as their custos several times from his usual base in the El Paso district. An Andalusian born about 1694, his assignment to La Junta in 1719 was probably his introduction to missionary life.[70] A zealous missionary and staunch defender of the Franciscans, he could be conciliatory when needed but also capable of biting sarcasm when offended. In 1750 he wrote a sharp rebuttal to the negative report of the viceroyal military inspector, Juan Antonio de Ornedal.[71] He was not a romantic, rather quite clear-eyed in his experience in the La Junta district, and not afraid to name names including those of the powerful.

The other three friars arriving in the La Junta district in 1719 are much less known historically. Already 42 years old, Father Lepiane had just transferred into the Santo Evangelio Province the previous year. He served for a year and a half as the vice-custos of the La Junta district before heading back to Central Mexico. His only other time in the San Pablo Custody was when he returned as custos from late 1723 to early 1727.[72] Martínez Clemente was only 27 years old in 1719, thus another young adult like Varo. The exact length of his time at La Junta is unknown, but certainly no longer than Varo. Aparicio was a Spanish friar who was in El Paso by 1708 and at Pecos in 1714–1715.[73] He would be the other friar besides Varo who was almost executed at La Junta in 1726.

The increased missionary presence in the La Junta district brought significantly more mission property in terms of livestock and supplies, as well as more widespread missionary presence and efforts to change the lifestyle of the people. Both of those factors promptly led to problems. In 1720 there was actually an uprising in the La Junta valley. Father Varo, who was present at the time, wrote in 1724 about two incidents, the second much more serious than the first. He related that Martín de Alday, who became the new governor of Nueva Vizcaya in 1720, received news of disorder in the La Junta district. According to Varo, this was due to "there not having been placed there the forces that were asked for in the beginning." Alday promptly made a military visit to La Junta, treating the people so well that he thought everything would remain calm. Therefore, he did not leave any soldiers there. But the result was the opposite of what he expected: the missions were subsequently plundered of almost all that they had. Varo was grateful for one thing, that Alday on his first visit had not punished any Natives, otherwise "we [missionaries] would have paid for it with our lives" during the plundering episode. "They would not have left us alone if they had been [punished]."[74] A Chihuahuan interviewed a few years later corroborated Varo's account, testifying that an uprising in 1720 caused Governor Alday to visit the Juntans "to calm them and contain them on account of the many petitions made by the Father Missionaries." Having left them in peace, "he got word that they had risen up again, so that he was obliged to send a force to contain them, and learned that they had carried away all the supplies, herds, tools, and worship items of those missions."[75]

Father Varo was particularly horrified that the Juntans had disrespected the vestments and other cloth items used during the celebration of the Mass, "tearing them apart to make loincloths as they did with a chasuble and cape, and using the corporals, albs, and altar coverings as bandanas and shirts." European fabric remained a valued item among the Natives, and some plunderers had not learned the high reverence for the Mass that the missionaries hoped to instill. Varo wrote that this uprising had occurred "after they harvested their plantings, in July or August, when the two rivers were swollen."[76] In his historical account of the La Junta missions twenty-five years later, he provided more details, including the motives for the uprising and the fact that once again some Juntans protected the missionaries:

> More and more disorders had been growing among the missionized Christian Indians, as had the depredations of the neighboring barbarians. . . . The Christians loved the freedom of the heathens, and both groups were led by the desire for plunder. . . . We owed the saving of our lives, and the fact that not all of the vestments and sacred vessels were lost, to a few Indians who faithfully protected us and took us out to the Villa of Chihuahua.[77]

The fact that there were Juntans who did not join in the uprising was corroborated by the Indian governor of the Julimes pueblo south of the La Junta district. He later testified that "there was an uproar (*alboroto*) in those towns that General Martín de Alday entered to calm, and it was said that they wanted to rise up. The declarant was told by many of those Indians that this was not on the part of all, rather only some. He did not know the cause of it."[78]

Two writers a quarter century later cited differing events that they said caused the discontent. Their information was secondhand at best, since neither was yet in northeastern Nueva Vizcaya in 1720. The fact that their accounts differ might be due to the fact that there were two incidents in 1720 as related above, the second more damaging than the first. In his 1748 history of military events and needs in Nueva Vizcaya, Captain José de Berroterán, who was stationed at the Mapimí presidio far below La Junta in the early 1720s, said that the missionaries took flight around September 1720. He said that Father Lepiane had twice ordered the Natives to dig a three-mile-long *acequia* (irrigation ditch) where he indicated, and twice the rising Rio Conchos had obliterated it. When the agronomically inexperienced friar obtusely ordered a third attempt, the Natives had him send their general to seek the help of an expert from the Spanish governor of Nueva Vizcaya. The general, however, for some unknown reason did not carry out the commission given to him. Upset at not receiving the desired help, the Juntans determined to remove the general from his position. The friars, suspecting that they were about to revolt, retreated to the safety of Chihuahua.[79] Although dated at the probable time of the second incident in 1720, Berroterán's account did not note any major plundering and did not mention the previous disturbance. Perhaps it was a conflation of the two episodes, reporting the reason for the disturbances noted earlier and the outcome of the second.

Father Miguel Menchero, the less reliable yet most quoted source for the ear-lier decades of the mission history at La Junta, wrote in 1744 that when some un-missionized Indians "on the other side of the Rio Conchos . . . where the fathers could not pass nor enter" were told to return some missing mission animals, they plotted to kill the missionaries and Francisco, a Native governor and his assistants, who were charged with guarding the herd. Francisco was the Juntan who sometime later very piously professed his Christian faith on his deathbed. Forewarned of the plot, the friars and Francisco fled during the night, managing to slip unseen past about thirty Native archers seven or eight miles up the Rio Conchos. Arriving at Coyame, they were assisted by its missionary to reach Chihuahua.[80] This was probably the actual uprising. Notably, in this account the instigators if not main perpetrators were not from the mission towns.

By February 1721 a member of the San Pablo Custody had collected 766 pesos in the province of Sonora "for the grave need being suffered by the religious of the new missions of La Junta del Río del Norte, where these missions have been seriously set back (*derrotadas*) by the uprising of the Indians with the damages of thus consuming the aid that these Religious had in their missions." In July of that year Father Gras at Coyame acknowledged receiving the donations. So he at least was not permanently dislodged from his mission and perhaps was always there.[81] Taken as a whole, all the accounts and testimonies make clear that in 1720 tensions developed to the point of an actual uprising. In accepting the missionaries and thus at least some of the direc-tives of the priests, the people now experienced lesser freedom than the neighboring non-missionized nations. The actual uprising may have been instigated by outsiders, but Juntans joined in. And yet some Juntans were devoted enough to the missionar-ies that they protected the Franciscans when the occasion called for it. The mission temporalities suffered serious losses, although perhaps Coyame remained unaffected.

Soliciting aid from regional benefactors, the friars promptly returned. Thus they did not consider this uprising to have been an outright rejection of the missions by most Juntans, and in fact counted upon being supported by them. By now, however, they were regularly petitioning for military protection, which they deemed to be essential to safeguard themselves from outside groups and to obtain more submission from the Juntans. Given the previous events, their continued presence was with a certain wariness and loosening of typical mission demands:

> We were always fearfully petitioning that a remedy be provided to undo the damages
> that threatened us on account of the Indians living with such freedom. For this
> reason we were unable to make any progress in their teaching. Although it is certain
> that the missions remained quieted for a time, it is also certain that this calm was not
> what was necessary to make them what they should be [*havitarlas*]. There occurred
> deception and perniciousness in many disorders that we were necessarily obliged to

endure in order to avoid greater inconveniences. These things were made tolerable for us by the infallible hope that we had on account of our petitions [for military protection], based on what had happened before.[82]

In no way, therefore, were the Juntans a people who were continually oppressed by missionaries—or any other Hispanics. The situation in the La Junta district forced the missionaries to put up with the freedom and "many disorders," as viewed by the Franciscans, among the people there. The friars often questioned what progress they were making, if any, in having the Juntans become their ideal of Christian.

Why, then, were there Juntans who repeatedly sought them out, asked them to come be with them, and protected them when they were endangered? Ironically, part of the answer was quite probably what Father Hinojosa had sought to avoid back in the 1680s. Repeatedly, the documents over the years speak of periods of extended drought alternating with the flooding of fields at La Junta, bringing about extended times of food scarcity. The Juntans continued to migrate voluntarily to distant Hispanic enterprises to work for better food security and a better standard of living. So if some Native religious or cultural gatekeepers, or even plunderers, actually turned on the missionaries, others would soon plead with the friars to return. Simply put, the missionaries were an assured link in the La Junta district itself to the benefits that could be had from Hispanics year-round, not just during planting or harvesting seasons in Nueva Vizcaya.

What is more, as Father Colina's 1704 note and events both before and after demonstrate, most dramatically in 1759, there were always Juntans who showed the Fathers genuine respect—no doubt varying according to the missionary—even if many Natives dodged or resisted in various "deceptive" ways the missionaries' efforts to govern or convert them more thoroughly. A decree by the Audiencia of Guadalajara in late 1716 had established that the Native governors of mission pueblos should be elected every two years by the majority of the males, always in the presence of the missionary.[83] If that was the case with the Native governor Francisco in 1720, the fact that he was a convinced Christian had not kept him from being chosen as governor of one of the La Junta towns. How many other Juntans were committed Christians is unknown; that remains between them and their God.

There are almost no descriptions of actual mission life in the La Junta district. The one bishop to visit, in 1742, left only population and confirmation statistics. The only known record of an outside Franciscan visitor, back in 1718, was equally laconic. There will be future indications of religious practice and attitudes, but they will be rare.

A Native Trading Center and Its Imperiled Guests, 1723–1746

After said Don Alonso was recently elected general, he gathered the people of the missions whom he harangued to rise up when the Spanish enter to settle in La Junta de los Rios—his presumption upon having seen them already in this Santiago de la Redonda [Coyame] when they entered looking for mines. The Indians fear that with subjection by the Spaniards they will lose the liberty in which they have lived and are living. That is the reason that the missions are a lost cause and without any progress after ten years.

— Fray Andrés Varo to Governor López de Carbajal, 1724

The Indians were happy to bring us here, and up to the present remain thus (God keep them so). . . . Nevertheless, Father, we need a presidio in these missions, and it needs to be numerous, because each one of these missions is on the frontier of enemies in all four directions.

— Fray Lorenzo Saavedra, San Francisco de la Junta, 1731

The next quarter century for the Juntans has gaps in the historical record, just as existed before. Except for a critical uprising in the Coyame valley in 1726, previous accounts have dealt with those decades in one or two sentences. And they contradict each other, asserting either a mostly continuous missionary presence or a mostly absent one.[1] This chapter fills in several episodes and takes a much closer look at the one in 1726, in the process revealing a basic pattern. Throughout this period some Juntans, not only prompted by labor engagements but also driven by droughts and hostile attacks by other Natives, migrated seasonally or moved permanently to the Chihuahua vicinity and its associated lower San Pedro River district. Juntans also continued to be important military auxiliaries with the Spanish troops. The 1726 uprising had a major impact on missionary policy. Thereafter there was an intermittent presence of Franciscans, very ill-defined at some points, within the La Junta valley, but apparently no more mission effort in the Coyame valley. The continued refusal of any Spanish military support at La Junta was a major factor, yet it did not completely dissuade the friars from renewed missionary engagement, always in response to repeated petitions by Juntans. What also emerges more clearly are the regional Hispanic political realities and the inter-Indigenous relations in the La Junta district, including the more frequent arrival of Apache traders.

Juntans and Labor Arrangements in the Lower San Pedro River District

The people of the La Junta valley continued their seasonal migrant labor, but now to the greater Chihuahua area. Some evidently ended up remaining there year-round. Their exact labor arrangements are unclear. Separated from their former *encomenderos* since 1715, they were not among the groups that were being distributed in *repartimiento* by Governor López de Carbajal in 1723–1726.[2] Some Juntans were clearly living along the lower San Pedro River by this time (see figure 3). By 1724 the Native governor of Santa Cruz was a Tapacolme, and his people were the principal group in the town. Indeed, persons from the other La Junta groups were also there, specifically the Cacalotes, Mezquites, Pocsalmes, Sopolmes (Oposmes?), Conejos, Pualacmes (Polacmes), and Cíbolos.[3]

The San Pedro River was the dividing line between the *repartimientos* for the San Bartolomé district and those for the Chihuahua district. It appears that Santa Cruz, located on that dividing line, remained the home base for the Tapacolmes, to go as laborers in one direction or the other. Between 1723 and 1726 the Natives of Santa Cruz were sent by Governor López de Carbajal in *repartimiento* southward to the haciendas along the Río Florido above the San Bartolomé Valley. According to Governor Alday's investigation of an incident in 1723 discussed below, some were also being sent in *repartimiento* to Chihuahua by the Zacatecan missionaries. At some point during these same years the Jesuit missionary Francisco de Navarette, intriguingly of the same name as the hacienda owner who had Tapacolmes in the middle Rio Conchos vicinity in 1715, obtained ten *repartimiento* Natives for an undetermined period to help build a church at the Jesuit mission of Satevó on the San Pedro River above Santa Cruz de Tapacolmes.[4] A credible guess would be that they were Tapacolmes and/or other transplanted Juntans from Santa Cruz or the nearby Native towns.

A small alarm over some Natives fleeing the San Francisco de Conchos mission in May 1723 led to an investigation of conditions not only there but also in the mission towns along the lower San Pedro River. Those were the closest to the La Junta district: San Pedro de Conchos, Santa Cruz, San Pablo, and San Antonio de Julimes.[5] All told, the actual incident was brief and without violence by the Natives. The reports of the investigation are somewhat suspicious, since even though the disturbance had been due to the alleged or actual actions of Nueva Vizcayan governors, the questionnaire used for the interviews of the Native governors was only about the missionaries. And the almost uniform responses consisted solely of grievances against the Zacatecan Province friars in charge of those missions. Among the several complaints was that of Don Marcos, governor of "the pueblo of Santa Cruz of the Tapacolmes nation" (the earliest known identification of this town as "de Tapacolmes"[6]), who said that the Franciscans were sending some Natives to Chihuahua as *repartimiento* workers. The Julimes governor, Don Sebastián, said that two men were punished by sending them to labor for two months in the stone grinders at Chihuahua.

Diego Salgado, "general of the Concha nation," who resided in San Pedro and also had in his charge the other lower San Pedro district towns of Santa Cruz, San Pablo, and Julimes, complained that the friars did not allow him to govern as he should. In fact, he asked to be relieved of that responsibility, since the complaints that the Natives at Santa Cruz had brought to the previous governor three years earlier had resulted only in the assignment of new friars but no change in their practices. Salgado did not want to be held liable for any disturbance or uprising that might occur. Governor Alday did not accept Salgado's resignation. He sent the entire record of the investigation to the viceroy, whose chief advisor merely recommended that the Franciscans be told to allow the Natives time to sow their own crops and that the Natives be paid by the people who employed them, with a reminder that such work had to be voluntary.[7]

To the extent that these charges of onerous Zacatecan missionary control were true, the increasing population of Norteños in the lower San Pedro River district, with their long tradition of autonomy in the La Junta district, would help to explain the complaints about Native subordination in the San Pedro one. What can be derived from all the comments is that the labor situation in the lower San Pedro River district was a combination of required working for the missionaries, already being challenged by some as without pay, and of *repartimiento* and voluntary working elsewhere. If there was indeed a general discontent or nervous volatility in these missions, it would have had some reverberations among the Juntans working and residing in the district as well as within the La Junta district itself.

Frontier Rumors and Reactions in the La Junta District
Native groups continued to arrive for trade purposes at La Junta, while hostile bands of other nations continued to raid the district. In November 1723 Father Lepiane announced from Santa Fe in New Mexico that he was the newly elected custos of the San Pablo Custody. He wrote that he would begin his visitation of the missions of the custody starting at La Junta in March of the following year.[8] If he did, he probably found his men on high alert. In late May 1724 Father Varo wrote from Coyame to Governor López de Carbajal that he had taken the precaution to remove to that mission—the closest to the Nueva Vizcayan settlements from which help might be needed—the sacred vestments from all the other missions. He had done so "in view of

the disorders of the Indians increasing more than usual, in dances, drunkenness from peyote, deliberative meetings (*tlatoles*), and other actions that always occur with greater excess when they are planning an uprising." Varo described the perceived instigators and the motives of the alleged plotters:

> The instigators are two Coahuiltecan Indians, who have been hidden in the *ranchería* of General Juan Sibula, a Cholome, who together with the General of the missions [of La Junta] Don Alonso, a very sharp enemy of our holy Catholic law, have admitted their *tlatoles* and stirred up the Indians to go to Coahuila to unite with the Coahuiltecans. I have known them to be bad before the arrival of those Coahuiltecans. After said Don Alonso was recently elected general, he gathered the people of the missions whom he harangued (*tlatoleó*) to rise up when the Spanish enter to settle in La Junta de los Rios—his presumption upon having seen them already in this Santiago de la Redonda [Coyame] when they entered looking for mines. The Indians fear that with subjection by the Spaniards they will lose the liberty in which they have lived and are living. That is the reason that the missions are a lost cause and without any progress after ten years.

That an alleged enemy of the "Catholic law" was elected as the new Juntan general demonstrates that the missionaries there did not control those elections. Varo argued that a presidio at La Junta was the only remedy, as the friars had urged previously. Not to do so, he stated graphically, "is to toss the workers like sheep to the slaughter." And, he added, making a play on words with the term *agua puerca*:

> The Venado captain who went to tell you that he wanted to be baptized and settle in this mission of the Redonda is already in foul water (*agua puerca*), having already forgotten and ceased to admit our holy Catholic law. He as well as the other (*los demás*) Cholomes who live upriver on the Rio del Norte that they call *agua puerca* go to see the [Spanish] governors more for what they give them than for the purpose of settling and subjecting themselves to any minister.[9]

In these two passages by Varo the dilemma confronted by many Juntans and the missionaries was clearly laid out. Although Varo portrayed Don Alonso, the new Juntan general, as a sharp enemy of Catholic law, the general's rallying cry was specifically against the settlement of Hispanics if that were attempted. Recently prospectors had appeared in the Coyame vicinity, and any Native of Nueva Vizcaya was well aware of what would happen if mineral deposits were discovered. Subsequent history would amply confirm that what most of the Juntans strongly resisted was any settlement of Hispanics, civilian or military, among them. Events in 1726 would demonstrate that General Alonso was far from being an enemy of the missionaries themselves. For their part, the Franciscans understandably felt too vulnerable to the hostile groups that surrounded La Junta for more than a hundred miles. And they wanted obedience to their missionary efforts to be more strongly enforced. Thus, they demanded a presidio, that is, a Hispanic settlement. This quandary would define the history of La Junta for several more decades. It was the Franciscans, prompted by their missionary zeal, who repeatedly gave in, returning again and again to La Junta without soldiers and with practically no other Hispanic presence.

In this episode the alleged instigators were Natives to whom Hispanics gave the generic name of Coahuiltecans, who were looking for allies to counter the Hispanic entrance into their territory to the east of Nueva Vizcaya.[10] The other suspected leader besides General Alonso was General Juan Síbula, called here a Cholome but actually a Cíbolo, who was harboring the Coahuiltecans at his *ranchería* to the east of the La Junta valley in the direction of Coahuila. Cholome could be a general indicator for Native groups traditionally surrounding La Junta, especially to the near southwest in the Coyame valley and extending to the northwest along the Rio del Norte to the border of the Sumas.[11] The Native captain identified as Venado was evidently not Apache, since Apaches were well known to Hispanics by this time. Two years later, in 1726, Varo would clearly distinguish him from the Apaches.[12]

Varo judged that the suspected uprising would not occur until after the Juntans had harvested their crops, that is in July or August when the rivers were swollen.[13] Before that time he would order the friars to leave, bringing with them the few liturgical vestments and linens that they had kept as strictly necessary in their own missions. It took over a month for Varo's letter to reach the governor, perhaps because the latter was traveling. When Governor Carbajal finally received the letter on July 4 at El Pasaje, far to the southeast of Parral, he judged from Varo's estimation that the time of the uprising was already at hand and immediately ordered that the presidios of Nueva Vizcaya detach a total of one hundred soldiers, to be joined by an equal number of trustworthy Indians, whom he would personally lead to La Junta. Gathering men as he headed north, he arrived in the San Bartolomé Valley, somewhat to the southeast of Parral, on July 15. The next morning, he met Father Pedro Sanches, one of the La Junta missionaries, who was passing through San Bartolomé. Father Sanches said that he had left "due to the hunger that he suffered in that land" and since he presumed that the Indians would rise up once they had gathered their crops. But they had not done so prior to his departure. The governor was told by those at San Bartolomé that they had not heard anything about any uprising other than from Father Sanches and that they would have heard something since they were in constant communication with Chihuahua and other places. So Carbajal ordered that several knowledgeable persons be interviewed about the situation.[14]

Four prominent persons of the San Bartolomé Valley gave their depositions. They all made very positive comments about the Juntans, saying that they had no reason whatsoever to believe that they would rise up against the missionaries, since they had been so docile when they had been working in the San Bartolomé Valley. Evidently these deponents were only too happy to seize this occasion to try to redirect the Juntan labor back to their valley. Two of them declared that the Juntans had been required to leave the San Bartolomé Valley against their will. One of them added that the majority of the Juntans were actually natives of the San Bartolomé Valley, and that he had heard some Natives from Santa Cruz say that the missionaries "weary (*aburren*) the Juntans by demanding more than is just from them." Was this actually about La Junta, or rather the complaint already noted about the Zacatecan missionaries in Santa Cruz itself? One of these interviewees had just seen several Juntans in Chihuahua who were going about peacefully visiting and laboring, without a word about an uprising. Another said that he had met Father Sanches about a week earlier but that the priest had already left, bound for Mexico City.[15]

Governor Carbajal decided to follow up on the reported statements from Santa Cruz. He sent for that governor and the one at Julimes, who arrived on July 21. Luis Caburraja of Julimes said that the Cholomes and the nations of La Junta continually passed through his town on their way to and from working in the Chihuahua area, and that many were *ladinos* (Spanish-speaking). He said that the Juntans who passed through his pueblo appeared content and that he had heard nothing about an uprising. Antonio Martín Talamantes of Santa Cruz described his town as composed principally of Tapacolmes but also containing people from all the La Junta towns, fleeing from the periodic droughts at La Junta. He too said that other Juntans passed through continually, and none of them had mentioned any uprising. In fact, they were busy gathering their harvest in the La Junta valley at this time. He added that four Juntans who arrived the same day on which he received the governor's summons said everything was calm. These Juntans had also reported that they had seen their missionaries at the Tabalaopa (today's Chuviscar) River that flows eastward from the Chihuahua district and did not know why they had left La Junta.[16]

These testimonies abundantly confirm that the Juntan labor had been redirected to the Chihuahua area, as Trasviña Retes had requested. But since Julimes and Santa Cruz were actually southeast of Chihuahua, not on the more direct route from La Junta to that town by way of the Chuviscar River, they also reveal the familial connections that many Juntans had established with Julimes and Santa Cruz. The testimonies affirm that the harvest was occurring in La Junta in July. They also reveal that the missionaries did withdraw from La Junta at that time. The Franciscans may have sounded a false alarm, but the fact that there was no uprising up to this point was what Varo had assumed—that is, that it would occur only after the harvest. Actually, the departure of the Franciscans with their more treasured supplies removed the supposed target of the alleged plot. If there had been a planned revolt, the conspirators now decided to lay low, with no missionaries to harass nor valuables to plunder. After all, news traveled both ways. The Juntans and the Cholomes had to have heard of the strong military force heading north toward them.

A month later a Hispanic wrote to the governor that some Julimes who had traveled to Coyame found everything peaceful there. They said that the Natives who had left Coyame were those of El Venado, and that the Sisimbles had stolen some animals from some Apaches who had come for the trading fairs in the La Junta district. They also said that the Junta general would be coming to see the governor to seek permission to attack the Sisimbles.[17] And indeed on September 19 Governor Carbajal in Chihuahua received Don Alonso Lopes, General of the Nations of La Junta, along with Manuel Ponze, Governor of the Mission of San Cristóbal; Juan Phelipe, Governor of the Mission of San Francisco; Juan, Governor of the Mission of San Juan; Antonio, alcalde of that mission; and others. In all they numbered twenty-eight to thirty persons.

In the name of the emissaries, Juan Francisco de la Cruz, captain of the mission of San Francisco, said in Spanish that it was not true that they had been planning to revolt, and that they had not given the Fathers any reason for leaving the missions. Governor Carbajal exhorted these leaders "to not allow public sins nor any offense, to keep in everything the law of God and those of the King, to not drink peyote because it is prohibited and those who do it sin gravely, and to be very obedient to the missionaries."[18] Notably, these leaders did not include anyone identified as from Coyame or San Pedro, the missions of the Cholomes. But they did include the Juntan general Alonso Lopes, presumably the same Don Alonso whom Varo had described three and a half months earlier as the new Juntan general allegedly fiercely hostile to the Catholic faith. Perhaps the Spanish governor took note of the fact that this Native delegation had not hurried to protest their loyalty upon the departure of the Franciscans. They came two months later, seeking to combine military strategies with the Spanish.

For their part, the missionaries remained absent from La Junta. On October 14 Father Varo wrote to the governor for the third time (he had written a second time on September 20) from the mission of Nombre de Dios next to Chihuahua. He insisted again on a presidio and for sustained military protection in the meantime. He noted that the governor had shown him the viceroy's response, telling the governor to protect the missionaries while the viceroy deliberated about such a move. In the same letter the viceroy had thanked the governor for having calmed the Natives. Recalling what had happened in 1720 after the very lenient response by Alday, Varo repeated that it would be insufficient if the governor merely escorted the missionaries back to La Junta and then left them there once more unprotected. He cited his own experience of six years in those missions, as well as "the notices that I had from the Reverend Father Preacher Fray Gregorio Osorio about those missions, of which he was the first founder and dwelled in them for a period of ten years." So Father Osorio had remained at La Junta up until this withdrawal of the missionaries in 1724. Varo named Fathers Domingo Villasiain, Antonio de Esquivel, and Diego Espinosa as the other friars who were with him earlier when they met with the governor.[19] Presumably they were those who had been in the La Junta district along with Varo, Osorio, and Sanches—the expected six for the six mission centers.

The governor's file on this matter ends with the record of a meeting he called of the leading military officials and citizens of Chihuahua on October 21 to get their opinions. The Chihuahuans were in much closer and more recent contact with the Juntans than the citizens of San Bartolomé, and they did not share the rosy views of the latter group. Their sense was that, even though an uprising had not taken place, the Juntans had not proven themselves to be completely loyal to the Spanish regime, "the cause being that they are so distant from the Spanish, very many in number, and do not have any military nearby to engender respect." They could not have put it more succinctly. Citing the 1720 incidents, these Chihuahuan leaders counseled against the governor reinstalling the Franciscans at La Junta before a presidio was placed there. Soldiers were already lacking in other areas of Nueva Vizcaya, and even a detachment of fifteen to twenty would be insufficient at La Junta. They supported the Franciscans' petition for a presidio. Adding a new charge against the Juntans, destined to reappear a quarter century later, they asserted that such an establishment would not only secure the Natives' loyalty to the king but also curb the robberies in Chihuahua and its surroundings that the Juntans were carrying out.[20] Presumably, all these proceedings were forwarded to the viceroy.

The 1726 Uprising in the Coyame Valley

At some point an undetermined number of friars returned to the La Junta district without military protection, perhaps with the assurance that it would be forthcoming as the viceroy worked things out. One returnee was the cautious yet intrepid Father Varo. When the year 1726 arrived, his greatest fears were realized. Much later, in 1749, he penned a very brief description:

> The year of 1726, the governor being Don Joseph Carbajal whom we had forewarned about our well-founded fears, the Sumas who live in between El Paso and La Junta rose up. They were accompanied by those from the Missions of Santiago de la Ciénega of Coyame, San Pedro, and Cuchillo Parado, with many others from the interior missions of the Cholome Síbolos, destroying almost completely the missions and placing us at the point of losing our lives. They would have killed us, as they did with two servants, had help not arrived in time by divine disposition.[21]

Some Sumas had been recalcitrant to Spanish imposition from the beginning of Spanish settlement in the El Paso region, and they would remain so. As revealed by the 1715 founding expedition, the people in the missions of Coyame and San Pedro in the Coyame valley who joined in the uprising were part of the extended nation of

Cholomes that bordered on the Sumas. Members of that nation had similarly joined the Suma insurgents in 1684, before missions were established at Coyame and San Pedro three decades later.[22]

Thanks to several contemporary documents, especially the diaries and letters of Joseph de Aguirre, one of the leaders of the Spanish rescue mission on this occasion, we have a much more detailed and contemporaneous account of what occurred.[23] Aguirre was for all practical purposes the successor of the deceased Trasviña Retes. Like the latter, he was the local military leader of Chihuahua and one of the six leading miners and hacienda owners of the district, together with former governor San Juan de Santa Cruz and the widow of Trasviña Retes.[24] The accounts are fascinating for what they reveal about the various relations and even intrigue among and within the various Native groups in or near the La Junta district at this time.

One of the persons interviewed in Chihuahua after the event was none other than General Alonso de Carvajal from the La Junta town of Guadalupe. The fact that he was from Guadalupe and general of the Juntans strongly supports the conclusion that the General Alonso López of 1724 was the General Alonso de Carvajal of 1726, with the double assigned Hispanic surnames of López de Carvajal. In both cases only two years apart the Juntan general was a General Alonso, and Guadalupe was the only principal town whose governor was not identified at the September 1724 meeting of Juntan leaders with Governor López de Carbajal at which General Alonso López was present.[25] In highly ironic contrast to Varo's charge in 1724 that he was anti-Catholic, General Alonso was the one who heroically saved Varo's life in 1726. Thus, religion was not the crucial issue for him; his call for readiness to battle in 1724 had been the prospect of Hispanic settlement in his valley.

Now, two years later, General Alonso asserted that the uprising was precipitated by the attempt to imprison a Cholome native in the Coyame valley who was trying to stir up the people. That instigator fled to the Sumas and returned with them to destroy the Coyame mission. It was in mid-March that Cholomes at Coyame and San Pedro, aided by Sumas, rose up against the two missionaries among them at the time, Andrés Varo and Antonio Aparicio. Killing two of the mission workers, a Sonoran Native and a Hispanic—one of only two Hispanics mentioned as briefly resident in the Junta district before 1760—they held the two Franciscans captive, planning to put them to death in a more spectacular and gruesome fashion. They also carried off all the iron objects and part of the vestments and precious items of all the missions that had remained stored at Coyame ever since 1724.

By this time Don Pedro Coyame was the general of the Cholomes in the Coyame valley. He himself was threatened by the belligerents and fled further south with some of his companions. But General Alonso (López) Carbajal hurried to the rescue from the river junction at La Junta with thirty of his men. Realizing that he was outnumbered at Coyame, he persuaded those up in arms to take the prisoners to the river junction, on the pretext that the people there wished to take part in the executions and the associated dances. When everyone reached the town of San Francisco, however, where General Alonso had ordered the valley Juntans to concentrate themselves for protection, the Juntans successfully attacked the belligerents, took the missionaries under their protection, and sent word to Chihuahua. Some Juntans had always protected missionaries, and now as a body they did so again. Reasons are not given, but one can assume the same as before: they wanted to maintain their alliance and trade relations with the Hispanics, and at least some were actually Christians defending their priests.

When news of the uprising reached Chihuahua on March 19, Alférez (Ensign) Joseph de Aguirre quickly organized a rescue expedition that included nineteen "Indios del Norte," among them Don Juan, the governor of San Francisco, and Fray Diego de Espinosa, one of the La Junta missionaries. Besides those visiting Chihuahua, the Juntans probably included some that resided in that district or were serving as military auxiliaries. No other missionaries beyond Varo, Aparicio, and Espinosa are mentioned in the accounts of this uprising. They were the three who were finally escorted to safety in Chihuahua. This would mean that Espinosa was the only Franciscan resident in the La Junta valley itself, unless another colleague was also temporarily absent and remained in Chihuahua when the rescue expedition left there. Ironically, perhaps at this time the Franciscans considered the missions in the Coyame valley safer, given what had occurred in 1720. Coyame was closer to Chihuahua and not separated by a very difficult mountain ridge. What is clear is that no missionaries remained in the La Junta district after this harrowing event, not for several years.

The expedition was joined by the Coyame general Don Pedro when they passed through his place of refuge. Arriving at the Coyame mission, they found it completely pillaged and abandoned. There they were joined by some "Indians of the North" from the town of Cuchillo Parado who had been working further south along the Rio Conchos in a hacienda at Chorreras. They had fled from there when some of the Sumas raided it also. The belligerent Cholomes, led by Diego, the governor of Coyame, and Lucas, the governor of San Pedro, refused the invitation to return to their towns. Among the belligerents from San Pedro were its cacique Cayetano and in particular the brothers Antonio and Santiago, known as the Toritos (the little bulls). This Santiago el Torito must have been the Cholome leader who welcomed the Hispanic missionizing party in 1715. Clearly his attitude and that of many of his townspeople had changed after a decade of mission efforts among them.

The mention of the cacique of San Pedro might well indicate a religious motive for the uprising, at least on the part of some. A cacique was a headman in the traditional Native system. Among the Pueblos of New Mexico he was the chief sacred leader, usually opposed to the missionaries and opposed by them. Was that the case with this cacique? It is hard to believe that there was not a formal religious leader in permanent sedentary communities whose cultural if not biological lineage included Mogollon-Anasazi ancestry. Remarkably, however, opposition by Native religious leaders is never mentioned in the known missionary correspondence about La Junta, unless this Cayetano in San Pedro is such a case. Only two caciques will be noted in the first known census list, in 1747. Caciques will be noted again in a listing of Native leaders at La Junta in 1759, but with no indication of their roles nor of their opposing the missionaries for religious reasons.[26]

Alerted to the arrival of the Hispanic force at Coyame, General Alonso left the river junction, bringing Fathers Varo and Aparicio and the liturgical items from the valley churches, in order to meet the Hispanic party at a place called El Álamo just across the Cuesta Grande on the Cuchillo Parado side. But, having arrived at the foot of that difficult mountain ridge on the La Junta valley side, he learned that other Sumas, lying in wait for such an opportunity, attacked his town of Guadalupe in his absence. So he hastily returned there, the missionaries always with him. He had a trusted Juntan carry a stark note to Aguirre from Varo: "Come for Fray Andrés Varo; do not delay." Upon reaching Aguirre the messenger explained why General Alonso had backtracked to the river junction. Given this news, Aguirre decided to delay entering the La Junta valley until he obtained more supplies, having been told that the distance from Coyame to San Francisco was twenty-five leagues. But he did send the Indians of the North who had joined him, by now almost doubled to thirty-four in number, to aid the threatened General Alonso and the others at La Junta.

Once resupplied and joined by another military force from Nueva Vizcaya, Aguirre and the other commander led this joint party of 295 men, half of them Hispanic (twenty-five soldiers, 122 citizen volunteers) and half Native allies (Chinarras, Conchos, Tobosos, Julimes, Tarahumaras) into the Embudo canyon and across the Cuesta Grande to arrive on April 4 at a place along the Conchos River above El Mezquite. General Alonso, who could count upon over 200 feared archers, met them there with the two friars. Juan Cíbolo, the general of the Cíbolos who were the Juntans' closest neighbors to the east, accompanied General Alonso as a supposed ally. This Juan Cíbolo was most probably the Cholome-Cíbolo Juan Síbula who had been the host of the Coahuiltecan instigators in 1724.

Don Alonso had just learned that the Cíbolo general had been persuaded to join the uprising and was now acting as a spy. Don Juan Cíbolo had actually called upon the Sumas, Cholomes, "the Captain Venado," and even some Apaches to join in attacking the valley Juntans for being allies of the Hispanics. Even though these hostile forces could allegedly draw upon more than 3,000 warriors from practically all of the surrounding nations, their resolve began to falter in view of the combined Juntans, Hispanics, and Native auxiliaries with the Hispanics. The Native governors of Coyame and San Pedro promptly arrived to plead that they had been cowed by the Sumas and that the real instigators were the two Cholome "Torito" brothers. While not really believing them, Aguirre treated them well, in order to encourage "their return and calm." He urged them to bring back their families.

Early the next day General Alonso led the combined forces three more leagues to San Juan and then four more to San Francisco. He informed Aguirre that the only reliably friendly Native leaders outside La Junta were their closest neighbors to the north, called El Tecolote and El Barrigón, who even though Cholomes were related to the Juntans. In fact, they had recently determined to come to live at La Junta. While Aguirre was there, those two Native leaders agreed to bring their people and settle one league from San Francisco. That this happened and endured would be verified two decades later by the Ydoiaga expedition.[27] Also judged loyal was Don Thomás, the old cacique and former general for many years of the Cíbolos now resident at La Junta. Aguirre also sent messages to El Venado, whose dwellings were more than twelve leagues up the Rio del Norte, and to El Pescado, whose usual encampment was eighteen leagues upriver. The fact that both arrived within a few hours, accompanied by General Bartholomé of the Sumas and "his unconverted (*gentil*) cacique named Cuchillo," demonstrated that they had indeed been waiting nearby to pounce upon the Juntans.

General Alonso and his aides urged Aguirre to make these suspected leaders and their companions prisoners, arguing that they had come only to treacherously see the Juntans' defensive situation. So, early the next morning as he lifted camp to return to Chihuahua, Aguirre took them all captive, including General Juan Cíbolo. No sooner had the march begun than the party saw the Cholome governors, the San Pedro cacique, and seventeen other Cholomes approaching from a very suspicious direction, through the woods upriver along the Rio del Norte and without any accompanying family members. Questioned, they had no good reply. The three Cholome leaders were then taken captive, while the other Cholomes were invited to bring their families and allegedly offered to settle at La Junta itself.[28] All the prisoners were led to Chihuahua as the rescue party escorted the Franciscans to safety there. The Torito brothers were not among those captured.

The valley Juntans' duplicitous protection of the missionaries and the imprisonment of the leaders of the uprising earned the Juntans the abiding enmity of the surrounding nations that were hostile to Hispanics.[29] Throughout these events Aguirre, the military commander, noted the linguistic ability of the Native leaders involved. Since some of them even knew how to read Spanish, certain messages were only sent orally in case the messengers were captured. General Alonso of La Junta and those accompanying him were all *ladinos* in that they could speak Spanish. So could the rebellious Cholome governors, who had at least some fluency (they were described as *algo ladino*) but preferred to speak in their own tongue.[30]

As for the Spanish-allied General Pedro Coyame, he knew he was a marked man among many of those in the Coyame valley. The following year, 1727, the Zacatecan

Franciscans allowed him and the forty families with him to settle on the San Pedro River below the San Pedro de Conchos mission. Finding that location either too unsuitable or too dangerous, they ended up living as wards of the Zacatecan convent in Chihuahua.[31] One can only wonder how they viewed this final disposition. As for the Cholomes who remained in the Coyame valley, they had definitely lost any good will from the missionaries. The Franciscans were not about to reestablish themselves in that valley unless a lot of things changed.

Stymied Efforts to Have Missionaries Again, 1726–1730

For eleven years in succession the Juntans had had missionaries in their midst, and three times the friars fled for safety. Their near brush with death in the Coyame valley in 1726 seared their collective memory like the 1680 Pueblo Revolt in New Mexico stamped that of their earlier Franciscan colleagues in the San Pablo Custody. For the next five years they refused to return to any place in the La Junta district, as much as the Juntans petitioned and as much as the friars wanted to do so, unless they obtained military protection—something that the Juntans did not want. That protection was against those outside the La Junta valley including some of the Cholomes, not the Juntans themselves. The 1726 uprising had made that clearer. In every case of threatened violence, at least some of the inhabitants of the La Junta valley had protected the missionaries, even though this put those Juntans themselves in danger.

The near martyrdom of two friars and the hostile Native alliance manifested at that time finally led to the serious consideration of a presidio at La Junta by the viceroyal officials. The Franciscans wrote that Aguirre, the leader of the rescue expedition, promised to support forty families who would settle at La Junta if Aguirre were named captain of a fifty-person cavalry troop stationed there.[32] This was part of a proposal being recommended by Brigadier Pedro de Rivera, who was in the midst of his highly consequential inspection tour of the military situation throughout the entire northern frontier of New Spain. Having taken stock of the situation in Nueva Vizcaya and New Mexico, Rivera wrote Viceroy Juan de Acuña, the Marqués de Casafuerte, in late September 1726 from El Paso, advocating the founding of a presidio at La Junta. He argued that by so doing "not only would those Indians who already were quiet and receiving instruction be protected, but, upon seeing those forces, the neighboring Indians who were disturbing all the surrounding ones would be calmed." As proof he cited the fact that the Sumas who had attacked the La Junta district were finally persuaded by the news of the projected presidio at La Junta to settle near El Paso. The viceroy approved this recommendation, and Rivera returned to Chihuahua in 1727 to carry out the plan after his inspection of Sonora and Sinaloa. Present in Chihuahua were Fathers Varo and Aparicio, awaiting their return to La Junta upon the founding of the presidio.[33]

But at the last minute, Rivera suspended the foundation "because of the serious difficulties that presented themselves," as he obliquely phrased it. Part of those difficulties was that in order to avoid any increased expense to the royal treasury, the provincial garrison commanders were to be required to detach several soldiers from each of their units to constitute the new presidial troop for La Junta. Those commanders drew up complaints that their troops would be left too reduced to carry out their duties, and their protests were supported by the governor of Nueva Vizcaya. Furthermore, a final assessment in Chihuahua concluded that even though more than one hundred Hispanics volunteered to be part of the founding, another thirty to fifty troops beyond those planned would be necessary. Such an increase in new troops was definitely not going to happen, as it went against the strong economizing strategies of both inspector Rivera and the viceroy.[34] Father Varo later alleged yet another reason for the suspension of the projected garrison:

> Don Pedro Rivera saw his plans frustrated due to the displeasure of the Chihuahuans that Don Joseph de Aguirre was not named [as projected captain] as they had desired. Their ardor thus cooled, they desisted from the help that they had offered for the erection of the garrison, such as the said Aguirre's promise of supporting forty families. These people put all their efforts into drawing up new reports contrary to their preceding truthful ones, in order to make the garrison founding vanish due to their own particular interests.[35]

Thus the combination of viceroyal economizing and conflicting interests in Nueva Vizcaya, both civil and military, ultimately blocked the sending of troops.

This disagreement over the founding of a presidio and possible civilian settlement at La Junta is the first known instance of a dispute, including charges of false statements, between the Franciscan missionaries of the San Pablo Custody and the Hispanic civil and governmental authorities in Nueva Vizcaya. It would by no means be the last. Sorting out the truth on such occasions can often be challenging. In this case, one can appreciate the insistence among the presidial captains and Hispanic settlers in Nueva Vizcaya for what best protected and improved their situation. It is no surprise that on a very recently expanding frontier, both civilian and military Hispanics would take a position more favorable to their communities than to restoring missions far from any Hispanic settlement, especially when the Juntans were already migrating down to serve them. One can also recognize the colonial government's concern about reducing financial burdens. On the other hand, the Franciscan call for returning to the spiritual care of willing baptized Natives and advancing their conversion is self-explanatory.

Not yet aware of Rivera's suspension of the presidio plans, authorities in Mexico City asked for an investigation of the supplies that would be needed in the La Junta district to replace those lost in the 1726 uprising. When these orders finally reached Nueva Vizcaya, Fathers Varo and Aparicio were queried in Chihuahua, between

December 6, 1727, and January 8, 1728. Varo presented himself as the missionary of San Cristóbal, probably because he had been the founder of that mission and perhaps that was still his official assignment. From the records that he had in his possession, he took the description of the liturgical items, livestock, and other supplies that the king had originally ordered to be provided to each mission. Most of these royal gifts had actually been lost in the 1720 uprising, but the missions had been resupplied through the generosity of benefactors. During the 1726 uprising many of the liturgical items, especially in the La Junta valley, had been undisturbed; others were returned by the belligerents. All of these were carried to safety in Chihuahua, but the rest of the mission property was lost. The few exceptions were the bells left hanging in the churches and perhaps one or the other large altarpiece painting. Three such paintings had been carried to the mission of Chinarras by the rescue party on its return trip southward, yet they were so mistreated that it would be cheaper to replace them.[36]

Sometime in 1728 Father Lepiane, who had finished his term as custos of the San Pablo Custody the previous year, wrote in Mexico City that Fernando de Castro was now with Andrés Varo in Chihuahua. The two ministered to those Juntans who voluntarily came to them and were ready to go to La Junta if a presidio were established. Hoping for this outcome, the Franciscans continued to list the six mission centers in the La Junta district in their mission plan. That plan called for royal subsidies for thirty-six Franciscans in the San Pablo Custody, two more than in 1712, since the positions of procurator (supply master) and lay brother had also been granted subsidies. This indirectly indicated that no additional subsidies had been given for the missions in the La Junta district, even though they were added after 1712. Rather, as the Franciscans would respond in their defense in 1748, some of the thirty-six subsidies for the custody were shifted as needed to provide for those missions.[37]

On October 14 that same year, Father Martínez Clemente, one of the 1719 founders of additional La Junta missions and now acting as official visitor of the custody, inspected the administrative ledgers of the La Junta district in the possession of Varo and Castro in Chihuahua. Martínez commiserated with his former companion Varo, who "shared with me his great sadness in being outside those missions without our being able to remedy it, since they are not being staffed due to the great danger they are in without having a presidio. And seeing his sadness to be well founded, I encouraged him to hope that divine providence would give some means for his solace."[38]

Still hopeful, in January 1729 the Provincial Chapter of the Holy Gospel Province continued to designate on paper six missionaries for the La Junta district, including Father Castro but not Father Varo, since the latter was named custos (and duly noted as a Spaniard, *gachupín*) of the San Pablo Custody. Thereafter, if Varo was to experience any consolation about the La Junta missions, it would have to be as a very interested leader or missionary elsewhere in the custody. He apparently never returned to La Junta. But in his long career, stationed mostly in the El Paso district, he would serve four times as custos of the San Pablo Custody and thus continue to be informed of conditions there. The same 1729 chapter appointed 34-year-old Juan Miguel Menchero (duly noted as a *hijo de la provincia*, a Spaniard who had joined the Franciscans in New Spain) as the new procurator for the custody. Menchero would exercise that responsibility for decades. The two Spaniards Varo and Menchero, with their long-standing positions of leadership in the San Pablo Custody, would figure prominently in the records of the La Junta missions.[39]

Writing in 1730, Bishop Crespo of Durango, who was battling with the Franciscans in an effort to assert his jurisdiction in the Custody of San Pablo that included New Mexico and the La Junta missions, declared that "for five years the five or six missions of the north at the Junta de los Rios . . . have been without ministers."[40] What continued, however, was the migratory travel of Juntans to the Chihuahua vicinity.[41]

The "Third Founding," 1731

The final recommendations of Pedro de Rivera upon the conclusion of his inspection tour of the northern frontier of New Spain were approved for the most part by the viceroy in 1729. The *Reglamento* published by the Marqués de Casafuerte soon thereafter altered the eastern and central frontiers of northern New Spain in fundamental ways that endured for decades.[42] A primary motive was to cut back on the costs of the greatly increased number of presidios on New Spain's expanding northern frontier since the 1680s. In Nueva Vizcaya the Conchos presidio, nearest to La Junta, was downgraded from forty-five to thirty-five soldiers. The other presidios in northeastern Nueva Vizcaya had been staffed by anywhere from twenty-nine to forty soldiers. The new regulations reduced all of them to thirty-five or fewer soldiers apiece, "to benefit the royal account."[43] No wonder that the Franciscans' repeated petitions for a presidio at La Junta would garner so little effective support from governors and citizens elsewhere in Nueva Vizcaya. The Crown was tightening its coin purse and military, not expanding them, even though frontier hostilities were unabated. Everyone was looking out for themselves.

It should not be surprising, therefore, that when Franciscans returned to La Junta in 1731, it would be with a promise of military protection that never materialized. The record of the friars' intermittent presence at La Junta during the next fifteen years is obscure. The 1731 return may have been a historical coincidence, a product of the Juntans' continued desire for missionaries, Father Varo's emotional ties to La Junta, and the novice frontier enthusiasm of Father Miguel Menchero. In early 1731 the Commissary General who had authority over all the Franciscans in New Spain appointed Father Menchero as his Visitor of the San Pablo Custody.[44] This meant that Menchero was to inspect all the missions and missionaries and make any necessary changes or recommendations. Thus he had the authority to do something about La Junta, and he seized the opportunity. In fact, he was actually implementing the order of Father Varo, who as the custos of the New Mexico Franciscans had passed through Chihuahua recently and had listened very sympathetically to the pleas of the Juntan leaders who sought him out there. Varo was most willing to send missionaries again. Yet, still keenly mindful of the events of 1726, he first obtained Governor Barrutia's promise of cooperation in terms of military support.

When Menchero arrived somewhat later in Chihuahua from Mexico City, the governors of almost all the La Junta district, accompanied by some other officials, met him and urged that he not wait any longer for the action of the Nueva Vizcaya governor. The petitioners were Joseph Martín and Pedro Moreno, generals of the La Junta missions and citizens of San Francisco; Juan Mateo, Juan Francisco Sonora, and Andrés, respectively chief *fiscal*, governor, and alcalde of San Francisco; Alonzo Joseph, governor of San Juan; Geronimo Mateo, governor of Guadalupe; Bernardo, governor of San Cristóbal; Francisco, governor of Coyame; Marcos, governor of the Cíbolos; and Manuel, "former governor." In their petition to Menchero, probably put in written form by a Franciscan, they took note of the missionaries "pertaining to the La Junta missions" who were ministering in Chihuahua and its environs to all the Juntans in that vicinity. They explained that they had appealed to custos Varo to order that those Franciscans enter the La Junta missions to "more exactly and immediately" administer the sacraments there, especially in view of those Juntans who were unable to travel to Chihuahua. Their petition also referred without explanation to "other inconveniences" due to the Franciscans' absence. The Juntan leaders were tired of waiting for Governor Barrutia's action, and told Menchero, "knowing that you have the authority to be able to command, you should deign to command to those Fathers that they enter with us."[45]

Menchero was a Franciscan in the mold of Varo but with less cautionary experience at this time. Resolute and zealous, he was sent as Visitor with special powers in response to Bishop Crespo's critique of the Franciscan work in New Mexico the previous year. Menchero was charged with defending the reputation of the custody while addressing any abuses that had crept in. Although he had already been appointed procurator (supply master) for the custody in 1729, he was still a relative newcomer as regards missionary experience on the frontier. After joining the Holy Gospel Province in 1714 at the age of nineteen and being ordained a priest several years later, he had held several religious offices in Puebla. Much later, in 1746, he himself would found the first Navajo mission, but this petition that was placed in his lap in 1731 was his first opportunity to send missionaries.[46] He did not hesitate. Father Varo probably would have waited upon Barrutia's commitment of troops.

On May 25 Menchero wrote that, in view of the Juntans' petition, he was of the opinion that one or more Religious should be sent immediately with the Juntans while the governor promptly prepared the expedition that would escort the others.[47] Governor Barrutia, also in Chihuahua, approved this action and asked Menchero to send him the names of the missionaries destined for La Junta. They were:

Reverend Father ex-Lector Fray Lorenzo Saabedra, vice-custos [leader of the group];
Father Preacher Fray Raimundo Gras who is not coming with the present Fathers
since he is ill, as is well known; Father Fray Antonio Manrique; Father Fray Juan
Mariano Rodríguez; and Father Fray Joachin de Amesti. Then there is the death of
Father Preacher Fray Ignacio Díaz of whom it is well and publicly known that he
was buried this year in the Third Order [chapel] of this Villa. He was a missionary
pertaining to those of the North or La Junta de los Rios.

This would have been a full complement of six missionaries designated for La Junta
prior to the death of Díaz. These assignments, and the fact that the Holy Gospel
Franciscans in Chihuahua were known as "on hold" for hopefully returning to the
La Junta missions, demonstrate the seriousness and perseverance with which Varo,
Menchero, and their superiors took the commitment to La Junta.

On June 7 Governor Barrutia asked his secretary to verify this list of missionaries,
since it was the basis for providing the government subsidies to those missions. The
secretary certified that Fathers Saavedra, Manrique, Rodríguez, and Amesti (as he
signed himself and was usually called, whereas his full surname was Amestigui) presented themselves to the governor that same day and said that Gras was also part of
their number. Being very precise, the secretary noted that Saavedra, Manrique, and
Rodríguez had arrived in Chihuahua on May 31, whereas Amestigui had arrived on
December 8 the previous year and Gras in mid-December. Díaz had arrived in the
beginning of March and died April 4. Thus Saavedra, Manrique, and Rodríguez must
have come from Mexico City in the slower part of Menchero's supply train, while the
other three were already in Chihuahua. Saavedra and Amestigui said that they were
prepared to leave on Monday, June 11, with the others only awaiting the governor in
order to make their entry.[48]

Father Amestigui had already formalized a detailed receipt for supplies that he
was given in Chihuahua on May 7 as the missionary destined for the mission of San
Francisco de la Junta. It was for 459 pesos' worth of supplies, plus 354 pesos that he
had received in cash in Mexico City for his provisions for the journey to the custody.[49]
Upon the arrival of Father Saavedra, Menchero changed Amestigui's projected assignment, handing over to him on June 1 the few inventoried items, mostly liturgical, of
the Guadalupe mission "and its annexes" (other places under the care of its missionary) that had been safeguarded in Chihuahua. A very similar inventory for the San
Francisco mission included the only statue noted, a wooden carving of St. Francis over
one-third vara in height (one vara is about 33 inches).[50] That was to be Father Saavedra's
mission center. On June 11, with the departure to La Junta imminent, Saavedra signed
a detailed receipt for 627 pesos' worth of supplies, plus 130 pesos he had received in
Mexico City for his provisions for the journey to the custody. The following day he
certified that he and his fellow travelers had been well taken care of by Menchero on

their journey from Mexico City.[51] All these receipts were in keeping with the viceroyal government's demands for an accounting for the monies that it distributed to missions. The Franciscans knew from experience that only detailed records would protect their reputation against false accusations.

Father Menchero, in his later historical account, called this 1731 sending of Fathers Saavedra and Amestigui the "third founding" of the missions at La Junta.[52] He had hastened ahead of the caravan from Mexico City to arrange for its supplies in Chihuahua. Needless to say, when the other friars arrived with the caravan they were surprised—and probably a bit shaken, considering the recent reputation of the La Junta missions—when they were greeted with the news of the immediate renewal of missionary work there. The arrangements had been made very rapidly, and with no provision of Hispanic escort.

Three weeks after Saavedra and Amestigui arrived at La Junta, Saavedra as the friar in charge wrote an account of their experience from his post at San Francisco in the La Junta valley. It bears citing at length, as a uniquely informative report of daily missionary life there:

> I left accompanied by Father Preacher Joaquin Amestigui. For such a dangerous journey we had no more escort than the principal Indians of these missions. There was also the serious scarcity of supplies occasioned by the speedy undertaking of a journey precisely for bringing us here, with the addition of maintaining at our cost the Indians who were conducting us until arriving in this region.
>
> Fr. Amestigui stayed in the mission of my Lady of Guadalupe, and I in that of St. Francis our Father. The Indians were happy to bring us here, and up to the present remain thus (God keep them so) with such affection that the great weakness of their little strength (*la mucha debilidad de sus pocas fuerzas*) is not being able to feed or help us in any way. We have had enough work in the vineyard of the Lord, with baptisms and other sacraments, as well as in Christian education and doctrine, in the afternoon and in the morning, with the docility, discretion, prudence, and patience that is required [of us], in order that they learn, as they have, up to the commandments of the Law of God, in the brief time of twenty-one days that they have been under instruction. They are helped by their great ability, with my dedication to teaching them. This has led to the interest of many heathen, who on the occasion of trading with these of La Junta have seen me. Through persuasive remarks I have placed the lodestone in their hearts for them to become Christian. And they have given and left me with great hopes. May God move and deliver them according to his will.
>
> Nevertheless, Father, we need a presidio in these missions, and it needs to be numerous, because each one of these missions is on the frontier of enemies in all four directions. That includes the two more distant ones, that are those they call Coyame and Cuchillo Parado, in which occurred the invasion now five years ago when the

Suma Indians wanted to kill the Religious and the latter miraculously escaped. Now in the present these same ones tried to do the same with us Religious who are here, and God held them back.

In these missions everything is needed. There is a scarcity of every kind of meat, of large and small livestock, and of seeds. We religious are very short of the necessities, especially of food. Recourse has to be had to Chihuahua, sixty leagues from here with most of the way dangerous. The closest to that Villa is Coyame at 38 leagues, the entire route without any settlement.

These lands of La Junta are very favorable for the sowing of diverse productive seeds, with the two rivers that abound in fish. There are many mineral deposits and lands between the Hacienda that they call Las Chorreras [to the south along the Rio Conchos] to ahead of these missions [across the Rio del Norte], while further north they are better according to what the Indians who have seen them have told me, and as their assays demonstrate.

The foundations of the missions and pueblos are poorly equipped [*mal aparatados*] and in the worst sites, while they have admirable sites where they could be well founded. But the Indian, Father, without the shadow of the Spaniard, does not take advantage, due to his laziness. The mission of Coyame has very rich lands, with very sufficient water, and a mineral hill. The mission at Cuchillo Parado is very pleasant with a river of good water and fish. The one at Coyame has an extensive and pleasant wetland with fresh water. In these missions are needed six Missionary Religious of a docile and capable nature, and may they come voluntarily by divine inspiration, because the unwilling come disconsolate, and thus do nothing profitable. A lay Religious is also needed to be school master for these poor creatures, who have a great ability and talent.[53]

Saavedra was apparently referring to the San Pedro village as Cuchillo Parado, since the latter had never been staffed with a missionary. Described for the first time in the known documentation was the typical mission routine of instruction in Christian doctrine in the morning and afternoon. Many things reported on previous occasions were again confirmed: the Juntans' welcoming attitude, the fertile lands but great lack of food in drought seasons, the Native trade carried on at La Junta, the great intelligence yet alleged lack of industriousness of the Natives, the great danger of hostile actions from all sides, and the need of a protective Hispanic military presence. One startling point is the alleged plot by Sumas to attack the missionaries within the first three weeks. One is left to wonder how "God held them back."

In the meantime, Father Menchero had continued up into New Mexico, where he finally began his official visitation of the custody on August 24 in Pecos. Returning to Chihuahua in mid-October, he was surprised to find Fathers Saavedra and Amestigui back in town. Saavedra explained that they had come to Chihuahua because the Rio

Conchos had overflowed and destroyed the plantings. The Juntans, he said, had urged the friars to go to resupply themselves (and, unspoken, also undoubtedly to provide for the Juntans). Saavedra was preparing to return to La Junta on the 22nd with the Natives who had accompanied them from La Junta, but this time with the additional missionaries still awaiting the governor's escort. With this reinforcement, Menchero planned to transfer Amestigui to San Cristóbal.[54]

But Amestigui had injured himself on a previous trip about halfway through his four months at La Junta and requested to return to Mexico City for his health. He explained that while attempting to ferry himself across the Rio Conchos on a raft at Las Chorreras, he had to jump off when the river threatened to carry the raft away. Striking against a boulder, he managed to cling to it until some Natives arrived to rescue him. The medicine that he had been taking for the groin injury that he suffered did not cure him, and the doctors in Chihuahua certified that he should not "exert myself, even less mount a horse, for this risks damaging my life."[55]

Menchero was undeterred by the fact that the governor had still not escorted the other friars to La Junta. Whether out of disgust or bravado or a combination of both, he decided to go ahead and send them all there on their own.[56] Although Father Gras was still among those waiting in Chihuahua, Menchero decided to send him back to the mother province in Mexico City. Gras was not happy about it, writing that he was being "excluded" from the San Pablo Custody due to being considered incapacitated for continued service on the frontier.[57] Rather, two new friars, Joseph Ortiz de Velasco and Rafael Padín, were now to join Manrique and Rodríguez who had also remained since June in Chihuahua. Manrique was to go to San Juan, Rodríguez to Guadalupe, Ortiz to Coyame, and Padín to "San Pedro de Cuchillo Parado," with Saavedra remaining at San Francisco. Surprisingly, this would put friars back in the Coyame valley, scene of the uprising five years earlier, at least temporarily without military accompaniment. These assignments confirm that San Pedro was now being associated with the distinctive Cuchillo Parado (Cuesta Grande) landmark.

Menchero sent this list to the governor sometime before October 26, proclaiming the audacious zeal of this move and asking for the necessary permission "until measures are given for their greater security more apropos for obtaining the goal." If this was an attempt to goad Barrutia into finally providing some military, it did not work. The governor thought Menchero's actions were foolhardy, citing the past history at La Junta and the opinion that the Juntans would not submit to the subjection that the missionaries sought. Barrutia declared that the viceroy, the Marqués de Casafuerte, was pondering establishing a presidio, and that he, the governor, would again petition the viceroy to that end. Yet he gave his permission for the missionary group to return to La Junta.[58] If that was a dare, Menchero did not back down, sending off the five missionaries. He as well as Barrutia probably knew that waiting for a presidio might mean waiting forever.

There was a sixth Franciscan initially slated for La Junta at this time. On October 18 Father Amestigui had handed over the worship supplies of the Guadalupe mission that he had been serving, along with an up-to-date inventory, to Fray Joseph Manuel de Eguia, since Amestigui was initially to be transferred to San Cristóbal.[59] Back in May when Menchero had first arrived in Chihuahua, Eguia was there as a member of the Zacatecas Province of the Franciscans and chaplain of the lay Third Order Franciscans. Father Eguia was so inspired by the zeal demonstrated by the Holy Gospel friars that either in May or October he asked Menchero to admit him into the San Pablo Custody "to give the life that God gives me for the Catholic faith that I profess, in order to live solely for charity among the heathen with every natural inconvenience, with only the desire to save myself by saving them." The zeal for martyrdom was not extinguished among the Franciscans. For some reason Eguia was not among the five on Menchero's list for La Junta, that assigned a different friar to Guadalupe. But then neither was there a missionary listed for San Cristóbal. If Eguia did go for a time to La Junta, by November 1732 he was in Santa Cruz, New Mexico, not exactly among the heathen with every natural inconvenience.[60]

What actually happened with these missionaries during the next five years is unknown. Menchero's historical notes in 1744 may be considered more reliable for the years beginning in 1731, since by then he was a member of the San Pablo Custody and the provider of the annual supplies to all the missionaries. He asserted that ever since 1731 the Franciscans "have maintained and do maintain themselves in said missions" of La Junta.[61] But this was a half-truth: the Holy Gospel Franciscans always maintained at least one missionary in Chihuahua who would attend to the Juntans who visited there, but by 1736 they seem to have again temporarily given up stationing anyone in the La Junta district itself. In a list of the missionaries of the San Pablo Custody in that year, totaling thirty-two priests and a lay Brother, only Antonio Esquivel was named for the La Junta missions.[62] From what occurred the following year, it is clear that Esquivel was residing in Chihuahua. Thus, at some point between 1731 and 1736 the Franciscans determined to no longer try to reside permanently in the La Junta mission district.[63]

The "Fourth Founding," 1737

Once again the Juntans sought to remedy this situation. In October 1737 the new Durango bishop, Martín de Elizacoechea, was passing through Chihuahua on his way to New Mexico. The Juntans asked him to send them ministers. Since the bishop was only in charge of priests who belonged to his diocese, not the Franciscans, the priests he sent would be diocesan priests. But even though some diocesan clergy at Chihuahua offered to go, the governor of Nueva Vizcaya, either on his own or in consultation with the bishop, tried to persuade the Juntans that the priests should be Religious since the priests at La Junta had always been Franciscans.[64]

Governor Vértiz y Ontañón asked Father Esquivel in Chihuahua to go in person to ascertain the situation at La Junta, where the missions "are alone and without ministers" due to the lack of military protection. With that information, the governor said, he could make the arrangements for a garrison there. Oh, oft-heard promise! Governor Vértiz deftly challenged Esquivel's missionary pride by asserting that if the Franciscans were unwilling to reestablish themselves in the La Junta district after having made this exploratory visit, he together with the bishop would place other ministers there. The challenge worked. Although apprehensive due to what had happened in 1726, Esquivel did not want to cede the Santo Evangelio Province's prior claim on missions at La Junta.

It so happened that two Santo Evangelio friars, Juan de Tejada and Francisco Lerchundi, were in Chihuahua at that time about to depart for Mexico City. Lerchundi was accustomed to very large and distant missionary territories. He had covered the huge western district of Laguna–Acoma–Zuñi in New Mexico from 1730 to 1733, and after that the Rio Arriba district of northern New Mexico until 1737. Esquivel determined on his own, by who knows what authority, to take the two friars with him to La Junta, even though once again they were given no military escort for fear that the Natives would be stirred up if other Hispanics came with them. By now Hispanics were very aware of the Juntans' emphatic safeguarding of their autonomy. The Juntans themselves provided couriers to accompany clergy who came to visit them. That was undoubtedly the case with Joseph Facundo, the priest who was Vicar and Ecclesiastical Judge of Chihuahua, who at that very time was at La Junta, "probably called there by the governor to test our spirit."[65]

Tejada and Lerchundi remained at La Junta after Esquivel conducted them there. But in January, Father Varo, once again custos, repeated the order that they go to Mexico City. His reasons for insisting that they go, even at the expense of depriving La Junta of missionaries, are unknown. He must have considered those reasons quite serious. Notified of Varo's directive, Esquivel wrote on January 19 that once the two friars at La Junta arrived in Chihuahua, he would send them on as ordered. But on January 28 the newly appointed custos, Father Juan García, wrote from Chihuahua that the Juntans "seem to be content" with the two friars there, and stated that he would ask Varo the reasons for recalling them. If they were still to depart, he would ask that replacements be sent for them from Mexico City. To the surprise of Father Esquivel, he himself was sent back to Mexico City, with a feigned pretext "to avoid dissensions, because it is not convenient that he be here," as García guardedly wrote in a postscript on February 9.[66]

Periods of drought continued at La Junta, as indeed in much of Nueva Vizcaya in the 1730s. A severe epidemic of *matlazáhuatl* (probably typhus) in the province in 1738–1739 further eroded the number of mission Indians. Deeds estimated the non-Native population of the future state of Chihuahua (northern Nueva Vizcaya) at 5,800 in 1700, compared to a Native population of 74,000, not including the La Junta district at that time. By 1750 the estimates stood at 30,300 non-Natives and 46,300 Natives including the La Junta district. That was a decline of more than 37 percent in the Indigenous population.[67] Although the years are not exactly the same, a comparison can be made with the La Junta valley between 1715 and 1747. In 1715 there were 1,405 resident Natives, not counting the eighty absent adult male migrants with their families. In 1747 the number of residents counted had declined to 1,132, with no calculation of absent migrant families. This comes to an almost 20 percent population decline in those thirty-two years. Since the statistics for the entire province covered eighteen more years, the rate of Native population decline in the La Junta valley appears to have been roughly comparable to that of the province as a whole.[68]

Once again no presidio was founded, but in this case there are various indications of a continuing missionary presence in La Junta. Menchero even gave as an example of the friars' conserving and augmenting of the La Junta missions the founding of three towns of Natives by Father Lerchundi, who "catechized and settled [redujó]" them.[69] This intriguing notice may reveal the origin of the temporary mission at Tapacolmes, at the present-day village of Polvo downriver from Presidio on the Texas side of the Rio Grande. One of these groups may have been the Pescados.[70] This had to have occurred before July 25, 1741, since on that date Lerchundi died in the Franciscan hospice at Chihuahua.[71]

The Hispanic military captains credited the Juntans during these years with recovering horse herds from the Apaches and repeatedly assisting in those captains' military operations. In the year 1740 one hundred warriors of La Junta joined fifty from the Native pueblo of San Francisco de Conchos, fifty Hispanic soldiers, and fifty civilians from Chihuahua in a military expedition led by Captain Berroterán that helped to subdue the general uprising of the provinces of Sinaloa, Ostimuri, and part of Sonora. Among the Juntan leaders at that time was Juan Antonio Príncipe, whose name will reappear in 1747, and several other town governors.[72] New mineral discoveries had brought greater Hispanic settlement into the formerly fairly autonomous areas of the Mayo, Yaqui, and lower Pima people frequented by Jesuit missionaries. This brought about rising tensions over perceived bad treatment and resulted in the first major Yaqui-Mayo revolt. Over a thousand Hispanics and more than five thousand rebels were killed. A new presidio was built in the middle of the rebel Yaqui territory and the new Hispanic governor imposed severely restrictive measures on the Indigenous population.[73] One wonders if some Juntans who helped destroy the autonomy of these nations realized the grim irony two decades later when they were resisting the introduction of a presidio in the midst of their own settlements.

Father Saavedra, who had entered La Junta in 1731, was elsewhere at least in 1736–1738 according to the events narrated above. In 1740 he was appointed commissioner of the Inquisition in two separate dispatches "for New Mexico's missions and also for Santa Fe." That made him the Church's officer for investigating any complaints about witchcraft, heresy, or serious immorality.[74] In order to receive this appointment Saavedra must have had a reputation for taking behavioral rules seriously. This is evidenced by a memorandum that he wrote around this time, sending recommendations to the Franciscan Commissary General in Mexico City about the appropriate conduct that should be mandated of Franciscans and others in the San Pablo Custody. Several items echoed general concerns—for example, missionaries should learn the Native languages, and therefore not be moved without just cause. In this memorandum Saavedra mentioned that "Father Fray Ángel García, missionary who left [Mexico City] destined for Zuñi (*salió destinado para la de Zuñi*), should fulfil that obedience." Saavedra listed García among the missionaries present in the custody.[75] And yet García does not appear in the known records of the missions of upper New Mexico until 1747, and he himself stated that he did not start ministering in the El Paso district until 1745.[76]

The only other place that García could have been in the custody between 1740–1741 and 1745 was La Junta, or else serving La Junta from Chihuahua. And so it was. In 1742, undoubtedly with a suitable military escort, the La Junta missions received their first and only episcopal visit. Bishop Elizacoechea of Durango reached the river junction in mid-November, exhibiting his unusual dedication to visit even the most remote missions of his diocese, as he had done in visiting Zuñi in far west New Mexico five years earlier. The bishop noted the "chapel" at San Francisco, where Father Saavedra himself was again missionary, and the "church" at Guadalupe, where the missionary was Father Ángel García. So evidently the church building at Guadalupe was of larger and better construction than the one at San Francisco. Since there had never been confirmations before, it is not surprising that Elizacoechea confirmed 210 people at San Francisco and 245 at Guadalupe. That was about 40 percent of the total population count in the La Junta valley in 1747, five years later. On the way back south, the bishop confirmed thirty-six persons at Coyame, which had no resident missionary.[77] This is the first specific notice of church activity anywhere in the Coyame valley since the 1726 uprising—and by the bishop, although a Franciscan probably accompanied the bishop. In 1731 Menchero had designated one of the new missionaries for Coyame, but there is no evidence that anyone actually resided or even ministered there.

La Junta Becomes Strategic

Prior to 1743 the Juntans had been in communication with El Venado, whom they reported that year as located way up the Rio del Norte, between El Cajón and El Paso. Two decades earlier, as noted previously, he had professed a desire to join the mission community at Coyame. But when a Hispanic force approached he had left for the upper Rio del Norte. Around that time the Venados had been reported as only about thirty miles upriver from La Junta. By 1743, even though now based farther away, El Venado together with Apaches-Cholomes and Sumas began to steal the Juntans' horses. Thereupon the Juntans declared him their enemy. After these allied hostile groups killed two men almost within the pueblo of Guadalupe that same year, one hundred warriors from all the La Junta valley towns engaged in a campaign of reprisal that "firmly punished *their* insolence." There were no more raids on La Junta the four years after that.[78]

As noted previously, Fr. Menchero reported in 1744 that missionaries were still "maintaining themselves" in the La Junta missions. Once again he pleaded for the establishment of a presidio, which in turn would draw Hispanic settlers to the valley with its alleged rich mineral deposits. He also voiced the increasing Hispanic viewpoint that La Junta was a gap in frontier defense that allowed the Cíbolos and Apaches to invade Nueva Vizcaya:

> As long as no directive is given to found and establish a presidio, which I requested back then, and which can be done without cost to His Majesty, for the protection of the missions and in view of the locality being the funnel and outlet of many nations of Cíbolos and Apaches, neither will fear dampen the boldness of the barbarians nor will the settlements increase with the families that with such protection will enter to settle there and work the rich mineral deposits, that will result in a great increase to the royal treasury, the cultivation of the unpopulated lands, and above all many souls for God.[79]

The Juntans would have cringed if they read or learned of Menchero's report, advocating not only soldiers but also Hispanic settlers in their valley.

In 1745 Juan Rodríguez de Albuerne, Marqués de Altamira, the military advisor to the viceroy, succeeded in having the viceroy order a secret investigation among the leading citizens of Chihuahua into the usefulness of all the presidios in Nueva Vizcaya. Altamira's policy favored self-sustaining civilian settlements over missions and presidios financed by the Crown. The report that he received must have delighted the Marqués. The great majority of those whose testimony was reported said that most of the presidios were useless, citing only that of Janos as essential, as well as keeping one of those along the eastern Camino Real up through Chihuahua. But several recommended that a new presidio be established at La Junta due to the hostile groups that menaced the Natives and missionaries there as well as the haciendas below La Junta. One witness reported that usually only one Franciscan ministered at La Junta, and only for three or four months at a time. Otherwise the friar came to Chihuahua due to the lack of companions at La Junta and the risk from hostile Natives, with no protection nor help from other Hispanics since they were over sixty leagues distant. Another stated that the presidio would help to keep the peaceful Natives in line and bring about the addition of some of the hostile Natives to the missions. The official from León who had been appointed to conduct this secret inquiry commented that indeed a Franciscan had arrived from La Junta during his inquiry in Chihuahua.[80]

A later report in 1749 on the San Pablo Custody by the governmental visitor Antonio Ornedal y Maza stated that he was told that Fathers Lorenzo de Saavedra and Francisco de la Concepción González were in charge of the seven towns in the Junta valley itself since 1746.[81] Since Ornedal was no friend of the Franciscans and was seeking to divert monies back to the Crown, he would have seized upon any opportunity to report a greater lack of presence in those missions. But there is a problem reconciling his statement in regard to Father González with other data from the same period that do not place González at La Junta until 1748.[82]

In early 1746 Father Menchero, appointed by the Holy Gospel Province authorities as official Visitor of the missions in La Junta and New Mexico, had intended to begin his inspections at La Junta and from there travel up the Rio del Norte to El Paso. But upon arriving in Chihuahua in March he was told about the dangerous conditions along the Rio del Norte including the earlier raid on La Junta, with "some Christian Indians shot with arrows, some *ahogados*" (drowned or suffocated). This was precisely when the 1743 raid was being magnified by the temporary governor of Nueva Vizcaya in his campaign against Captain Berroterán.[83] Menchero wrote to the viceroy to ask that a military escort be provided immediately so that two missionaries could reestablish a permanent presence at La Junta. He also asked for a military escort for himself upon his return from upper New Mexico to El Paso near the end of August, so that he could make a reconnaissance of the Rio del Norte from El Paso down to La Junta.

Upon receiving Menchero's messages and the simultaneous complaints against Berroterán, in late June the Viceroy approved both of the Franciscan's requests and had the necessary orders sent out. The Marqués de Altamira was perturbed that news of the raid at La Junta, now exaggerated even further to causing the death of "around thirty Christians," had only reached the viceroy through the April letter against Berroterán, and then only "in passing and lightly, without ever being reported by the Conchos captain." The raid on La Junta was thus not only being misdated but continually inflated, with the authorities mystified as to why such an event had not been immediately reported to them.[84] The reason was that the Juntans themselves had given a stern military rebuke to the attackers, and Berroterán was busy establishing peaceful terms with the Apaches near his district.

The viceroy's directives had not reached Menchero by the time he passed back through El Paso and Chihuahua, and thus his approved reconnaissance down the Rio del Norte did not take place. Back in Mexico City, he wrote to the new viceroy in April 1747, asking that the previous directives "to construct a presidio" (an exaggerated interpretation of those orders) at La Junta be implemented. With this request

Figure 8: Franciscan Custody of San Pablo, 1747. (By Fray Miguel Menchero. Courtesy of Staatsbibliothek zu Berlin, Germany)

he included the report sent to him by Father Francisco Sánchez. Sánchez had been the Franciscan inspector of the custody in early 1745 before Menchero and by order of the custos "had gone to be informed and carry out the prior investigations in this matter." Menchero wrote that "the Apaches and Sumas continue to raid, the Native Christians abandon the missions, and due to the imminent risk the Missionaries follow them, withdrawing to the Villa of Chihuahua, in great spiritual detriment both to the Missionaries and to the Natives who go about dispersed."[85] A product of this official visit of the Franciscan custody by Menchero was a map of all of New Mexico and northern Nueva Vizcaya, dedicated to the new Viceroy Güemes y Horcasitas "so that His Excellency might protect the greater increase (*incremento*) of these missions."[86]

The Quarter Century in Retrospect

Taken together, two mid-eighteenth-century summaries of the Franciscan presence in the La Junta district balance each other out. Captain Berroterán wrote in 1748 that after 1720 all the missionaries who provided pastoral care to the Junta settlements resided in Chihuahua, "entering only for a time (*en una temporada*), and the Indians have always received them without incident [*sin novedad*]."[87] Seeming to state the opposite, in 1750 the Franciscan provincial wrote that after 1726 "for some periods [*por algunos tiempos*] two Religious have served those missions, in others three, and sometimes four."[88] While the first statement overly minimizes the missionary presence at La Junta since 1720, the second could be taken to overly exaggerate it. The history recounted up to this point demonstrates that there were real times of prolonged residency in La Junta, especially before 1726, but also periods when no one went to the missions—for as long as five years between 1726 and 1731.

The accounts in this chapter do uphold Berroterán's statement that there were no more violent attacks on the missionaries themselves between 1726 and 1747. In 1731 Father Saavedra wrote that the Suma Indians had wanted to attack, but they were "held back." Just as notable is the fact that in the three verified entries to La Junta by missionaries in 1731 and 1737 they were given no Hispanic military escort, trusting themselves to their Juntan guides. One has to admire the friars' zeal and the Juntans' loyalty. In that decade the Juntans at least twice took the initiative to petition for missionaries. And they protected them. What they did not want was any Hispanic settlement, whether military or civilian. Yet the Franciscan leaders did not cease to advocate for a presidio, to increase not only their security but also the Juntans' obedience. What no one explicitly noted at the time, nor indeed has noted since, is that there is no evidence of a missionary resident in the Coyame valley, or even ministering in that valley, after the 1726 uprising. The inhabitants of that valley, or at least the Cholomes, had earned the Franciscans' great distrust.

Yet frontier strategy in regard to La Junta was finally shifting, due to the push for an altered frontier policy by the Marqués de Altamira and the mounting concern of the *hacendados* to the north of Chihuahua about Suma and Apache raids in their territories. As a result, the La Junta district was about to receive its second and most thorough military inspection.

CHAPTER 6

Between Converging Hispanic and Apache Realms, 1747–1749

These people barter with the heathen Apaches and get the tanned skins and bison hides that they take to sell at the Villa of Chihuahua. And in that way, they acquire there what they need for themselves and their family. If they ransom some child, they add him to their pueblo and his baptism is secured and the community nurtures him.
—Fray Lorenzo de Saavedra, San Francisco de la Junta, January 1748

Suppressing all the presidios [in eastern Nueva Vizcaya] might well be advantageous due to the savings from military salaries, but if their demolition results in the coming of the nations to dominate those places, it will be the same as cutting off the roads for commerce and giving opportunity for frequent thefts and deaths.
—Captain Joseph de Berroterán, April 1748

T he ever-present Sumas and Cholomes were now being joined by dominant groups of Apaches pushing relentlessly southward, and the Juntas
were caught in the middle of the converging Apache and Hispanic realms.
Raids were increasing in the greater Chihuahua district with its expanding ranches
and important mines. The repeated requests of Fathers Menchero and Varo for the
establishment of a presidio and even a Hispanic settlement at La Junta finally dove-
tailed with an emerging realization in Mexico City that they could no longer leave an
extremely large gap in frontier defenses between El Paso and Coahuila. Varo's proposed
inspection of the lands along the Rio del Norte between El Paso and La Junta was
now expanded into a much broader reconnaissance by three military expeditions.
And Captain Joseph de Berroterán, initially summoned in disgrace to Mexico City
to answer charges made against him, was now asked to write a report on the history of
military operations in the region as the most experienced commander in northeastern
Nueva Vizcaya. The resultant reports by all the military commanders give the first

detailed picture of the Juntans, the entire La Junta district, and the lands beyond it since the 1715 expedition of Trasviña Retes.

The Juntans in 1747

Menchero was as insistent as his previous colleagues. About a month after his letter in April 1747 he wrote again to the new viceroy, asking that he revalidate the order for a military reconnaissance and the reestablishment of permanent missions. Unknown to him, the Marqués de Altamira had been at work devising a more ambitious plan. On June 12 Altamira laid it out before the viceroy. Describing the defensive line of New Spain along its entire northern frontier, he pointed out that there was no presidio between El Paso and San Juan Bautista in Coahuila (the Presidio del Rio Grande) (see figure 1). The stretch between La Junta and San Juan Bautista had never been charted. The Rio del Norte below, at, and above La Junta should be scouted for presidio sites. Altamira remarked that the missions in the La Junta district, in which he included Coyame and San Pedro, contained "a large number of settled and Christian Indians bordering the heathen Apaches, Natages, Faraones, Sumas and others who are on the other side of the Río del Norte."[1] With the viceroy's approval, three concurrent military expeditions from Nueva Vizcaya and Coahuila were ordered to converge on La Junta. At the same time, the veteran Captain Berroterán was ordered to compile and submit a background report on the history and current state of military conditions on the frontier.

The first expedition to arrive in the La Junta district was the one commanded by Joseph de Ydoiaga, captain of the San Bartolomé presidio. Traveling in mid-November more or less down the Rio Conchos from Julimes, he came upon a recent settlement of Cholomes and Tecolotes twelve leagues south of Cuchillo Parado at an old Native site called Santa Cruz, more than a hundred miles north of Santa Cruz de Tapacolmes on the San Pedro River. The Cholomes said that they were former inhabitants of Coyame and Cuchillo Parado. Given that in 1715 the people of Cuchillo Parado were said to be distinct from the Cholomes, but that in 1731 a missionary was to be sent to "San Pedro de Cuchillo Parado," either the Cholomes at the newly settled Santa Cruz were actually from Coyame and San Pedro or else the Cholomes had come to make Cuchillo Parado their own settlement. In addition to the sixty-two Cholomes from El Coyame and 128 from "Cuchillo Parado," the new Santa Cruz village also had Tecolotes from the Rio del Norte above La Junta, eighty-three professing to be Christian and forty-nine unbaptized. They all told Ydoiaga that they had totally abandoned their former homes the past June due to frequent Apache attacks, coming together for defensive purposes to repopulate Santa Cruz. Finding this site also more agriculturally favorable, its new inhabitants had brought their church bells with them. Many spoke Spanish "reasonably well," and their continued migrant work in Chihuahua and other area ranches provided them with Spanish clothing and blankets.[2]

According to Lieutenant Joseph de Vargas, Ydoiaga's ad hoc military secretary for the expedition, the people at the new Santa Cruz expressed a desire for having priests among them. When he reached the La Junta valley, Ydoiaga twice tried to persuade the two Franciscans there of the "serious necessity" for missionaries at Santa Cruz. But they would not hear of it. They regarded these Cholomes as "arrogant Indians beyond control." When Ydoiaga persisted in trying to convince them, they replied that these Natives should return to their pueblos and restore the bells that they had carried off.[3] Clearly whatever experience these latest missionaries had of the Cholomes in the Coyame valley had only renewed the Franciscan distrust of them ever since the 1720s. From this new settlement Ydoiaga headed due north twelve leagues to Coyame, rather than continuing down the river to Cuchillo Parado. This was to unite his forces, as previously arranged, with the militia from Chihuahua captained by Domingo Antonio García, who arrived at Coyame three days before Ydoiaga. García wrote that Coyame had been abandoned "years ago" (*hace años*), and that the priest's house and church were "all deteriorated." Ydoiaga had a scouting party visit the abandoned Cuchillo Parado.[4]

Taking a direct route from Coyame to the mouth of the canyon where one began the arduous ascent of the Cuesta Grande, Ydoiaga marched the entire eleven leagues without water until reaching the Rio Conchos again. Rumors that the expedition was coming to establish a presidio preceded it to the La Junta valley, and several Juntan envoys crossed over the mountain ridge to parlay. Among them was Juan Antonio Príncipe, who had assisted Captains Berroterán and Ydoiaga in suppressing the Yaqui uprising in 1740 and was now a general at La Junta. One can imagine what was going through Príncipe's mind as Ydoiaga's force of ninety Hispanics and fifty-four Native auxiliaries now approached his own land. Another Juntan envoy was the "very Ladino" (fluent in Spanish) Pedro Mulato, who would play a similar mediating role twelve years later when troops again approached to actually found a presidio.

The envoys alerted Ydoiaga that the people in the towns below the river junction in the La Junta valley had fled. The same group of towns would act in a similar way twelve years later. The envoys delivered a note from Father Saavedra at La Junta, written the previous day, that urged Ydoiaga to curtail his forces (*que abrevie su campo*). General Príncipe reported that he had tried to dissuade the people from leaving but to no avail. Saavedra later learned that the people of San Juan and San Francisco, his assigned missions, had also wanted to rise up. Ydoiaga assured the envoys verbally, and Saavedra in a reply note, that he was coming only to make an inspection and asked Saavedra to call the people back and calm them. The captain remained firm that he would enter the valley, and the messengers headed back across the ridge.[5]

The next morning, November 21, the expedition traveled six very difficult leagues through the canyon and across the rough mountain ridge. After resting for the night to allow the pack train to catch up, they proceeded four more leagues through the hills

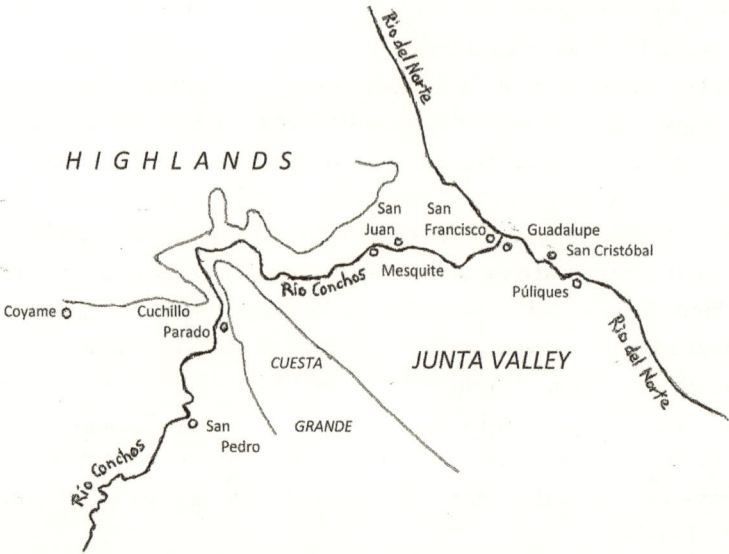

Figure 9: La Junta district in 1747. (By Robert E. Wright)

to San Juan Bautista, preceded by the nearby El Mezquite. The Natives ahead were notified that they could give the customary demonstration of arms as they went out to greet Ydoiaga upon his approach to Mezquite. They were probably led by Príncipe, since he was at the head of the census list for San Juan Bautista, as General of the Pueblos del Norte. He informed Ydoiaga that almost all the towns that had risen up had been restored. By this time the people of Mezquite were living with the Cacalotes in San Juan Bautista due to fear of the Apaches. But each group still worked their traditional separate fields. There were also Conejos and Cholomes at San Juan Bautista, making a total of 314. Thus, San Juan Bautista had become the largest town in the La Junta valley, guarding its southern flank but least exposed to the north and east. Ydoiaga gave the distance from San Juan Bautista to San Francisco at the river junction as four leagues.[6]

Ydoiaga found the veteran La Junta missionary Lorenzo Saavedra at the San Francisco mission, where Saavedra had first served beginning in 1731 and had been present during the bishop's visit in 1742. No other missionary in La Junta's history would span such a long time, going back seventeen years. Saavedra also ministered to San Juan Bautista. At San Francisco Ydoiaga found that a group of Tecolotes had joined its traditional inhabitants. At the Guadalupe mission just across the Río Conchos, Fray Francisco Sánchez, "with the attentions corresponding to his urbanity," was waiting at the church door for the expedition. The town census of Guadalupe noted a cacique, Gerónimo Tennato, besides the usual Hispanic-titled officials. In addition to the people at Guadalupe, Sánchez was also charged with caring for San Cristóbal and Púliques, the two missions downstream along the Rio del Norte.[7] This was apparently the same Father Sánchez who was the Visitor of the San Pablo Custody in 1745 and who went to investigate the situation at La Junta. There is no other known record of him in the custody.[8]

Table 3. 1747 Census of the La Junta Missions

	Couples	Widowed with children	Total individuals in families	Single or solitary widowed	Total
San Juan Bautista	66	13	298	16	314
Cacalotes	34	6	148	8	156
Mezquites	17	3	75	4	79
Conejos	8	3	38	3	41
Cholomes	7	1	37	1	38
San Francisco	49	8	205	15	220
San Francisco	38	6	158	12	170
Tecolotes	11	2	47	3	50
Guadalupe	45	2	166	6	172
San Cristóbal	31	7	147	11	158
Púliques	61	8	250	18	268
Púliques	26	4	109	6	115
Cíbolos	23	3	88	5	93
Pescados	12	1	53	7	60
Total	252	38	1,066	66	1,132

At this point the expedition journal noted Don Bartholomé de Porras, alias Mahoma, "the Indian Commander of these pueblos," who was described as very astute and intelligent. In 1750 he would be identified by Captain Rubín de Celís as a *lobo*, a mixture of Native and Black African descent, knowing Spanish, with the appointment of lieutenant general of La Junta by the Spanish governor.[9] He must have been one of those Juntans conceived when his Juntan parent met an African worker during the migrant season. This probably happened at the hacienda of Bartolomé de Porras in the San Bartolomé valley, one of the litigants in 1715, who might well have been the future Native general's godfather. Generals Porras and Príncipe led Ydoiaga with about half of his men to the settlements on the Rio del Norte downriver from Guadalupe.

On the southwest side of the river three short leagues from Guadalupe was the Púliques village, whose inhabitants now included Cíbolos and Pescados, making this the second largest town in the valley, guarding its eastern flank. Ydoiaga called the town San Antonio de los Púliques, whereas in 1715 it had been called San José. Thus in the consolidation of towns it had taken on the San Antonio title of the formerly neighboring village of the Conchos. The Cíbolos had their own general, Francisco Palacios. The census of the Púliques nation was the only one other than that of Guadalupe where a cacique, Bartholomé Gonzáles, was noted. Ydoiaga explained the presence of the Pescados:

> [These] not too long ago lived downriver, moving their rancherías from one part to another, according to their will and the convenience of the *humedades* that the river left to them to make their small plantings of corn and pumpkins. Because of fear of the Apaches and seeing themselves to be too few in number for their own defense, they came together and are now to be found in the aforementioned Pueblo.

The Pescados were happy that now they had lands properly assigned to them, apparently by Ydoiaga, since previously the lands they were using had only been lent. Ydoiaga urged all these groups in the settlement to become even more united by interrelating through marriage without heeding minor ethnic differences. They should construct a suitably spacious church and houses of adobe.[10] Apparently, therefore, they did not have any adobe structures up to this time.

The inspection party then explored further downriver led by the Cíbolo general. On the way they saw in the floodplains "halfway to the edge of the river, on the northern bank . . . the former pueblo they call 'Tapacolmes,' of whose vestiges there may be observed only some remains of thick walls of what was a church or chapel of adobe." This is the first mention in any document of a former Tapacolme mission at this site. More recently, Ydoiaga was told, the Pescados had lived there before moving for greater safety to Púliques.[11] For their part, the Cíbolos had lived in the mountains around fourteen leagues north-northeast of the river junction until, attacked by Apaches, they had been persuaded by Father Gregorio Osorio to resettle at La Junta. The mention of Osorio apparently places this move of the Cíbolos at least two decades earlier, and the Apaches as already roaming about thirty-five miles north of La Junta by that time.[12]

Returning upstream past Púliques, Ydoiaga crossed the Rio del Norte to visit San Cristóbal, where he saw the old general Bernardo. In a very rare note about land distribution in the La Junta documents, Ydoiaga related that he was told at San Cristóbal that "each one planted more or less, according to the land they had owned from the time of their ancestors, because there was no equality of land ownership." Communally, each town clung to its lands, since "they had no other ones anywhere else . . . there being few surplus ones." Later Father Saavedra affirmed the same, noting that lands "belong to each one in each pueblo. And furthermore, said pueblos have retained possession of their lands ever since their ancestors, even though it is from the time of Heathendom." This and the previous information that the Pescados were initially loaned land at Púliques and that the Mezquites and Cacalotes continued to work their own lands, even though residing together, all demonstrate the strongly rooted practice of heritable land ownership within the Juntans' communal lands.[13]

Ydoiaga urged the people at San Cristóbal to move to the south side of the river, where they could have more regular access to Mass and the sacraments

> without the necessity for crossing the river in a canoe with the sick so that the Padre might confess them. From this ceremony, a graver ill, and even death, could result for them, by their being taken out from their little houses to the air and the dampness of said river. They informed me that such a case had not happened more than twice, with two sick persons whom the aforementioned Reverend Father of Guadalupe, who administers them, had ordered to be crossed over to a brush shelter that had been prepared for these occasions due to his fear of crossing said river. But he now crossed it without fear whenever it was not high.

The people reported that previously Father Andrés Varo had contemplated moving the pueblo to the south bank, but no suitable place had been found between Guadalupe and Púliques.[14] The militia captain of Chihuahua, Domingo Antonio García, whose squad had been ordered to join Ydoiaga's expedition, wrote that "the five nations of Púliques, Cíbolos, Pescados, and Tapacolmes with those of San Cristóbal are united and in friendship." Indeed, he lumped their families together in a single total.[15]

All these statistics and observations manifest the centuries-old stability of the principal towns of La Junta clustered around the river junction (San Francisco, Guadalupe, San Cristóbal), and, perhaps for not quite as long a time, a few leagues upriver on the Conchos (San Juan) and a few leagues downriver on the Rio del Norte (Púliques). They also reveal the absorption into the core La Junta towns of former outlying villages and of new nations that were formerly in neighboring territories. This concentration of settlement was due to the threats from the dominant non-missionized nations of the region, many of whom were Sumas and, increasingly, various bands of Apaches. The ethnicity of the people at San Francisco, Guadalupe, and San Cristóbal was not mentioned in any journal. These developments are presented in the following table, with italics indicating those groups moving into towns not originally theirs.

In comparing the total population numbers in the La Junta valley towns reported in December 1747 with those given in early June 1715, one notes that there was an almost 20 percent decline in resident population, from 1,405 to 1,132, without including absent migrants in either case. This was in spite of the new nations that had moved into the towns during those three decades. Father Saavedra said that the decrease was due to plagues and flight in the face of hostile raids. In fact, disease struck on January 11 while Ydoiaga was still at La Junta, with three natives dying at San Francisco alone on that day.[16]

Table 4. La Junta Valley Towns, 1715 and 1747

Towns in 1715	Towns in 1747
Aranzazu (Conejos) Mezquites San Juan Bautista (Cacalotes)	San Juan Bautista (Cacalotes, *Mezquites, Conejos, Cholomes*)
San Francisco (Oposmes) Guadalupe (Polacmes, Cíbolos) San Crístóbal (Pocsalmes) San José (Púliques) San Antonio (Conchos)	San Francisco (--------, *Tecolotes*) Guadalupe (---------) San Cristóbal (---------) San Antonio de Púliques (Púliques, *Cíbolos, Pescados*)

Relations with Apaches and Other Nations

Even though some Apaches threatened the La Junta settlements, several towns were on friendly or at least trading terms with certain Apache groups. Those at Púliques had "somewhat good relations" with the band of El Lijero, whose members came only a few at a time and only for a few days. By this time El Lijero was judged to be well into his eighties. Ydoiaga wrote that his elderly status was why he was given command of his people. This was the closest group to Púliques, where they traded tanned deerskins for tame horses, rawhide bridles, and things like corn and beans. On February 1, 1748, while Ydoiaga was awaiting new orders, El Lijero arrived in San Juan to make Ydoiaga's acquaintance and to urgently ask for a written attestation of peaceful relations with the Spanish. He said that his people were about 150 families. Ydoiaga provided him with the note.[17]

Natagé Apache bands traveled from farther away and would bring bison skins and dried meat. They cut their hair as did the friars, so the Juntans called them *Friales*. When Ydoiaga asked El Lijero about them, the chieftain said through an interpreter "that they were very far away; that they were very many and very handsome; that they had good weapons and many big harquebuses; that they had much meat of bison and deer, and a large horse herd—excellent for running. And due to these circumstances, they were reputed to be very wealthy among the rest of the nations."[18]

The band of Captain Berroterán's compadre, Don Pascual, came frequently and remained close by without any hostilities—as the Conchos captain himself affirmed the following year. Don Pascual's people knew all the ins and outs among the Hispanic presidios as well as the Toboso lands. Finally, at least one Apache family, that of an Alonzo appropriately surnamed Baptizado, actually lived in Púliques. The people at San Cristóbal also engaged in trade with Apaches, "haggl[ing] for tanned skins when the Apaches come in with them."[19]

The second expedition to arrive in the valley was that of Governor Rábago y Terán and his men from the Coahuila presidios. Approaching from the southeast while Ydoiaga and some of his men were absent exploring upriver along the Río del Norte, they reached the town of Guadalupe on December 18. The next two days they quickly passed through the downriver settlements. They too noted the old adobe walls of demolished houses (*cassas demolidas*) of a former mission at the Tapacolmes site. Returning to Guadalupe, they saw various herds of mares, horses, and mules bearing brands of their fellow citizens from Coahuila, Saltillo, and northern Nuevo León. Thus they discovered that the Apaches who were raiding in those eastern provinces were bartering what they captured with the Natives at La Junta, with whom they were maintaining peaceful relations.[20]

To avoid upsetting the Juntans, rather than reclaiming the stolen animals Rábago y Terán ordered his men to trade for them, but to be careful of the Juntan skill in negotiating. Aided by the two Franciscans, he also prevailed upon the Juntans to release to him two baptized Native women captured in the Rio Grande missions of Coahuila by the Apaches. One was a married Pampopa from Mission San Bernardo traded at Guadalupe, and the other was from the San Juan Bautista mission traded at San Francisco. The governor sought to assuage the Juntan owners of these captives with some gifts, "having noted in [those owners] much vileness and boldness, and no fear of God nor his ministers."[21]

As for the nations to the northwest of La Junta toward El Paso, the people of Púliques and San Cristóbal told Ydoiaga that they had been in communication with El Venado prior to his participation in the raids against La Junta in 1743, after which they viewed him as an enemy. They declared that it was only these groups to the northwest who were harassing the Chihuahua vicinity. In his reconnaissance far up the Rio del Norte in the latter part of December, Ydoiaga stopped at the "old ranchería called 'of the Venados'" at a place that he named Los Pilares (a name that would last among Hispanics).[22] This harkens back to the mention of the Venados along that stretch of the Rio del Norte a few years earlier.

Knowing the danger of hostilities along the upper river, General Juan Antonio Príncipe offered himself and forty of his best warriors to accompany Ydoiaga along that route. Ydoiaga actually hoped to give battle to the hostile groups as well as examine possible presidio sites. At first he passed through mostly flat land comprising the former area of the Tecolotes, who had abandoned it due to hostilities by the Apaches-Cholomes. One abandoned village site was seven leagues above San Francisco (the former San Bernardino?), and another seven leagues farther was called La Ruidosa. Five leagues beyond that, and now traveling through rougher undulating country, was a place also named La Ruidosa. Ydoiaga continued his reconnaissance upriver for another twenty-six leagues before finally turning back toward La Junta.[23]

Conflicting Presidial Recommendations

Having thus completed his inspection in every direction, the San Bartolomé captain came to the conclusion that there were insufficient agricultural prospects in the La Junta valley and upriver for the proposed presidio and an accompanying Hispanic settlement. At every stop on his journey he had noted the unreliable agricultural conditions due to cycles of repeated flooding or dry spells with the consequent sandy soils and impossibility of sustained irrigation, all confirmed by the people. He also consistently noted grasses of bad quality for grazing animals.[24] Of course, the Juntans were not about to give glowing assessments of their lands, since they were all too aware of the purpose behind these expeditions.

Expedition members noted evidence of a previous unsuccessful attempt by one or two Hispanics to develop farming in the nearby flatlands along the Rio del Norte above the river junction. Ydoiaga merely mentioned it as one more example of failed attempts due to the cycles of flooding and drought. The lieutenant of the Chihuahua militia accompanying Ydoiaga's troops said that Father Saavedra had told him that in earlier times, when the missionaries had attempted irrigation projects, two Hispanic farmers, Juan de Acosta and Francisco de Aguirre, failed at such an attempt due to flooding and "departed in poverty." Rábago y Terán gave a different reason for the failure. Encountering the ruins of a house and acequia in the lowlands above San Francisco, he wrote that it was where a Hispanic citizen, now of Chihuahua, had farmed years ago (*años pasados*) before he gave up, "oppressed by the damages these Indians made to his herds and other goods on account of not wanting any Spaniard in the vicinity."[25] This is the only other notice before 1760 of non-Franciscan Hispanics attempting to reside in the La Junta district, the first case having been the assistant of the missionaries who was killed in the 1726 uprising.

Rábago y Terán's blaming of the Juntans for running off the Hispanic farmer, rather than attributing the farmer's departure to natural factors, may have been due to his opinion, contrary to Ydoiaga's, about the feasibility of a presidio. The Coahuila governor held that the Native seasonal agriculture in the low-lying wetlands, although without irrigation, demonstrated that there was a sufficient basis for a presidio in the long lowland to the north of the San Francisco settlement. The presidio would contain the hostilities of bordering nations. It would "subject the Conejos, Cacalotes, Mezquites, Síbolos, and others who live with too much pride and vile subterfuges (*vilantes socapados*) . . . in a disorderly manner" in the valley towns. And it would prevent the "illicit" commerce with the "Apaches, Sumas, Nataje, Colomes [*sic*], and others that come among them."[26]

Rábago y Terán's opinion of the Juntans' troubling independence was fostered upon his arrival at the Guadalupe mission by Father Sánchez, with whom he had a long conversation the night of his arrival in the valley:

> He shared with me the total desolation (*desconsuelo*) that he was experiencing in this place, on account of the complete lack of subjection of its Indians with no fear nor recognition of Spanish authority. To enjoy their laziness, they did not consent to any Spaniard (*español*). For this reason they did not respect the missionaries who

vexed them very much, and the latter find it necessary to absent themselves. When they do not, the people ask him, "When are you going, Father?" Such expressions, and others that are omitted, made me feel compassion for him.[27]

Yet the Coahuila governor called the various Native groups that he encountered on the right bank of the Rio del Norte below Guadalupe Christians. And on his quick trip up the Rio Conchos, he noted that the people there (the very same ones that he criticized as disorderly) "hear Mass when it is offered [and] pray if they want, as all the other towns (as reported by their ministers)." Although he alleged that they "have no other occupation (*asilo*) than horse-riding and trading with the Apaches," he also noted that they planted in the lowlands in the appropriate season. Thus he undermined his own stereotypes. What he did see clearly in his brief visit was the traditional autonomy enjoyed by the Juntans. Adding to our knowledge of their sense of ethnic identity, he stated that the various groups in the Mezquite–San Juan vicinity lived in distinct cottages (*jacalillos*) about one or two leagues from each other.[28]

Having finished his lightning inspection of the entire La Junta valley on December 23, Rábago y Terán waited four days at San Francisco for Ydoiaga's return while resting his horses and mules. When some of his soldiers became infected with an illness (*tabardillo*) spreading through the towns, he departed on the 28th, leaving a letter for Ydoiaga as he headed back to Coahuila.[29] Upon receiving the letter that strongly advocated for the establishment of a presidio, Ydoiaga again argued against the agricultural and grazing potential of the lands. He also advised much caution about domesticating the Natives' pride and preventing their centuries-old commerce with other nations. He and other witnesses related previous attempts to establish irrigation canals, all ending in ruin. Ominously for the Juntans, two of Ydoiaga's men declared that the very lands farmed by the Natives were "the most reasonable or the least bad," but held that even those lands were insufficient for pasturing large herds of horses and cattle.[30]

Father Saavedra concurred with Ydoiaga that there was no suitable place in the valley for both a presidio and a Hispanic settlement. But he hastened to add that he had been informed by Father Varo and others that there might be a suitable location for a presidio at Tecolote, seven or eight leagues upriver. The Franciscans had also been told that the former Cíbolo encampment in the mountains fourteen leagues to the north of the Rio del Norte would be a suitable presidio and settlement site. Ydoiaga, however, had inspected both places and reported no positive results. Saavedra repeated the missionaries' earnest desire that a presidio be established. But he counseled that it would be necessary that the officer given that charge be gentle and calm, otherwise "the predicted flight will take place and all will be lost." Prophetic words, in view of what happened a dozen years later.[31]

Both the Franciscans and the military were on the proverbial horns of a dilemma. There was no room for a presidio, much less a Hispanic settlement, among the long-established Native towns in the valley, and the people of La Junta had clearly expressed their resistance to any Hispanic settlement being established in their midst. Thus the friars, anxious to have a military presence to protect themselves and the Native settlements and to make the Juntans more amenable to their direction, were reduced to recommending distant sites that would be of little use in the event of attack and that were still judged to be unsuitable.

Saavedra also spoke against eliminating the trade with the Apaches, since through that barter the Juntans acquired the tanned skins and bison hides that they took to sell in Chihuahua to acquire such items as Hispanic clothing. Through these exchanges they might also ransom some *indito* (Native child) to add to their community and its future generativity.[32] The Franciscan also had a silent reason for supporting the Apache trading. The tanned skins acquired by the Juntans were an important element of the material support of the mission economy, as reported by Ydoiaga's secretary Vargas. The secretary's comments also shed some more light on mission life there, mentioning the patronal feasts that all colonial society, Hispanic and Native, usually embraced:

> And it is evident from listening to Their Paternities, that the Indians support them without reluctance with some of the grains that they harvest so they can maintain themselves, and this gift they call "alms." And I have also seen the said Reverend Father, Vice-Custodian, give their alms of corn to the poor and elderly Indians who have nothing. And it is public and common knowledge and I have heard the Indian General and the governors say that for each baptism they contribute a tanned skin; for each marriage, another; and for each burial or Requiem Mass, an excellently tanned skin; and that is not counting the ones they contribute for the festivities of the titular saints of each pueblo.[33]

This important trade in animal skins also offers an added lens through which to view Father Sánchez's reported comment that if he stayed too long the people at Guadalupe would ask him when he was leaving. As reported by Rábago y Terán, Father Sánchez was very discouraged by the attitude of the Juntans and took the people's question about his departure in a negative sense. The people undoubtedly noticed his dispiritedness. But another motive for their query might have been that they wanted the friar to help justify and provision a trading trip to Chihuahua, since he would need them as an escort.

That is what one gathers from the reply of Father Saavedra to Captain Ydoiaga when the captain protested Sánchez's announced departure for Chihuahua on January 11. Ydoiaga asked how Sánchez could leave when many Natives were dying from illness. Saavedra replied that Sánchez was exhausted. Ydoiaga countered that there did not seem to be that great a need for corn or other things at Guadalupe, to which Saavedra responded, playing upon a biblical phrase (Matthew 4:4), that "man does not live by corn alone." Saavedra assured Ydoiaga that he would write to Sánchez to return quickly. When Father Sánchez left by the road of La Mula he was escorted by ten Indian archers—and he had a load of tanned skins. He arrived back at La Junta on February 1, most probably with the same Juntan escort. If they had only wanted to be rid of him, why would they escort him back?[34]

Mission Arrangements

The viceroy's instructions to Ydoiaga included the "reestablishment" of the official six missions (two of which had been in the Coyame valley) "or the ones of those which may be formed with no less than one hundred families each, and whose adminis-tration is to be restored to the corresponding religious missionaries who had retired from said Missions to the Villa of Chihuahua."[35] In other words, missions with large populations were to be retained or formed through mission consolidations, and the number of Franciscan priests at La Junta should be readjusted accordingly. None of the existing five towns in the La Junta valley had one hundred families (see table 3). In fact, the directives would seem to require, as Ydoiaga concluded, the consolidation of those five towns into only two. But the two missionaries at La Junta had received no instructions from Father Menchero about what was to be done, and Menchero himself never arrived.[36]

Consulted by Ydoiaga on this point, Father Saavedra was definitely not in favor of the consolidation of the settlements. He asserted that the Juntans would find such a move harsh and that it would cause them to flee. True, "today the few remaining towns will be found with 40–50 families, few families more or less with enough boys and girls of daily-catechism age." But just as these families might come to an end, they might increase with procreation, or with those who come from the unconverted (la gentilidad).[37] As already noted, other groups had been joining the towns, with many being catechized and baptized. Saavedra related how he had done this with the now deceased Native chief named "El Barrigón," who had been given the Christian name Bruno and had been happy as a Christian. He noted how the Tecolotes had joined San Francisco and other towns. Thus we learn that the people whom the Native leaders El Barrigón and El Tecolote had brought to live at San Francisco at the time of the uprising in the Coyame valley in 1726 had remained, with various ones becoming Christian. The Pescados at Púliques were now Christian, as were the Cíbolos at San Cristóbal. At San Juan there were other groups who were being catechized.[38]

Upon Ydoiaga's order, his secretary Vargas certified that the Natives and others told him that there had not been more than two missionaries at La Junta for some years. In fact, he was told that at various periods Saavedra had found himself companionless at La Junta—as he himself witnessed when Father Sánchez left for Chihuahua with his Juntan escort and the tanned skins. And yet, he observed, the Franciscans claimed that there were five missions supported by the Crown.[39] These comments would soon be employed against the Franciscans by others.

The third expedition of the planned reconnaissance, captained by Fermín de Vidaurre of the Mapimí presidio, did not arrive until the last days of January. With the La Junta valley already scouted by then, Captain Vidaurre stayed only a week, limiting his report to confirming what Ydoaiga had written. Ydoiaga and his force remained in the valley, as he had been instructed. On February 7, 1748, he declared at the San Juan Bautista mission that he would stay there, or at Coyame if necessary to graze his horses, until further notice from the viceroy about the erection of a presidio.[40] It was not until April 1, after the viceroyal authorities had compared the various expedition reports, that he received the order to return to his presidio of San Bartolomé. Before departing, he learned that Father Saavedra was seriously injured or ill; in fact, on April 5 a party of twenty-five Juntan archers led by the governor of Guadalupe passed near San Juan Bautista carrying Saavedra on a litter as they left for Chihuahua. Ydoiaga offered a military escort but was told by the Juntan leader that the Native escort would be more secure on its own—a terse commentary on relations of non-mission Natives with Hispanic military in the changing power dynamics of the region.[41]

Father Saavedra did return to La Junta for at least another year.[42] As for Father Sánchez, in January 1749 Varo noted that he had just arrived in Mexico City from the custody, "having made it known that he has no desire to return there."[43] Thus Sánchez was disenchanted not only with La Junta but also with the entire Custody of San Pablo, to which he had been sent as Visitor in 1745. He was evidently not cut out for frontier life. His "urbanity," as noted by Ydoiaga, found little outlet in a place so remote from other *gente de razón*. The Juntan disregard for his authority cemented his determination to return to the social life and clerical prestige of the viceroyal capital. According to Father Varo, there was a third missionary assigned to the La Junta district who was absent at the time of Ydoiaga's visit. Commenting on Ydoiaga's report, Varo wrote in 1749 that José Páez "had gone to the Villa of Chihuahua to seek help for his needs."[44] In that case, he was absent during at least the five months of Ydoiaga's presence in the La Junta district, since he was never mentioned in the captain's reports.

Three expeditions had come and gone. The resultant reports gave the first census of individuals in the district and provided much information about the land for many miles above and below the river junction, the increasingly prominent Apache presence and the diverse relations with them, and the resultant shifting demographic realities. They also brought to light the system of land ownership and how the Juntans contributed to the missionaries' upkeep. And they affirmed once more the people's abhorrence at the prospect of a Hispanic settlement in their midst. In that regard, once more, nothing happened. But a presidio was on the viceroyal prospectus sheet, even though it would still take more than a decade to bring it about.

The Apache Threat and Frontier Deliberations in Mexico City

Captain-for-life Joseph de Berroterán felt misjudged and slighted. He had been captain of the Presidio of San Francisco de Conchos since about 1727. Thus he was the most experienced commander of the northeastern military salient of Nueva Vizcaya. But in 1746 he was falsely charged by the temporary acting governor of Nueva Vizcaya with failing to come to the aid of the Juntans when they were attacked. He and the other commanders of the eastern line of presidios in Nueva Vizcaya were also charged with putting their own business ahead of defending the province. The viceroy ordered that secret testimony be taken from local witnesses, after which Berroterán was to be notified "to present himself as a prisoner in this Captaincy General" to answer the charges. In late October of that year the four presidial captains wrote their joint defense, asserting that their efforts had brought about complete peace in their territory since 1743, and that the territory being raided to the north and northwest of Chihuahua was the responsibility of other military units. Sometime thereafter Berroterán was taken to Mexico City.[45]

Thus the Conchos captain was in the viceroyal capital in 1747 when the major reconnaissance of the Rio del Norte between El Paso and Coahuila was ordered. Taking advantage of his presence and recognizing his unmatched experience on the northern frontier, in October 1747 the viceroy ordered that he write a report of everything that had transpired in the region, to serve as background and context for the reports that would be received from the new expeditions. In the spring of 1748 Berroterán submitted his final report. By that time the officials were mulling over the expedition reports, trying to determine what to do about the defenses of Nueva Vizcaya. The aggrieved Conchos captain handed in a monumental sixty-page manuscript in April that also served as a defense of his own reputation.[46]

In Mexico City Berroterán learned that the viceroy's advisors, especially the Marqués de Altamira, had concluded from the captains' reports of peace in eastern Nueva Vizcaya since 1743 that the presidios there were no longer needed. The viceroy and Altamira would love nothing more than to be able to report more savings to the king by eliminating them. Berroterán sought to disabuse them of this idea. Harkening back to the previous military reductions taken as a result of Rivera's inspection of the northern frontier in the late 1720s, he asserted that they had allowed more than 400 Apaches to take the place of the former hostile nations that had been painstakingly subdued or removed from the frontier. So far, he declared, the Apaches had not begun to commit thefts or murders in northeastern Nueva Vizcaya.

He credited this success to the peace and friendship that he personally had established with the Apache captain Pascual. In fact, the two were *compadres* or spiritual kin, since Berroterán had served as godfather to one or more of Pascual's children. But being a compadre did not mean that he trusted Pascual. Rather, he wrote that it was necessary to be on one's guard with the Apaches, "given their numbers, valor, inconstancy, and reserve until they become confident of knowing the passages that guarantee them safe haven in the mountains." He warned that the peace experienced since 1743 was really a period of preparation by the Apaches for even greater hostilities along the whole frontier from Coahuila to El Paso. Leaving it unguarded would threaten the continued existence of the two provinces of Coahuila and Nueva Vizcaya.[47]

Decrying the measures that had weakened the forces of Nueva Vizcaya, Berroterán pointed to the new presidios that had been founded in Sonora and Coahuila and the ones being considered for Sonora (Tubac), Texas (San Xavier), and New Mexico. Availing himself of a Catholic metaphor, he declared that this was "giving cult to a saint who is not beatified while abandoning the canonized one."[48] In other words, Nueva Vizcaya was an established and very productive province, while the other cases were efforts at expansion. A more strategic process would be first to safeguard what had been gained—namely, Nueva Vizcaya—and, with this in hand, expand beyond. But the viceroyal officials realized that they did not have such a choice. Certainly Nueva Vizcaya was important, but so were the mines in Sonora. New Mexico had to be preserved on account of both its population and the maintenance of Spanish dominion in the center of the continent. Texas was a crucial strategic block to the continental ambitions of other European powers as well as the expanding Comanche empire.

In his closing comments Berroterán repeated that the eastern line of presidios in Nueva Vizcaya—Pasaje, Gallo, Mapimí, Cerrogordo, San Bartolomé, Conchos—was necessary, and he declared that those presidios were well situated. He did allow that the one at San Bartolomé could be moved forward to Guajoquilla, while the Conchos presidio itself could be moved "to the east part of La Junta de los Rios that has its river banks populated." But while this might improve security for the missions at La Junta, it would require the expense of constructing new soldiers' quarters and chapels at the two new locations.

It would also lessen the protection of commerce and travelers leading up to Chihuahua, since moving the Conchos presidio to La Junta would place it far beyond the route to Chihuahua. No longer able to contain his pent-up sense of grievance, Berroterán ended with a hardly veiled criticism of the bureaucrats in the metropolis: "There's a huge difference and disparity between the practical and the speculative." The proposal to extinguish the current presidios would leave the haciendas and towns of Nueva Vizcaya wide open to attack. "Those who live in this capital do not experience in the slightest way such bad effects. . . . The difference is that between peace and war."[49] The Marqués de Altamira could not have taken kindly to such remarks.

Not to be lost in this voluminous report is Berroterán's concession that a presidio could be established in the populated eastern part of La Junta along the Rio del Norte. That is, in fact, where the presidio would be built in 1760. Berroterán is the only one known to have made this specific recommendation as to the presidio's location; his view must have carried weight. And the Conchos captain would promptly be proven correct in his assessment and warnings about the impending Apache hostilities. The increasing pressure by those Native groups all along the colonial frontier was due to their flight in the face of the Comanches, Wichitas, Pawnees, and other northern nations armed with French guns. Along the central Hispanic corridor northward, the El Paso district had already been experiencing Apache raids since 1707. Taking Berroterán's warning as a marker, military inspectors in the following decades dated the surge in raids into north-central Nueva Vizcaya from 1748.[50]

In these circumstances the placement of a presidio along the Rio del Norte between El Paso and the Presidio de Rio Grande in Coahuila took on more urgency in Mexico City. But initially the inveterate insistence on economizing, and thus lower military expenses, would continue to get in the way at the viceroyal capital. Also, as long as economizing meant taking soldiers from other posts in the interior of Nueva Vizcaya to staff the new presidio, there would be foot-dragging by local officials in those places. Actually, the preferred policy of the Marqués de Altamira was to "transform all the troops into farmers," as the Franciscan chronicler Juan Agustín Morfi wrote around 1780.[51] Additionally, Altamira was one of the earliest reformers of the Bourbon era who "saw missions as places that isolated rather than integrated Indians" into Spanish colonial life. Indeed, that separation from Hispanics, even if those Hispanics were settled adjacent to the Native town, was the missionary ideal. Altamira hoped to accomplish the twin goals of economizing and yet permanently settling the frontier by promoting to the extent possible the establishment of self-supporting civilian towns rather than presidios and encouraging the integration of contiguous Native settlements with those Hispanic ones. He actually accomplished this objective in the establishment of the Colony of Nuevo Santander along the Gulf Coast between the provinces of Texas and Tampico with a plan approved in 1746 and carried out in 1748–1749.[52]

The Marqués made the same kind of proposal in December 1749 for eastern Nueva Vizcaya: replace the presidios so ardently defended by Berroterán with new civil settlements with their militia.[53] In the case of La Junta, however, while the conflicting reports being received in Mexico City made it unclear whether a presidio could be materially maintained there, those reports seemed to agree about the impossibility of any civilian settlement. Given the increasing threat of Apaches joining raiding Sumas and the great isolation of La Junta from the rest of Nueva Vizcaya, no civilians would dare to venture there without a presidio. Furthermore, there was no suitable land for both institutions.

The Varo Report on the San Pablo Custody in January 1749

In early 1749 Father Varo had an opportunity to place the situation at La Junta before the viceroy, the Conde de Revillagigedo. Varo was in Mexico City by January 3, seeking to restore his health, and was immediately asked by the provincial of the Santo

Evangelio Province to write a detailed report on the state of the San Pablo Custody in response to a royal request. He completed his extensive mission-by-mission report on January 29. Given the time required for Varo to travel from El Paso to Mexico City and for messages from La Junta to make the same journey, the report was not up to date on the most recent events in that district.[54] In some descriptions Varo undoubtedly relied on his own personal experience in the La Junta district more than two decades earlier. But he also drew upon the information circulated among the Franciscans in the custody since then. Consequently, the information that he provided has varying degrees of reliability.

Varo evidently relied mostly on his own memories from the 1720s in giving the locations and titles of the various towns along with the ethnicity of the inhabitants. Although he mistakenly reversed the locations of the Oposmes and the "Pozalmes" (Pocsalmes), placing the former at San Cristóbal and the latter at San Francisco, he stated that they both spoke "Pozalme." As noted in the first chapter, this correlates with those two places being the towns of the Abriache with their common language in 1582. He correctly had the "Poxasmas" (Polacmes) at Guadalupe and the Cacalotes at San Juan Bautista. His most striking statement was that the Cacalotes spoke "Patragueye," as did those in the two attached towns of Aranzazu and Nuestra Señora de Begoña. Although Varo was thus unaware that Aranzazu no longer existed and he confused the rarely used religious titles given to Mezquite and Cuchillo Parado in 1715, his identification of "Patragueye" as a common language on the upper portions of the Conchos and Norte Rivers in the La Junta valley is another astounding linguistic correlation with the Patarabueye of the 1582 Luján journal.

Understandably unfamiliar with the most recent events in the now abandoned Coyame district, Varo still had Cholomes at San Pedro Apóstol and Cholomes and Sumas at Santiago de la Ciénega y del "Coyamet," where he noted that the various springs made a very beautiful wetland. That latter place and name he remembered well, since it was where he was almost executed. He gave Cuchillo Parado the mistaken name of San Pedro de Alcántara, probably in an effort to make sense of the earlier confused references to San Pedro de Cuchillo Parado. Varo listed Pedro Esquer for San Pedro Apóstol and Joseph Páez for Coyame, but supposedly those two places no longer had Cholome residents and thus no call for missionaries. He had two missionaries in the La Junta valley. Lorenzo Saavedra was correctly listed for San Francisco, but also as caring for Guadalupe. Francisco de la Concepción González was listed for San Cristóbal and also responsible for the two downriver towns of San Antonio with the "Puricas" and San Joseph with the "Síbolos" as well as San Juan Bautista. These alleged mission assignments for the La Junta valley do not make sense geographically, particularly San Juan Bautista being taken care of from San Cristóbal rather than the much closer and more accessible San Francisco.

Varo stated that in a letter from Father González dated July 28, 1748, the friar reported that he had catechized more than 460 Cholomes in a place in the immediate vicinity of the San Pedro mission in the Coyame valley. This catechizing incident was probably while passing through there on his initial entry to La Junta after having been exiled from New Mexico for a second time in March of that year. This explains why Inspector Ornedal had him at La Junta rather than Sánchez, who had left the San Pablo Custody sometime after Ydoiaga's departure in April. By sending González to La Junta in the civil province of Nueva Vizcaya, his superiors placed him out of the reach of the New Mexico governor who banished him.[55]

Whether it was González himself or Varo who identified the Natives that González catechized as Cholomes, the fact that he catechized so many there indicates that there was no resident missionary at the former mission. If they were Cholomes, then they had not completely abandoned the area. The latest news about Father González had not yet reached Varo in Mexico City. According to Ornedal, González abandoned his post at the Guadalupe mission with its attached responsibilities of San Cristóbal and Púliques on December 11, 1748, allegedly out of dire necessity. That was undoubtedly a more accurate statement of González's mission assignments than the one Varo gave. The Franciscan provincial later commented that González had fled to the protection of the new governor of New Mexico, Tomás Vélez Cachupín, as soon as the latter took office in April 1749.[56]

Missionary lists drawn up in Mexico City are one thing; actual presence is another. It is practically inconceivable that Joseph Páez was at Coyame in 1748. As previously noted, Coyame had been abandoned by the Cholomes in June 1747 and neither Lieutenant Vargas in February 1748 nor Captain Ydoiaga in April that year noted any Natives or missionary when they passed through there. What is certain is that by November 1748 Páez was stationed in El Paso, where he was the president of the Franciscans in that mission district.[57] If Pedro Esquer was ever at San Pedro, it had to have been after Ydoiaga left the district in April 1748 and Father González passed through there the following July. What is known for sure is that by March 1749 Esquer was back at the mission of Zia in central New Mexico, where his previous extant entry was in May 1746.[58] The same considerations apply to the sworn affidavit by Father Menchero in 1751 that the Religious on the Franciscans' assignment list for La Junta during 1748 were Saavedra, González (noted as subsequently deceased), Páez, Esquer, and Joseph [Ruizo?].[59]

In his January 1749 report Varo stated that he was unable to provide the population numbers for the missions, since it was said that there were far fewer inhabitants due to the invasions of infidels. He held that if a presidio had been founded "many would not have left (as they have) for the haciendas, mines, and other missions with more security." He dwelt upon how this situation of great insecurity affected the missions and the missionaries, who often in the past had had to flee to Chihuahua "until the Christian Indians have been left in peace and come to seek their Fathers." He also repeated his longtime allegations that the founding of a presidio was always blocked by local presidial captains and elites out of self-interest. Varo reasserted that there were appropriate places for a presidio and Hispanic settlements. He held that the only difficulty to be overcome was the lack of irrigation, since rain was very scarce, but acequias could easily provide a solution. On this point, he ignored his own early experience and that of subsequent decades.

In view of charges made at the end of 1749 against the Custody of San Pablo, it should be noted here that Varo reported a temporarily enlarged contingent of forty active Franciscans. Thirty-three priests and one Brother serving as a teacher were the usual number supported by the government. Four more positions had been subsidized in 1746–1748 for the new effort among the Navajos. Additionally, there were two Franciscans—a priest and a lay Brother—serving beyond the subsidized quota.[60] Varo asserted that the missionaries' work would be helped by having even more friars, since they were so spread out and isolated from each other. With more friars other nations could be reached.

He also claimed that the missionary effort in New Mexico would be facilitated by a corresponding increase in the number of military, led by men "who attended to the principal purpose of their assignment rather than the greed that drives them into committing many hostilities against the Indian neophytes." He could afford that unvarnished language in this internal Franciscan report. Although rarely one to mince his words, perhaps he would have been more circumspect if his report had been sent instead to the viceregal administration—especially since the protégés of Viceroy Revillagigedo who were sent to New Mexico at this very time were about to unleash a scathing verbal and political attack on the Franciscans of the custody that would infuriate Varo and his fellow friars.

CHAPTER 7

From Allies to Enemies, 1749–1758

In this census there are lacking some families who are dispersed at the Villa of Chihuahua, the Real of Santa Eulalia, and various ranches around the Villa of Chihuahua, due both to the lack of provisions that has occurred for the past three years in these Missions of the North, and to various invasions of enemy Indians.

—Fray Joseph Páez, San Juan de la Junta, December 1750

Those Pueblos or settlements, under the pious title of missions and Christians who do not even understand how to make the sign of the cross, as the captain informs me, and tolerated unbelievers, are the origin and refuge of the uprising and apostasy of the Sumas. For these latter depend totally on those at La Junta . . . [and are] in league with Apaches, all joining together to attack the road to the town of Chihuahua.

—Governor Vélez Cachupín of New Mexico, March 1751

Even though the ten years between 1749 and 1758 seemed to begin as usual for the Juntans and the Franciscans, attitudes were shifting dramatically among distant Spanish authorities. While various groups of Apaches were now common visitors in the La Junta valley, Apaches along with other nations were soon conducting damaging raids to within the very environs of Chihuahua. Furthermore, Hispanic suspicions that the greater La Junta district was becoming a refuge for Native and multiracial runaways from Hispanic localities were soon borne out—even though only in the Coyame valley. This important distinction was lost on the Spanish authorities beyond Nueva Vizcaya, however, who were quick to disregard decades of loyal military assistance by the Juntans in accusing them as the source of all the troubles. The Franciscans were also blamed by viceroyal officials for this alleged state of affairs due to their supposed neglect.

Actually, hostilities by certain Native groups along with renewed prolonged drought brought to an end any extended residence of missionaries in the La Junta valley, even while other Native groups accepted refuge there. It was during this period that the viceroyal administration in Mexico City for the first time began to determinedly press temporizing Nueva Vizcayan officials to establish a presidio near La Junta, convinced as they were that the river valley was the major gap in their defensive line on the northern frontier.

Condemning the Juntans and the Franciscans

It may have been Father Varo's resoluteness in the face of New Mexican officials that brought about once again his selection as custos of the San Pablo Custody at the chapter of the Holy Gospel Province in Mexico City on February 8, 1749. He did not arrive back in the El Paso district until August.[1] In March of that year he was still in Mexico City, once again petitioning Viceroy Revillagigedo for a presidio at La Junta. Repeating the charge of self-interest by the military captains and their associates in Nueva Vizcaya, he magnified the settlement potential at La Junta beyond what he should have remembered, even though his one piece of evidence may have been true:

> They say that in La Junta de los Rios there is no place suited for a presidio, nor fields to maintain the horse herd, whereas there are so many and such good locations there that surpass those of El Paso del Rio del Norte. . . . The proof that there is no lack of grazing fields is that the captains who entered there and remained in the depth of winter and with the greatest drought experienced in those northern lands brought out their horse herd (that was vast) so fat and vigorous that all the Vizcayans were amazed.[2]

As further persuasion for a presidio, Varo stated that favorable witnesses were interested in the mines in the Sierra del Ojo de Agua of the Cíbolos north of La Junta and other mineral sites that could be worked with the protection of a suitable guard. Coming to a conclusion, he asserted that "the efficacious means of immediate respect for military force" was the only hope for "the protection and restoration of the missions of La Junta, that were as weakened (*decaidas*) as their Natives were disorderly."[3] Those independent Natives!

The reports of the "outspoken" Father Varo did not fall upon receptive ears at the viceroyal headquarters. Asking for more missionaries, more military, and more presidios ran counter to the economizing goals of Viceroy Revillagigedo and the preferred strategy of the Marqués de Altamira, still Auditor de Guerra. Charging the military commanders in the region with greedy mistreatment of the Natives could not have helped either. Perhaps unknown to Varo, the recently arrived cavalry captain in Santa Fe, Tomás Vélez Cachupín, was a protégé of Viceroy Revillagigedo, indeed a member of his household in Mexico City. In late 1748 Vélez Cachupín was named interim governor of New Mexico when the new appointee declined. The viceroy selected another of his household protégés, Juan Antonio de Ornedal y Maza, as his emissary to deliver that appointment. Ornedal was also to conduct the administrative review of the outgoing governor and an inspection of the military situation in Nueva Vizcaya and New Mexico. He may or may not have also been given secret verbal instructions to size up the mission situation. The reality is that he did, with hardly veiled hostility. Once he reached upper New Mexico in April 1749, Ornedal and the "hotheaded" Vélez Cachupín, who "was already in the habit of exaggerating his own merits and the faults of others," set to work to levy every charge that they could against the Franciscans.[4]

In late July 1749, as Varo was returning to the San Pablo Custody, Inspector Ornedal sent a scathing report from El Paso to the viceroy about the work—or lack thereof, in his view—of the Franciscans.[5] Speaking of the custody in general, with no distinctions about different regions, he charged that the missionaries gave almost no attention to the Natives, with months passing without Mass, due to the absence of the missionaries on commercial trips. He said that the Natives were not being taught Spanish and the missionaries did not know the Native languages, with confession occurring only at the point of death and through an interpreter. According to him this was due to the too frequent transfers of the missionaries, transfers that were taking place without the allegedly required approval of the governor. The result, he declared, was that there was no spiritual progress; in fact, matters were as if the missions were only just beginning.

Ornedal asserted that the missionaries were forcing the Natives to give them more of their produce than the Natives had agreed to contribute and that they were compelling the Natives to engage in weaving without pay. When the local Hispanic officials intervened or tried to intervene, the missionaries replied insubordinately. This was because the majority of the Religious in the custody were sent there as a banishment and punishment. Ornedal also argued that Santa Fe and all the missions at El Paso were prosperous enough to support secular priests rather than having government-subsidized missionaries. He recommended that practically everywhere else the number of missionaries be severely reduced by consolidating every three missions under one missionary. This was a frontal attack, no holds barred.

Some of Ornedal's charges were not without some basis, but they were unrelentingly negative and too universally applied. The study by Jim Norris of the causes of the diminishing power of the Franciscans of the San Pablo Custody provides the larger context for assessing the inspector's charges.[6] He related how Franciscan leaders dutifully enjoined the friars to learn the Native languages and teach them Spanish, while acknowledging that the great diversity of languages and the frequent transfers of the missionaries were an obstacle to this effort. The transfers were often necessary to compensate for illnesses, deaths, retirements, and suitable matches between missionary and people.[7] Although Norris did not directly challenge Ornedal's charge that the majority of missionaries in the custody had been banished there as a punishment, the data that he provides argue against it. A good number of the friars studied by Norris were sent as recently ordained or quite young—that is, relatively untested.[8] Norris also noted that the affidavits from New Mexicans in 1750 collected in their defense by the Franciscans praised the friars' missionary diligence and alleged that many Puebloans were fluent in Spanish while Native languages were diverse and difficult to master.[9]

When Governor Vélez Cachupín learned that the Franciscans were gathering affidavits of support from Hispanics in New Mexico, he shut the door to any further communications not obtaining his approval: "No New Mexico official was to attest to or certify any Franciscan reports. . . . Franciscan mail could not leave the Kingdom, except for correspondence pertinent to the Inquisition, without the governor's approval." The governor who succeeded Vélez Cachupín in 1754 was also antagonistic to the Franciscans and continued the same embargo policy, with the result that there is very scant documentation from the friars in New Mexico including El Paso during the 1750s. Since these Franciscans led the custody that included La Junta, information on this decade at La Junta after 1750 is minimal, and even then was often delayed.[10]

The last subject that Ornedal treated in his report was La Junta,[11] where he guessed that the government was providing subsidies for four missionaries (the number of missionaries named by Varo earlier that year). Ornedal asserted that only two were needed, since he was told that there had only been two since 1746, with Father Saavedra and Father González as missionaries until the latter's departure in December 1748. No one else came to help until Father Ángel García left El Paso bound for La Junta on June 10 or 12, 1749. Ornedal was told that each mission had at least thirty families, all peaceful and well inclined to speak Spanish. This latter statement was one of the many contradictions in his report, as the Franciscans would be quick to point out, since Ornedal had previously stated that the Natives in the custody did not know Spanish.

At the same time that Ornedal was sending his accusations, the new governor of Nueva Vizcaya, Juan Francisco de la Puerta y Barrera, was sending proposals to lessen the number of presidios on the eastern flank of the province. He was prompted by the miners and merchants of Chihuahua, who were mostly concerned about the increasing raids of Apaches and Sumas along the trade routes to the northwest, to El Paso and Sonora, and asking for a military buildup in that direction.[12] In December 1749 the Marqués de Altamira offered his favorite solution: replace all the eastern presidios with settlers who would act as civilian militias, as they were doing in Nuevo Santander. For civilian expansion below El Paso and to fill the military gap down to La Junta, add a new presidio at Pilares or some other appropriate site between the two places.[13] Captain Berroterán's warnings the previous year did not seem to be carrying much weight.

The Marqués read the 1748 expedition reports on La Junta in the most negative sense possible, giving weight especially to the remarks of Rábago y Terán and any others like him. The Juntan self-autonomy was now described as open hostility. Altamira wrote that the Juntans were "more than a little suspect" in the raids being committed in the Chihuahua vicinity. Their towns "are missions in name only and the Natives are subjected (*reducidos*) in name only," due to the lack of a nearby presidio and Spanish settlements. The people continued to trade with former missionized and enemy Natives. Altamira's conclusion was stunning: "The Indians of those five missions with the name of Christians are the worst enemies, the abettors (*alcahuetes*), recipients, and directors of the gentile apostates." He was not that pleased with the Franciscans either. He found their refusal to serve in the new town of Santa Cruz of the Cholomes "a very lamentable scandal."[14]

The Juntans' perennial position as middlemen for Native traders made such charges plausible to many. Indeed, within a few decades it became clear to Spanish officials that "the transfer and exchange of animals was the activity that involved a great amount of inhabitants of Nueva Vizcaya in the theft of livestock." It was not only nor perhaps even principally the Apaches who were engaged in this activity, nor solely other never-missionized Native groups. Some of the lower strata of colonial society—mulattos, mestizos, former mission Natives—were implicated more and more. And they had some powerful abettors among some of the supposed Hispanic elite.[15] In the case of the Juntans, however, the consternation of far distant authorities blinded those officials to important countervailing realities well known by better informed Nueva Vizcayans: the Juntans themselves continually had to fend off hostile attacks by Native groups unhappy with their relations with Hispanics and consistently fought as valued allies with the Hispanic military.

The Franciscans Defend Themselves

By 1750 the Franciscans began to learn what the 1748 inspection reports had said about them and their ministry. At the beginning of that year Father Varo informed the new provincial of the Holy Gospel Province that Captain Ydoiaga had reported to the viceroy that he had found only two missionaries at La Junta for five missions, and therefore the royal treasury was being defrauded. This is when Varo wrote that Páez was also a missionary in the La Junta district in 1747 but absent at the time of Ydoiaga's visit. Varo declared that since even before the founding of the La Junta missions there had always been thirty-three priests and one lay Brother allotted royal subsidies in the San Pablo Custody, and that the La Junta missionaries had always been supported out of those same thirty-four allotments. A postscript added by someone else clarified that the five La Junta subsidies were drawn from the additional ones assigned to El Paso, Zuñi, Santa Fe, Taos, and Pecos. On the rare occasion when there was a full complement of six priests at La Junta, the sixth one, called a "supernumerary" since he was beyond the subsidized number, was supported out of the cumulative funds provided for the other missionaries.[16]

By the time the Franciscan provincial in Mexico City received Varo's message, he was angrily composing a response to Ornedal's damning report, a copy of which he had received from the viceroy in December. The provincial, Father Jimeno, expanded a draft point-by-point rebuttal into his formal animated response in March 1750. In regard to La Junta, he very briefly summarized the mission history there since 1715, stating that since the hostile invasions in 1725 [*sic*] two to four missionaries had ministered in the district. But he emphatically denied the charge that the friars were defrauding the government, explaining how the La Junta district was supported without ever having received additional stipends. Jimeno also explained the situation involving Father González, who was being protected by Vélez Cachupín.[17]

La Junta under Stress

By September 1749, if not earlier, the veteran El Paso missionary Father Joseph Páez had been assigned to the La Junta district. It may have been Varo who gave him that assignment, when Varo returned to El Paso in August as custos. Fathers Saavedra and García must have been gone by then, if the latter indeed ever arrived there. From this point on, it is clear that Páez was the only missionary to La Junta and that he visited from his base in Chihuahua. That fall, Captain Berroterán conducted a campaign from his Conchos presidio against the Sumas and Apaches upriver from La Junta. The following April while in Chihuahua, Berroterán certified that the Native leaders at La Junta had told him that the Franciscan had made two visits there from September 1749 until the present, "being unable to remain in them as in previous times due to the continual hostilities by the Indians of the Suma nation with the Apaches and to the great lack of provisions for the past two years."[18]

The following year, in February 1751, the corregidor of Chihuahua made a similar certification, in which he also noted the presence of Juntans in the vicinity of Chihuahua:

A little more than a year ago Father Páez left the missions in his charge, and has been in this Villa of Chihuahua making visits to those missions every two months [*de dos a dos meses*] ... as well as to those who are dispersed in this Villa and its surroundings due to the many invasions that the enemies have made, and to the lack of provisions for more or less the past two years.[19]

Three days later, the lieutenant governor and captain general of Nueva Vizcaya wrote a very similar testimonial. He remarked that even the Natives of La Junta, "fearful of being attacked, go about in other places."[20]

Berroterán's fall 1749 campaign against the Sumas and Apaches had been precipitated by the Marqués de Altamira. Incensed by the Concho captain's protestations in 1748 about the need to maintain the eastern line of presidios, the Marqués had written a fiery opinion on December 5 of that year, threatening severe actions against all the commanders, whom he viewed as inexcusably idle in the face of the increasing hostilities in northern Nueva Vizcaya. Rather than befriending the Apache Pascual, Altamira declared, Berroterán should bring about the settlement under Spanish control of his group and any other suspected ones. Sixty or more soldiers should immediately be sent with an equal number of Native auxiliaries to bring that about, or, failing that, to capture the Natives and send them to Mexico City.[21] Berroterán undertook another campaign at the end of 1749 and early January 1750, but the Natives he brought back were Venados, not Apaches. There were 101 who were settled at the Guadalupe mission at La Junta.[22]

Altamira's directives only succeeded in alienating all the Apaches. In February 1751 the Marqués wrote that the attacks of the Natagé and Faraón Apaches, allied with the Sumas, in the triangle between El Paso, La Junta, and Chihuahua were only getting worse in spite of the directives of the viceroy to form civilian militias and have the presidial troops patrol the land. Even though Altamira noted that the La Junta missions themselves were being invaded, this did not deter him from his prejudgment of the Juntans. On the contrary, since they no longer had missionaries among them, it was all the easier to accuse them of "robbing and attacking without fear of Hispanic reprisal (*muy a su salud*), as they attributed their hostilities to the neighboring Indian nations." The Marqués presumed that they were a significant cause of all the damage being experienced, probably disguising themselves as Apaches.[23]

Altamira expanded on his earlier argument that the eastern presidios of Nueva Vizcaya were useless, located where there was no longer any Native hostility and far from the northern triangle where military forces were needed. Comparing these presidios with all the others along the northern frontier, he declared that those others faced much more danger with fewer soldiers and yet managed to hold their own with the help of the militias. Showing increasing exasperation, he urged that no further time should be spent in seeking additional information; there was more than enough at hand. It was time to act by completing the frontier line of presidios from El Paso to Coahuila through the transfer of the posts along the Camino Real below Chihuahua to the Rio del Norte.[24]

Faced by the divergent assessments of the leaders of the 1747 expeditions, Altamira declared that a presidio should be established not too far from La Junta. To his credit, he recognized that it should not be built among the La Junta missions themselves "nor so close that the Indians of La Junta judge that its purpose is solely to restrain them, yet not so distant that their movements could not be observed and efforts to bring them into the desired order (*reducirlos y arreglarlos*)" be rendered impossible. He continued to think that Pilares, whose location he misjudged, or some similar location would probably be suitable, to be determined by a new captain not having the vested interests of the eastern-corridor commanders. Altamira urged the viceroy to call a military council that included persons with experience on the Nueva Vizcayan frontier in order to make these decisions once and for all.[25]

Ethnic Changes in the La Junta Valley

Near the end of 1750 the viceroy, prompted by Altamira, had asked Captain Berroterán about the status of the Venados whom he had brought to La Junta at the beginning of that year. Berroterán had Father Páez certify that all had remained quite content, allowing thirty children to be baptized. Páez added that since then fifteen other Venados had arrived, as well as eighty-five Sumas, with twenty-eight of the latter being baptized. The drought, the increasing Apache threat, and the Spanish captains' stepped-up campaigns must have all been motivating factors. Páez made a surprising suggestion in regard to these newcomers: "They are all inclined toward Christianity, and only as such could they be moved to Coyame, about 14 leagues away, with some volunteer Natives of the five [La Junta] missions who might like to go. Granting them the plentiful lands and springs of Coyame and treating them well, they would be joined by the non-missionized Natajé [Apaches] and other groups."[26]

Even Pascual and his people allegedly promised to accept being missionized, but they did not follow through. They undoubtedly felt betrayed by their former Hispanic "friends." Berroterán did capture some Apaches, whom the governor of Nueva Vizcaya distributed among some haciendas and bread-making operations. These captives gradually made their escape.[27] Altamira would never admit it, but the implementation of his directives changed an Apache group that had been at peace with Hispanics into their enemy. The Marqués was pleasantly surprised by the reported good behavior of the Venados, Sumas, and Juntans in the river junction towns. He endorsed the recommendation by Father Páez, subsequently approved by the viceroy, about the possible new mission settlement at Coyame.[28] Evidently any hope of pacifying the nations that had been the scourge of the frontier was welcome. However, there is no known record of a move to Coyame taking place.

These Native arrivals in the La Junta towns in 1750 explain the high number of Natives under instruction for baptism in the census report that Páez made that year. As part of a detailed census of the entire San Pablo Custody, he submitted reports for the missions of San Francisco, Guadalupe, and San Juan.[29] Giving the complete names including surname of almost every head of family in the already baptized and thus longer-settled population, Páez also named their spouses and children. The family heads included one widow with children and widowed or single individuals without children.

Listed as a separate group and only by first name at San Francisco and Guadalupe were those he labeled "doctrineros," that is, those receiving religious instruction in preparation for baptism. But for San Juan he wrote instead "single boys and girls receiving religious instruction" (*muchachos y muchachas de doctrina solteros*), again listed only by first name. Paternalistic missionaries would sometimes refer to all those under their care as *muchachos*.[30] But in this case, the fact that only at San Juan were those under instruction introduced as *muchachos* and *muchachas* who were single may have been because they were sexually "eligible" young people. This would fit with the practice of missionaries to separate younger singles from the rest of the mission population in an effort to control sexual relations.[31] How this was managed at La Junta, however, is an open question, given that Father Páez only visited every three months or so.

Table 5. 1750 Census of Three La Junta Missions

	Couples	Widow with children	Total individuals in families	Single or solitary widowed	"Doctrineros"	Total
San Juan	39		161	8	83	252
San Francisco	27	1	108	9	64	181
Guadalupe	31		133	17	71	221
Total	97	1	402	34	218	654

In his census for each of these missions Páez noted that some families were missing, being dispersed in Chihuahua and ranchos in its vicinity, in Santa Eulalia, and in Julimes, "due to the lack of provisions that has occurred for the past three years in these missions del Norte, and to various invasions of enemy Indians." This mirrored the earlier certifications of Berroterán and the Chihuahua corregidor. The serious impact of the three years of drought and raids on the already settled population of the three towns can be roughly gauged by comparing the census counts by Ydoiaga in late 1747 with those of Páez in late 1750, not including the new arrivals the latter year. A plausible interpretation gives 170 people counted at San Francisco in 1747, down to 117 in 1750. At Guadalupe there was less of a decline, from 172 in 1747 to 150 in 1750. San Juan, including the Mezquites and Conejos, dropped from 276 in 1747 to 169 in 1750.[32] Not knowing the exact time of year of this census, there is no telling if among the absent were those involved in the customary migrant work.[33]

In all three towns the newly arrived Venados and Sumas constituted a third or more of the census count, making these places still active posts of new conversion efforts in the minds of the Franciscans. Of course, for the Juntans they represented bolstered defensive forces if they remained as faithful allies, as well as increased progeny as previously noted by Father Saavedra. Páez indicated the men holding official positions in each town. In San Francisco they were Governor Nicolás Mamuqui, Alcalde Andrés Cacolehi, Alguacil Manuel Mauricio, and Fiscal Joseph de la Cruz. Only in San Francisco did he identify a sacristan, Bernabé Jurum Juñote. In San Juan there were Governor Domingo Finis, Alcalde Juan el Yaqui (and another Yaqui and a Manso), and Fiscal Juan Antonio Finis. In both of those towns this mixture of Indigenous and Hispanic surnames was also present among those in the general population.

At Guadalupe, on the other hand, there were only two Indigenous surnames, and none among the town officials: Governor Rafael de los Santos, Alcalde Matheo Ponze,

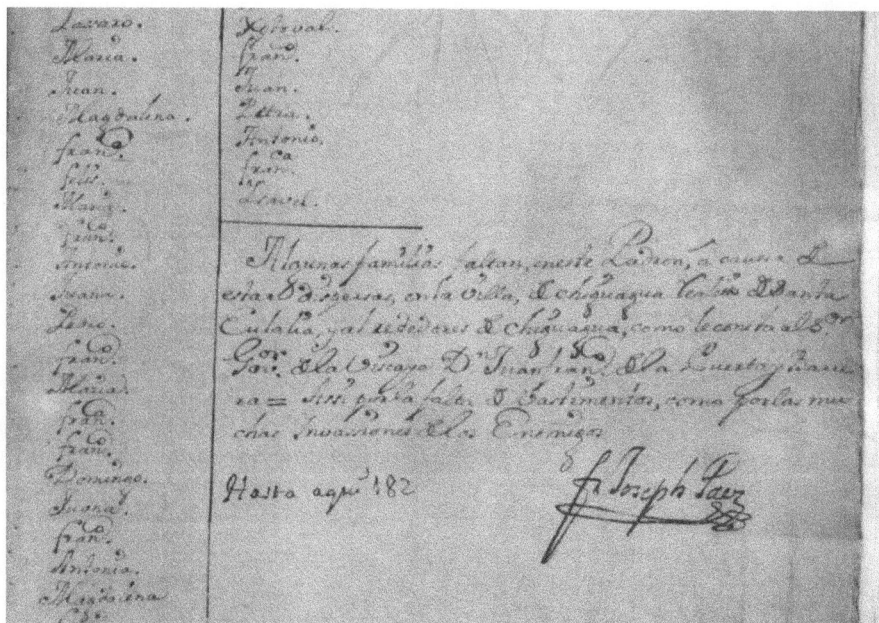

Figure 10: 1750 census by Fray Joseph Páez. (Courtesy of the Center for Southwest Research, Zimmerman Library, University of New Mexico)

Alguacil Pedro Pablo, and Fiscal Joseph de Arriendas. Could this point to a greater degree of Hispanicization or at least a greater degree of dealing with Hispanics by those at Guadalupe, just below the river junction, than among the towns along the Rio Conchos that were located on the route into and out of the La Junta valley? This might correlate with the bishop's observation in 1742 that Guadalupe had a church (a more solid edifice) while San Francisco had a chapel. Such questions make the different responses of these towns to the imposition of a military fort at the end of this decade all the more interesting.

Among the already established Juntans (thus not including the Venado and Suma newcomers) in each of the three town censuses there was an average of about two children per family. Guadalupe had a slightly higher average (2.29, San Juan 2.13, San Francisco 2.0). On the other hand, Guadalupe had a much greater proportion of widowed adults (ten compared to thirty-one couples) than the other two towns (San Juan seven to thirty-nine, San Francisco three to twenty-seven). The only widowed person having children with her was at San Francisco. But Guadalupe also had as many never-married adults (four maidens and three bachelors) as San Francisco (two maidens and five bachelors); San Juan had none. Although ages were not given in the census, these several statistics taken together might postulate both a greater number of older people and a more multigenerational community at Guadalupe.

Ethnic Changes in the Coyame Valley

Even more significant population changes were taking place across the Cuesta Grande in the Coyame valley. This was strikingly revealed by an expedition coming out of El Paso in late 1750. Realizing that Captain Ydoiaga had only surveyed half the course of the Rio del Norte between La Junta and El Paso, and that there had been conflicting opinions about possible presidio sites, in May 1750 the viceroyal officials sent orders for Captain Alonso Rubín de Celís at the El Paso presidio to reconnoiter between El Paso and La Junta and make his own recommendations. His observations at first hand in the La Junta district would be every bit as negative as those of the Marqués de Altamira at long distance.

The El Paso captain was having his own image problems. Word spread quickly among the Franciscans that in a fit of anger in 1749 he had some of his soldiers execute the Suma sacristan of the San Lorenzo mission near El Paso. The real culprit, actually a servant of the captain, had falsely accused the sacristan of stealing from Rubín de Celís's corn supplies. In reaction to the unjust execution of one of their own, the Sumas started to rise up, but were restrained. To stamp out any further commotion, Governor Vélez Cachupín ordered a large group of Sumas of both sexes to be sent to Mexico City. According to Father Carlos Delgado, three cripples—a woman and two men—were ordered beheaded and left unburied by the corporal leading the group because they were not able to keep up with the march. The military guard even allegedly sold these Sumas' little children as slaves in various places along the way. This was one of many accusations that Delgado made against the governors and alcaldes of New Mexico, in an account obviously penned to support a counterattack to the Ornedal report.[34]

Rather than heading directly down the Río del Norte that he was ordered to inspect, Rubín de Celís took a very southerly loop through northern Nueva Vizcaya to reach the Río Conchos and descend it to the La Junta valley. A probable explanation for this very large detour was that he was responding to the concerns of the hacienda owners in those districts, who wanted him to show military force in their domains beleaguered by Sumas and Apaches. Departing from El Paso on November 9, the expedition traveled south toward Chihuahua and then south-southeast through the haciendas of Aguanueva and las Hormigas, delayed a week in the latter part of the journey by sleet and snow.[35]

Finally, guided by five Sumas—one "an expert in Castilian"—whom they encountered on their way and who identified themselves as Christians, they reached the Río Conchos many leagues south of the La Junta district. Descending that river toward the La Junta valley, in one of the cottonwood (álamo) groves along its banks they came across five Native encampments called El Venado by their Suma guides. One can only puzzle about a possible connection with the Venados being settled at La Junta during this time. These people had no Christian items with them, at least not visible to the eye. Two Suma men, their wives, and another Suma woman were found among the

Natives at this place. The expedition members recognized them as fugitives from the uprising in 1749, that they said took place at Santa María de las Caldas below El Paso. One of the Sumas found at El Venado, in fact, had been among those sent in chains to Mexico City by Rubín de Celís. All five of these Sumas were forcibly brought back to El Paso by the captain.[36]

Continuing further, they came across the encampment of the Suma leader called El Bagre, father of one of their guides. He said he was Christian and had a rosary around his neck. He said that he had served Doctor Ubineta in Chihuahua, and that his current settlement was subject to the government of Nueva Vizcaya and served by the priests at La Junta. Father Páez, in fact, had witnessed his marriage. This or the next settlement was most probably in the vicinity of the former San Pedro mission where Father González had catechized almost 500 people in 1748, people identified in Varo's report of the incident as Cholomes. Rubín de Celís did not call any of the people in this 1750 visit Cholomes. Captain Ydoiaga and his detachments had not passed through this section of the Río Conchos and thus left no record of people there.

A little over a league farther along the river was the much larger encampment of Captain Mathias el Venadito. These people spoke the Suma language, but their dwellings and clothing were like those of Apaches. El Venadito's people had fled to the top of a mountain across the river, but he was persuaded to come down with forty of his men. He said that they had been living in Coyame, the former mission of the La Junta district, until they were attacked by Apaches. So they had moved to this site on the Río Conchos to start their settlement there. Rubín de Celís noticed signs of beef having been eaten, but the people were not raising any animals. So he concluded that they were responsible for the raids that were being suffered by the haciendas of Nueva Vizcaya.

The next day the expedition traveled eight leagues to the west, crossing over a very rugged ridge since the river was impassable, and arrived at a small valley with a little marsh created by the water flowing down from the springs at Coyame. From there the stream or creek continued down to the Rio Conchos, where there could be seen a small settlement across the river at the place called Cuchillo Parado. Its inhabitants were said to be of the same nation and way of life as those at El Venadito's. From afar Cuchillo Parado was judged to be unsuitable for a Hispanic town. In the meantime, two soldiers had gone back along the trail in search of two horses that had been lost. Back at El Venadito's they found the horses, and also saw many people still coming down from the mountain and fording the river, among whom were noted specifically "negroes, mulattos, coyotes, etc."[37] To Rubín de Celís this was proof that this encampment was "the unruly site (*rochela*) of all the fugitive and delinquent people of Nueva Vizcaya and its haciendas."[38]

These populations containing Sumas, Suma speakers with some Apache cultural traits in an encampment led by El Venadito, and another encampment named El Venado, with at least several declaring themselves to be Christian, certainly make one think of the Sumas and Apaches-Cholomes allied with El Venado in 1743. It should be noticed, however, that Rubín de Celís in this account did not call any of them Apaches. The fact that in El Venadito they were accompanied by mixed servant races of the Hispanic frontier would be taken by the Marqués de Altamira as definite confirmation of his strong suspicions. It was at this same time that other Venados and Sumas were entering the missions in the La Junta valley. The La Junta district was certainly undergoing some important transformations.

An Alleged Reconnaissance of the La Junta Valley

The next day the expedition of Rubín de Celís traveled nine leagues over hills, through ravines, and across precipices to once again reach the Río Conchos. The following day, December 9, they marched east and over the Cuesta Grande into the La Junta valley, a full month after they had set out from El Paso. Arriving at the Río Conchos they met a very old Native who could not or would not give them his name nor respond to the "Ave Maria" salutation.[39] At El Mezquite nine men, some wearing a cross, others a rosary around their necks, emerged from three pole houses and lined up in double file to formally receive the expedition. Before the captain's party reached San Juan, the General of the Juntans named Bernardo[40] came out to meet them with the same formalities, accompanied by more than fifty mounted warriors bearing a banner of red silk with a cross in its center. A little farther on appeared Bartolomé de Porras, who had been described as commander of the Juntan towns back in 1747. Rubín de Celís identified Porras as a *lobo* (predominantly Black and Native mixture), with the title of lieutenant general given him by the governor of Nueva Vizcaya. Both generals knew the Spanish language. They told Rubín de Celís that the people ate what naturally grew on the land, scarce for the past two years due to the alternating floods and droughts, combined with the unsuitability of the land for irrigation. They also reported that the Franciscans had never been able to raise a crop at Coyame, since it too was unsuitable for irrigation.

The El Paso captain used this initial meeting to castigate the Juntan leaders. After what he had seen on the other side of the Cuesta Grande, and probably even before that, he had already prejudged the residents of the La Junta valley as a worthless and vile people. He held the La Junta generals responsible for what he had encountered previously, reprimanding them for permitting "so many settlements of bandit Indians, without schooling or Christian discipline or political order, nor even signs among most of being Christians, thus manifesting that those Indians were the ones who maintained themselves by the robberies and raids that were continually occurring in Chihuahua . . . and beyond." In response the Juntan generals, dumbfounded (*sorpresos ó confundidos*) by this charge as Rubín de Celís himself noted, granted that there might be some bad persons among those encamped across the mountain ridge. But they explained that those people's scattered sites and the lack of suitable places for establishing towns for them prevented their subjection. Indirectly asserting that this situation was not their responsibility, the generals said that they would inform the governor of Nueva Vizcaya so that he would take the appropriate measures.[41]

By this time the primary goal of Rubín de Celís was apparently to make up the time spent on his great southern detour through the Chihuahuan haciendas. His actions— or rather lack of action—were certainly not in keeping with his charge to carefully examine the La Junta valley and the territory between it and El Paso for a presidio site. Whereas he had taken a month to get to La Junta by an out-of-the-way route and did not even inspect the site at Coyame proposed by some for a presidio, this day he had pushed ahead for fifteen leagues, including the very difficult passage of the Cuesta Grande, to reach San Juan in the late afternoon. There he was told that San Juan had forty families (very close to Páez's census count of thirty-nine couples, not counting single households) who were out hunting, and that it was not known where they had gone. Seeing tracks that led to the Rio Conchos, the suspicious captain concluded that the people were actually hiding on the other side where some small thatched-roof huts could be seen. But he did not bother to cross over to verify his presumption.

It is not surprising that the people of San Juan decided to remove themselves upon the approach of the captain. After all, one-third of them were Venados and Sumas. The Sumas had to be well aware of what Rubín de Celís had done to people of their nation in the El Paso district, and that he was now arresting any who were recognized as from there. Perhaps Berroterán had been able to convince so many people upriver from La Junta to settle in the valley towns at the end of 1749 not only due to the increasing Apache threat but also on account of the harsh treatment of their people by Rubín de Celís and his men.

Since the horse herd of the Hispanic party was still negotiating the Cuesta Grande due to the great distance traveled that day, the El Paso captain had to remain the next day at San Juan. He took the occasion to reprimand the La Junta generals again in insulting terms "about their obligation to live as Christians, maintaining themselves through work and not merely the 'grass' [*zacate*] they supposedly fed on like beasts, nor from what they robbed, causing so much damage to Nueva Vizcaya." Otherwise, he threatened, the viceroy would become fed up and send troops to destroy them. Thus he accused the Juntans not only of tolerating the alleged misdeeds of those across the Cuesta Grande but also of actually directly participating in them. How could one reply to such intemperate language? "They only responded that they would try to not be bad."

It so happened that at this time Father Páez was in the La Junta valley to celebrate the annual feast day of the mission of Guadalupe, December 12. He had arrived a few days previously and planned on departing shortly afterwards, since the valley was still experiencing a severe drought. This may have been when he carried out his census. The few provisions the friar had brought with him from Chihuahua were running out, and the Natives had nothing to give him. Páez went to San Juan at midday to see Rubín de Celís, and the next day, December 11, the captain's entourage and Páez went down the river to San Francisco. With the justification that the river was too swollen, Rubín de Celís did not cross to visit any of the towns below the river junction. His hosts, undoubtedly aware of the purpose of his visit, were only too happy to tell him that the lands downriver were also unsuitable for farming.

The captain made no mention nor gave any description of the groups of Natives that inhabited any part of the valley, whereas he had been careful to describe those on the other side of the Cuesta Grande. He already had all the description he wanted in order to illustrate his highly negative portrayal. Without halting at San Francisco, he continued on for two leagues into the lowlands upriver on the Rio del Norte, that he described as also mostly unsuitable for farming. He pitched camp there to rest the horses that had caught up with his party. In the meantime, Father Páez, undeterred by the swollen river, was carried across it on the shoulders of some Natives in order to be there for the evening vigil of the feast day of the Guadalupe pueblo.[42]

Guided by the two Juntan generals, Rubín de Celís proceeded rapidly up the Rio del Norte that he was supposed to be inspecting. Within three days he arrived at the place called Los Pilares that had been indicated as a possible site of the future fort. On the way, somewhere between forty-two and sixty-five miles (sixteen to twenty-five leagues) from San Francisco, his party passed by the empty encampments said to be of El Venado. One of the generals said that El Venado and his people had been in La Junta for a few days—thus no longer as enemies, perhaps visiting the Venados who had settled there—but he did not know where they went afterwards. Both generals were being tight-lipped after their treatment at San Juan. They turned back before reaching Los Pilares, after pointing out its location from the ford downriver called La Ventana, saying that they did not dare to venture into hostile territory. Whereas he had taken a month to reach La Junta on the circular route through the hacienda owners' lands, Rubín de Celís reached El Paso by the more or less direct river route that was the official reason for his expedition in less than one-third of that time, arriving on December 20.[43]

If the captain's own recorded actions and words were not enough to discredit his supposed reconnaissance visit, Father Páez's certainly were. The missionary, thoroughly disgusted, dashed off a note on December 11 so that, ironically, it could be carried by someone in the captain's party to Father Varo in El Paso. Páez criticized Rubín de Celís for what he considered a very perfunctory inspection. He reported that when the El Paso officer arrived in the valley, he sent the Natives who had gone out to meet him to tell Páez that if the missionary wanted to visit, he should come to San Juan, since the expedition was hurrying back to El Paso. When the priest asked the captain if he had passed through the Coyame mission site, Rubín de Celís said no, that his guide had said that it was four or five leagues out of the way. Páez noted that this was a small distance, given that the purpose of the captain's expedition was to scout out appropriate sites like Coyame for a presidio (indeed, Coyame would later receive one).

Páez remarked that the captain made the quick trip through San Francisco and three leagues up the Rio del Norte without inspecting anything along the river below its junction with the Conchos. Even while in San Juan, according to Páez, Rubín de Celís did not leave his tent nor send any of the Hispanic citizens traveling with him to investigate. Rather, he told Páez that doing such would serve nothing, since Páez himself, being there, should be the one to send information. He even remarked, Paéz exclaimed to Varo, that "it was a sin that Religious were in such places, that only bringing girls from El Paso would make it good, and other such indecorous foolishness of which you and others are not unaware."[44] This was not Father Páez's first experience with the captain, since the friar had been stationed at El Paso. It would not be his last either. The fate of the two would become closely intertwined at the end of the decade.

Rubín de Celís did give some rare information about the state of three church buildings in the La Junta valley, corroborating and amplifying earlier indications. The Native generals told him that the town of Guadalupe "was similar to San Francisco, with the only difference being that it had its church finished." So evidently the church at San Francisco, that Bishop Elizacoechea had called a chapel, was still incomplete. At San Juan what served as a church consisted of "an adobe house with its portal, containing a bare (*desnudo*) adobe altar, an old canvas painting of St. John the Baptist more than two yards high, a little room with an attached cell or sleeping compartment, a small supply room (*dispensa salita*), and corral." So the painting of John the Baptist that had survived the 1726 uprising was evidently still extant. The town had four other small adobe houses and others of plastered pole construction. A more formal church had been started, some 14–15 varas in length and five varas wide with a transept, but its walls were only about a yard high. The outlines (*muestras*) of a sacristy and baptistry were also visible.[45]

Two years later the Franciscan custos wrote that only one mission at La Junta had a church and priest's dwelling. From the previous reports, this would have been Guadalupe, as the only mission with both a suitably completed church and missionary dwelling. From the other reports, we know that San Francisco had lesser constructions, and San Juan even less, but at least both were adobe structures. The status of church buildings at San Cristóbal went unreported. The custos also wrote that there was no provision of resources for maintaining what existed, with the missionaries lacking military protection and any other kind of support.[46]

Rush to Judgment

Rubín de Celís's very disparaging account of the entire La Junta district became even more accentuated in his accompanying recommendations. Stating that La Junta was 126 leagues (about 325 miles) from El Paso by the river route, he declared that the only suitable place in that whole distance for a Hispanic settlement was at El Palo Clavado or the Plain of Peace (the first site of the future San Elseario fort), twenty-five to thirty leagues below El Paso. But he also asserted that the lowlands at La Junta above San Francisco—that is, more or less where he camped December 11—could be considered for a fort, and also the place called San Diego about midway between La Junta and El Paso along the Río del Norte. This aim could be accomplished in both places, he declared, by developing suitable earthworks to contain the seasonal flooding. In fact, he recommended that both presidios be established, so that the sight of the one at La Junta might

> bring into submission, make vassals, and gather into the lap of our Catholic religion and royal dominion so many uncivilized (*barbara*), apostate, outlaw (*foraxida*) people whom we encountered hidden away—Indians, mulattos, negroes, and the rest—in the settlements or so-called towns and missions of said La Junta, along the lower banks of the Rio del Norte and the upper ones of the Río Conchos.[47]

Governor Vélez Cachupín of New Mexico had ordered Rubín de Celís to share the expedition report with him before sending it to the viceroy. Upon reviewing it, the governor was only too happy to use it as further proof of the allegedly decadent state of the missions of the San Pablo Custody, including those at La Junta beyond his jurisdiction. Vélez Cachupín, after all, was probably the primary promoter behind Ornedal's earlier condemnation of the Franciscans' work or lack thereof. Writing from El Paso at the end of March 1751, he urged the viceroy to take very prompt action in regard to "the supposed five missions of La Junta," citing the El Paso captain's report as irrefutable evidence that they were the source or support of all the disturbances from the Chihuahua district to that of El Paso. The fact that Vélez Cachupín was a protégé of Viceroy Revillagigedo gave particular weight to his words, assuring an appreciative hearing that would be strengthened later as he began to demonstrate an ability to bring the hostile nations surrounding New Mexico into peaceful relations.[48] His comments to the viceroy, therefore, should be noted at length:

> Those Pueblos or settlements, under the pious title of missions and Christians who do not even understand how to make the sign of the cross, as the captain informs me, and tolerated unbelievers, are the origin and refuge of the uprising and apostasy of the Sumas. For these latter depend totally on those at La Junta, and have established themselves in its vicinity protected among the mountains and forests of this Rio del Norte and that of the Conchos, having secret communications and paths for their commerce, in league with Apaches, all joining together to attack the road to the town of Chihuahua, the haciendas of Enseñillas, Hormigas, and Agua Nueva, and the immediate vicinity of that town [Chihuahua] for two or three leagues. This is

likewise the place of retreat for all the perverse Blacks, mulattos, *lobos*, and coyotes who flee from the mines of Chihuahua and the haciendas of Vizcaya, all cooperating in the atrocious hostilities and ruin occurring in this Presidio of El Paso. For if the Natives of those five missions were under proper subjection, the Sumas would be subdued and not so insolent and the Apaches would not be able to have free entry along this part of the Rio del Norte, since these latter [the Apaches] were very ignorant [of this territory] until those of La Junta with the Sumas guided them, as the Sumas themselves have declared and confessed to me. And Captain Don Alonzo [Rubín de Celís] understood and observed that the horse herds and cattle and sheep that they steal in all the above-noted haciendas, as also from the pack trains of merchants between here and Chihuahua, enter into the infamous bosom of the five missions and the close-by canyon through out-of-the-way routes. There they are divided up and traded for skins with the Natagé Apaches and others that they invite and convoke from the plains.[49]

From being a remote and isolated afterthought on the colonial north-central frontier, La Junta and its missions were now being cast as the source and abettor of turmoil for the whole region, with no distinction between them and the people occupying the Coyame valley. And upon what evidence? Certainly there was the observation of Rábago y Terán three years earlier of some stolen animals from the northeastern frontier being traded at La Junta. But Rubín de Celís had only specifically noted the bones of roasted animals, as well as the presence of Negroes and mixed-race people, at one settlement in the San Pedro vicinity. Similarly, Vélez Cachupín turned Rubín de Celís's mention of one very old man who did not respond to a Catholic greeting into a blanket declaration that none of the Juntans knew anything about Christianity.

Leaving aside the allegations of the El Paso captain and the New Mexico governor, what does clearly stand forth from the report of Rubín de Celís is the greatly shifting demographics occurring in the Coyame valley and south of there along the Rio Conchos. Attacks by certain Apaches had driven the Cholomes from their settlements, and now those places were becoming large encampments of Sumas and possibly Venados, who even themselves were driven out of Coyame by Apache attacks. Their settlements were becoming refuges for disaffected or oppressed Blacks, mulattos, and coyotes from the interior of Nueva Vizcaya. The practically simultaneous report and census of Father Páez reveals that at this same time there were numerous Venados and Sumas apparently settling into the La Junta valley missions. Those missions had received contingents of other surrounding groups in previous decades, especially the Cíbolos, but the long-settled Juntan townspeople were still the majority. One would like to know much more about these demographic processes in the following years, but the sources so far investigated shed very little light.

When the reports of Rubín de Celís and Vélez Cachupín reached Mexico City in mid-June 1751, the Marqués de Altamira triumphantly asserted: "If before it was only upon the presumption that they [the Juntans] might be bad that it was resolved to create a new presidio, now with the experience reported by the captain of El Paso . . . it is clearly much more urgent and necessary to establish immediate respect for the royal arms." Always attentive to reducing costs, Altamira recommended that Rubín de Celís be the one to choose the site of a single presidio. Acknowledging that it might be difficult to find an appropriate location, he recommended San Diego about midway to El Paso or some other site below it such as Los Pilares. Asserting that the troops should continually be on the move, the Auditor declared that they could thus "easily" observe the proceedings of the Juntans. Experienced officials on the north-central frontier must have rolled their eyes in disbelief upon reading this lack of geographical comprehension. The Marqués could not conclude without firing another salvo at the Franciscans:

> And since notice has been taken of the state of total abandon in which the missions of La Junta have been, and their yearly support (sínodos) effectively having been paid without the missionaries having perfectly assisted them in so many years, now with the erection of the new presidio whatever excuse that could be given for the previous omission and neglect will cease, and Your Excellency [the Viceroy] will deign to order that the Very Reverend Father Provincial of this Province [of Mexico City] be asked and charged to give the most efficacious provisions so that those missions be perfectly assisted from now on, being made aware of how much the greater service of both Majesties [God and king] is at stake in this.

The viceroy immediately ordered that letters be sent out as Altamira recommended.[50]

In the meantime, in order to provide a more substantial rebuttal to the entire Ornedal report, the next Franciscan provincial had tasked Father Varo, with his decades of experience in the San Pablo Custody and still its leader, to draw up a response. Varo did so with a vengeance, going point by point. The result was an extensive document finished at El Paso on January 29, 1751. Either the mail embargo by Vélez Cachupín was not yet in place there, or somehow the Franciscans slipped it through to Mexico City. It certainly would not have made it past the New Mexico governor. Varo's anger would have been stirred even more if the report by Rubín de Celís, further exaggerated by Vélez Cachupín, had been completed and in circulation at this time. A decade later Francisco Figueroa, the archivist of the Santo Evangelio Province, described Varo's document as somewhat satirical, but very learned and zealous. It was actually so bathed in sarcasm that the provincial decided not to send it to the viceroy, especially since it targeted Ornedal and Vélez Cachupín, two of the viceroy's favorites.[51] Varo began by taking the El Paso missions, with which he was very familiar since he normally served there, as his primary arguments to discredit Ornedal. Then he turned to those in upper New Mexico with some inclusion of those at La Junta. In paragraph 34 he admitted that some missions were in a bad state, namely San Lorenzo near El Paso, Zuñi, and those at La Junta.

In fact, he called the La Junta missions lost (*perdidas*) on account of not having a presidio there. Repeating for the umpteenth time his accusations about the self-serving reports of the military captains after their inspections, in this diatribe he asserted that now "all the town and mine of Chihuahua and all the neighboring citizens" wanted the presidio. Having just received Father Páez's note from La Junta criticizing Rubín de Celís, he charged in paragraph 72 that the El Paso captain was so at ease (*sosegado*) that his forces were asleep. "Many times he has said: '*cumplir y mentir*'"—that is, say that you are carrying out what is ordered, while actually lying. It was evident to Varo that Rubín de Celís would do nothing serious to fulfill the orders of the viceroy to establish a fort near La Junta. Varo was so disgusted and frustrated with the governing authorities in New Mexico that he finished by exclaiming that "all of us missionaries want, if God permits, that there not be in our time nor have any longer in this Kingdom [of New Mexico] friars of St. Francis, so that there no longer be anyone who, coming out to meet us, says what Ahab said to the most zealous Elias [Elijah]: 'Is it you, you disturber of Israel?'" (para. 77).[52] Ornedal and those frontier officials whose views he parroted had certainly stoked an already simmering fire of Franciscan discontent.

The Decade of the Fifties: Military Politics Far and Near

Altamira's frontier reform was finally approved in 1751. It eliminated the five existing government-supported presidios on the east, including that of Conchos, but placed the seat of operations of a new sixty-man mobile cavalry company at Guajoquilla, the eastern site that Berrotrán had recommended three years previously. Besides patrolling the eastern frontier, this cavalry unit was also made responsible, incredibly, for visiting the western regions of Nueva Vizcaya, that is, the Tarahumara and Tepehuan country. To block the Apaches on the north, a presidio was to be established at or near Pilares on the lower course of the Rio del Norte between La Junta and El Paso, while a civilian settlement was to be founded closer to El Paso. Rubín de Celís was to transfer his military company at El Paso to found the new presidio near Pilares, while a new captain would recruit a new company for El Paso.[53]

As Berrotrán had predicted, the new measures were dismally incapable of containing the Apaches and other hostile groups. Furthermore, the governor of Nueva Vizcaya and Rubín de Celís were in no hurry to bring about a presidio at Pilares. With the argument that the site lacked water three months out of the year, the cavalry troops of Rubín de Celís were "temporarily" stationed at the hacienda of Agua Nueva, some sixty miles north of Chihuahua and in the midst of the haciendas of Rubín de Celís's colleagues through which he had detoured the previous year. True indeed, they were thus better positioned to defend the settlements and ranches nearer to Chihuahua. But Agua Nueva was about the same distance from La Junta as Chihuahua, only more to the northwest. This left the vast expanse of northeastern Nueva Vizcaya utterly defenseless. That was because the new cavalry unit of Guajoquilla, supposedly charged with that responsibility, was actually occupied for the near future in the transfer to the diocesan clergy of the more established Jesuit missions of the Tarahumara, far from eastern Nueva Vizcaya. Meanwhile the province was under siege. By 1755 the income of the *diezmos* (church taxes on produce) of the Durango diocese had been reduced to half its former amount.[54]

In 1752 the corregidor of Chihuahua once again gave the necessary certification that "in all of the past year 1751 the missions of La Junta de los Rios del Norte y Conchos have been administered by the Reverend Father Preacher Jubilado Fray Joseph de Páez."[55] This succinct and careful wording allowed both the corregidor and the Franciscans to dodge the question of whether Páez had actually resided at La Junta all that time—a viceroyal requirement—which of course he had not. Due to the continuing lack of security, and probably other reasons dealing with both colonial and missionary strategies, during the remainder of the 1750s Father Páez appears to have been the sole priest serving those missions. There were, however, Franciscan attempts to improve that situation. It was apparently in the year 1752 that Fray Manuel Rojo, just arrived in northern New Mexico in 1751, was sent back south to serve at La Junta. That was probably in response to the viceroy's order for more missionaries the previous year with the foreseen founding of a presidio there. But "because of the failure of the escort Captain Rubín de Celís had promised for those missions," Rojo took the next convoy back to the New Mexican interior.[56]

In January 1753 the new custos, Fray Jacobo de Castro, who had again attempted to send more missionaries, reported a repeated lack of response by Rubín de Celís as well as an "uprising" by the Juntans:

> In fulfilment of the order that Your Reverence gave me . . . that I place Religious in the missions of La Junta de los Rios, I sent the Father Preachers Fray Joseph Páez, Fray Juan Sanz de Lezáun, and Fray Manuel Bermejo, who remained in the Villa of Chihuahua with this assignment more than four months . . . but there was no provision for the security of these Religious. The captain of the [planned] Presidio of Pilares, Don Alonso Victores Rubín de Celís, was entrusted by the viceroy with the care of those missions. But it must be noted that the location of Pilares where the new presidio is to be founded is 70 leagues distant from the missions of La Junta de los Rios over a very bad route. The natives of La Junta are in an uprising and very involved with the infidels—that is why all the depredations occurring daily in the Villa of Chihuahua and its environs are attributed to them. And that is very believable, due to the sociability that they have with the gentiles, and also since they

themselves told me that it has been five years that they have not harvested a grain of corn or other crops to maintain themselves. Consequently, it is natural that they turn to robbing, since they neither work nor have from whence to obtain what is necessary.

The custos decided to leave only Father Páez for La Junta, with the understanding that the priest would have to travel sometimes to Chihuahua for his needs since "everything is lacking" at that river junction. But Castro declared that he was ready to send as many Religious as necessary, as soon as the viceroy placed a presidio in the La Junta valley itself.[57]

How much the people of the La Junta valley were involved in raiding, a charge dating from the Marqués de Altamira and Rubín de Celís in 1749–1750, or even in an uprising, should be open to question, given their continual relations with the Franciscans and the people in the Chihuahua vicinity. Castro found that accusation "very believable," without asserting it outright. It was certainly true that the Juntans were sociable with "gentiles" such as the Apache traders. But the new custos accepted too easily the stereotypical charge that they did not work, a charge that almost a century of reliable migrant labor demonstrated as highly inaccurate.

Two weeks before Castro wrote about the captain's failure to provide military security to the missionaries, Rubín de Celís at Aguanueva wrote to the viceroy that it was the fault of the two missionaries whom Custos Varo had earlier placed in Chihuahua, and after them the two friars whom Father Castro brought, who "did not come see the captain [himself] nor ask him for an escort."[58] It is hard to believe that he was not notified, twice, about the missionaries awaiting an escort. Given the timing of his letter, one has to ask if he had learned about or suspected the Franciscans' discontent with him and their intention to write about it to Mexico City. Be that as it may, in September 1753 the viceroy was told by his advisors, whom he had ordered to look into the matter, that La Junta was listed for subsidies for one missionary each at San Francisco, San Juan, and Guadalupe, and for two shared by San Cristóbal, Coyame, and San Pedro.[59] This is the first official government statement encountered that gave the number of subsidies designated for La Junta. The number five corresponds with the number that the Franciscans had been stating all along as drawn from the 34-person plan for the entire custody.

The viceroy ordered the head Franciscan in all of Mexico, Commissary General Abasolo, to provide missionaries at once. Upon asking the Holy Gospel provincial for information, Abasolo was given Custos Castro's January letter faulting Rubín de Celís. Forwarding Castro's letter to the viceroy, Abasolo in his cover letter wrote that apparently the captain was at most offering only an escort, not on-site military protection at La Junta nor any needed supplies. And the Commissary General repeated the assertion of the Holy Gospel provincial in 1750 that these missions had never received royal subsidies—that is, monies granted specifically for them above and beyond the original 34-person plan. Rather, they had been maintained by taking missionaries from those places assigned two friars in New Mexico "in order to save new costs to His Majesty." The Commissary, however, concluding with the usual act of deference, declared that he would order whatever the viceroy might determine.[60]

In his mission-by-mission report written in distant Mexico City the following year, in July 1754, Father Manuel de San Juan Nepomuceno y Trigo wrote much more positively about the Juntans than Castro had the previous year. Stating that he had no firsthand knowledge of the six missions at La Junta, he wrote that he had heard very positive things about their inhabitants: "I have been assured that its Natives are good and that, not having fields in which to plant, they make repeated absences to Chihuahua, where with their labor they acquire what they need, being very vigilant and in no way lazy in seeking (en solicitar) work."[61]

Viceroy Revillagigedo was determined to have a post established along the Rio del Norte in spite of the maneuvering of the frontier officials. That was one of his first orders to the newly appointed governor of Nueva Vizcaya, Matheo Antonio de Mendoza.[62] Accordingly, in June 1754 Mendoza called a provincial Junta de Guerra (war council) of his military captains—Berroterán (retired?), Rubín de Celís, and Carpio—along with the corregidor of Chihuahua, representatives of the Chihuahua elite, and Father Páez. The objective was again to determine where to locate the presidio. The veteran Berroterán now recommended Coyame or a place called Pecho Viejo, from either of which places the troops could note "which Indians (of those they call Norteños) are friends and which are not." The Chihuahua representatives, predictably, argued that no fixed site should be selected, rather that the two existing compañías volantes (mobile cavalry troops) including that of Rubín de Celís should remain as such, in order to better protect the dispersed haciendas. The opinions of Rubín de Celís and Father Páez went unnoted in this report by the governor. However, at a critical juncture in 1759–1760, Mendoza would cite an opinion allegedly given to him by Rubín de Celís three days after the 1754 junta, strongly advocating that the presidio be established at La Junta. That was the recommendation that Mendoza himself made in 1754 to the viceroy.

At the same time, the governor praised the Juntans who acted as auxiliaries with the Hispanic troops, stating that "obedient to the orders of the Commandant they went on sallies by themselves various times to seek out the enemies, and succeeded in capturing many." Mendoza wrote that this "necessary assistance" of the Juntan warriors could only be maintained by paying or gifting them for such service, in order to provide for them and the families that they left at La Junta while they were engaged in military movements. He asked that such funds be made available. Mendoza also noted that Juntans continued "to go to Chihuahua and its haciendas and ranches to work in alternating crews (por tandas) and for other business." Thus while officials outside the region, in El Paso and Mexico City, rained harsh criticism upon the Juntans, those regularly interacting with them in Nueva Vizcaya continued to experience and value them as faithful allies and workers.

Nothing happened for three more years. So a Junta de Guerra was convoked in Mexico City in 1757 by the next viceroy, the Marqués de Amarillas, to settle the matter once and for all. Rubín de Celís was summoned to the meeting as the commander of the troops still "temporarily" headquartered at Aguanueva, serving as a mobile cavalry company charged with patrolling the territory above Chihuahua. This council agreed with Governor Mendoza and similar earlier reports (such as those of Rábago y Terán and Rubín de Celís) that a presidio should be established at or near La Junta, whereupon the viceroy immediately ordered that this decision be implemented without any further delay.[63]

Yet again nothing happened, to the great frustration of the Mexico City officials. In the meantime, throughout the 1750s the entire country between Chihuahua and the Rio del Norte was rife with Native hostilities. In 1760 a Franciscan who had served in New Mexico, and most recently though very briefly at La Junta, wrote that the Sumas and Apaches now "harried all the roads with armed bands which could not be exterminated." The haciendas of Ojo Caliente and Carrizal about seventy miles below El Paso were raided repeatedly, forcing their abandonment for several years. Haciendas and mining operations in the vicinity of Chihuahua suffered continuous incursions. The Rio Conchos was left unprotected, its ranchers having withdrawn to its southern headwaters on account of the continuous robberies and murders.[64]

Throughout this decade, Father Páez remained faithfully and courageously traveling to La Junta to minister there, as certified once more for the year 1757 by the authorities in Chihuahua.[65] But the situation was about to change dramatically.

The Inglorious Founding of a Presidio, 1759

They reacted strongly with total resolution, shouting No! No! No! They would not allow it in their lands that God had given them. Let it be placed in El Cajón or at Coyame!

— Juntan leaders, San Juan Pueblo, 17 December 1759

Having conferred with each other in their language, the Juntan representatives replied unanimously, most in Spanish, that they agreed with the introduction of a presidio.... And that they are ready to indicate tomorrow the site where the presidio should be placed, leaving undisturbed their fields for planting.

— Captain Leizaola, Guadalupe Pueblo, 26 December 1759

Once Governor Mendoza in Chihuahua finally decided to make a presidio happen at La Junta, he and his agents had no moral scruples as to how they brought it about. Quite a few Juntans were initially persuaded to allow this radical change in their valley, but they bitterly learned what the great majority had strongly anticipated: these Hispanic officials could not be trusted. The fact that two different parties, the Hispanic officials and the Franciscan missionaries, were the contemporary participants in and relators of these events allows one to see through the official smokescreen, following step by step what actually occurred.

The First Presidio Test

In mid-February 1759 Father Castro, once again the Franciscan custos in El Paso, wrote Governor Mendoza of Nueva Vizcaya that his superiors in Mexico City were sending two Religious for the La Junta missions at the viceroy's order. But the custos was still not ready to send resident missionaries without soldiers who would remain with them. Consequently, Father Castro told the governor that "when you deign it appropriate you determine when they will enter La Junta with Father Páez and how their persons will be secured."[1]

Both officials undoubtedly were shocked, like the rest of New Spain, by the total destruction of the San Saba mission in Texas the previous year by powerful northern nations, putting an end to Spanish expansion on the northeastern frontier. The rude awakening in Texas could only have strengthened the resolve to more forcefully confront the growing threat by hostile Native alliances across the northern borderlands. The viceroy and his advisors ordered a vigorous military response to the San Saba attack to instill respect for the Spanish realm. But the punitive expedition in north Texas in fall 1759 was another disaster, not so much in terms of loss of life but definitely in regard to an embarrassing demonstration of Spanish futility at a distant and strongly fortified Native town swelled by allied forces. Perhaps that result helped determine the duplicitous strategy that Governor Mendoza and his subordinates eventually adopted in regard to La Junta.[2]

Possibly Governor Mendoza wanted to add a major gesture of obedience and military achievement to his resumé, since he was about to retire and ask for rewards. For whatever reason, this time he acted. However, he did not reply to Father Castro until late March, and then only to state that the matter was being deliberated. It was not until mid-May, having consulted with Father Páez, that he issued his decision to his military commanders. He stated that the same reason that had delayed this project still remained, that is, the need to employ the available troops to restrain the hostilities being committed against the Hispanic haciendas and towns of northern Nueva Vizcaya. Nevertheless, he was now ordering Captain Rubín de Celís to prepare a detachment of sixteen soldiers who were to conduct the three missionaries to La Junta with provisions for three months for the friars and the soldiers.[3]

Eleven days later the governor notified Páez that the operation was on. Both men realized that this would be a very delicate project to bring about. Everyone was well aware of the Juntans' antipathy to having any Hispanics other than missionaries reside in their midst. Mendoza assured Father Páez that the cavalrymen being sent were "the oldest and most prudent" ones. They had orders to follow the Franciscan's directions, effectively making him the leader of the expedition. The governor wrote Páez to be supremely tactful and indeed to not reveal to the Juntans the true purpose of this initiative. The friar was to tell them that the military were only there temporarily to scout the territory and to hinder the entrance of the Natagé Apaches and their allies. At the same time the Franciscans were to try to induce the Juntans to recognize the advantages of having a presidio. If, on the other hand, the people evidenced such repugnance to this proposal that an uprising seemed to be imminent, then the soldiers should remove themselves and return to their military company.[4]

Up to this point all the Hispanic actors appeared to be in agreement. But when the project encountered the predictable Juntan opposition, the reports began to diverge.

As customary, Governor Mendoza ordered that a record be kept of the ensuing correspondence with his military commanders and Father Páez. This would be the official narrative. But another witness who wrote about the events over the next year was Father Juan Sanz de Lezáun, who together with Fathers Manuel Ysidoro Abadiano and Páez entered La Junta at this time. His account was for his superiors, and in many ways it differs radically from the governor's version.[5] As tensions between the governor's party and the Juntans increased, the Franciscans found themselves precariously in the middle. Mendoza and his associates—always as recorded by Mendoza—became very hostile critics of anyone standing in their way. That included Rubín de Celís, the initial captain charged with the La Junta venture, and eventually Father Páez as the Franciscan leader. The lengths to which the governor and his men went and their patent sanitizing of their own actions strongly undermine their credibility at important junctures, although their accounts still provide important information.[6]

Second Lieutenant Juan Hidalgo, the commander of the detachment sent by Rubín de Celís to escort the Franciscans, wrote the usual military journal of their experience. He reported that they arrived at Cuchillo Parado with its Cholome natives on June 8, El Mezquite on June 10, and San Juan on June 11. The report of Cholomes at Cuchillo Parado is one more part of the ethnic puzzle there, where Rubín de Celís had identified people with Suma-Apache traits in 1750. Páez ordered Hidalgo's squad to remain at San Juan while he himself went ahead in order to smooth the way for their arrival at the river junction itself. Three days later Hidalgo's men moved to "near" San Francisco. Finally on June 15 they crossed over to Guadalupe, where Páez had arranged for some houses to be given over to store the troop's provisions and to house the women who had accompanied the soldiers. In view of their foreseen stay of at least three months, the military had brought along their wives. The choice of Guadalupe is one more indication that it had the most developed town structures.[7]

During the time he was at Guadalupe, Lieutenant Hidalgo heard that all the caciques and governors were saying that no presidio could be located in La Junta due to the limited land and the lack of pasture for the horses. When Hidalgo lamely replied, as he had been directed by Mendoza, that he was not establishing a presidio, rather solely serving as an escort to the Franciscans to protect them from hostile enemies, the people knew better. They responded that they had already heard in Chihuahua that a presidio was going to be built. Such news was hard to keep secret, and Juntans were always in Chihuahua. Up to that point, Hidalgo noted, things appeared calm.[8]

That was also the tone of Father Páez's report to the governor penned on June 20. He wrote that they had arrived on June 9 without incident and had been welcomed by the people. Placing Father Abadiano in San Juan and Father Sanz de Lezáun at San Francisco, Páez installed himself at Guadalupe. Noting that they were lacking some supplies, he remarked that they also had "worries about fears occasioned by the inconstancy of the Natives of these Missions as also by the unsubdued groups (*barbaros*) who were entering and leaving these places. Accustomed as they all are to live without being reined in by fear and respect, they are finding it strange to see the squad of sixteen soldiers in these lands." Páez repeated what he had stated to Mendoza back on September 2, 1754, that there existed suitable places at La Junta to establish the presidio.

Coming back to the worries he had mentioned earlier, he said that the Natives were convinced that a presidio was being planned "in their lands, within their towns," and that they wanted to continue with the complete liberty they had "in order to live in vices and laziness and mixed with the gentiles" without recognizing all the benefits that would come to them with a presidio. Paéz's decade of brief visits to La Junta did not appear to have endeared its people to him. He again recommended that the presidio be established, arguing that not doing so would result in a greater self-sufficiency (*abilantez*) of the Natives, discredit to the Hispanics, and the insignificance (*inconsecuencia*) of the Catholic religion. To underline this point, he added that about forty Apaches arrived to trade with the Hispanics, and that when they came near the convent they saluted him with the discharge of about twenty firearms. Then they went to the soldiers, trading about twenty mules for the same number of horses of the soldiers.[9]

Lieutenant Hidalgo's journal picks up the story at this point, expanding on the successive arrivals of Apaches. First to appear was the band of Pasqual, already noted as trading with the Juntans back in 1747:

> On the 21st, while I was sick in bed and nine of my men away guarding the horse herd, a large number of gentile Indians of the band of Pasqual, who was carrying a *bastón* [Spanish rod of authority] in his hand, entered the pueblo, arriving at the very door where I was lying ill. The Indians of the town said that the Apaches had come to sell meat and hides, which they did, and in the afternoon they crossed over to the other side of the Rio del Norte where I was told there were many Apaches.

Things became definitely more threatening the next day when the "enemy" Natagé and Salinero Apaches arrived with a display of power and disdain for the Hispanics that ended with defiant warmongering:

> Without giving the customary notice, on the 22nd, while I was still ill, there arrived another large number of enemy Apache Indians, Natajés and Salineros, with their two captains with rods of authority, well armed, all on horseback with short shotguns in holsters, some with pistols and swords, all with leather vests and no bows and arrows.[10] Formed in two rows and discharging their pistols and shotguns, without speaking they dismounted and began entering the houses to trade mules and skins for horses at the rate of one female or male mule for a horse. They also wanted to buy gunpowder and bullets, but I ordered on pain of death that no soldier

nor Christian Indian give or sell gunpowder, bullets, or weapons. Upset by this, the Natajé captain went to where my horse herd was located and arrogantly told its corporal to gather them together. That soldier said that only his lieutenant could give that order, upon which the Apache captain said that he knew all the soldiers and questioned what they were doing at La Junta, being as they were from El Paso. [Told that it was upon the orders of the governor of Nueva Vizcaya] the chief disdainfully went back to his people and crossed to the other side of the Rio del Norte, where it was known that there were more Apaches.

On the 23rd the Indians of the La Junta towns crossed over to the other side where those Apache captains and their Indians were in order to buy the skins and other things. Returning that afternoon, they told me that the Apaches wanted to attack and kill the soldiers and the women that we had brought. I replied that if the warrior Indians of Guadalupe and San Juan and San Francisco aided me, even though I was ill and had few soldiers they would see how I punished those Apaches for their audacity to say that they wanted to attack. But when I asked them to gather their people, they did not consent. Lacking their support, I did not attack, but neither did those enemy Indians.

Three days later yet another, but less threatening, group of Apaches described as Rayados and Vermejos arrived at Guadalupe carrying only bows and arrows and trading buffalo meat and pecans.[11]

The day after the arrival of the Rayado and Vermejo Apaches at the Guadalupe settlement, Father Páez summoned Lieutenant Hidalgo, still ill, to a meeting at his convent:

I found said Reverend Father in his room with the caciques, governors, and justices of all the La Junta towns. In Father Páez's presence they said that they did not want a presidio nor soldiers in their lands, that only the Reverend Fathers could be there, and that I could leave with the soldiers before the Apaches committed some offence. Hearing this and seeing the resistance and resolution of those caciques and justices, said Reverend Father ordered me to prepare to leave as soon as possible. I left July 1.

Thus, not wanting a presidio and once again facing a threat from other Indigenous nations for harboring Hispanics who hampered trading activities, the Juntans saw no recourse but to dismiss the Hispanic military while keeping the presence of the friars. Following Páez's instructions, Hidalgo only withdrew across the Cuesta Grande to "El Pueblito," the site previously called San Pedro, to await further orders or the arrival of Páez himself. The three Franciscans remained in the La Junta towns, but Páez finally arrived at El Pueblito on July 11, leaving Sanz de Lezáun and Abadiano at La Junta. He stayed with Hidalgo's men three days, and then left on the 14th with two companions to report to the governor. Páez told Hidalgo to remain at El Pueblito until he returned, but on the 28th the lieutenant received orders from Rubín de Celís to return to Chihuahua.[12]

Fathers Abadiano and Sanz de Lezáun were apparently left in the dark as to the Apache threats and the decision of the La Junta leaders to banish the Hispanic military. Páez probably did not want to leave them terrified with such news. In his written recollections, Sanz de Lezáun indicated that he had been very much caught off guard by the lieutenant's decision to depart so soon after having arrived, "giving for a pretense I don't know what dream or fiction—the beginning of the scheme."[13] The scheme to which he was referring was the one that the Franciscans later came to attribute to Governor Mendoza as events unfolded. As of July 1759, however, they had no suspicions. Upon Páez's return to Chihuahua on July 19, he handed Mendoza the letter he had composed back on June 20, that spoke only of worries about the inconstancy of the Natives, but he undoubtedly added a verbal update about what transpired afterwards. According to Mendoza, Paéz explained that he had not altered or added to his written account because he had not changed his mind about the importance of placing a presidio near La Junta. Consequently, the governor decreed that, "given that his Paternity [Páez] does not detect any effective inconvenience to the transfer of the troop" to La Junta, Rubín de Celís be instructed to set out with his company within twenty days—that is, by August 8—to found the presidio.[14]

Five days later Mendoza had a peremptory letter written to the La Junta general, Francisco Arroyo, and the governors, alcaldes, and captains, ordering them to come to meet with him in Chihuahua on August 9.[15] This would very conveniently, for the governor, place the Juntan leaders on the last stage of their journey to Chihuahua the day after the troops of Rubín de Celís departed for La Junta. In this way the Juntan leaders would meet the Spanish cavalry on the road near Chihuahua, far from any reinforcements from La Junta. But while the governor was waiting for the Juntans' response, Lieutenant Hidalgo and his men arrived back in Chihuahua. Hearing their stories and reading Hidalgo's journal, Rubín de Celís had misgivings about directing his men to La Junta without giving the situation more thought. After all, nine years previously he himself had experienced the difficulty of access to the La Junta valley and the presence of many nations on both sides of the Cuesta Grande.

On August 6, two days before Mendoza's deadline for the troops' departure, the captain wrote him recommending that time be allowed for a full and complete inquiry into the matter. He said that Father Páez agreed with him "and has explained himself in the same terms with myself and many other persons of considerable distinction." In order to deal as planned with the Juntans, he asserted, "skill and the right occasion and troop strength" were necessary. Rubín de Celís added that Mendoza should give no weight to the apparent disagreement between the report that Father Páez had given and Hidalgo's journal, since Páez had told him that the lieutenant's journal was true and had assured him that he had told the same thing to Mendoza, "even though in his [Páez's] report he had written differently due to who knows what influence or act of respect." Perhaps, the captain suggested, the Juntans would not resist if the presidio were placed a good distance from their towns.[16]

With that, Mendoza told Rubín de Celís to suspend the departure of his troops and sent Hidalgo's journal and Rubín de Celís's letter to Páez for his comments. Páez replied that Rubín de Celís had pointed out the same difficulties that Páez had. The Franciscan asserted that the captain should be able to work out whatever might need to be done in order to address those difficulties. Was Páez perhaps reflecting back on the captain's negligent performance at La Junta in late 1750, and thinking that the captain was shirking again? He pointed out that Rubín de Celís himself had previously urged the importance of placing a presidio at La Junta precisely in view of the difficulties now being noted. When it came to the captain's assertion that Páez had dissimulated in his written report, the friar practically sputtered with indignation:

> Does the military journal speak more truth than my report? Are the captain and his lieutenant more truthful than I? Where is the disagreement? . . . Could it be that the journal is an authorized testimony and my report some tall tale? In what inconsistencies does the captain find me so that he denigrates my person and state by affirming to Your Lordship that I vary in my recommendations, saying verbally [to so many] the contrary of what is in my report? I am not a military soldier for making military journals. . . . What I am is a minister working for souls.

Now, however, Páez added in written form the rationale for why the military squad had left La Junta, agreeing in his statement with that of the lieutenant. In doing so he gave further insight into his own reasoning: "Since I was coming to this town to inform you of the new events and of the inconstancy (*veleidad*) of the Indians and I had noticed the faintheartedness of the lieutenant, I feared that with my absence some mishap would occur" if the soldiers remained there.[17]

By August 13 the governor realized that the La Junta leaders were not responding to his summons. They were no fools and demurred from delivering themselves into his hands. Mendoza now had a major act of disobedience confronting him. To dispel that situation, he had a letter written, pre-dated to August 5, that ordered the Juntans to suspend their trip to meet with him until further notice. In that way it would appear that he had changed his mind days before the Juntans were supposed to arrive in Chihuahua. This would hopefully calm the Juntans' heightened state of alert over defying the governor by making it seem that he was unaware of their defiance. The letter was given to Páez to be delivered.[18]

The governor was not the only person concerned about the Juntans' reaction to his original summons. The two Franciscans still at the river junction later claimed that when they relayed Mendoza's first message to the Native leaders, the Juntans became very upset. The friars even offered to accompany them to Chihuahua as hostages—as ineffective as that probably would have been in assuring the Natives' safety. Fearing for their lives with the people so agitated and also lacking supplies, the two missionaries fled on August 12 in spite of the dangers of the journey. Upon arriving in Chihuahua, Sanz de Lezáun immediately went to explain the situation to the governor. He was not well received: "Since we priests (thanks be to God) are so well thought of by these gentlemen, they don't agree with anything." Shades of Father Varo's exasperated remarks a decade earlier.[19]

"The Theater Act Had Begun to Be Played Out"

Mendoza was now faced not only with the Juntan leaders' refusal to come but also the return of the fearful missionaries. He sent Father Páez, presumably with some persons to accompany him, to ascertain the situation at La Junta and hopefully calm the people.[20] Páez left on August 29 and did not return until September 22. He must have spent two weeks at the river junction, eventually succeeding in persuading a sizeable group of leaders to come to Chihuahua. Accompanying him upon his return were the governors and other Juntans, totaling about thirty in all. But General Arroyo was not among those present. According to Mendoza, the Juntan delegation demonstrated appropriate submission as he explained to them the advantages of having a presidio. Indeed, he recorded, "they happily consented, as long as they would not be adversely affected (*no se les perjudicara*) in their towns and lands that they need for their planting and maintenance, to which I agreed (*lo que les ofrecí*)." Thereupon the delegation returned to La Junta on the following day.[21]

On this occasion Páez delivered his own note to Mendoza, again urging that the plan for the presidio be carried out. According to the copy of the letter that Mendoza had entered into the record, Páez reported that he had not found the people disturbed. He asserted that the agreement of the Juntans to come to Chihuahua with him demonstrated this. In fact, Páez wrote that Pedro el Mulato had asked him if Sanz de Lezáun had given him Pedro's letter. Pedro told Páez that he had asked Sanz de Lezáun why the missionaries were leaving, as the Juntans had given no motive for it and everything was very calm, and had asked the missionary to send his regards to Páez. This Pedro el Mulato, who had served as an envoy fluent in Spanish in 1747, would play an important role as an ally of the Hispanics in subsequent events. Páez said that given the peaceful state of the Juntans, he had decided not to give Mendoza's pre-dated letter to them suspending their visit, but rather to bring their representatives to Chihuahua.

No explanation is given in the record for the alleged undelivered letter from Pedro el Mulato. Evidently Father Páez was as determined as Mendoza, if not more so, to make the long-desired presidio a reality. He too was not going to accept any more delay. Páez must have viewed Sanz de Lezáun as an unexperienced alarmist in regard to conditions at La Junta. He confirmed what Mendoza himself reported about the meeting that took place with the Juntans in Chihuahua:

> You know well that they themselves said in my presence that they were loyal subjects of His Majesty, as experience had demonstrated in the military campaigns and outings in which they had participated, and that what they refused and still refuse is that a presidio be placed in their own lands that they need for their crops. [The Juntans say:] let the Spaniards search for a place where the Juntans will not suffer damage. In view of this, it seems to me that the presidio should be placed where they are not negatively affected and yet are within sight, as I said in my report, so that these people once brought into line (*reducidos*) might live an ordered (*sociable*) life and not go wandering about in this town [Chihuahua] and the others of its jurisdiction. . . . At the same time this would remove the communication they have with the Apache nations that are frequently among (*assisten con*) those of the North.

Páez went on to say that the Juntans were opposed to the presidio "since they have lived a free life and find subjection a burden"; thus, the royal arms should be established "to contain whatever boldness those Sons might consider." He asserted that they said that Sanz de Lezáun and Abadiano had left them to get the provisions that they needed, and repeated that the Natives denied having given the priests any motive to declare that they had sensed a great change in the Juntans.[22]

These communications of Paéz, always as copied by Mendoza's secretary, clearly assert his determination to go against the Juntans' traditional autonomy and open trading economy. He wanted them well subordinated to the Spanish church and state. This included preventing their trade with those who were not Spanish allies, their traveling freely among Hispanic towns, and their following their own cultural mores. Yet he still had enough standing among their governors to get them to come meet the Spanish governor. If they had been able to read his note to Mendoza, he would have lost any authority that he had among most of them. He was advocating everything that most of them intensely resisted.

Things were not as simple as Páez wanted to make it seem, nor as those Juntans who came to Chihuahua with him were hoping. One has to ask why Páez had to spend two weeks at La Junta to persuade a delegation to go to Chihuahua with him. General Arroyo was still refusing to come. Much more resistance would be evident as events unfolded. But Mendoza now had the assurances he wanted, and indeed needed to have recorded on file. On September 27 he ordered that Rubín de Celís be notified to be ready to set out with his troops on October 5 to establish the presidio "in La Junta or the location that you find more suited and opportune, without negatively affecting the people in their towns and lands that they need for their fields." Those were his instructions for the official record. Events would prove that his verbal instructions were quite different. The presidio was to be given the title of Nuestra Señora de Bethlem y Santiago de las Amarillas. Two days later the governor wrote the Franciscan custos, still Father Castro, telling him to send as soon as possible the two priests that were lacking in order to have a missionary in each of the supposed five mission centers.[23]

Reflecting back on these events the following May, Sanz de Lezáun wrote that this second expedition of troops to set out for La Junta was preceded by "great conniving (already the theater act had begun to be played out)" by three principal actors in Chihuahua: Governor Mendoza, an "interim captain" named Manuel Muñoz, and Father Ángel López, the custos of the Zacatecan Franciscans in Nueva Vizcaya.[24] Here Muñoz, the future governor of the province of Texas, first appears on the historical stage of the northern frontier. It turns out that he was every bit as much of a manipulator as Governor Mendoza would prove to be. Mendoza must have recognized this affinity in Muñoz and set him up as his agent.

Up until this time Muñoz had never been even a soldier in the troops of New Spain. Born in the town of Matamoros in the archdiocese of Burgos in Spain, he had come to Mexico City as a 16-year-old. He spent six years engaged in commerce in the employ of Francisco Canal, who at that time served as a tutor to the Uranga sons from Chihuahua. It was probably this connection to that influential Chihuahua family that prompted Muñoz to move to Chihuahua in 1752 and establish his own trading company. He was a 29-year-old merchant in 1759 when Mendoza drew him into his schemes, elevating him abruptly into a career as presidio captain that would eventually lead to the governorship of Texas.[25]

Even though Mendoza dictated a message for Páez on September 29 about the troop departure, for some reason he did not hand it to him until October 3, merely two days before the set date. The note informed Páez that the Franciscans were to return to La Junta with the troops, and that Páez was not to leave the other two by themselves again. It also told him that the governor had written to Custos Castro about promptly sending two more friars. Mendoza added that he felt that Páez should tell Castro that, "on account of what I know, and you do not ignore," two more Religious should replace Sanz de Lezáun and Abadiano "since they do not seem appropriate for that destination."[26]

Mendoza brought to a close the voluminous set of documents compiled up to this point in regard to the establishment of a presidio at La Junta by listing the mission centers in the La Junta district along with their *visitas*, that is, the other places served from those centers:

1. The town of San Cristóbal, its *visitas* the town of Púliques and the town of the Cíbolos;
2. Nuestra Señora de Guadalupe—it does not have *visitas*;
3. The town of San Francisco, its *visitas* the little town (*pueblito*) of the Conejos

and the little town of the Tecolotes;

4. The town of San Juan de los Caballeros, its *visita* the little town of the Mezquites;

5. Town of San Antonio de Pueblito, its *visita* the little town of Cuchillo Parado.[27]

Since Mendoza had with him in Chihuahua the missionaries and the soldiers who had been in the La Junta district most recently, one would be inclined to judge this list as accurate regarding Native communities. But it reflected the "ideal" mission plan rather than the actual situation. Previous known documentation does not speak of any missionary residing at San Cristóbal since the 1726 revolt in the Coyame valley, even though an attempt was aborted in 1731 by the departure of the designated friar. There may have been one or two missionaries in the Coyame valley for at least a brief time before the summer of 1747, but it appears fairly evident that there were none after that. Two new items are the appearance of San Antonio de Pueblito in place of San Pedro at the Cuesta Grande end of the Coyame valley, and the association of the Conejos with San Francisco rather than with San Juan, as had been the case in 1747.

Supposedly four days after having closed this batch of documents destined for the viceroy, Mendoza added one more. He stated that it was the recommendation by Rubín de Celís back in August 1754 to build a presidio in La Junta on the lands of the San Francisco pueblo, where the presidio would thus be "within sight of" the La Junta towns.[28] In his cover letter on October 13 Mendoza explained to the viceroy, the Marqués de Amarillas, that he was adding this document "since I have noticed in him [Rubín de Celís] some repugnance, founded in pretexts about whether or not there is a place in the North for that construction, which is not what he believed in his earlier report. It will be him who will have to build it, something that it has seemed to me I should make present to you in view of what might occur."[29] What would occur would be the removal of Rubín de Celís from command. Was the governor now setting the stage for that move?

As described later by Sanz de Lezáun, when the captain's troops and the Franciscans arrived at the Álamo site at the base of the Cuesta Grande blocking the entrance to the La Junta valley, two emissaries from La Junta boldly (*con bastante denuedo*) confronted them, warning against the entrance of the troops.[30] Rubín de Celís was thus faced with the strong probability of having to fight his way into the valley. That was a daunting prospect, given the great difficulty of the terrain ahead that would not allow the use of the military's weapons to advantage. They had to first pass through narrow canyon walls for more than half a league and then over the Cuesta Grande and several crossings of the swollen Conchos River. The captain decided to retire to Coyame, with no note of any inhabitants there, and send for the governor's directions. Receiving this news, Mendoza sent back orders for the troops to remain at Coyame, but for the Franciscans to return to Chihuahua. The missionaries did so, "knowing the ill will we were likely to encounter" from the governor, arriving on November 8.[31]

The next day the governor wrote a letter to Páez and a separate one to Fathers Sanz de Lezáun and Abadiano. He was still counting on Páez as a possible ally. The letter to Sanz de Lezáun and Abadiano had a different tone, asking them various "impertinent questions repugnant to our dignity." When the Franciscans did not give the desired response, the following day the governor called Sanz de Lezáun to his presence and asked him more questions, behind which the friar detected the hidden intention of trying to trick him into saying something that would aid the governor's plans. Failing again, Mendoza invited all three Holy Gospel missionaries to "a splendid meal and some drinks" in an effort to weaken their alertness and resolve. Also attending were Manuel Muñoz, who was always in the governor's company on these occasions, and the Zacatecan custos. Muñoz would later employ the same wining-and-dining tactic to greater effect with Native leaders in La Junta. But it did not work with the friars. They smelled a rat, and it turned out that they were not wrong.

Realizing that he was making no headway, Governor Mendoza finally declared that the Fathers should return unaccompanied to La Junta so that if by chance there was any unrest among the Natives they could get them to accept the presidio. But, he said, they were to get some benefactor to provide what they needed for the trip; there would be no provision made for them by the governor. He assured them that he would see that their expenses be reimbursed later, but they no longer believed him. Meeting afterwards among themselves, the three priests decided to give no response to this "poisonous proposal." Even Páez realized by now that there was indeed major unrest at La Junta and that they would be possibly risking their lives going back there alone.[32] Up to this point Páez had been the governor's strongest ally and messenger. No longer. Now the disabused friar would also be on the governor's hit list.

A Presidio at Last, By Hook or By Crook

At the beginning of December the friars noticed preparations being made for some expedition and heard that it might be destined for La Junta.[33] When they asked Governor Mendoza what was happening, he said that they could make their own way to La Junta following the military, but financed by some benefactor as he had stated in early November. If they did not go, he had decided to name a friar from the Province of Zacatecas, Miguel González, as the pastor there and send other missionaries from that province. He asserted that he could do this as vice-patron, that is, as sharing in the viceroy's authority in church matters. Actually, he did not have the authority for assigning missionaries, as noted above in the case of Father Francisco de la Concepción González and Governor Cachupín of New Mexico a decade earlier. But aggressive governors like Mendoza and Cachupín assumed that they did and would brook no opposition.

Sanz de Lezáun replied that he and his companions would not stand for this, that they would be going even if it cost them their lives, and only asked to be told the day of the march. Mendoza shot back that he did not know the date, and that they could follow the troop movements. When Father Abadiano told the governor that evening that a friend had supplied some funds for the journey, the governor "let loose with so many shouts and offensive words that the poor man [Abadiano] was stunned." Sanz de Lezáun commented parenthetically: "said gentleman regularly offends everyone regardless of who they are, as all Chihuahua can swear." Mendoza's effort to rid himself of the friars in order to carry out his own designs at La Junta without anyone who might challenge him was now openly declared.

Promising never to bother "said gentleman" again, the Franciscans suspected that a group that left the afternoon of December 4 led by Captain Leizaola, the commander of the other cavalry company in north-central Nueva Vizcaya, was probably heading for La Junta. When they asked the Zacatecan Franciscan custos, he tried to mislead them, saying that it was leaving for Mexico City. No longer trusting him either, the three missionaries set out on their own for La Junta on December 5. They could find no mules for their supplies, since Mendoza had ordered the people not to provide them any. Only able to obtain three Juntans in Chihuahua to help carry their goods, they were forced to leave behind almost all that they had acquired. On their way that first day, they were overtaken by Muñoz, now Captain Muñoz, who also left Chihuahua the day after the advance party. Governor Mendoza had determined to remove Rubín de Celís from command of his military company and replace him with Muñoz, who was already proudly displaying his new baton as commander of the projected presidio.

Early the next morning, without alerting the missionaries, Muñoz left with his soldiers, leaving the Franciscans to catch up with him. One day during the journey the friars got into an argument with him over what had transpired in Chihuahua before their departure. Muñoz angrily denied that Mendoza had said what the friars stated, and yet declared that the governor had all the authority he claimed and more. Muñoz curtly told the missionaries that they always had the option of turning back to Chihuahua. "From then on," Sanz de Lezáun wrote, "we confirmed what we had previously thought about him; we now knew him as a declared enemy."

When the friars arrived at Coyame on December 14, where Muñoz had gone ahead with Leizaola to formally depose Rubín de Celís from his command, they were not allowed to visit privately with the disgraced captain. Páez was told by Leizaola, as the governor had said before, that the Franciscans could precede the military company into La Junta, so that they could calm the Natives if there was unrest among them. Seeking to avert a disaster, Páez asked Sanz de Lezáun if he was willing to come along with him, and the two agreed to cross over into the La Junta valley. They were accompanied by only four people: Lieutenant Juan de Luna of the Conchos presidio; Bartholo Porras alias Maoma, "former general" of the Juntans—actually commandant or lieutenant general in 1747 and 1750—who was now living near Chihuahua; Joseph Saldierna, the servant of Sanz de Lezáun; and an unnamed Juntan who had been assisting them.

From this point on the accounts of Governor Mendoza's military officers as copied in his official record contrast in essential ways from the recollections of Sanz de Lezáun. On the 16th the small embassy arrived at Los Mezquites, a village of about twenty families at that time, and encountered only an old woman who boldly stared at them. When asked by Porras in her own language where the others were, she said that they had all fled to San Juan, since the Hispanics were coming to kill them. As the priests' party drew near San Juan, eight mounted men in battle gear approached them. Seeing that they were the priests and relatively alone, they were allowed to enter. In San Juan itself all the men were armed, while the women hurried to prepare food for the visitors.[34] With difficulty the friars were able to calm the people.

The next day more than 500 armed Natives arrived on foot and on horseback. After holding a meeting among themselves, they came to the priests' residence, where they were told that the king had ordered that a presidio be established, but that they would not be harmed since it was to be placed at a distance from the towns. The people were told that to disobey the king was a serious offense and that if they did the friars could not defend them. The Juntans would not hear of it: "They reacted strongly with total resolution, shouting No! No! No! They would not allow it in their lands that God had given them. Let it be placed in El Cajón [60 leagues away up the Rio del Norte] or at Coyame!" The missionaries tried to assure them upon the friars' lives that neither they nor their lands would be harmed. But the Juntans were adamant that the troops' entrance would mean war, and upon departing spit on the ground.

The friars continued to try to persuade those who came to see them for the next two days, but they realized that it was useless and began to deliberate how to flee. They became more alarmed when on the night of the 18th more warriors began arriving, both Christian and pagan. When the women noticed the priests' party preparing to leave the next morning, they broke out crying, "Now it is certain that they are coming to kill us, since the Fathers are leaving." What was a missionary to do?!

> An old man called Mendilote who had been a general of the Juntans came in tears and crying out, pleading with my servant Saldierna that the Fathers not leave. With this uproar, I had the baggage put back, promising them that we would die with them. God willing, they calmed down. Don Juan de Luna decided to leave with Bartholo Porras alias Maoma and Pedro, the Indian mulatto of the town of Guadalupe. Already mounted, Bartholo Maoma told me: "Fathers, more news. These Natives are saying that many people are coming and without a doubt some will kill your Paternities. So let's go!" I replied with the crucifix in my hands: "If there are no Christians who would defend us, this Divine Lord whom I have in my hands will send angels from heaven to defend us. In no way will I leave, so that our Sons will see that if they die, we also die."

With that, the three mounted men left to tell the captains across the mountain ridge what was happening, while the two missionaries remained.

On reporting about this entry of the Hispanic emissaries into the La Junta valley, Leizaola recorded not a word about the turmoil and massive military buildup occurring there. Rather, he simply stated that he had sent these delegates to persuade the La Junta leaders to come meet with him in Coyame. He declared that those who came were not only Pedro el Mulato but also Juan Trinidad, governor of San Juan, and a few others from that same town. Muñoz wined and dined them, and Leizaola wrote that these Juntans agreed to having the presidio and asked to be allowed to go back to persuade the others to also come to meet with him.[35]

Sanz de Lezáun wrote that at this time the Hispanic troops moved up to the Álamo site at the base of the Cuesta Grande. Father Abadiano, who had remained with them as their chaplain, later told him that when the inexperienced Captain Muñoz was apprised of the war preparations by the Juntans and their allies, he wanted to enter the valley with guns blazing. Sanz de Lezáun asserted that if Captain Leizaola, a veteran soldier, had not opposed Muñoz, all the troops would have died as well as Páez and himself, because more than 500 warriors on high alert were above the canyon walls and along the very difficult mountain ridge blocking entry. Furthermore, all the women, children, provisions, flocks, mules, and horses in the Hispanic camp would have been left exposed.

Back at San Juan, Natives were entering and departing cursing the presidio without paying attention to the priests. The two missionaries spent the entire night trembling in fear, listening to the cries of war outside their dwelling. The next day they again tried to persuade the Juntans who would listen to them to allow the soldiers to enter and establish the presidio at what they thought was the selected place beyond the La Junta towns. They even offered their lives as a guarantee for their words. Some people from San Francisco and San Juan began to soften. According to Sanz de Lezáun, by the time that Lieutenant Luna and Pedro el Mulato reappeared the next afternoon, December 21 (he did not mention any other Juntan accompanying them), about sixty Natives had already been persuaded. Be that as it may, Pedro el Mulato—and the San Juan governor if Leizaola is to be believed—certainly must have at least helped to support that argument. On the 22nd Luna and Pedro el Mulato led those Juntans to "render their banners to the Royal Standard."[36]

In Leizaola's version of these days, again there was no credit, indeed not even any mention, given to the Franciscans at La Junta for influencing these Juntans. Rather it was all due to Leizaola's persuasion when they arrived at his camp and Muñoz's wining and dining and gifting again. Leizaola recorded the names and offices of those who met with him this second time. From San Francisco there was close to a full slate of officers—governor, cacique, fiscal who was also war captain, alcalde, and second lieutenant—and twelve others. San Juan had an even stronger list of officers—governor, cacique, three former governors, fiscal, second lieutenant, corporal, alguacil, former alcalde or fiscal, former alguacil—and twenty others. San Juan's associated settlements of Los Conejos and El Mezquite had an additional eighteen persons between them: the governors of both, three former governors of Los Conejos of whom one had also been cacique, a former governor and a former alcalde of El Mezquite, and eleven others.

In striking contrast, on the other hand, almost no one had come from the towns below the river junction. Guadalupe, the town of General Arroyo, had only three, and one of them was Pedro el Mulato, identified (accurately?) as cacique and former general and governor. Of the other two, one was a corporal. Judging by this minimal response from his own town, Pedro el Mulato obviously carried very little weight there on this occasion, if he ever had. There was absolutely no one from San Cristóbal or Púliques. The total was actually sixty-nine persons.[37] At first glance this was an impressive list for San Juan and its associated settlements as well as for San Francisco. Reflecting more carefully, however, it is long on officials acknowledged if not appointed by Spanish officialdom and thus possibly more aligned with them—governors, alcaldes, and fiscales—and short on native caciques and especially war captains.

Back in San Juan, more armed men were arriving, yet they doffed their hats as they passed by the priests. Meanwhile, Muñoz, "now thinking that he had a bird in the hand" with the Juntans who had submitted, marched to near the canyon mouth on December 23, a Sunday.[38] But he halted there when he was told that the canyon and mountain ridge ahead were crowned with Native warriors. According to the Franciscans, Muñoz was struck with fear and called for Father Abadiano to hear his confession, which the priest was not able to do "on account of the great uproar" (*alboroto*) at the time. Muñoz called for the Juntans in his camp to meet with him and swore to them upon the cross "that if the Juntans let him enter, his intention was to go travel around (*pasearse*) with the Fathers, in order to fulfil the King's command, and then leave." If he really swore to that, it is hard to believe that anyone accepted it.

For whatever promise and for whatever reason, the Juntan delegation went to see the insurgent general Arroyo, "a very brave Indian with a great following among all of them," and told him that, having received Munoz's assurance, they had pledged to help the troops enter. Not wanting to fight against their own, the La Junta defenders very reluctantly relented, but they cursed their submissive fellow townsmen and the presidio, shouting that the others had been deceived by wine and brandy and some blankets, and asserting that "once the presidio was inside they would rise up with their lands"—as in fact they did a few months later. With that, Muñoz led his troops over the Cuesta Grande and into the La Junta valley that same day of December 23, halting for the night at El Mezquite.[39]

Predictably, Leizaola's account as recorded by Mendoza had no mention of the insults hurled by the hostile Juntans upon their brethren who had allied themselves with the Hispanics. He did note that his troops were met at the Cuesta Grande by a hostile force, but only gave credit again to his persuasion and Muñoz's largesse in persuading sixty more Juntans who came to parlay with him to desist, not noting at all the decisive role of their fellow Juntans. Again Leizaola listed the names and offices of this second contingent of Juntans. From San Francisco were another cacique who was also a former general and governor, three other former officials, and seven others. San Juan was represented by an alcalde, two former officials, and seven others; Los Conejos four others; and Los Mezquites one former official and three others. What had to have especially relieved and gratified the Hispanic military were the twenty-eight from Guadalupe, including above all Francisco Arroyo—"cacique, general," who was also either governor or former governer and former captain—and five former officials. From San Cristóbal, however, there was only the governor and one other, and from Púliques only one.[40]

On Christmas Eve the Hispanic troops marched through San Juan, where the relieved Fathers Páez and Sanz de Lezáun went out to meet them, even though by this time the latter priest was "quite broken down" (bien accidentado) in health. Sanz de Lezáun wrote that he remained for the "three days of Christmas" with neither bread nor tortillas, only some chocolate bars. Abadiano, arriving with the troops, took up residence at San Juan, while Sanz de Lezáun went to San Francisco and Páez to Guadalupe. The troops, or at least their officials, took up residence at the convent of the Guadalupe mission at the invitation of Father Páez. Sanz de Lezáun wrote that on that day the majority of the Natives of Guadalupe fled and all of those at San Cristóbal, as well as the Púlicas, Venados, Pescados, and various families from a settlement next to San Francisco and others from San Juan. Thus, some Venados had indeed continued to reside at La Junta. This Christmas Eve was far from being a peace-filled night of Christmas carols. Centuries of Juntan autonomy had come to an abrupt end.[41]

A Presidio in the Heart of La Junta

The governor's orders as represented to Sanz de Lezáun had been to build the presidio in the large flatland outside San Francisco (as recommended by Rábago y Terán and Rubín de Celís). It was the friar's opinion that if this had been done, since those lands were three leagues long, things might have gone better. But Muñoz operated with the same tricks and deception he shared with his patron Governor Mendoza. Sanz de Lezáun's account of this key event demands quoting at length:

> The second day of Christmas [Muñoz] invited to a banquet the governor (governa-dorcillo) of Guadalupe, another leader called Mapuchí, and the mulatto Pedro with their women and children, who were all seated at the table and in the principal place. Father Páez, the minister of that mission, and Father Abadiano, who had been invited to sing the Mass of thanksgiving, were seated at the table abashed and embarrassed, seeing at the table and in the best place such [---?] agents, something that never had

been done among people of distinction. They [Muñoz's people] set about getting them drunk with toasts. Seeing that he had achieved what he intended, when they got up from the table the captain led them to the hill (*loma*) of that town, a shotgun blast (*tiro de escopeta*) away [from the convent]. There he made his measurements for the founding of the presidio. Since the Natives were inebriated, they went along with it. The two Fathers, seeing this disrespect for the people, and seeing that it was done without calling the three Fathers to see the plans for the presidio as was mandated, mounted horses and went to the San Francisco mission, where I was ill [to inform me]. . . . Finding himself without the Fathers on that hill, the captain went ahead making his lines for the presidio. The few Natives who had remained in that mission of Guadalupe together with the few from the other missions went to protest to the captain that this was not what had been agreed upon, rather that the presidio was to be placed at a distance from their towns and fields. Of what use was the oath he had made? From then on they would believe nothing that he or the Fathers said. If he made the presidio there, the few who had remained would go with the others who had risen up. Three times they made this demand, and he rebuffed them each time, but they bravely persisted. The following Sunday Captain Francisco Leizaola, having concluded his preparations, departed for Chihuahua as commissioner for the said presidio. He took Father Páez with him.[42]

To be noted in this report is that, according to Sanz de Lezáun, only alleged leaders from Guadalupe were invited. All three were Hispanophiles—certainly Pedro el Mulato, most probably the former governor Mapuchí (as shown by later events), and clearly the governor.[43] This latter was none other than General Arroyo's son-in-law, Ygnacio, as will become clear in later accounts, as will also the fact that he was definitely allied with the Hispanic military. He had most probably just been elevated to governor by Muñoz, thanks to his Hispanic leanings and his relation to the highly respected Arroyo, who was notably not present. Not to be missed either is the departure of Páez, to be discussed below.

In glaring contrast was the report by Leizaola as copied into the official record by Mendoza. Once again making himself the principal actor, Leizaola described a sober meeting, not a drunken banquet, on December 26, and had it including a much larger number of people. He listed twenty-four of them, adding that there were "many more who are listed elsewhere." This other alleged list is not in the Mendoza packet of documents. All but five of the listed names were already at Leizaola's disposal, appearing on the lists of the two delegations that met the Hispanic force on the other side of the Cuesta Grande. Leizaola (or Mendoza) could have simply copied these names from those previous lists.[44] Thirteen were on his first list, those who were the first to travel to render obedience to the invading troops, and thus presumably the most Hispanophile. One of the six names from the second list stands out: it was given simply as Francisco

Arroyo from Guadalupe, with no title. This was the most obviously false entry, since Leizaola himself went on to note that General Arroyo did not show up for this meeting. Three of those on this "approving" list now had different official designations than they had before the occupation of the valley by the troops. Apparently all three had been promoted by the Hispanic officials, two to governor and one to alcalde. One of these was the previously unlisted governor Ygnacio at Guadalupe, thus identifying him as Sanz de Lezáun's *governadorcillo*.

Leizaola noted the absence, besides that of Arroyo, of any from the Cíbolo, Venado, and Pescado nations. He stated that almost all those attending knew Spanish. Most patently lacking credibility, as demonstrated by events both before and after, was his assertion that this was a representative group of attendants who unanimously agreed to the presidio, with the understanding that their lands for planting would be left free. The identification of almost everyone on the list as a cacique, an office of leadership bestowed by Natives only, was an obvious effort to give legitimacy to the claim of this being a representative group. This fabricated version of the December 26 event, as recorded by Governor Mendoza, was clearly drawn up to justify the military officers' lying actions. Its obvious falsehood negates not only the validity of the sham consultation but also that of the captain's entire report as recorded by Governor Mendoza.

But that was not the only objective of Mendoza's rendering of Leizaola's "report" on this meeting. A major part of the captain's account was dedicated to relating damaging testimony by the Juntans against not only Rubín de Celís but also Father Páez. What Governor Mendoza and his henchmen wanted, they got, at least according to the official record. The report stated that the Juntans blamed all the discord and tumult prior to the entrance of the troops on the deposed captain and the missionary slated to be removed.

Allegedly asked for their reasons for not allowing Rubín de Celís to enter to found the presidio back in October, they were said to have brought up the widespread reports of his mistreatment of the Sumas while he was still in El Paso before 1752. They also said that due to him they were being blamed for the subsequent hostilities carried out by the Sumas and others.[45] Indeed, both these charges were true. The Juntans did have good reason to be very distrustful of Rubín de Celís, above and beyond their long-standing defense of their autonomy. Even if Leizaola and/or Mendoza fabricated much of the official record, the Juntans' negative sentiments in regard to Rubín de Celís were probably already well-known to Hispanic officials. But, astoundingly, there was not a word in this alleged testimony about the Juntans' opposition in principle to the presidio, whether Rubín de Celís was present or not. If one was to believe this account, their only problem was with the deposed captain. That left begging the question why, once Rubín de Celís had been removed from command, they had resisted Leizaola and Muñoz at the Cuesta Grande and why General Alonso and others were absent from this called meeting.

To answer that question, Father Páez was targeted as the sole cause of the continued opposition:

> They have had and have even greater distrust of Father Fray Joseph de Páez, since his reverence has given them bad treatment without having any love for them. Indeed, he has expressed and sworn to them that once the presidio was established there would not remain any Indian in the town [Guadalupe]. To that the governor of this town, Ygnacio, added more particularly that everyone was displeased with said Father Páez for harassing them, since besides the more than 300 pesos given him by our Lord the King (may God protect him) for his maintenance, he wants the Natives to contribute to him (as they have done with the little that they have) whenever he desires. And yet he is tepid in the administration of the holy sacraments due to spending most of his time in the town of San Felipe el Real, where he has a small shop where he sells what he takes from the Natives, that is, the hides that they give him and that he makes them acquire from the Apaches. When that does not happen he gets upset, mistreating the Natives by his words. Thus they point only to this obstacle to their better life, and would be happy with another missionary who is not said Father Páez, now that they are pleased to have Captain Muñoz who they say sits very well with them and with whom they have no mistrust. Therefore if said Father is removed, they will seek to have the General [Arroyo] and all the other Natives who have disappeared due to fear return to their towns. . . . For their total relief they ask that until Your Lordship [the governor] sends them a Religious to minister to them in their town, Father Páez be removed and Father Manuel de Abadiano minister to them and the soldiers, since they are satisfied with him.[46]

In this case, it should be noted that the newly installed *governadorcillo* Ygnacio was the one explicitly credited with testimony against Páez.

Just as with Rubín de Celís, there was some basis for the charges made against Páez. He did not esteem the Juntans; rather he criticized them and sought a presidio in order to impose Hispanic order upon them. Everyone including the Juntans knew that he was a champion of placing a presidio close by in their valley. He resided mostly in Chihuahua, not at La Junta. A lay representative (as required by Franciscan rules) undoubtedly sold hides in Chihuahua given to Páez by the Juntans, a practice between Juntans and Franciscans already noted in 1748. But the charges went way beyond that, to the point of absurdity.

Even if the natives disliked Paéz, they had continually received him without harm as he had been the only one to brave the dangers of the journey to La Junta to minister to them for a decade. Why would they be so resolutely ungrateful to him? Páez advocated a presidio in order to bring about more control over the Juntans; in no way would he have predicted to the people of Guadalupe that they would all be removed or flee from their town once the presidio was founded. The charge about financial misbehavior of the friar was a maneuver often employed by Spanish officials when opposed by missionaries.[47] Whether or not that was true of Páez, it was absurd to allege that his presence was the sole reason that Arroyo and the others had resisted and left the settlements. They could have done that at any time in the past decade.

Even more absurd was the assertion that they harbored no mistrust of Muñoz. How could they have such confidence in this neophyte captain after having known him for only a few days and when he had just seriously broken his oaths about the establishment of a presidio? Finally, the Juntans' alleged request that Father Abadiano remain with them until the governor sent a new minister betrays the fact that this declaration was at least doctored if not totally written after Sanz de Lezáun left La Junta at the end of January. Before that Sanz de Lezáun was actually the closest minister to Guadalupe from his post at San Francisco and he, not Abadiano, was actually ministering to Guadalupe after Páez's removal.

Only Leizaola and two Hispanics, and not a single one of the twenty-four Juntans listed by Leizaola who had been declared to be almost all Spanish-speaking, signed this document. Not even Pedro el Mulato, who had supposedly written the note to Father Páez earlier and in that case certainly knew how to write. Since this document was drawn up as a report and not an official record of testimony, strictly speaking it did not need any signature besides that of Leizaola. Yet realizing the document's actual legal import, the captain did have two Hispanics witness to it. But they were not the ones making the charges. Why was there no Juntan signature or, failing that, an X with the name written in, as occurred in many Spanish colonial documents among Hispanics themselves?

What was the real reason for the attack on Páez? Some motive for Juntan resistance had to be provided, since they were all allegedly happy with the presidio and its captain. Páez was the leader of the Franciscans who were witnesses to what actually occurred, and in particular to the charade carried out on December 26 by Muñoz and Leizaola at the behest of Mendoza. Páez was also the veteran missionary to La Junta, so he above all had to be discredited or at least removed from the entire affair.

No credence is due either to what Mendoza had transcribed as Leizaola's statement about the selection of the presidio site. It asserted that the Juntans themselves chose the location at a place that they assured Leizaola did not disturb their towns and fields. This was said to have taken place on December 28, two days after the "meeting" at which he supposedly obtained their agreement:

> They went out with me from this pueblo [Guadalupe], and at a distance of a fourth
> of a league [about two-thirds of a mile] upriver on the Conchos along the royal road
> they said that it was their desire that the presidio be built there since it was good
> land where they would not be adversely affected in any way, and indeed would be

convenient for them in having at hand the aid of the Spaniards and being able to help them against enemy Indians when they were asked to do so. They did this very happily, even though I proposed to them that it was my desire to do whatever they asked, even withdrawing the horse herd so that it would not disturb them, nor have soldiers in close proximity. To that they replied that I should do as I saw fit, and that they did not reserve even their houses, since already in the meantime that the presidio was being constructed they had lodged the soldiers in them.

The Juntans would never have accepted a presidio in the heart of their settlements, and Sanz de Lezáun noted above that it was actually even closer to Guadalupe. The fact that soldiers were lodging in the Juntans' houses was most probably without their voluntary acquiescence. The happy portrait being painted by Mendoza and his lieutenants would soon be exposed as counterfeit.

What Leizaola wrote about laying out the site, however, remains invaluable. He summoned Muñoz, and the two together agreed that the site was appropriate. Under the supervision of Joseph Saens Sagardia, who was in charge of the actual construction, they immediately set about marking off the presidio lines. This event, on whatever day or however it occurred, was the beginning of the Presidio del Norte, today's Ojinaga. Leizaola provided very specific detail:

> One hundred thirty-four varas on the front from north to west (*de frente de norte a poniente*), squaring off equal distances on the other sides, with the main gate (*puerta*) facing north-northeast. Additionally, to the back of the square and next to it another one hundred three varas in width with the same one hundred thirty-four varas in length for the presidio's corral. The presidio faces the junction of the Norte and Conchos Rivers a half a league away in their lowland (*ancon*). The left corner of the presidio's front has the Río Conchos to the west, the middle of the front line faces the town of San Francisco at a distance of about a league, and from the right corner the town of Nuestra Señora de Guadalupe lies a quarter of a league to the east. Both of those towns are within view of that location, from which one sees all the splendid [*sic: explendido*, probably the transcriber's error for *extendido*, outspread] terrain, sufficient (*capaz*) and in a place suitable for its protection. And in consequence of this having been executed with no opposition from the natives previously named, we the two captains ordered that beginning tomorrow the 29th of this month the work on the fort begin.

Again only the Spanish officials signed this document. This time its writer was careful to point out that "the Natives did not, saying that they did not know how." Believe that as one sees fit.[48]

The great irony in all of this was that the Franciscans' repeated demands for military protection ever since 1715 were finally met, but by placing the presidio where they had warned that it would not be accepted. The Juntans and their Native allies had mobilized impressively to prevent such an occurrence, and only very reluctantly and in order not to engage in battle with their own had they given in to the Hispanic officials' hardly credible protestations that they were not coming to establish a presidio. The friars' predictions that the Juntans would flee was borne out by the towns below the river junction. Now the die was cast, by governor and Juntans alike.

Autonomy Unbowed, 1760–1786

These Norteños provided us a considerable increase to our forces, thanks to their fighting prowess and the enmity with their neighbors the Natagés that was introduced among them, ever since the first attacks in which they acted in unison with the troop of the presidio with the heroic deeds reported in its journals.

—The Marqués de Rubí to Viceroy Croix, 1768

They give repeated motives for suspecting that, when they do not join the Lipan Apaches in hostilities, they serve as spies for them or alert them to the state of our settlements and the movement of the troops.

—Viceroy Conde de Revilla Gigedo, 1793

The placement of a presidio in the heart of their settlements did not destroy the Juntans' determination to be an autonomous people. An armed uprising put down with the aid of troops from throughout Nueva Vizcaya was followed by the flight of many to Coahuila, where they managed to establish a relative autonomy within the mission system there. When those who remained in their homeland despite their unhappiness with the military's presence were removed along with the presidio in 1766, most of them fled to join their compatriots in Coahuila. The few who remained in Nueva Vizcaya, almost none at La Junta itself, often continued to act as prized military allies and scouts with the Hispanic forces, as they had for a century. Their relatives in Coahuila were highly valued by the military there for the same reason, even as all of them continued to be viewed by outside officials as treacherous allies due to their continued trading relations with Apaches. This new era of geographic relocation and cultural preservation begins with the dramatic events of 1760—the Juntan equivalent of "the year 1680" among the Pueblo Natives of New Mexico.

The Lies Unravel: Juntan Flight
In a memo written to Governor Mendoza by Captain Leizaola on December 28, the

same day that he recorded the marking off of the presidio site, some of the real state of affairs began to be acknowledged in writing. At first it is surprising that the governor included this memo in the official record to be sent to the viceroy, in view of his party's previous machinations and proclamations of the happy receptivity of all the Juntans. But the captains and the governor had to deal with the actual reality, and the memo admitted it. Leizaola requested more soldiers and laid out the reasons why. Even though he claimed that the people of Mezquite, San Juan, Conejos, San Francisco, and Guadalupe were all supportive—still a major overstatement—he reported that the Hispanic force was exposed to the east and north.

That was because the people of San Cristóbal, Púliques, and Santa Cruz [?] did not respond to the summons to assist at the founding of the presidio. In fact, they were opposed to it, and had withdrawn and joined the Pescados, Venados, and Cíbolos, all of whom were allied with the "enemy" Apaches. Those Apaches were the bands of Pasqual, el Lijero, Sebastián, Alonso, the Natagés, and other chiefs. In view of this, Leizaola asked that thirty more cavalry be sent to La Junta to join the fifty already there.[1] Several of the Apache groups named by Leizaola were traditional trading partners of the Juntans and would logically ally with them against Hispanics. All of them had already been recognized at La Junta in 1747 except Sebastián, and some had actually been living at La Junta, especially if Alonso was the Alonzo el Baptizado at Púliques that year.[2]

The captain must have hand-delivered this memo to Mendoza at the same time as the two reports about the meeting with the Natives and the site selection for the presidio.[3] With Father Páez in tow, Leizaola arrived in Chihuahua by January 2. On that date Páez in Chihuahua wrote his provincial that Mendoza was trying to replace the Holy Gospel Franciscans at La Junta. The governor had had several conversations to that effect with the Jesuits, even summoning to his presence their Father Visitor, who at the time was passing through the mission of Coyáchic to the west of Chihuahua. But the Jesuit official was well informed and told Mendoza that La Junta was a mission district assigned to the Franciscans and that the friars had not been remiss there.[4]

Rebuffed by the Jesuits, Mendoza notified the viceroy in mid-January that Leizaola had removed Páez from La Junta, and that he had approved this action. He defended it as indispensable in order to satisfy the Juntans and offered Leizaola's trumped-up report as demonstration. Not yet revealing to the viceroy his desire to replace the Holy Gospel Franciscans altogether, Mendoza wrote in such a way that he would not only be rid of the other two Franciscan witnesses to all that had transpired in 1759 but also open a door to having the Franciscans he wanted and in the way that he wanted:

> Nor do I find it convenient or apropos that the Reverend Fathers Fray Juan de Lezáun and Fray Manuel de Abadiano remain, the one due to his age, the other due to being ill. So I ask that Your Excellency in your kindness request that the Very Reverend

Father Commissary General destine for those five missions that number of robust Religious who are hardworking, understanding well that with the alms that they receive from the King they have to maintain and vigilantly attend to the cultivation and benefit of the souls of those townspeople without thinking of other interests.... He should appoint one of those five as Custos.[5]

With a person like Mendoza, one has to read between the lines. He was no longer requesting different missionaries from the custos of the San Pablo Custody, nor even from the provincial of the Holy Gospel Province. Rather he wanted to bypass that province of Franciscans altogether by having the viceroy directly address the Franciscan Commissary General, the head of all the Franciscans in New Spain. This would make possible a request that Franciscans come from their Zacatecas Province whose members served all the other Franciscan missions in Nueva Vizcaya. As previously noted, the governor and the Zacatecan custos in Nueva Vizcaya were co-conspirators. Mendoza was also hedging his bets by requesting that the missionaries assigned to La Junta be given their own custos. If perchance he had to remain with Holy Gospel friars, then at least he could deal with them through a custos in his own playground of Nueva Vizcaya, rather than having to deal with the custos in El Paso outside his jurisdiction.

Meanwhile, Captain Muñoz at La Junta had written Mendoza on January 12 that he had tried to coax back the Juntan general Francisco de Arroyo. But in spite of handing out daily gifts at La Junta, "he observed rumblings among the people, begotten by the unsettled and rebel spirit of General Arroyo."[6] Fathers Sanz de Lezáun and Abadiano remained in the valley but wrote that the honor of their word among the Juntans had been left in shambles by the treachery of Mendoza's party:

> The Indians that had remained threw in our faces the oath the captain had made, as well as the word that we had given them that the presidio would be placed ... at a distance from the towns. In the future they would not give us any credit, no matter how much we preached to them. It was a total contempt. I went back and forth to the mission of Guadalupe [since Páez was gone] to give them Mass even although very broken in health. I had various run-ins with the captain [Muñoz], both on account of the presidio and because he told me that we missionaries had a precise obligation to minister to the soldiers and that they were exempt from paying religious fees, that the King paid us missionaries for this; to which I responded all that was pertinent to the many faculties that he claimed to have.[7]

In a letter written on January 15 Sanz de Lezáun added that the Natives were exasperated not only by the building of the presidio in their midst but also by the damages being caused to their crops by the cattle, sheep, mules, and horses of the military.[8]

Governor Mendoza was right about one thing: the health of one of the missionaries. Sanz de Lezáun himself wrote that by this time he was totally broken down and completely without sustenance. Mendoza had seen to it that they were unable to bring any substantial supplies with them in December. Apparently they were getting no help from Muñoz, who nevertheless demanded that they minister to his soldiers without recompense. Sanz de Lezáun also said that he was threatened "at every step" by both the insurgent Natives and those who had remained. Perhaps he was being too alarmist, but circumstances had changed dramatically. He determined to leave when the supply train that came in late January returned to Chihuahua. Notifying Muñoz so that the captain would tell him when the pack train was departing, he was told that it would pass through San Juan on January 27. Accordingly, Sanz de Lezáun went there on that day, joining Abadiano, the resident missionary. But he found himself still waiting the following afternoon. The friars finally found out from some passing muleteers that Muñoz had severely charged the pack train operators to go by a different route through La Mula, thus avoiding San Juan. Having learned from the muleteers that they were going to halt for the night at the Boca Grande, Sanz de Lezáun and his two servants set out after them, reaching them at 11 p.m. The next day they made their way over the mountain ridge, and they finally reached Chihuahua around February 5.[9]

That left Father Abadiano on his own at La Junta. The presidio construction went ahead, not without difficulties, and the attitude among the Juntans only worsened as it impacted their lives and livelihood. By February 21 Muñoz dropped any further pretense of calling them friendly. He wrote Mendoza that despite all his good efforts, "as they are people who are not thankful for the benefits we offer them, I need and am obliged to proceed with caution, having detected that through some persons the Indians that appear obedient are communicating news of what is happening with the rebels, with messages going and coming from one side to the other." Upon receiving this news and learning that those Natives still at La Junta "are deserting daily and withdrawing to the open country and mountains, joining those already dispersed," Governor Mendoza ordered that Muñoz publish Mendoza's decree that if within a month they returned to their towns they would be treated well, but if they did not, war would be waged against them.[10]

Writing from Chihuahua on the same day that Muñoz sent his decree to La Junta, Sanz de Lezáun stated that even in San Juan, where Abadiano had remained, half of the natives had departed. Two months later Abadiano himself came down to Chihuahua. On May 2 he wrote to his provincial that even though in La Junta he was surrounded by dangers and without food, he had intended to return there, newly provisioned, but was being prevented by Mendoza. The governor was asking the Zacatecan Franciscans to provide missionaries for La Junta.[11] Sanz de Lezáun, still in Chihuahua at that time, added to the picture. He affirmed that Abadiano had come to get supplies once Lent had passed. Abadiano also told him that he had made the very dangerous eighty-league journey on his own due to the great disrespect shown him and the Church by Muñoz.

A soldier at La Junta had tried to desert, and Muñoz preempted the porter's lodge of the convent at Guadalupe as a guardhouse. Abadiano, who perhaps had moved to the Guadalupe convent by then, protested to no avail. When the soldier managed to escape and take refuge in the church, Muñoz paid no attention to the right of sanctuary. At issue was the legal right of avoiding arrest by claiming asylum in a church, a right still considered sacrosanct at that time.[12]

Disgusted, Abadiano had left for Chihuahua. On May 5 two Religious of the Franciscan Province of Zacatecas appeared in Chihuahua to take over the La Junta missions at the order of the governor. Mendoza was determined to see his plan through. By then Abadiano together with Páez, who had somehow managed to remain in or return to the area, had provided themselves with supplies and made known their intent to go back to La Junta. But Mendoza sent them notice that if they tried to enter, he would send soldiers to intercept them and bring them back tied to the tails of horses. Sanz de Lezáun, the source of this information, was unaware of how this episode turned out, since he himself planned to leave for Mexico City on May 11, still trying to recover his health.[13]

As Father Saavedra had predicted over a decade earlier, so it had come to pass. With the presidio placed in the midst of the La Junta villages, most of the people had fled. On July 11 Muñoz wrote to Mendoza about the state of the presidio construction and his difficulties with the Natives who had been put to work on it. The laborers were drawn from La Junta, the Cholomes, and the Tarahumaras:

> There are forty-two houses on lots [*en soleras*] for the soldiers. That comes to forty-four with two more that were added with their hall and corral along the interior circumference of the wall. Six more that I hope will be in the same state tomorrow make fifty. After that we will continue with the rest of the number until they are in proper shape. Then we will continue the roofing, which has not been possible due to the scarcity of carpenters. There are forty-two natives of La Junta and Cholomes at work on this. They tend to slack (*fallar*), nevertheless they serve as relief since some of the Tarahumaras are ill and others have fled without our being able to remedy it. Out of the last forty that the justice of Cusiguiriachi sent, twenty-six have gone. And that is even though we are guarding them. So I and the soldiers are on high alert, but with no clear remedy with which we can stop their flight.[14]

No wonder that the Jesuit visitor to the Alta Tarahumara the following year recorded a significant population decline among the mission centers there, with many persons having fled the labor exactions.[15]

Counterattack and Reprisal

On the same day of July 11 that Muñoz wrote about the presidio construction, he also reported that seventy-one of the Juntans had returned, as well as the Cholome general with his people who had been raiding in the region. Muñoz was told by a Native who came for horses that the rest of the Juntans were on their way with General Arroyo. He assigned the Cholomes the place named Los Tecolotes for their residence. With these returnees the insurgents repaid Muñoz's deceit in kind. The Spanish troops had to be extremely grateful that the walls of the presidio had been completed by July 22, since at dawn that day General Arroyo and the Cíbolo general attacked with hundreds of Natives from the La Junta towns and the Apaches. According to the young private Narciso Tapia, there were 800 attackers; according to Muñoz, more than 200. The private's eyes may have grown large at his first large-scale combat; on the other hand, Muñoz may have still been trying to minimize the degree of opposition. Muñoz wrote that the battle lasted two hours, Tapia that it lasted about an hour. Seven Natives (Tapia: nine) were killed, all from the towns below the river junction, and more than sixty wounded before they fled. One Hispanic soldier died and four others were wounded. During the fight Fathers Páez and Abadiano, who had returned by then, were in Guadalupe pueblo with three soldiers guarding them. Those soldiers said that throughout the battle the Fathers were in the church prostrated on the floor, praying with their arms extended in the form of a cross.[16]

Immediately after the attack, Muñoz wrote Mendoza with the stark news that the only Juntan leaders who remained with him were Ygnacio the governor of Guadalupe and his family, Pedro Mulato and his family (also of Guadalupe), "Chepe" from Guadalupe and his family, and Joseph de la Cruz of San Francisco and his family.[17] The first two men were the ones whom both Sanz de Lezáun and Leizaola had identified as agreeing to where the presidio was located. Pedro el Mulato and Joseph de la Cruz were members of the first Juntan delegation at Coyame that championed the troops' entry into the valley. These men, therefore, had already cast their lot with Muñoz, and there was no turning back.

The defeated Juntans took to the mountains again with their families, both up and down the Rio del Norte. Muñoz sent for even more troops. Given the depleted military in Nueva Vizcaya, it took a while to gather them. At the beginning of September one hundred soldiers led by Lieutenant Manuel Gómez de la Torre arrived.[18] The augmented troops headed up the Rio del Norte on September 7, being told by Native spies that ahead were the "insurgents"—more like refugees—from the towns above the river junction: San Francisco, San Juan, Mezquite, and Conejos. On September 8, more than eleven leagues from the presidio at the ford called Agua Ruidosa, they captured thirteen Juntans without any shedding of blood. The other Juntans on the mountain heights at first prepared to fight, but the prisoners asked for truce terms. At that, the Native justices came down from the heights and, after all the Juntans conferred among themselves, proposed that if they were pardoned they would return to their towns and surrender the instigators of the uprising. Since this arrangement was in keeping with what Governor Mendoza had ordered, it was accepted. The colonial troops returned downriver to pitch camp across from Guadalupe the next day. They remained there three more days ferrying supplies across the swollen river.

The surrendered Juntans had also allegedly agreed to help locate General Arroyo's campsite downriver from La Junta. Spies under the Guadalupe governor Ygnacio finally located them beyond the Boquillas canyon. After a pitched battle on both sides, Muñoz and De la Torre reported 177 insurgents captured. This number was not quite as impressive when later described by the soldier Tapia as forty-seven warriors and more than one hundred women and children. Generals Arroyo and Joseph el Cíbolo were urged to surrender by the Natives who cut off their flight, including Ygnacio, who was identified at this point as General Arroyo's son-in-law. Refusing to do so, the two were killed along with five to nine others. Their heads and the right hand of Arroyo were severed. Tired and concerned about guarding such a large number of prisoners and the horse herd, the officers decided not to advance against the camps of the Cholomes, Venados, and Cíbolos but rather to return to the presidio. After this, according to Tapia, all the other insurgents began to submit, with the exception of the Cíbolos who took refuge in Coahuila in the mission pueblo of San Antonio [sic] de Peyotes.[19]

This choice of refuge by the Cíbolos was to be of major consequence for the Juntans. Dulce Nombre (not San Antonio) de Peyotes was about ten leagues to the west of the Presidio of Rio Grande. In 1737 the San Francisco de Vizarrón mission for Pausanes was founded one-quarter league—two-thirds of a mile—to the east of Peyotes.[20] This Rio Grande mission area in Coahuila had already become familiar to some of the Natives in the Julimes district in Nueva Vizcaya. This is known from events in 1754–1755, when some Natagés and Cíbolos who asked to settle with lands of their own were given a new mission at a place called San Yldefonso, between the Peyotes-Vizarrón missions and the new town of San Fernando de Austria to the north-west. The Native leader was Joseph Antonio Carabeo, a supposed Christian who spoke fluent Athapaskan and Castilian. The friar at the new mission soon concluded that many of those who actually entered it were "ladinos and deserters from the missions of Julima [sic]." After ten months they burned the church and went to live with three Apache bands in the mountains nearby.[21] Thus some Apaches and Cíbolos with experience in the Julimes district were already aware of settlement possibilities in the upper Rio Grande area of Coahuila. This helps to explain why refugee Cíbolos made that Peyotes-Vizarrón mission district their destination in late 1760. They would not be the only ones.

After the punitive Hispanic expedition arrived back at La Junta on September 17, the justices of the towns there were told to prepare their people for the taking of a census. It was carried out September 20–23 (see table 6). The following day ninety-two people—children and adults—were marched off as prisoners to the governor in Chihuahua from the Álamo site across the Cuesta Grande. Clearly the four

Figrure 11: Rio Grande settlements of Coahuila in the 1750s. (Courtesy of the Benson Latin American Collection, LILLAS Benson Latin American Studies and Collections, University of Texas at Austin)

towns above the river junction had benefited from the pardon that they received on September 8. Of the 483 persons in total, not counting the prisoners, 384 were from those communities.[22] Only sixty-five were at Guadalupe, with less than 40 percent considered loyal to the Hispanic occupiers. San Cristóbal and Púliques were practically depopulated at this time. The greater compliance or submission of the towns above the river junction compared to the greater defiance and resistance by those below it had been manifest ever since the initial standoff on the other side of the Cuesta Grande before the entrance of the Spanish troops.

Table 6: La Junta Census, September 1760

San Juan	189	
Los Mezquites	45	
Los Conejos	72	
San Francisco	78	other families still among the insurgent Cholomes and Cíbolos
Guadalupe	65 (only 27 considered loyal to Hispanics)	various families still fugitive
San Cristóbal	19	
Púliques	7	
Cholomes	4 in the same family	
Conejos	4 in the same family	
TOTAL	483	
Prisoners sent to Chihuahua	92 adults and children	

Governor Mendoza was jubilant upon receiving the news of the suppression of the uprising on September 26. Bishop Pedro Tamarón y Romeral of the Durango diocese was in Chihuahua at the time, near the middle of his twenty-one months' pastoral visit of the vast northern section of his diocese that embraced all the provinces on the northwestern frontier except Baja California. The bishop and the local clergy happily obliged Mendoza when they were asked to have the church bells pealed to announce and celebrate the event. The traditional *Te Deum* of thanksgiving was sung in the parish church, and the next morning a Mass of thanksgiving was celebrated, again at the request of the governor. On the morning of September 29, the shackled and chained-together Juntan captives arrived in Chihuahua, just before the bishop departed the town to visit the missions to the northwest of Chihuahua as far as the Cosihuiriachi district on the eastern edge of the Upper Tarahumara country.

At the mission of Santa Ysabel on September 30 Bishop Tamarón was received in the church by none other than Father Abadiano, since the resident missionary, Joseph Trujillo, had gone the night before to meet the bishop at a hacienda several leagues distant in order to escort Tamarón to the mission. The visitation journal noted that Abadiano, even though a missionary at La Junta, "had come to help" Father Trujillo. The bishop, Abadiano, and Trujillo must have had quite a conversation, since by now Trujillo was the new custos or director of the Franciscans of the Zacatecan Province in Nueva Vizcaya. That may have been precisely why Abadiano had come to that mission, that was outside the route to Chihuahua, in view of the intrigues of Governor Mendoza attempting to impose his own will on the missionary presence at La Junta.[23]

Tamarón's conversations with Abadiano and others during this trip clearly impacted his views on both the governor and the Juntans. This was evident by his actions and his words when he returned to Chihuahua for the greater part of October. Wanting to intercede for the Juntan prisoners, he encountered the Mendoza that everyone else knew:

> A good portion [of the Juntans] in the acclaimed victory were seized with their arms crossed without making any defense and yet locked up in the Chihuahua prison to suffer much hunger. Having compassion for them, and knowing how they had given themselves up, I wanted to plead for them to the Governor, since I was told that they were crying out in the prison that they were loyal and good Christians. I wanted to ask that they be distributed among other Native towns, or that we discuss giving them some relief, but once he began to hear my topic he blew up and was so indisposed that I stopped and did not dare to continue.[24]

No one, not even a bishop, should suggest that Mendoza ever reconsider anything.

One of Tamarón's principal reasons for his extensive pastoral visitation was that he shared the opinion that the increase of Native raids was due to the reduction of the presidios carried out a few years earlier. He wanted to gain firsthand credible information in order to appeal to the king to strengthen the frontier defenses.[25] On October 28 and 29 he visited the mission towns along the lower San Pedro River near its junction with the Rio Conchos. The situation farther north toward the La Junta district was still too volatile to consider traveling there. He was not able to visit Julimes on the other side of the swollen Rio Conchos a little north of the river junction but was informed that the village had only seven families of Concho natives, with fifty-two persons in all. Its Hispanic inhabitants had abandoned the town due to its exposed position in "a land very at risk from enemies who are desolating it rapidly." The missionary at Julimes also cared for San Pablo a few leagues up the San Pedro River from the junction. San Pablo had eight Native families but a total of only thirty-six persons. Yet in between Julimes and San Pablo there were fifty-two Hispanic families and a total of 454 persons.[26] The lower San Pedro district had clearly become dominated by Hispanics with their haciendas.

Bishop Tamarón then visited the districts of San Francisco de Conchos, Parral, and the Lower Tarahumara zone. By then he had heard enough opinions criticizing the installation of the presidio at La Junta to write to the viceroy, retracting his uninformed praise three months earlier:

> I have been generally informed by captains and persons of intelligence that it is not good to have the Presidio of Las Juntas in the site of Bethlehem [*sic*: he switched the fort name with that of the place] and that it has been the cause of the loss of those towns and of seeing its unhappy Natives offended, some in the mountains, others who returned, not a few who go about conducting hostilities, and a good portion who in the acclaimed victory were seized with their arms crossed without making any defense.[27]

In organizing his voluminous notes in mid-1765 into a major report on his pastoral visits, the bishop reflected further upon the presidio at La Junta. He thought that the presidio would be much more useful near Julimes, where it could defend the San Pedro River towns and more quickly come to the aid of the Chihuahua vicinity, while still being able to reach out to La Junta. He added that there would be lands available for soldiers and horses near Julimes, leaving the Juntans able to benefit from the little good land that they had and "freed from many pressures that can have very bad results"— as the year 1760 had demonstrated.[28] Viceroyal authorities would come to the same decision in 1766 but reverse it only a few years later. These successive Spanish shifts in strategy would completely undermine the centuries-old presence of the Juntans as a people in the region.

Autonomous Refugees

The events of late 1759 and 1760 marked the conclusion of seventy-seven years of a unique experience between Natives and Hispanics on the northern frontier of New

Spain. During those eight decades the Juntans had managed to maintain their political and religious autonomy in their relations with Hispanics by participating in a system of long-distance migrant labor and serving as military allies while welcoming only Franciscan missionaries to their river valley. Upon the installation of the presidio in their midst, the Juntans who still remained there were finally subordinated—but not ultimately. That is because Cíbolos were not the only defeated Natives to seek out a relatively autonomous new location within the Rio Grande country of Coahuila.

Father José Antonio Rodríguez happily received a group of refugees at his San Francisco Vizarrón mission in January 1761. Ever since its lands were greatly enlarged in 1753 to encompass fifty *sitios de ganado mayor y menor por mitad*, he had been hoping to entice "some non-settled Christian Indians without any home property" to help make it more productive. That was the radically new situation of the forty-six refugee families comprising 160 persons whom he described as "terrorized by the Spanish military," who gratefully accepted his offer that month. In May another thirty families from the same people arrived, probably bringing their total number close to 300. Much later, in 1793, Viceroy Conde de Revillagigedo reported that the fugitives who entered the Vizarrón mission were Julimes, Venados, Cíbolos, Norteños, and Cholomes from Nueva Vizcaya.[29] Other than the Julimes, those were nations resident at La Junta since 1750 if not much earlier, and noted in 1760 as refusing to submit to the Hispanic forces in the La Junta valley.[30] That fits with the fact that those were the townspeople who were notably missing in the census taken in the La Junta valley after the defeat of the belligerent Natives.

The mention of Julimes among these refugees, whether they were among the first to arrive or only came later, is a reminder that for more than a century Juntans had been passing through this town, the closest to them on the Rio Conchos, in their migrant journeys. The town's sacramental registers show the original Julimes people being replaced by Apaches by 1729—probably very young captives taken into Hispanic households—and groups on the outer edges of the La Junta district, particularly Cholomes. Coyame and Cuchillo Parado began appearing in the Julimes records as specific origin sites in the mid-1730s. In 1751 the groups with the largest number of sacramental entries were the Tarahumaras and those "from el Norte," followed by the Apaches and the Cholomes. The overall impression after 1728 is of an original Julime population giving way to immigrants from the greater La Junta district and Tarahumaras, along with "home grown" Apaches.[31]

Given this strong connection of Natives at Julimes with those in the La Junta district, it is probably not just a coincidence that with the defeat and flight of the Natives in the La Junta district those at Julimes also began to disappear, while the Hispanic population rebounded dramatically. Between 1761 and 1767 only ten Native children were baptized at Julimes, and the only two given an ethnic identification were Tarahumara. During the same period ninety-four Spaniards and sixty mixed-bloods

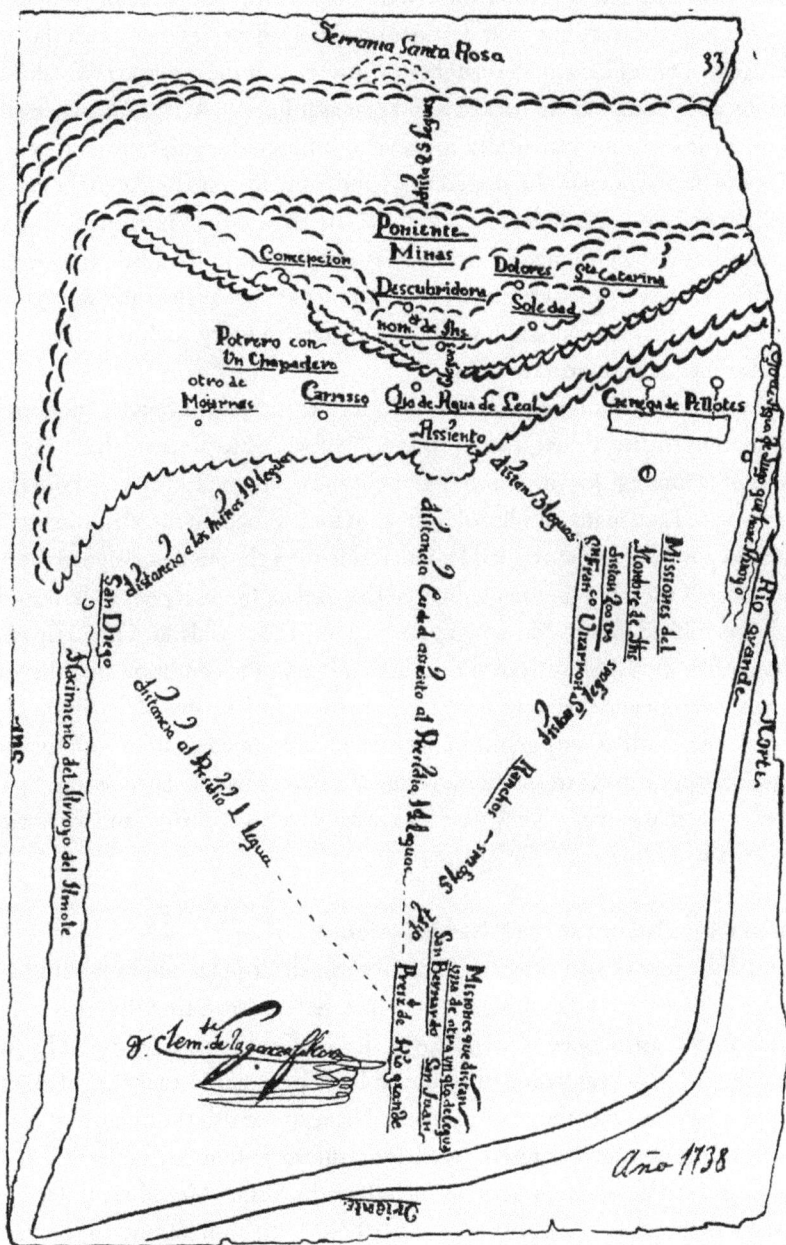

Figure 12: The Peyotes-Vizarrón district with the Carrizo and Mojarras lands in the southwest (upper left) quadrant. (Courtesy of the Archivo General de la Nación, Ciudad de México)

(including sixteen mulattos and two *lobos*) were baptized. The marriage records followed the same pattern.[32] Indeed, in 1762 a squad led by the lieutenant captain of La

Junta left Julimes heading east to track down some Natives, including women and children, who had fled. Whether these were people from La Junta or Julimes—or both—was not reported, but their destination closely identifies them with the previous refugees. The soldiers finally caught up with them at the presidio of Coahuila in Monclova, and brought them back at least as far as Julimes.[33] After 1766, when all the Natives still at La Junta were forced to move to Julimes, their flight from there soon after (as will be discussed in the next section) undoubtedly contributed to the fact that by 1767 all the La Junta-Julimes refugees at El Carrizo near the Vizarrón mission were commonly known as "Julimeños" by the Hispanics in Coahuila. Their knowledge of the frontier between Nueva Vizcaya and Coahuila as well as their military prowess promptly made them scouts employed by the Spanish military, such as the expedition of the Marqués de Rubí in 1767–1768.[34]

In Coahuila these "Julimeños," principally former Juntans, once again showed their determination to direct their own lives. In 1778 Father Morfi wrote that when "the missions of la junta de los rios Norte y Conchos rose up, the Indians of those eleven towns dispersed and many families of Julimeños took refuge" in the Vizarrón mission. The Native governor of the original Pausan residents of the mission assigned the newcomers most of the labor in order to lighten the work of his own people. In response, the refugees robbed the mission at night and fled into the brushland. They only agreed to return after several pleas from the authorities upon the condition that they have their own governor and their own fields separate from the Pausanes. Thereupon 160 of them and their families were granted a very fertile site named Carrizo with two good springs about four miles to the south of the Vizarrón mission, later becoming that mission's principal granary. They were also assigned a large grazing land for horses at the place named Mojarras.[35]

Imposed Co-Existence at the River Junction

Back in the La Junta valley after the flight of those determined not to live under the control of a Spanish presidio, things seem to have settled down after the crisis of 1760. Fray Jacobo de Castro, once again custos of the San Pablo Custody, visited La Junta in November 1762. Even while he wrote to Bishop Tamarón that the inhabitants remained "disgusted with the nearby presidio," he reported that the number of Natives had increased, although the towns had been reduced to four (see table 7). The San Juan Bautista settlement, now actually including the former Mezquites and Conejos villagers, was about the same as in September 1760, with both numbers approaching the high of the year 1747. San Francisco had doubled its population and Guadalupe had tripled, even with the presidio located between it and San Francisco. That brought both places not too far below their 1750 numbers. The continuing major decline was downriver. With Púliques now vacant and San Cristóbal reportedly moved across to the south bank, the population below Guadalupe was only about one-quarter of what it had been in 1747. Bishop Tamarón stated, presumably echoing Custos Castro, that usually three friars resided in the valley, with royal stipends of 300 pesos each. The fifty military families at the presidio had only attracted two civilian ones at this date, giving the fort a combined population of 138 persons.[36]

Table 7. Native Population Estimates, 1747–1762

	1747	1750	September 1760	1762
San Juan (with Mezquites and Conejos)	314	252	306	309
San Francisco	220	181	78	167
Guadalupe	172	221	65	194
San Cristóbal	158	Unknown	19	117
Púliques	268	Unknown	7	Vacant
Total	**1,132**	**Unknown**	**475**	**787**

Manuel Abadiano, the recently ordained native of Veracruz who had received his baptism of fire in the San Pablo Custody as a missionary at San Juan in the La Junta valley in 1760, wrote that after 1761 he moved from there to "Guadalupe at that place, five years, all alone." This may indicate that there were indeed other missionaries before 1762, probably including Páez, after which Abadiano, left alone, moved to the more developed church and convent at Guadalupe in the near vicinity of the presidio. Thus he remained until the end of the mission period at La Junta in 1766, evidently alone in the valley.[37] He was probably also the chaplain for the military families at the presidio.

So neither the Native settlements nor the missions had been dealt a death blow by the presidio after all. Rather a cluster of three Native towns remained close by the river junction and its new presidio, but now all on the south side of the Rio del Norte, while the larger town of San Juan remained to the west upriver on the Conchos. One may presume that a good number of the previous residents remained, drawn back by their ties to the land, but it is also probable that there was an increased number of other groups, brought in or attracted by the military economy. Whatever their ethnicity, Natives were no longer in charge in the valley. However, they had the added protection of the presidio, as much as the remaining Juntans despised it, since its domination of their lives meant among other things the end of trade with the Apaches and the consequent hostility of the latter.

Besides the hundreds of Juntans who fled to Coahuila, others probably migrated to Chihuahua or haciendas in northern Nueva Vizcaya where some Juntans had already settled previously. The merchants and miners of Chihuahua generally hired "Norteños" for periods at a time as their armed escorts in the 1760s.[38] The inspection tour of the northern frontier by the Marqués de Rubí in 1766–1767 did not pass through La Junta, since that valley had just been abandoned. Nevertheless he later wrote that the Natives at La Junta had shown "the fickleness and slowness common to all the new [*sic*] missions." But he praised how they had served as military auxiliaries to the Spanish forces in the 1760s: "These Norteños provided us a considerable increase to our forces, thanks to their fighting prowess and the enmity with their neighbors the Natagés that was introduced among them, ever since the first attacks in which they acted in unison with the troop of the presidio with the heroic deeds reported in its journals."[39] This was no small recognition and praise from the Marqués, even if couched in the cultural stereotypes of Native Americans by many Hispanics. What a marked contrast to the continued certainty of non-local Hispanic officials in the 1750s that the Juntans were the major supporters and co-perpetrators of all the Native raids within Nueva Vizcaya, a charge that was the primary excuse for establishing the presidio at La Junta.

This radical change in missionary conditions at La Junta, finally conforming to the Hispanic model customary elsewhere that gave Hispanics the upper hand, hardly had a chance to be tested. Ironically, whereas the missions had not been ended as the missionaries had feared by the establishment of a presidio in the very heart of the Native settlements, they came to an abrupt demise in 1766 due to the continued colonial debates over the allocation of military resources.

La Junta without Juntans

The move of troops from Agua Nueva to La Junta in 1759 had not resolved the defensive weaknesses of northeastern Nueva Vizcaya, particularly in the San Pedro River and Chihuahua districts. The wisdom of the placement of the new presidio at La Junta was contested by many besides Bishop Tamarón. This led the new viceroy, the Marqués de Cruillas, to order another inspection visit there in 1762. In 1765 the viceroy's council decided to provide better protection for the Chihuahua vicinity by reestablishing one of the presidios in eastern Nueva Vizcaya that had been abandoned in 1751 and permitting the governor of Nueva Vizcaya to move the presidio at La Junta to a more serviceable location. But the governor did not act until the Marqués de Rubí was about to carry out his inspection of the entire northern frontier in 1766.[40]

The governor had the La Junta presidio removed to Julimes, closer to Chihuahua, as Bishop Tamarón had recently recommended. The Juntans were also moved to that place. But judging by their subsequent actions, they were far from pleased. Neither was the Marqués de Rubí when given the bad news upon his arrival in Nueva Vizcaya. In his report in April 1768 upon the conclusion of his inspection tour of the entire northern frontier, he condemned the move to Julimes as reducing to naught the great effort and expense that had gone into the founding of the presidio at La Junta. After reviewing Captain Muñoz's documents about the presidio construction, he called them *poco calificados* (not very competent) and the actual site plan "ridiculous." Be that as it may, he reported that the presidio's woodwork and beams were now destroyed.

The harm did not stop there. In moving the Juntans to Julimes, the Hispanics lost an important corps of military auxiliaries, since the transferred missions had "dissolved (*se disiparon*) in a brief time." The current location of the displaced Juntans was unknown to Rubí's informants, but the Marqués suspected that they had "reconciled with their new enemies [the Apaches] and were together in their former dens, due to the natural attachment of every Indian to the place of his birth." That would make them "our 'domestic' and most fearful enemies, introducing outsiders . . . now unhampered by the presidio, to the Río Conchos, Laguna of Parras, and routes they can take all the way to Durango." The presidio had to be reestablished at any cost, he asserted.[41]

The move of everyone in the La Junta valley to Julimes also meant the end of the eight-decade work of the Franciscans of the San Pablo Custody of the Santo Evangelio Province with the Juntans. The La Junta district and the Juntans no longer figured in the listings of the custody's missions. The village of Julimes continued to belong to the missionary territory of the Zacatecan Province Franciscans, outside the territory of the San Pablo Custody.[42] Furthermore, the prompt flight of most Juntans from Julimes made any discussion of missionary jurisdiction over them at that place a moot question.

Major international events had made military changes clearly necessary throughout the northern frontier of New Spain, not only in Nueva Vizcaya. Peace talks in Paris in 1763 had ended the Seven Years' War, with Great Britain triumphant. The treaty resulted in a major realignment of the European presence in North America. France lost Canada and the eastern part of Louisiana to Great Britain, while ceding trans-Mississippi Louisiana to Spain in compensation for its ally's loss of Florida to the British. France would no longer be a colonial presence in North America, and Spain had to adjust its colonial organization to the new reality. In response to the havoc being wrought by hostile groups in Nueva Vizcaya, four companies of *dragones* (mounted infantry) were recruited from within the province in 1768. Rubí also recommended redrawing the entire frontier map, establishing a line of presidios spaced about a hundred miles apart more or less along the 30th parallel. This would include returning the presidio at Julimes to La Junta. When Rubí's recommendations were finally approved and promulgated in 1772, 37-year-old Hugo Oconor was entrusted with implementing them. He had been interim governor of Texas during Rubí's inspection and was appointed Commandant-Inspector of the northern frontier in mid-1771.[43]

Upon his arrival in northern Nueva Vizcaya in December 1771, Oconor had found twenty-five Norteños (Juntans) serving there as paid scouts, at half the salary of the Hispanics. Thus some highly valued Juntans remained with the military. Oconor praised them and insisted to the government that they remain in service.[44] Through such reports, the framers of the 1772 regulations for the presidios were well informed of what had taken place at La Junta since 1766. The regulations asserted that the "prejudicial novelty" of abandoning the Norteño towns there had resulted in their destruction and had given free access to the hostile nations "who occupied and demolished a great part of the buildings of the former presidio." The presidio was to be restored, and its captain should "endeavor to gather into their deserted towns at the proper time those Norteño Indians, who are of accredited valor."[45]

That very valor, however, continued to promote negative suspicions about the rest of the Juntans, their location still apparently unknown by those in Nueva Vizcaya. Oconor himself, planning for the reestablishment of a presidio at La Junta in September 1772, wrote to the viceroy: "It is suspected that the Norteño Indians have also involved themselves in the infestation of Nueva Vizcaya, which news if confirmed will make its pacification more difficult."[46] This suspicion might have arisen from the report that he received in his first two months at Chihuahua, that "a very large group of Apaches, Cholomes, Norteños, *criados* [former Hispanic-raised Natives], and Tarahumaras" had set on fire the houses at Guajoquilla and its haciendas and other places downriver, killing thirty-nine people and wounding sixteen.[47]

When Oconor finally set out from Chihuahua in early December 1772 to reconnoiter the Rio del Norte to determine the exact locations for the presidios to be established along its course, he headed up through the abandoned hacienda of Hormigas toward La Junta. At Coyame Fray José Ignacio María Alegre y Capetillo from the Franciscan missionary college of Queretaro, who accompanied Oconor in his expeditions, praised the beautiful spring of water and noted that Captain Muñoz, he of the La Junta/Julimes presidio, had built a house there and dug an irrigation canal. There was no mention of anyone living at Coyame. Climbing over the Cuesta Grande, the expedition arrived at San Juan, "one of the abandoned towns." Alegre y Capetillo wrote that the troops saw San Juan, San Francisco, San Cristóbal, Guadalupe, "and others of Julimes." He described the presidio itself as "very deteriorated, built of adobes, the Natives having burned almost all the woodwork." It was not suitable for a settlement, since the Río Conchos flowed there through very low and harsh land with no place for even an agricultural field. Inspecting the Arroyo de la Mula (across from today's Redford valley) about seventeen miles down the Rio del Norte, they also found the land there harsh and sterile.[48]

On his march back up the Rio del Norte from Coahuila in May 1773, Oconor received word that the Gileño, Natagé, and Mescalero Apaches had gathered in the La Junta vicinity, planning to surprise him upon his return. When he arrived at the abandoned pueblo of Los Púlicas, he could tell that Natives had encamped there. On the way his men captured about 250 head of livestock and killed some Apaches in one skirmish. Five months later, on October 28, 1773, he installed the Julimes troops with their families back at their old site at La Junta. He gave them possession of the small houses while ordering that there be carted in "the wood and other materials suitable for placing the presidio in a defensible state and protecting the families from the inclemencies of the weather." Ten days later he placed the troops of Cerro Gordo at the new presidial site of San Carlos downriver, returning to La Junta on November 13. From there he took his men to seek out Apaches to the north of the river in what are now called the Davis Mountains, finally succeeding in routing about 500 Apaches with more than forty killed. Returning once more to La Junta, he departed up the Rio del Norte on December 9 to continue inspecting and establishing the rest of the presidial line.[49]

The return of the presidio did not mean the renewal of formal mission efforts with any Natives who might have returned there or newly settled there.[50] Native relations in the area would henceforth be solely under the direction of the military and their chaplains at the presidio. La Junta had changed from a valley of centuries-old autonomous Indigenous trading settlements with the occasional presence of Franciscan missionaries to a Hispanic frontier outpost without missions. Apaches and other hostiles occupied the surrounding territory. Attempts in the 1780s to settle several bands of Mescaleros in the abandoned La Junta towns failed. That is a different story, partially chronicled by others.[51]

The initial overture from some Apaches in 1779 to be given settlements in the La Junta valley included a hope to be accompanied and taught by some of their "Julimeño relatives" in Coahuila. Several Mescalero chiefs asked to be allowed:

> to settle in the abandoned pueblo of San Francisco a short distance from the presidio of El Norte . . . they have petitioned for bringing in some of their relatives, the Julimeños, reduced in the mission of Peyotes [sic], belonging to Coahuila, and the Suma who are now in the nearby missions of the pueblo of El Paso, for the purpose of aiding and teaching them to build their houses, grow crops, and perform the rest of the labors of the field.[52]

But the former Juntans would have no part of such a plan, if indeed they were actually given the invitation. They chose relative cultural autonomy over former homeland, where they would be clearly subordinated. The permanent absence of the aboriginal Juntans from their river valley is demonstrable, among several indicators, by the church records there.[53] Even at Julimes the Juntans were gone, both those who had been present up to at least 1751 and those who had been transferred there in 1766. In the 1778 census there were not even any Julimes. The missionary in charge reported that the four Julime families were absent as auxiliaries in the presidios, and six other Julimes were fugitives—five men and one 12-year-old girl.[54]

Julimeños in Coahuila

By the time the Juntans and their allies who fled with them to Coahuila became known as Julimeños, Mescalero and Lipan Apaches had thoroughly established themselves in the mountainous ranges between Coahuila and Nueva Vizcaya. These were the former homeland of groups the Hispanics had called Tobosos, who had raided in Nueva Vizcaya and both traded and robbed in Coahuila. Most of those bands were eliminated in the 1720s. Now Apaches were doing the same thing.[55]

The Juntans' experience with Apaches had been not just war but also trade. They and various Apache groups continued that relationship in Coahuila. The Juntan/ Julimeño willingness to interact peacefully with both Apaches and Hispanics was an autonomous stance that Hispanics being raided by Apaches could not tolerate. Jacobo Ugarte, freshly arrived from Spain as the new governor of Coahuila in early December 1769, was already convinced by the end of that month that "the Julimeños, especially in the mission of San Francisco Bizarrón, could no longer be trusted as guides and scouts." He wrote to Viceroy Croix that they were serving as informants and collaborators with raiding Apaches, and even causing more damage than the Apaches! They should be removed from the frontier.

There was only one problem: it was impossible to prove their guilt in the raiding. They were known, however, to be in possession of stolen goods (trade items in their view) and supposedly to engage "in scalp dances and other acts of idolatry." The viceroy replied by asking for a full report, including what the missionaries had to say. Even though Ugarte assumed that the missionaries would side with the Julimeños—a point to be noted—he sent the report as specified, but now asking that the Julimeños be banished to Spain's factories in Havana. The "evidence" he presented was largely from the past, not the present, and the viceroy thought so little of it that he took no action. Ugarte continued to urge removal through the year 1776.[56]

Inspector General Oconor did listen. In 1776 he singled out the Julimeños among all the mission-related natives in Coahuila as suspects for the robberies in that province due to their "constant friendship" with Apaches.[57] He may or may not have been aware of the Norteños' long-standing and openly conducted trading with Apaches prior to 1760, something that had upset the Hispanics in Nueva Vizcaya. The Juntans/Julimeños were not the only ones in the Hispanic realm trading with Apaches who raided elsewhere. One wonders what Oconor's successor, Teodoro de Croix, thought when he received word from the Texas governor in 1779 that a majority of the Hispanic civilians in San Antonio were "very anxious about the harm which will befall their friends the Lipan Apaches" upon hearing of a proposed Coahuila campaign against them.[58]

In 1778 Father Juan Agustín de Morfi gave a more careful assessment. He was accompanying Croix, the first Comandante General of the Provincias Internas, on that official's inspection tour of the north. Morfi remarked that the Julimeños remained peaceful, "although with the general displeasure of all Indians subject to mission." They were part of an established mission system in Coahuila that perhaps limited them more than had been the case at La Junta. "They continue to work their fields without giving a motive to distrust them; and yet there are various opinions about their fidelity."

TEXAS

Presidio del Norte

del Norte

Rio Conchos

Chihuahua

Julimes

Vado San Vicente

Rio Grande

San Antonio

S. Pedro

San Fernando
Vizarrón

Presidio del Rio Grande

NUEVA

Santa Rosa

Laredo

VIZCAYA

COAHUILA

Monclova

Figure 13: The Rio del Norte / Rio Grande frontier in the 1780s. (By Robert E. Wright)

What was certain, Morfi asserted, was that they were frequently sought as military auxiliaries by the captains of all four presidios of that province, since they were the ablest and most daring at war. The captains had no complaints against them; in fact, the majority of these auxiliaries had died in combat.[59] The last remark was a reference to the ambush of seven Norteño scouts—thus explicitly identified as former Juntans— as they were leading the way for Comandante General Croix and Father Morfi. The expedition had just crossed the Rio Grande del Norte into the Big Bend country at the San Vicente ford on the way from Coahuila to the presidio at La Junta, that was already becoming colloquially known as the Presidio del Norte. The Norteño scouts were surprised by Apaches hiding in deep gullies that crisscrossed a large plain, and only one survived.[60]

Franciscans from the Pachuca missionary college took over the direction of the Coahuila missions in 1781. A few years later their religious superior noted some distinctive traits of the Julimeños. They were traits that had been noticed among their Juntan ancestors since the 1580s. These Julimeños cultivated their own plots besides the communal lands, and they were sharp traders whom Hispanics could not hoodwink. With the viceroy's permission they grew a plant they called Julime tobacco that the Apaches sought in exchange for deerskins and buffalo hides, items that the Julimeños bartered with the Hispanics. They were "very clean in their clothes, with attractive cloth pants, boots, shoes, and sombreros." They gambled, but not with their clothes like the other natives. And they did not flee in the face of danger. On the contrary, many had been taken into the presidial companies.[61]

Nevertheless, and in notable contrast to the positive comments of the Franciscans who dealt with them on a more regular basis, they still could not shake the suspicion that fell upon them by outsider officials due to their autonomous manner. In 1793

Viceroy Conde de Revillagigedo wrote that they and the rest of the mission Indians of Coahuila could not be more perverse—marked by all kinds of vices, especially drunkenness, avoiding work, and carrying out robberies. "They give repeated motives for suspecting that, when they do not join the Lipan Apaches in hostilities, they serve as spies for them or alert them to the state of our settlements and the movement of the troops."[62] Self-reliant traders they had been, self-reliant traders they would be, maintaining and defending their autonomy as best they could.

Epilogue

Two centuries had elapsed since the first Spanish expeditions passed through the La Junta valley. In terms of national and international geopolitics, the Juntan Natives were never a major player, even in the Indigenous world. But they certainly were important actors in the regional context, as traders, military allies, and migrant workers. At their core in the La Junta valley itself, they were sedentary and peaceful, although quite capable warriors when they needed to be. The major hostile nations recognized by the Spanish in northeastern Chihuahua were the Tobosos, Cholomes, Sumas, and eventually the Apaches. That in itself made the river valley, already very distant from colonial settlements, difficult for Hispanics to reach and all the more isolated.

However, precisely due to its sedentary stability, peaceful character, and location at a watered oasis in the center of the great Southern Plains, many of the warlike groups surrounding La Junta, as well as some more peaceful ones to the east toward the Tejas Natives, preferred to respect La Junta as a valued trade center rather than attack it. A constant throughout the history of the Juntans was their position as Native trading middlemen. For the sake of their own economy as well as to forestall hostile attacks by other Indigenous nations, they always maintained those trading relationships, even in the face of opposition from Hispanic officials. Thus they would simultaneously, and contradictorily, be praised by different officials in the later 1700s as the best of military auxiliaries and the worst abettors of hostile raiding in Nueva Vizcaya and later Coahuila.

After one or the other slaving raid on their outer settlements, for more than a century Juntan contacts with Hispanics were solely through long-distance migrant labor and serving as military auxiliaries. The only exception was three years of a small missionary presence in the 1680s. The first Spaniards to encounter the Juntans found them to be the most intelligent, physically well-built, best featured, socially adept, and militarily skilled people that they had seen for hundreds of miles. The Juntans, for their part, experiencing frequent hardship due to the cyclical droughts and floods that bedeviled them and also the occasional attacks by other Native groups, recognized the benefits of association with Hispanics in order to have a more permanent food and economic resource as well as a military ally.

That did not prevent, however, their being taken advantage of as a migrant labor pool by at least some. They were a highly valued labor source noted for their reliability, and some became permanent residents on Hispanic haciendas and later in the lower San Pedro River towns and the Chihuahua vicinity. At the same time, their strong determination to maintain their autonomy kept them intent on Hispanics remaining at a very respectable distance from their own river valley. They were greatly abetted in this desire by the lack of mineral discoveries in their district and the hostile Native groups who roamed between them and the Hispanic settlements.

Juntans began inviting Franciscans to their valley by the 1670s and in the following decade formed an alliance with Hispanic officials that made them formal military allies. Through their migrant labor they had come to recognize Franciscans as Hispanics who were more protective of them, even if trying to change their religion and acculturate them to Hispanic ways. For the Juntans the missionaries were guaranteed links to the benefits of Hispanic colonial society. The Juntans liked some of what the Hispanic culture had to offer, including European clothing and a food supply. Thus they were generally willing to go along with the missionaries in some things that pleased those Franciscans, like memorizing some prayers and doctrine and getting baptized.

Although the initial missionary effort in the 1680s was derailed by Native hostilities, the return of Franciscans in 1715 introduced more than five decades in which the Juntans would walk the political and cultural tightrope that hosting missionaries from the Custody of San Pablo would involve. Those decades revealed more and more clearly a fundamental difference in disposition toward the missionary presence between most Juntans on the one hand and most Cholomes in the Coyame valley on the other. The inhabitants of the La Junta valley generally tended to protect and respect their missionaries, escorting them to safety when the occasion demanded. That respect and care were most dramatically demonstrated at times of extreme missionary vulnerability, during the 1726 Coyame revolt and again during the 1759 prelude to the Hispanic military occupation of the river junction.

The missionaries complained about the Juntans' autonomous ways and the lack of real conversion on the part of most, at least according to Hispanic standards. Yet there was never any explicit mention of Native religious leaders at La Junta, other than the outsider Taagua in 1684. Juntans got baptized, especially their children, and attended religious instruction and Mass. For whatever reason, they valued Christian rituals enough to give valuable hides for them at baptism and marriage, and especially on the occasion of burial. And they enjoyed, as in most other mission districts on the frontier, the special patronal religious celebrations associated with their community. Among them there were at least some who genuinely became Christian in their faith and practice.

Whatever attitude one might have toward missionaries in general or Franciscan missionaries in particular, one has to judge most of the Franciscans who served at La Junta as very courageous and dedicated. Nowhere else on the entire northern frontier of New Spain did they find themselves so alone for so long as the only Hispanics, hundreds of miles from anyone else. Indeed, at various times there was only one of them serving the Juntans. The great paradox that faced the missionaries from the beginning was the need to have a stronger Hispanic presence in the valley to enable a more protected and standard program imposing Hispanic Christianity and culture along with the realization that the Juntans would never allow any additional Hispanic presence in their midst.

When the Juntans became the scapegoats in the 1750s for Hispanic fears due to increasing hostile raiding in northeast Nueva Viscaya, and the Hispanic military finally planted themselves in their midst, hundreds fled to Coahuila while others remained rooted in their valley but unhappy with the situation. But when these latter were forced to abandon their towns a few years later, most fled to join those in Coahuila, where they established a relative autonomy within the extensive mission lands there. Although they continued to be known by Hispanics as valued military auxiliaries and shrewd traders, their decades-old commerce with Apaches branded them as highly suspect by many. Life in their native valley of La Junta had ended for practically all. Now known as Julimeños by most Coahuilans, they began a new chapter in their highly unusual history.

In exploring this saga of Natives and Hispanics at La Junta, even though the resources are very thin on many occasions, we get some revealing glimpses at times of the human personalities and deeper emotions that were at play: Juan Sabeata, the international diplomat trying to build alliances to save his Jumano people; Father Nicolás López unfazed by viceroyal authorities in his determination to extend the frontier mission field; Father Agustín de Colina outraged at injustice against the Natives; Father Joaquín de Hinojosa idealistically determined to convert only by means of true faith; Sergeant Major Juan Antonio Trasviña Retes abetted in his economic aggrandizing by the corrupt Governor Manuel San Juan de Santa Cruz; the Juntan governor Francisco urging his family to follow the Christian ways; the Juntan general Alonso López de Carbajal leading his people in opposing Hispanic settlement but courageously defending the Franciscans; Father Andrés Varo, doggedly realistic and bluntly combative; Father Lorenzo de Saavedra with the most appreciative understanding of the Juntans from his long experience there; Captain Joseph de Belaunzarán, the veteran and aggrieved frontier commander; Pedro el Mulato, the mixed-race Hispanophile; Governor Antonio de Mendoza, highly autocratic, treacherous, and vituperative; Father Juan Sanz de Lezáun, ravaged by Hispanic officials' machinations and their devastating impact; General Francisco de Arroyo, a universally admired Juntan leader who would not surrender his people's independence; the inexperienced and brash Captain Manuel Muñoz playing the career game. Typically, due to the sources, we get much rarer glimpses of the inner thoughts of the Juntans themselves. But what a glimpse in 1759!

Hopefully this story extending over most of the Spanish colonial period sheds much more light than before on the history of human habitation and interaction in the still remote borderlands of northeastern Chihuahua and West Texas, as experienced by the people of the La Junta valley and their neighbors. May it yield a deserved appreciation for the Juntans as a people and contribute to a better understanding of the complex interactions and demographic shifts among the Indigenous nations in that area. It certainly brings out of obscurity the work of the Franciscans of the Custody of the Conversion of San Pablo, so well-known for their ministry in upper New Mexico, at the hardly recognized far southeast end of their huge mission field. Now the international boundary between the United States and Mexico runs through the La Junta valley, and its original inhabitants are long gone from there, refugees with a history still to be completed. They and the Franciscans whom they welcomed among them share a unique story of determined autonomy on the one hand and dedicated intrepidness on the other.

Appendix: The Frontiers of Northern New Spain

T his study claims that the La Junta district is almost unique in the missionary annals of the north frontier of New Spain in regard to the decades-long absence of any Hispanics other than missionaries for hundreds of miles. For the sake of brevity, that claim is held to be evident among those knowledgeable in the history of the Spanish provinces or colonies of Texas, Coahuila, Nuevo Santander, central Nueva Vizcaya, Sonora,[1] and Baja and Alta California. There were Jesuit missions among the Seris for only two decades, with a garrison about forty-five miles distant.[2] The mission districts bearing more similarity to La Junta, and yet not as unique in regard to the combined characteristics of long-term geographical isolation from Hispanic settlements and the absence of Hispanics other than missionaries, are those of the Zuñi, Hopi, and Yaqui people. Since some might want to propose the Rarámuri (Tarahumara) due to their situation in later historical periods, they are also discussed.

Northern Nueva Vizcaya and the Tarahumaras

Along the primary corridor of Hispanic advance up the central plateau of New Spain, the mission frontier moved beyond Durango in the 1590s. Susan Deeds has made abundantly clear that in the Tepehuan and southern Tarahumara regions of Nueva Vizcaya, and even in the eastern and central districts of the Alta (northern) Tarahumara, missions and Hispanic settlements developed fairly concurrently in close proximity. This circumstance was almost always to the detriment of the missions, due to demands for Native labor in the nearby mines and haciendas. The result was that the members of those nations who did not take refuge in the high Sierra Madre were turned into laborers, involuntarily or voluntarily, for the Hispanics. Hispanic encroachment on Native lands, including those of the missions, was common.[3]

After efforts in 1649–1652 to establish the first Hispanic presence in the Papigóchic river valley in the center of the Alta Tarahumara country failed, there was no further attempt to enter that region until 1675. Within three years there was a mining camp and twenty Hispanic farms. By 1688 the Jesuits had formed the new mission jurisdiction of the Alta Tarahumura with nine permanent mission centers; two more were added by 1720. Nine of those centers were within the area of the very productive mines and Hispanic farms in the southeastern corner of the territory and in the fertile Papigóchic valley. This new presence within the Tarahumara lands, as few in comparative numbers as it was, predictably led to two serious uprisings in the 1690s, the last uprising being severely crushed.[4]

The soldiers who arrived to put down the insurgencies protected all the missionaries at least briefly after both events, but otherwise the Jesuits were frustrated that the scattered dwellings of the Tarahumaras and the lack of enforced mission discipline left the people free in regard to Christianization. The Natives could live in a ranchería outside the mission center, leave to labor for Hispanics elsewhere either voluntarily or involuntarily, or withdraw to the more inaccessible country on the other (western) slope of the Sierra Madre.[5] If they remained, many might disregard the missionaries' directions, but they could not avoid the labor demands of Hispanics in mines and haciendas near and far. Thus, the experience of those of their nation in the southern Tarahumara region repeated itself for the northern Tarahumaras, if only with lesser intensity.[6]

The Western Pueblos: The Zuñis and the Hopis

The "western pueblos" of Ácoma and the Zuñis and Hopis were distant from the central corridor of missions and Hispanic settlements near the Rio Grande in New Mexico. Ácoma, however, is only about sixty miles from the Rio Grande. Its people thus had more interaction with Hispanic civilians, especially after the new Laguna district developed only twenty miles away in the 1700s. But the Zuñi district is around seventy miles further west, and the first Hopi town another 120 to the northwest. With these latter mission sites, therefore, there is a similarity to the La Junta district at least in terms of distance from Hispanic settlements. In fact, the Hopis were much further away than the Juntans from Hispanic civilization.

Given the paucity of information for the seventeenth century—the only century that there were missionaries residing among the Hopi—comparisons can only be very sketchy for that period. Unlike what happened in the core La Junta settlements, the first experiences of the Zuñis and the Hopis with Spaniards were violent. Ever since 1539 they had come to know them as brutal invaders, liars, and worse. Unsurprisingly, therefore, missionaries were not initially invited by either nation. When the Franciscans came seeking admittance in 1629, the initial reception was definitely unwelcoming, with the Franciscans who were grudgingly tolerated being killed within a few years by the townspeople. In the La Junta district, to the contrary, although the Franciscans were also under threat at various times, they were repeatedly warned and led to safety by Natives of the La Junta valley. The subsequent history in the western pueblos before 1680 is little known. The presence of one or two priests in the Zuñi towns is mentioned in documents for 1660–1666, 1671–1672, 1675, and 1680. Similarly, documents mention missionaries living in the Hopi district until at least 1640 and in 1654–1655, 1662–1666, 1669–1672, and 1680. In the Great Pueblo Revolt of 1680, all the missionaries in both districts were killed.[7] The five decades from 1629 to 1680 are similar to the almost five decades that Franciscans were alone in La Junta in the eighteenth century, from 1715 to 1759. And it is quite plausible that the missionaries' presence was intermittent among the Zuñis and the Hopis just as it was at La Junta.

Were there any other Hispanics residing among or close by the Zuñis or the Hopis during those fifty years, unlike at La Junta?[8] Brew wrote that "no Spanish farmers or traders, . . . as far as is known, ever settled in the Hopi country."[9] That may be, but only if one limits Hispanics to farmers or traders. Sheridan wrote more circumspectly: "The missionaries were the only Kastiilam [Spaniards] who lived among the Hopis for any length of time."[10] In fact, even though the records are scant, there are several notices that Hispanic citizen-soldiers were present there and in the Zuñi district for extended periods in the 1600s, not just as soldiers merely passing through.[11]

And there were others who at least visited annually if not more often. These were the *encomenderos* or their delegates and the *alcaldes mayores*. By royal decree Hispanic *encomenderos* were to receive an annual tribute or portion of the products made by the Native communities assigned to them. In 1662–1663 (and undoubtedly not only those years) the *encomienda* tribute was collected from the Hopi towns of Shongopavi and Awatovi by a Hispanic officer.[12] Around 1643 *alcaldes mayores* were appointed for the first time to supervise the western pueblos.[13] Since these officials were usually expected to live within the district that they governed,[14] was that the case for the Zuñi and Hopi towns? Simmons commented:

In some areas, however, as in the jurisdictions of Laguna-Acoma, Jémez, and Zuñi, there were no true Spanish towns, only Indian Pueblos. Since Spanish law forbade outsiders in Indian villages, the officials in such districts usually applied for a grant of unoccupied land near the chief population center and established themselves in their own haciendas. In such instances, the prohibition against property owning [by *alcaldes mayores*] was clearly not observed.[15]

In 1659 the *alcalde mayor* of the Zuñi-Hopi jurisdiction apparently visited both places regularly, and on one occasion he quoted a Hispanic colonist actually living in the Zuñi area.[16]

Admittedly, these are sparse indications due to the scant historical record for the pre-1680 period. But they undeniably demonstrate a Hispanic presence besides the missionaries among the Zuñis and the Hopis that did not exist at La Junta. A further important difference is that many Juntans established a regular contact with Hispanics by migrating a long distance to work for them, whereas the Hopis and the Zuñis never did, as far as the very meager record reveals.

After Hispanics reestablished themselves in upper New Mexico in 1692, repeated efforts to reconnect with the Hopis foundered due to their refusal to the demand that they accept Christianity.[17] The Zuñis, on the other hand, beset not only by Apaches but also by Utes, Havasupais, and even Hopis, were more than willing to allow proselytizing missionaries among them if that meant military help. They could always still follow their own consciences. By 1700 a Franciscan was at Zuñi and a guard of eleven soldiers was stationed there. But the abusive behavior of the soldiers and three settlers who had been exiled to serve there led to the killing of the settlers in 1703 while the military squad was absent. The Zuñis temporarily fled to a mesa top and the governor recalled the priest, whose life had been spared.[18] The friar was back at Zuñi in 1705,[19] and soldiers were again stationed there until at least 1715.[20] Furthermore, the *alcalde mayor* of the district was buried there in 1706.[21]

The Zuñi mission records are missing from March 1712 until December 1725. Subsequently there appear to have been residential priests until 1760, but with many gaps ranging from a few months to one or rarely two years. After 1760 there was almost never a residential Franciscan, rather friars visiting from Ácoma or Laguna.[22] The secondary literature is mostly silent in regard to non-Franciscan Hispanics in the Zuñi district after 1733. *Alcaldes* are identified in 1750, 1754 (with two other Hispanics), and 1779. That there were others present after 1776 is demonstrated by the fact that the few non-Zuñis appearing in the sacramental registers during that time "were for the most part connected with the families of the *alcaldes mayores* or were soldiers periodically stationed at the pueblo."[23] So again, even given the scant record, there was certainly much more of a Hispanic presence at Zuñi than there was at La Junta before 1760.

The Yaquis

Moving finally to the northwestern frontier of New Spain, one must consider the case that is most similar to La Junta in terms of being very isolated from Hispanic settlements, not having resident Hispanics other than the missionaries, and engaging in long-distance migrant labor. This was the mission district among the Yaquis for the first few decades after its founding in 1617. The Yaquis lived in a fairly compact district on the west coast of Sinaloa along the Gulf of California. The closest Hispanic settlement was the new presidio of El Fuerte about 130 miles south, until mining camps such as Piedras Verdes (later Baroyeca) and Álamos began to develop after 1675 from thirty to seventy miles distant. Along with the mining operations came the cattle and farming haciendas, thus ending the relative geographic isolation of the Yaqui towns.[24] In 1633 there were still no resident Hispanic soldiers. The missionaries reported before 1645 that male Yaquis "travel outside the province sometimes 50 leagues or more to be able to buy smart-looking (*galano*) clothes through their work. . . . Some return, others adapt to living among Spaniards (*se hacen a la vida entre españoles*) and remain with them or in mining settlements."[25] Thus far went the similarities with La Junta. Indeed, Edward Spicer, who specialized in studying the Yaqui, observed that "Yaqui independence of European penetration, other than that of the Jesuits, was almost unique."[26]

But there were also significant differences, even just in terms of relations with Hispanics. Spicer claimed too much in asserting that "for nearly a century and a quarter, from 1617 to 1739, the Jesuits needed no military backing."[27] He conveniently omitted the fact that very early on, sometime before 1620, the captain of El Fuerte responded to a Jesuit appeal for help in view of a potential uprising. Arriving among the Yaquis in the guise of peace "with a good number of soldiers and armored horses," he hung a Yaqui shaman and several of his accomplices.[28] And what it would cost Yaquis to resist Hispanics had been amply demonstrated eight years prior to the arrival of the Jesuits, when about fifty mounted soldiers accompanied first by 2,000 Native allies, and then in a second attempt by 4,000, engaged in day-long hard-fought battles with Yaquis whose forces were several thousand more than the ones recruited by the Hispanics. The Yaquis successfully repulsed both advances but lost many fighters, and afterwards invited a peace agreement that allowed for the missionaries' entrance. More missionaries arrived in 1621, and eventually solid churches were built and decorated. A very intriguing statement, not further explained, from these first years was that soldiers "would come at times to obtain the produce of the planted fields."[29] Very little is known about events in the Yaqui missions after 1626, less than a decade after their founding. Just as among the Zuñis and the Hopis, the current state of research makes a more detailed comparison with La Junta impossible. But as sparse as this record is, it can be seen that ever since the initial advance to the Yaqui settlements, Hispanics were more of a frequent presence and imposing player there than at La Junta.[30]

Notes

Introduction

1. Jefferson Morgenthaler, *La Junta de los Rios: The Life, Death and Resurrection of an Ancient Desert Community in the Big Bend Region of Texas* (Boerne, TX: Mockingbird Books, 2007), 3 (first quote); J. Charles Kelley, *Jumano and Patarabueye: Relations at La Junta de los Rios* (Ann Arbor: Museum of Anthropology, University of Michigan, 1986), 47 (second quote).

2. The La Junta district on both sides of the Rio del Norte (Rio Grande) was the northeastern limit of the Spanish colonial province of Nueva Vizcaya and subsequently of the state of Chihuahua under independent Mexico. The eastern side of the river only became part of the state of Texas with the Treaty of Guadalupe Hidalgo in 1848.

3. The military chaplain at the river junction in 1817 gave the distance to Chihuahua as eighty leagues: Fray Francisco Buenavida to Bishop Castaniza, 6 November 1817, Archivos Históricos del Arzobispado de Durango (henceforth AHAD) microfilm, AHAD-233, frame 436, Special Collections, New Mexico State University Library, Las Cruces, New Mexico. In northern New Spain a league was generally about 2.6 miles: John L. Kessell, *Spain in the Southwest: A Narrative History of Colonial New Mexico, Arizona, Texas, and California* (Albuquerque: University of New Mexico Press, 2002), 423. The great distance from any Hispanic settlement places La Junta outside the sphere of "settler colonialism" that has been a recent almost obligatory focus of Indigenous studies. In fact, I would agree with Allan Greer, Jennifer Spear, and Samuel Truett that this concept, unless morphed way beyond its strict meaning of Native elimination, actually does not fit most French and Spanish colonial enterprises in North America. See their essays in the forum on "Settler Colonialism in Early American History" in *William and Mary Quarterly*, 3d ser., 76 no. 3 (July 2019).

4. The term Native is capitalized to indicate the original peoples on the American continent, those whom the Europeans called Indians, in distinction from those of European or African descent who were born in, and thus also "native" in the larger sense to, the Americas. This practice is similar to the use of First Nations in Canadian historiography.

5. Scholars stating that there were no permanent ethnic locations date back to James Manly Daniel, "La Junta de los Rios and the Despoblado, 1680–1760" (MA thesis, University of Texas at Austin, 1948), 27, 29, and Howard G. Applegate and C. Wayne Hanselka, *La Junta de los Rios Del Norte y Conchos* (El Paso: Texas Western Press, 1974), 8–9. Among others since are Gary Clayton Anderson, *The Indian Southwest, 1580–1830: Ethnogenesis and Reinvention* (Norman: University of Oklahoma Press, 1999), 17–28, 63–65. For his part, Morgenthaler, *La Junta de los Rios*, mistakenly had several non-Juntan groups resident there in 1683 (69) and core Juntan communities not arriving until around 1715 (91). Bradley Folsom, "Spanish La Junta de los Rios: The Institutional Hispanicization of an Indian Community along New Spain's Northern Frontier, 1535–1821" (MA thesis, University of North Texas, 2008), 64, 68, accepted Anderson's thesis.

6. This study employs the ethnically-mixed term Hispanics after 1600, as does Kessell, *Spain in the Southwest*, 75, 110–11, 200–201. Peter Gerhard, *The North Frontier of New Spain*, rev. ed. (Norman: University of Oklahoma Press, 1993), 27, noted that by 1600 the *gente de razón* (Hispanics) in the frontier provinces "included many Africans and others of mixed race. . . . Perhaps from mid-sixteenth century, the Spanish conquest of the frontier gradually became in effect a multi-racial advance." When referring specifically to the colonial government, however, I will use the term Spanish, since Spaniards remained definitely in charge of colonial policy.

7. William B. Griffen, *Indian Assimilation in the Franciscan Area of Nueva Vizcaya* (Tucson: University of Arizona Press, 1979), 37, 94, uses "La Junta district" or "La Junta province" in the same way that I do. He employed "La Junta proper" to refer to the closer vicinity of the river junction (28, 37, 94).

8. Griffen, *Indian Assimilation*, 29, 34. This should not be confused with the unrelated nations known as Norteños in colonial Texas. See the index entries in the classic study of Luis Navarro García, *Don José de Gálvez y la Comandancia General de las Provincias Internas del Norte de Nueva España* (Sevilla: Consejo Superior de Investigaciones Científicas, 1964), 580: "Norteños, indios de la Junta de los Ríos," "Norteños, indios de Texas." However, Navarro García incorrectly stated that "Norteños" only began to be used for the Juntans in the 1750s (113, no. 147); as will be shown, it was already in use in 1715.

9. The Native struggle to preserve or gain autonomy, and its success or failure, plays out in many different ways, depending on various factors. Juliana Barr, *Peace Came in the Form of a Woman: Indians and Spaniards in the Texas Borderlands* (Chapel Hill: University of North Carolina Press, 2007), studied in temporal succession the relations of three different groupings of Natives with Hispanics in the Spanish province of Texas. Most of those Native groups—Caddos, Karankawas, Tonkawas, Apaches, Wichitas, and Comanches—never or rarely settled with

Hispanics; they managed to retain their autonomy, if not actually dominate over the Hispanics. Barr even argued, unconvincingly to this writer, that the groups who entered the San Antonio missions "could, in fact, exert control over the terms by which they lived together with Spaniards" (118) in "part-time residence" as "visitors" at these "sites for socioeconomic alliance and communal ritual" (119).

10. The late-colonial history of the La Junta valley remains to be thoroughly written. Pioneering essays appeared in the *Journal of Big Bend Studies* 3 (1991), one by Oakah L. Jones, "Settlements and Settlers at La Junta de los Rios, 1759–1822," 43–70, and the other by Elizabeth A. H. John, "Spanish-Indian Relations in the Big Bend Region during the Eighteenth and Early Nineteenth Centuries," 71–80. See also Morgenthaler, *La Junta de los Rios*, 128–58, that covers up to 1795.

11. Chantal Cramaussel, *Poblar la frontera: La provincia de Santa Bárbara en Nueva Vizcaya durante los siglos XVI y XVII* (Zamora: El Colegio de Michoácan, 2006), 356 (my translation, as will be the case for all Spanish documents and resources quoted hereafter unless otherwise noted). This meticulously researched study by Cramaussel has been of great benefit in providing many details helpful to this work, as the reference notes will show, even though I disagree with some of her conclusions.

12. Morgenthaler, *La Junta de los Rios*, "Preface." The purpose of this study is not to engage in a general comparative history of frontier districts. However, since some scholars have questioned the uniqueness of the La Junta story, in the appendix there is a brief analysis of the other northern frontier districts in regard to the two characteristics of geographic isolation and the absence of non-missionary Hispanics. Given particular consideration are the Rarámuri/Tarahumara, Zuñi, Hopi, and Yaqui cases.

13. This was the assumption of Kelley, the first major ethnographer and archaeologist of La Junta, in his *Jumano and Patarabueye*, 66–67, 111. This 1986 volume was the first published edition, with only a few notes of revision, of his 1947 dissertation.

14. Probably due to his own early academic employment in West Texas, Carlos Castañeda did the pioneering historical studies relating to La Junta in his monumental *Our Catholic Heritage in Texas, 1519–1936* (Austin: Van Boeckmann-Jones, 1936–1950), vol. 1, 269–75; vol. 2, 317–18, 326–27; vol. 3, 211–32; vol. 4, 236, 247–48. Kelley significantly advanced the field with his 1947 doctoral dissertation combining archaeology and history, *Jumano and Patarabueye*. In 1948, Daniel wrote his important master's thesis, "La Junta de los Rios and the Despoblado, 1680–1760," using archival documents pointed out to him by Castañeda. A few years later, Kelley made his continuing scholarship available to the general public in his best-known "The Historic Indian Pueblos

of La Junta de los Rios," *New Mexico Historical Review* 27, no. 4 (October 1952): 256–95, and 28, no. 1 (January 1953): 20–51. This two-part essay has been reprinted in facsimile in *The Native American and Spanish Colonial Experience in the Greater Southwest. II: Introduction to the Research*, ed. David H. Snow (New York: Garland Publishing, 1992): 117–93. It has since been made readily available through links in the *Texas Beyond History* website, "La Junta de los Rios" (texasbeyondhistory.net), in its Credits and Sources section. The only substantive study of the colonial period since these earlier works is Morgenthaler's *La Junta de los Rios*, privately published in 2007. It is well written, but I disagree with his basic thesis as well as many minor points. In fact, there is a long history of mistaken assertions about La Junta from reports as early as the mid-1700s.

Chapter 1

1. Álvar Núñez Cabeza de Vaca, *Naufragios y comentarios* (México: Porrúa, 1988), 59–61 (quote on 60).

2. Ibid., 18–47.

3. The contemporary summary by Oviedo y Valdés of the journey account sent by the three Spanish survivors in 1539 from Havana to the Audiencia of Santo Domingo, a report since lost, noted that blessing with the sign of the cross and blowing upon the ill was "the way that those in Castile whom they call healers (*saludadores*) do it": Basil C. Hedrick and Carroll L. Riley, eds., *The Journey of the Vaca Party: The Account of the Narváez Expedition, 1528–1536, as related by Gonzalo Fernández de Oviedo y Valdés* (Carbondale, IL: University Museum, Southern Illinois University, 1974), 133. The Native healers along the Texas coast also blew upon the ill as part of their practices (Núñez Cabeza de Vaca, *Naufragios y comentarios*, 29).

4. Núñez Cabeza de Vaca, *Naufragios y comentarios*, 47–59. The route cannot be definitively determined, but most recent scholars have the Spanish party passing through the La Junta valley after crossing back over the Rio Grande from the Bolsón de Mapimí in Coahuila: Donald E. Chipman, "In Search of Cabeza de Vaca's Route across Texas: An Historiographical Survey," *Southwestern Historical Quarterly* 91, no. 2 (October 1987): 127–48. Andrés Reséndez, also opting for the La Junta route, capably summarized the arguments pro and con up through 2002 in his *A Land So Strange: The Epic Journey of Cabeza de Vaca* (New York: Basic Books, 2007), 294–95.

5. Núñez Cabeza de Vaca, *Naufragios y comentarios*, 61. There are various scholarly conjectures as to the exact place where the Spanish party arrived. After reviewing all the literature, Jefferson Morgenthaler concluded that it was in or near a town later named San Bernardino, some twelve miles above the river junction: *The River Has Never Divided Us: A Border History of La Junta de los Rios* (Austin:

University of Texas Press, 2004), 249n2. But he did not explain this conclusion.

6. Núñez Cabeza de Vaca, *Naufragios y comentarios*, 61–63. The Oviedo summary similarly noted for the first time in this journey through the continental interior the cultivation of beans, calabashes, and corn, with a special notice of bows that would indicate that these were of uncommon quality (Hedrick and Riley, *The Journey of the Vaca Party*, 142–43)—as the later expeditions would remark.

7. Núñez Cabeza de Vaca, *Naufragios y comentarios*, 63. Nueva Mexico with the feminine adjective is not a grammatical error. It referred to the hoped-for new *city* of Mexico—*la nueva ciudad de México*—whose prospects impelled adventurers northward. As such, the name continued in use for some time.

8. Morgenthaler, *La Junta de los Rios*, 7, with a map on page 10.

9. J. Charles Kelley, "Factors Involved in the Abandonment of Certain Peripheral Southwestern Settlements," *American Anthropologist* 54, no. 3 (July 1952): 358–60 (quote on 358).

10. Nancy Parrott Hickerson, *The Jumanos: Hunters and Traders of the South Plains* (Austin: University of Texas Press, 1994), xxvi–xxvii, explains why the La Junta valley was perhaps the most important crossroads of very long-distance trade routes below New Mexico. Kelley, *Jumano and Patarabueye*, 128, 132, 174n7, pointed to the Opata as a source of desired goods to the west, noting the quantity of trade pottery from northwestern Chihuahua at La Junta in the 1200–1400 period.

11. Kelley, *Jumano and Patarabueye*, 130. In his earlier writings, Kelley was ambivalent on the ethnic-origins question (see "Factors Involved in the Abandonment," 361–62 versus 383). On the basis of much later archaeological discoveries by Robert Mallouf and others, in 1990 he favored the migration hypothesis: "The Rio Conchos Drainage: History, Archaeology, Significance," *Journal of Big Bend Studies* 2 (1990): 38. A few years later Mallouf favored the cultural diffusion hypothesis: "Comments on the Prehistory of Far Northeastern Chihuahua, the La Junta District, and the Cielo Complex," *Journal of Big Bend Studies* 11 (1999): 81–85.

12. Mallouf, "Comments on the Prehistory," 83.

13. This "pre-history" (before written records) of La Junta is fundamentally based upon the archaeological investigations by J. Charles Kelley and his colleagues between 1937 and 1949. The only significant excavations since then were in 1994 by a team led by William A. Cloud in a peripheral site, El Polvo. For the various detailed excavation reports, see the bibliography under those two authors' names plus William Shackelford. Robert J. Mallouf in his work in the late 1980s on regional arrowheads and the Cielo Complex at higher bluff elevations along the edge of the La Junta valley (see his "Comments on the Prehistory," cited above) emphasized the hunter-gatherer culture in his interpretations of La Junta

pre-history.

Nancy Kenmotsu authored the archaeological background summary in the 1994 report of the Cloud-led excavation noted above and co-authored or authored more recent summaries including new developments: Myles R. Miller and Nancy A. Kenmotsu, "Prehistory of the Jornada Mogollon and Eastern Trans-Pecos Regions of West Texas," in *The Prehistory of Texas*, ed. Timothy K. Pettula, 238–41, 256–60 (College Station: Texas A&M University Press, 2004); Nancy A. Kenmotsu, "Jornada Connections: Viewing the Jornada from La Junta de los Rios," in *Late Prehistoric Hunter-Gatherers and Farmers of the Jornada Mogollon*, eds. Thomas R. Rocek and Nancy A. Kenmotsu, 177–203 (Louisville, CO: University Press of Colorado, 2018). For another presentation of the historical cultural development of the Juntan people and their relations with the various Native groups in the larger region beyond them before 1700, see Morgenthaler, *La Junta de los Rios*, 15–22.

14. Miller and Kenmotsu, "Prehistory of the Jornada Mogollon," 238.

15. Kenmotsu, "Jornada Connections," 191–202, argued for only a seasonal residency by people throughout the La Junta valley, whom she viewed as primarily hunter-gatherers, although acknowledging that supportive data are "thin." Her arguments [with my comments in brackets] were Cabeza de Vaca's experience *before 1550*; Juntans' alleged intimate knowledge of surrounding groups and distances [only to the northwest, and they had many trading visitors]; the strong predominance of fine-grained (hunting) over coarse-grained (plant-processing) stone materials; rock art styles in the region [there is no known rock art close to La Junta]; the lack of offerings at burials; limited ceramic inventories; and fluency in multiple languages [not so]. She did not note that her hypothesis of the practice of heritable land tenure at La Junta (confirmed by later Spanish reports) challenges the primarily hunter-gatherer thesis.

16. Robert James Mallouf, "A Synthesis of Eastern Trans-Pecos Prehistory" (MA thesis, University of Texas at Austin, 1985), 146.

17. J. Charles Kelley, "Archaeological Notes on Two Excavated House Structures in Western Texas," *Bulletin of the Texas Archaeological and Paleontological Society* 20 (1949): 99. Given the size, 15.5 x 11 x 9 cm, and fertility symbology, this was most probably a local agricultural fetish rather than one carried around by a mostly mobile hunting group.

18. Kelley, *Jumano and Patarabueye*, 129–30, summarizes most of these traits. They are abundantly demonstrated in the narrative that follows.

19. Scholars who have studied the emergence of this initial type of pueblos with block units and other structures have generally concluded that the units were for small extended families organized according to either paternal or maternal descent. Such groups tend to have unambiguous social boundaries that help to

preserve their traditions and to assert land ownership: John A. Ware, *A Pueblo Social History: Kinship, Sodality, and Community in the Northern Southwest* (Santa Fe: School for Advanced Research Press, 2014), 85–87.

20. Kelley, *Jumano and Patarabueye*, 127. Kelley theorized that the Southwestern cultural element ceased to be reinforced in the La Junta district with the disappearance of the pueblos in the northern Chihuahua area by the 1500s, probably as the result of intensifying hostile raids. At this same time, Plains hunters with their Southeastern connections were appearing on the scene (*Jumano and Patarabueye*, 132). Although Kelley did not suggest this, could this be one reason that a more complex religious culture apparently did not develop at La Junta? Kelley also found very few references to religion among the Jumanos, the group who became seasonal visitors if not residents in the La Junta valley during this period (*Jumano and Patarabueye*, 138).

21. Kessell, *Spain in the Southwest*, 29–45.

22. Oakah L. Jones Jr., *Nueva Vizcaya: Heartland of the Spanish Frontier* (Albuquerque: University of New Mexico Press, 1988), 21–23, 26.

23. Robert C. West, *The Mining Community in Northern New Spain: The Parral Mining District*, Ibero-Americana 30 (Berkeley: University of California Press, 1949), 52, and Edward H. Spicer, *Cycles of Conquest: The Impact of Spain, Mexico, and the United States on the Indians of the Southwest, 1533–1960* (Tucson: University of Arizona Press, 1962), 28–29. For slave raiding in other frontier areas, see Gerhard, *The North Frontier of New Spain*, 345–48 (Nuevo León), and Patricia Osante, *Orígenes del Nuevo Santander (1748–1772)* (México, D.F.: Universidad Nacional Autónoma de Mexico / Universidad Autónoma de Tamaulipas, 1997), 34–39.

24. George P. Hammond and Agapito Rey, ed. and trans., *Obregón's History of 16th Century Explorations in Western America* (Los Angeles: Wetzel Publishing Company, 1928), 269, 272, 277. Unlike the authors of the other accounts of the 1581–1583 expeditions, Obregón was not a participant. For the Espejo expedition of 1582–1583 he had access to the account of Bernaldino or Bernardo de Luna, who took part in that venture (*Obregón's History of 16th Century Explorations*, 333, 316).

25. George P. Hammond and Agapito Rey, *The Rediscovery of New Mexico, 1580–1594: The Explorations of Chamuscado, Espejo, Castaño de Sosa, Morlete, and Leyva de Bonilla and Humaña* (Albuquerque: University of New Mexico Press, 1966), 71. For the death of Francisco Ibarra, see Jones, *Nueva Vizcaya*, 26.

26. Hammond and Rey, *The Rediscovery of New Mexico*, 158–59. In this journal by Diego Pérez de Luján of events in 1582, the boy Pedro was reported as having been brought up by him and to be "as much as (*hasta*) thirteen years" old. From this I estimate that Pedro was probably seven years old or younger when captured,

and that this slave raid occurred in the first half of the 1570s. This corresponds with the New Mexican practice when taking Native slaves, whose average age upon baptism when noted in the Parral church records between 1640 and 1700 was under ten years old, with many quite younger: Paul Conrad, *The Apache Diaspora: Four Centuries of Displacement and Survival* (Philadelphia: University of Pennsylvania Press, 2021), 50.

27. Cramaussel, *Poblar la frontera*, 188.

28. Hammond and Rey, *The Rediscovery of New Mexico*, 6–8, 69–70. This published translation of the expedition account by Hernán Gallegos, one of the participants, has been checked against the only known manuscript copy (made in 1602), photocopied and transcribed by Barbara De Marco and Jerry R. Craddock, "Relación de Hernán Gallegos sobre la expedición del padre Agustín Rodríguez y el Capitán Francisco Sánchez Chamuscado a Nuevo México, 1581–1582" (Berkeley: Research Center for Romance Studies, University of California, 2013), preface updated 2015, https://escholarship.org/uc/item/4sv5h1gz. I cite the original foliation (the first folio number given in the transcription). Obregón's account of this expedition, drawn from several participants including Gallegos (Hammond and Rey, *Obregón's History of 16th Century Explorations*, 296), will also be cited at times. These accounts are given here in some detail, since they provide the indispensable ethnographic basis for all efforts to identify and differentiate the various people encountered. The distances occasionally given for the Chamuscado expedition are calculated from Obregón's account and modern maps, since those given (in leagues) by him and Gallegos are confusing and at times underestimated.

29. Hammond and Rey, *The Rediscovery of New Mexico*, 70, 72. Hammond and Rey misinterpreted "raya" (dividing line) as a Spanish name (Raya) for the Yoslli, and also mistakenly had the Conchos and the Yoslli residing in the same territory and speaking the same language. The De Marco and Craddock transcription is "despues de aver salido de la nación concha fueron a dar en la raya que se divide la dicha lengua e tierra de los conchos y otra nacion de gente" (folio 28r). The Obregón account, built out of several sources, is clearly fragmented and hopelessly confused in its remarks about the groups encountered before entering the La Junta valley (Hammond and Rey, *Obregón's History of 16th Century Explorations*, 273–77).

30. Hammond and Rey, *The Rediscovery of New Mexico*, 70–71. The following year Espejo described "mescal" as a very sweet preserve made along the Rio Conchos by boiling agave leaves (Hammond and Rey, *The Rediscovery of New Mexico*, 215). Other descriptions from this period indicate that Natives termed naked usually referred to men, not women, and even then as still partially clothed. See the description by Luján in his account of the Espejo expedition below.

31. Hammond and Rey, *The Rediscovery of New Mexico*, 71.

32. Ibid., 72.

33. Hammond and Rey, *Obregón's History of 16th Century Explorations*, 280. The fame that Cabeza de Vaca and his companions had gained as healers had led to their being called children of the sun by the Natives and being escorted safely the rest of their journey across the continent. For "sons of the sun" and "coming from the sky/sun," see Núñez Cabeza de Vaca, *Naufragios y comentarios*, chapter 22 (p. 44), chapter 31 (64) and the famous passage in chapter 34 (69).

34. Hammond and Rey, *The Rediscovery of New Mexico*, 72–74; Hammond and Rey, *Obregón's History of 16th Century Explorations*, 278. Luján's account of the Espejo expedition the following year is the source for the capture of the boy Pedro, thirteen years old in 1582, in this vicinity (*The Rediscovery of New Mexico*, 159). Obregón noted this previous slaving raid and is the source for the gift-giving by the Spaniards. He also wrote that the people were weavers of cloth, but this must have been a confusion with those encountered later in New Mexico. No other account of the Juntans described any as weavers of cloth.

35. Hammond and Rey, *The Rediscovery of New Mexico*, 74. This shortcut to the Rio del Norte still exists. Obregón wrote that the Spaniards found more than 2,000 Natives in this district of the Rio del Norte (Hammond and Rey, *Obregón's History of 16th Century Explorations*, 280). Hammond and Rey, *The Rediscovery of New Mexico*, 75n2, mistakenly assumed that the Spanish party went down to the river junction. They also mistakenly asserted that the Spaniards found the houses here similar to those in the village on the Rio Conchos visited the previous day. The manuscript text is "en el qual rio y valle hallamos mucha gente de la lengua que el dia antes aviamos pasado y casas en que habitaban" (De Marco and Craddock, "Relación de Hernán Gallegos," 30v). This was a declaration of similarity in language but not necessarily in houses.

36. Juan Cantor was not mentioned in the chronicles of the Chamuscado expedition. But in the reports of the Espejo expedition the following year he is noted as having accompanied the Chamuscado expedition into New Mexico (Hammond and Rey, *The Rediscovery of New Mexico*, 162; *Obregón's History of 16th Century Explorations*, 318). For the use of Nahuatl in central Nueva Vizcaya, see Susan M. Deeds, *Defiance and Deference in Mexico's Colonial North: Indians under Spanish Rule in Nueva Vizcaya* (Austin: University of Texas Press, 2003), 17, 37, 79, 121.

37. Hammond and Rey, *The Rediscovery of New Mexico*, 74–75.

38. Hammond and Rey, *The Rediscovery of New Mexico*, 74–75 (quote), 78 (Turkish bows). For the obtaining of buffalo hides through trade at San Bernardino, see Hammond and Rey, *Obregón's History of 16th Century Explorations*, 280.

39. Ramón A. Gutiérrez, *When Jesus Came, the Corn Mothers Went Away: Marriage, Sexuality, and Power in New Mexico, 1500–1846* (Stanford: Stanford University

Press, 1991), 3.

40. Hammond and Rey, *The Rediscovery of New Mexico*, 77. A good example of how oral memory can be "prompted" is that the following year the Juntans, having already discussed the Cabeza de Vaca story with the Chamuscado expedition a year earlier, had sharper memories of three Christians and a Negro (Hammond and Rey, *The Rediscovery of New Mexico*, 164, 217).

41. Hammond and Rey, *The Rediscovery of New Mexico*, 77–78, but amending in italics the dance description according to the De Marco and Craddock transcription; Hammond and Rey, *Obregón's History of 16th Century Explorations*, 278, 280–84.

42. Hammond and Rey, *The Rediscovery of New Mexico*, 162, 165; Hammond and Rey, *Obregón's History of 16th Century Explorations*, 318. For the Chamuscado expedition's experiences in New Mexico, see *The Rediscovery of New Mexico*, 81–111.

43. Hammond and Rey, *The Rediscovery of New Mexico*, 14–19. Unless otherwise noted, the source for the following account of the Espejo expedition is the Luján report as translated by Hammond and Rey in their *Rediscovery of New Mexico*. This has been reprinted in facsimile in *The Native American and Spanish Colonial Experience in the Greater Southwest*, vol I: *Introduction to the Documentary Records*, ed. David H. Snow, 179–238 (New York: Garland Publishing, 1992). There is also a very summary account by Espejo himself, discussed below. *Obregón's History* is almost silent on the La Junta district during this expedition. I am very grateful to Nancy Brown-Martinez at the Center for Southwest Research and Special Collections in the Zimmerman Library at the University of New Mexico for directing me to the photocopy and transcript of the earliest extant manuscript copy of the Luján document: Diego Pérez de Luján, "Relación de la expedición de Antonio de Espejo a Nuevo México, 1582–1583," transcribed by Jerry R. Craddock, revised by Barbara De Marco (Berkeley: Cíbola Project, Research Center for Romance Studies, Institute of International Studies, University of California, 2013), preface updated 2015, http://escholarship.org/uc/item/5313v23h (accessed 20 July 2017). I have relied upon this for certain corrections to the Hammond and Rey translation, citing the contemporary foliation (the first folio number given in the transcription). Another photocopy of the 1602 Spanish script is at the Center for Southwest Research and Special Collections, MSS 841, vol. 113B, AGI Patronato (hereafter UNM-AGI), legajo 22, ramo 4, folios 60r–104v.

44. Hammond and Rey, *The Rediscovery of New Mexico*, 153–55, 214–15; Hammond and Rey, *Obregón's History of 16th Century Explorations*, 316–17.

45. Hammond and Rey, *The Rediscovery of New Mexico*, 157–58 (Luján report).

46. Ibid., 155, 158 (Luján report), 215 (Espejo report). Previous scholars have concluded that the Pasaguates were Chamuscado's Cabris just across from the

La Junta valley, based upon Luján's statement that the next day his expedition traveled four leagues to reach a settlement in the La Junta valley. On this point the Luján document has to be seriously questioned. The distance from the Concho boundary to within the La Junta valley was much more than four leagues. The Espejo report translated in *Rediscovery* relied upon an at-times-faulty nineteenth-century transcription of the no longer extant original document. A copy contemporaneous with the original, judged by Jerry R. Craddock to be the most reliable document extant, is photocopied and transcribed in his "Antonio de Espejo's Report on His Expedition to New Mexico 1682–1683 with Associated Documents" (Berkeley: Cíbola Project, Research Center for Romance Studies, Institute of International Studies, University of California, 2017), folios 6r-20v, https://escholarship.org/uc/item/8rg671zm. For the rendering of Pasaguates, I follow the Luján (pasaguates) and Espejo (paçaguates) transcripts, and not the versions given in *Rediscovery*.

47. Hammond and Rey, *The Rediscovery of New Mexico*, 158 (Luján report), 215–16 (Espejo report). I follow the Espejo manuscript transcript in using Tobosos, not the *Rediscovery* Jobosos. Trying to harmonize the Luján and Espejo accounts, Hammond and Rey surmised that the "Jobosos" were Otomoacos (216n5), but everything points to this being an erroneous conclusion.

48. Hammond and Rey, *The Rediscovery of New Mexico*, 211. The first quotation is my translation of *"escarmentada de pressas que alli se auian hecho"* (Luján, "Relación de la expedición," 103v, lines 1–3), rather than Hammond and Rey's "having taken warning from the captives that had been seized there."

49. Some more recent scholars, studying the use of the terms "chichimeca" in the 1500s and "toboso" in the 1600s, have come to the conclusion that "toboso" was applied in a generic sense the same way that "chichimeca" had been applied in the previous century. In both cases, they were terms applied to all non-sedentary Native peoples who continued to engage in hostilities in a region recently penetrated by Hispanics. These same Natives may have been given different names when living at peace in later times. In Nueva Vizcaya in the 1600s, the "Tobosos" were the warring people who frequented the rugged mountainous country to the north and east of the central agricultural and mining districts of the province. Cramaussel, *Poblar la frontera*, 75–77, provides a good summary of the argument. This would help to explain the use of "chichimeca" in Obregón's account of the 1581 expedition and "toboso" by Espejo and Luján in their accounts of the 1582 expedition.

50. Hammond and Rey, *The Rediscovery of New Mexico*, 216–17. Kelley called Espejo's population estimate for the five towns "certainly excessive" ("Historic Indian Pueblos," 27 no. 4, 266n21).

51. Hammond and Rey, *The Rediscovery of New Mexico*, 158–59. Kelley, *Jumano*

and Patarabueye, 52, 168n7, identified Luján's Otomoacos with Gallegos' Amotomanco speakers, thus placing them along the upper portion of the Rio Conchos in the La Junta valley. The distance (5.5 leagues) given by Luján between the Otomoaco town and San Bernardino on the Rio del Norte points to the same conclusion.

52. Hammond and Rey, *The Rediscovery of New Mexico*, 153, 161, 162. The Spanish phrase is from Luján, "Relación de la expedición," 66v, line 19. There was no notice by the chroniclers of the Chamuscado expedition of the planting of a cross among these people near the Mezquite site, unlike at San Bernardino. That omission would have left them open to Spanish raiding.

53. Hammond and Rey, *The Rediscovery of New Mexico*, 159–60. The italicized words in the quotation are my translation of "escriptos diciendo como quedaban de paz" (Luján, "Relación de la expedición," 65v, lines 4–5), rather than Hammond and Rey's "signs stating that they had been pacified." As will be noted below, a very precise translation is necessary here. The information that the hostile people included Pedro's father and relatives comes from Hammond and Rey, *Obregón's History of 16th Century Explorations*, 318.

54. Hammond and Rey, *The Rediscovery of New Mexico*, 160–61. Luján did not describe the dwellings. His account is very helpful here, as well as his description of the Conchos previously, in detailing what the common Hispanic description of "naked" Natives actually meant, at least in this expedition account. Barr discussed Europeans' frowning upon exposed bodies and noted that in the San Antonio area (just as with the Otomoacos and others at La Junta as described here) Native men had minimal clothing while Native women were praised by missionaries for their "modest" dress (*Peace Came in the Form of a Woman*, 149).

55. Hammond and Rey, *The Rediscovery of New Mexico*, 161.

56. Ibid., 162.

57. Ibid., 162–64 (quotation on 162). The italicized words in the quotation are my translation of the original manuscript's *poner de paz* (Luján, "Relación de la expedición," 67v, lines 11–18), rather than Hammond and Rey's "pacify." Villages raided for slaves are not "left in peace," nor are crosses placed in them as signs of peaceful alliance. There is no incident in any of the documents about the La Junta district, or in any other documents of which I am aware, when crosses were planted at the conclusion of a visit that was a raid for captives. Other scholars, in part misled by the Hammond and Rey translation, have universally misinterpreted this passage. For more recent examples, see Chantal Cramaussel, *Diego Pérez de Luján: Las desventuras de un cazador de esclavos arrepentido* (Ciudad Juárez: Gobierno del Estado, Universidad Autónoma de Ciudad Juárez, 1991), 23, 25; Nancy Adele Kenmotsu, "Helping Each Other Out: A Study of the Mutualistic Relations of Small Scale Foragers and Cultivators in La Junta de

los Rios Region, Texas and Mexico" (PhD diss., University of Texas at Austin, 1994), 191, 220; Morgenthaler, *La Junta de los Rios*, 44; Andrés Reséndez, *The Other Slavery: The Uncovered Story of Indian Enslavement in America* (Boston/ New York: Houghton Mifflin Harcourt, 2016), 116–17.

58. Hammond and Rey, *The Rediscovery of New Mexico*, 163. The italicized text is where the manuscript differs from Hammond and Rey. The text is confusing: "esta jente tiene en sus casas y bestidos arcos como los demas yndios otomoacos" (Luján, "Relación de la expedición," 68r). Hammond and Rey translate: "These people have houses, clothes, and arrows of the same type as the other Otomoacos Indians." This is the only place where Luján seemingly identified Abriaches as Otomoacos. It was probably a slip of the pen or of the original transcriber, since Luján had clearly differentiated the two before.

59. Hammond and Rey, *The Rediscovery of New Mexico*, 163–64. San Juan Evangelista has been identified as a site directly north of the river junction already deserted in the 1600s. After some initial confusion, Santiago has been identified with the town later named San Cristóbal on the same (now Texas) side of the river a few miles below the river junction (Kelley, *Jumano and Patarabueye*, ix, 52–53, 62 fn.).

60. Hammond and Rey, *The Rediscovery of New Mexico*, 164, checked with Luján, "Relación de la expedición," 68v.

61. Hammond and Rey, *The Rediscovery of New Mexico*, 217. The Spanish text is from Craddock, "Antonio de Espejo's Report," 8v.

62. Hammond and Rey, *The Rediscovery of New Mexico*, 165–68 (quotations on 167–68, with italicized words being corrections from Luján, "Relación de la expedición," 71r–71v). The number of men in the expedition as it entered New Mexico is given in Hammond and Rey, *Obregón's History of 16th Century Explorations*, 321.

63. Craddock, "Antonio de Espejo's Report," 9r. Espejo described the mantillas as blue-and-white-striped cotton shawls like some from China. Hammond and Rey followed Forbes in identifying the Otomoacos in general as Cholomes (*The Rediscovery of New Mexico*, 11, 19, 21), which is very questionable at least in regard to the La Junta district, given the identification of the Native groups there by the late 1600s. It is much more likely that the Yoslli/Pasaguates were Cholomes.

64. Hammond and Rey, *The Rediscovery of New Mexico*, 209–11 (quotations on 210). I have corrected in italics some important mistranslation details in regard to the Jumanos above the Davis Mountains and the food and trade items at Santo Tomás, based upon Luján, "Relación de la expedición," 102r, 103r.

65. Hammond and Rey, *Obregón's History of 16th Century Explorations*, 338.

66. Morgenthaler, *La Junta de los Rios*, 13–14.

67. The failure to make this distinction consistently by Morgenthaler is the great

weakness of his otherwise substantive account. Once past the initial encounters, his general tendency was to portray everyone in the La Junta district as at best reluctant about missionaries and always oppressed by Hispanic conquistadors, slavers, and scalp hunters (*La Junta de los Rios*, "Preface," 24, 33–37, 45, 47, 55). Anderson did not make any distinctions at all, writing simply about La Junta or the Juntans, all erroneously considered to be Jumanos, whose settlements he claimed extended all the way to El Paso and included the Concho and Toboso natives to the south of La Junta (*The Indian Southwest, 1580–1830*, 15, 17, 21–22). He presented the history of La Junta by 1683 as one of a basically transient population of many groups coming and going with little cultural continuity, most of them having a continual distaste for missionaries, if not actual rejection of them (26, 65, 79, 94). This study presents a very different assessment.

68. See Kelley, *Jumano and Patarabueye*; J. Charles Kelley, "Juan Sabeata and Diffusion in Aboriginal Texas," *American Anthropologist* 57, no. 5 (1955): 981–95, facsimile reprint in David H. Snow, *Native American II: Introduction to the Research*: 195–209; Hickerson, *The Jumanos*; and Anderson, *The Indian Southwest, 1580–1830*, 13–66.

69. Hammond and Rey, *The Rediscovery of New Mexico*, 158–59; Kelley, *Jumano and Patarabueye*, 57.

70. This leaves out the people at the towns of Guadalupe and Púliques on the right bank of the Rio del Norte below the river junction, not visited by the 1580s expeditions. Varo's report in 1749 will be discussed more fully at that period in this history.

71. Kelley, "Historic Indian Pueblos," vol. 27, no. 4 (1952), 277–78.

72. Some scholars have asserted that slaving continued at La Junta for decades, if not a century, while providing no evidence whatsoever. See Applegate and Hanselka, *La Junta de los Rios del Norte y Conchos*, 9, 15, 17, 20. Unfortunately, this booklet was apparently the source for the same assertions being made over and over again in a recent major Texas educational resource for classroom use, "La Junta de los Rios" (texasbeyondhistory.net) (see "Early Encounters" and "Spanish Frontier").

73. Jack D. Forbes, *Apache, Navaho, and Spaniard* (Norman: University of Oklahoma Press, 1960), 34.

Chapter 2

1. Hammond and Rey guessed that the Morlete party in 1590–1591 followed the Chamuscado and Espejo route up the Rio del Norte from La Junta but in returning pioneered a new route more directly from what is now the El Paso district to Santa Barbara. Whether the illegal expedition of Leyva de Bonilla in 1593 followed the 1581–1583 routes or the "new" one is unknown (*The Rediscovery of New Mexico*, 44, 46–47, 49–50).

2.   Castañeda, *Our Catholic Heritage in Texas*, vol. 1, 186–87.

3.   This listing is a confirmation of the conclusions of the previous chapter. Indeed, the rough similarity between Julimes and Yoslli-mes is striking.

4.   All these nations, named as such or in close approximations, were those indicated by Alonso de Posada in the 1680s as those encountered in the large territories through which one approached the La Junta district from various directions: Alfred Barnaby Thomas, trans. and ed., *Alonso de Posada Report, 1686: A Description of the Area of the Present Southern United States in the Late Seventeenth Century*, Spanish Borderlands Series, vol. 4 (Pensacola: Perdido Bay Press, 1982), 23, 36–37. My interpretation of certain names and locations disagrees with what Thomas took from Anne E. Hughes, *The Beginnings of Spanish Settlement in the El Paso District* (Berkeley: University of California Press, 1914). A photocopy and transcription of the Posada manuscript is provided by Barbara De Marco and Jerry R. Craddock, eds., *Alonso de Posada's Report on the Geography of North America, 14 March 1686* (Berkeley: Research Center for Romance Studies, University of California, 2021), https://escholarship.org/uc/item/6gx2x5gd. For the assimilation of the Conchos and Julimes and the continued hostility of Tobosos, see Griffen, *Indian Assimilation*, 2–3, 14, 70, 109–10.

5.   William B. Griffen, *Culture Change and Shifting Populations in Central Northern Mexico* (Tucson: University of Arizona Press, 1969), 1. The debt of historians of northeastern Nueva Vizcaya, including La Junta, to Griffen's extensive research is immense, as will be apparent in this study. Anderson, *The Indian Southwest, 1580–1830*, 4, concurred with Griffen's conclusion of relative Native autonomy in this region.

6.   William B. Griffen, "Southern Periphery: East," in *Southwest*, ed. Alfonso Ortiz, 340–41 (Washington, DC: Smithsonian Institution, 1983).

7.   Griffen, *Culture Change and Shifting Populations*, 9–12.

8.   Griffen, "Southern Periphery: East," 341. Based upon Captain Retana's reports in 1693, the visiting military inspector stated that the nations from the La Junta valley eastward toward Texas were "more peaceful than warlike" with the exception of the Apaches: Joseph Francisco Marín to Viceroy de Galve, 30 September 1693, Parral, in *Historical Documents relating to New Mexico, Nueva Vizcaya, and Approaches Thereto, to 1773*, 3 vols., ed. Charles Wilson Hackett (Washington, DC: Carnegie Institution, 1923–1937), vol. 2 (1926), 392.

9.   Forbes, *Apache, Navaho, and Spaniard*, 33–34. As previously noted, Applegate and Hanselka, *La Junta de los Rios del Norte y Conchos*, 9, inexplicably claimed that slave raiding continued at La Junta for a century after 1580. Their only reference was W. W. Newcomb Jr., *The Indians of Texas: From Prehistoric to Modern Times* (Austin: University of Texas Press, 1961), 232–37, who, as had Forbes, noted only the slaving raids before 1582. Their repeated allegations (15,

20) cite incident reports that stated no such thing.

10. Max L. Moorhead, *The Presidio: Bastion of the Spanish Borderlands* (Norman: University of Oklahoma Press, 1975), 6–15.

11. David J. Weber, *The Spanish Frontier in North America* (New Haven: Yale University Press, 1992), 124–25, discussed the *encomienda* system in general and in seventeenth-century New Mexico. See also John L. Kessell, *Kiva, Cross, and Crown: The Pecos Indians and New Mexico, 1540–1840* (Washington, DC: National Park Service, U.S. Department of the Interior, 1979), 98–99, 186–90, and David H. Snow, "A Note on Encomienda Economics in Seventeenth-Century New Mexico," in *Hispanic Arts and Ethnohistory in the Southwest*, ed. Marta Weigle, Claudia Larcombe, and Samuel Larcombe, 347–57 (Santa Fe: Ancient City Press, 1983); facsimile reprint in Snow, *Native American II*, 469–79.

12. Susan M. Deeds, "Rural Work in Nueva Vizcaya: Forms of Labor Coercion on the Periphery," *Hispanic American Historical Review* 69, no. 3 (August 1989), 433. Gerhard, *The North Frontier of New Spain*, 9–10, compared the practice of *encomienda* in the different frontier areas. For Nueva Vizcaya in particular, see 165. See also Griffen, *Indian Assimilation*, 46–49, and Deeds, *Defiance and Deference*, 12–15, 74.

13. West, *The Mining Community in Northern New Spain*, 60–61, 71. Sara Ortelli, *Trama de una guerra conveniente: Nueva Vizcaya y la sombra de los apaches (1748–1790)* (México, D.F.: El Colegio de México, 2007), 190, cites two sources for slightly different times in Mexico in general: wheat sowing in October–November and harvesting in June, and maíz sowing in May and harvesting in November.

14. Deeds, "Rural Work in Nueva Vizcaya," 434, 437–38. For *encomienda* and *repartimiento* in the central Nueva Vizcaya area, see also West, *The Mining Community in Northern New Spain*, 47–53, 72–74, and Keith Wayne Algier, "Feudalism on New Spain's Northern Frontier: Valle de San Bartolomé, a Case Study" (PhD diss., University of New Mexico, 1966), 103–20.

15. Cramaussel, *Poblar la frontera*, 207–8 (quote on 208); see also 22.

16. Ibid., 207.

17. William B. Griffen, "A North Mexican Nativistic Movement, 1684," *Ethnohistory* 17, nos. 3–4 (Summer–Fall 1970): 99.

18. Chantal Cramaussel, "The Forced Transfer of Indians in Nueva Vizcaya and Sinaloa: A Hispanic Method of Colonization," in *Contested Spaces of Early America*, eds. Juliana Barr and Edward Countryman (Philadelphia: University of Pennsylvania Press, 2014), 190. Reséndez, *The Other Slavery*, has echoed Cramaussel in considering *encomiendas*, *repartimientos*, and debt peonage as "generally shar[ing] four traits that made them akin to enslavement: forcible removal of the victims from one place to another, inability to leave the workplace,

violence or threat of violence to compel them to work, and nominal or no pay" (10).

19. Cramaussel, *Poblar la frontera*, 233.

20. Cramaussel, *Poblar la frontera*, 222 (1630s), 224–26 (1680s), 233–34 (1700s), 237–40 (permanent workers); see also the transcribed document limiting the free movement of Natives (369). Cramaussel simply qualified as self-serving subterfuge the statement of a missionary in 1649 that all the Natives of his mission were in the haciendas of Indé since there was no military escort to keep them in the mission (229). In her 2014 essay she acknowledged that the Yaquis moved about more freely but again resorted to the debt-peonage argument without offering any specific evidence ("The Forced Transfer of Indians," 194–95, 204–5). For the Yaquis' voluntary long-distance migrant labor as early as the 1640s, see the appendix to this study.

21. Conrad, *The Apache Diaspora*, 61 (quote), 63–64, 67–68, 71–72; James F. Brooks, *Captives and Cousins: Slavery, Kinship, and Community in the Southwest Borderlands* (Chapel Hill: University of North Carolina Press for the Omohundro Institute of Early American History & Culture, 2002).

22. [Lieutenant] Governor of Nueva Vizcaya to Viceroy, 1 September 1744, Chihuahua, in *La historia eclesiástica y civil de la Nueva Vizcaya, 1554–1831* (Durango: Editorial de la Universidad Juárez del Estado de Durango, 2009), 51–59. This volume is a printed digitalized edition of the very rare *Documentos para la historia eclesiástica y civil de la Nueva-Vizcaya*, Documentos para la historia de México, Cuarta Série, vol. 4 (México: Imprenta de Vicente García Torres, 1857). The lieutenant governor's report is given in English translation in Thomas E. Sheridan and Thomas H. Naylor, eds., *Rarámuri: A Tarahumara Colonial Chronicle, 1607–1791* (Flagstaff, AZ: Northland Press, 1979), 95–101. For very similar complaints about the operation of the *repartimiento* system in the early 1700s in Sonora, see Robert C. West, *Sonora: Its Geographical Personality* (Austin: University of Texas Press, 1993), 63–64. Citing a governor's decree in 1600, Cramaussel stated that the *repartimiento* system in Nueva Vizcaya had allowed for one-sixth of the group to be put to work and "took the form of forced labor of two months each year and by each person and was applicable to both men and women" (*Poblar la frontera*, 219 (quote)–220).

23. Cramaussel, *Poblar la frontera*, 221–22. The cited viceroyal document is WBS (Stephens collection) 842 in the Benson library at the University of Texas in Austin.

24. Griffen, *Indian Assimilation*, 5–7; José Arlegui, *Crónica de la Provincia de N.S.P.S. Francisco de Zacatecas* (reprint ed. México: Cumplido, 1851), 231–32. The notice of the "bishop" is from Francisco Javier Alegre, S.J., *Historia de la Provincia de la Compañía de Jesús de Nueva España*, tomo III (Roma: Institutum

Historicum S.J., 1959), 40.

25. For the Cholomes, see Griffen, *Indian Assimilation*, 31–32. The names of most of the nations inhabiting the La Junta district become known to us with the first missionary efforts there in the 1680s and are solidly confirmed with the refounding of missions there in 1715.

26. Griffen, *Indian Assimilation*, 70 (historical summary); Brian Imhoff, ed., *The Diary of Juan Domínguez de Mendoza's Expedition into Texas (1683–1684): A Critical Edition of the Spanish Text with Facsimile Reproductions* (Dallas: William P. Clements Center for Southwest Studies, Southern Methodist University, 2002), 145 (1684).

27. Griffen, *Indian Assimilation*, 34. An argument for this position, not given by Griffen, is the listing of nations under the Native governor of the Eastern Conchería, discussed below.

28. Griffen, *Indian Assimilation*, 6–7. It should be noted that in this revolt the Julimes, erroneously equated by some authors with the Juntans, made peace separately from the Juntans.

29. Pedro Vázquez Cortés solicitando mandamiento, 9 January 1645, Parral, Archivo Histórico Municipal de Parral, Fondo Colonial, https://www.rootspoint.com/fondo-colonial/ (henceforth AHMP-FC), Gobierno y administración, serie encomiendas y repartimientos, AHMP.FC.A05.001.006 (accessed 28 March 2021). The word *nación* applied twice to the two groups together is clear in the manuscript: "la nacion mamites y gorretas" and "la nacion de gorretas y mamites."

30. Cramaussel, *Poblar la frontera*, 65, 364 (*encomiendas*). For the Ochanes, see Griffen, *Indian Assimilation*, "Auchanes" (30). For La Chorrera, see Gerhard, *The North Frontier of New Spain*, "Chorreras" (196 map, 200).

31. Chantal Cramaussel, *La Provincia de Santa Barbara, 1563–1631* (Chihuahua: Secretaría de Educación y Cultura, Gobierno del Estado de Chihuahua, 2004), 124–25.

32. "Francisco Martínez Orejón . . . solicitando se le restituya su encomienda," 6 June 1655, AHMP-FC, Gobierno y administración, serie encomiendas y repartimientos, AHMP.FC.A05.001.009 (accessed 30 January 2018). The existence of this *encomienda* in the 1640s is derived from the statement that it was granted by Governor Francisco Bravo de la Serna, who is listed as governor in 1638–1639 in Jones, *Nueva Vizcaya*, 238. The name of the hacienda and the fact that some of these "Conejos" were married by the parish priest in the Valley of San Bartolomé is found in Cramaussel, *Poblar la frontera*, 214.

33. Title of *encomienda* to Bernardo Gómez, 28 November 1653, Parral, AHMP-FC, in "Francisco Martínez Orejón" appeal cited above. The *media anata* was a fee paid to the royal treasury upon receiving a government office or position

(Gerhard, *The North Frontier of New Spain*, 370).

34. Cramaussel, *Poblar la frontera*, 190, 216, 363.

35. Pedro de Ortega statement, 2 September 1715, San Bartolomé, in the file "Los labradores del Valle de San Bartolomé solicitando se les devuelvan los indios mansos ... que han vuelto a sus pueblos de las Juntas [*sic*] del Norte," AHMP-FC, Gobierno y administración, serie encomiendas y repartimientos, AHMP. FC.A05.001.018. This file of 116 pages will henceforth be designated as "Los labradores," since it will be cited frequently in chapter 4.

36. Griffen, *Indian Assimilation*, 57–59. Apparently counting all the baptisms of Tapacolmes in the entire records, Chamaussel gave the number of forty, "of whom 25 are *gentiles*" (*Poblar la frontera*, 214), eleven more than Griffen's more temporally limited count.

37. Cramaussel, *Poblar la frontera*, 200.

38. Fernando Ocaranza, *Crónica de las Provincias Internas de la Nueva España* (México: Editorial Polis, 1939), 164.

39. Griffen, *Indian Assimilation*, 68; decree of Governor Lope de Sierra Osorio, 19 January 1678, Parral, Libro de Gobierno de Lope de Sierra Osorio, folio 18, AHMP-FC, Gobierno y administración, serie libros de gobierno y conocimiento, AHMP.FC.A14.001.004 (accessed 27 March 2021); Hackett, *Historical Documents*, vol. 2, 360 (1693). Santa Cruz was a satellite of the San Pedro mission center until at least 1693, and Griffen could find no local documents nor parish records for San Pedro during the seventeenth century (Griffen, *Indian Assimilation*, 66).

40. Cramaussel, *Poblar la frontera*, 208n141, 213. She also stated that "their pueblo and corresponding mission [of Santa Cruz de Tapacolmes] go back to 1677," but gave no reference for this apparently inaccurate information. Perhaps she was relying on the first known reference to the village of Santa Cruz (without the added "de Tapacolmes') in 1678, noted above.

41. Griffen, *Indian Assimilation*, 57. Cramaussel, *Poblar la frontera*, frequently made the same observation and added that the farm owners probably often avoided paying for sacraments by not having them administered to their seasonal Native workers (152–53, 162).

42. Griffen, *Indian Assimilation*, 45–46, translated sections of the 1653 document. I use the mostly identical decree made in 1666 and transcribed in its entirety by Cramaussel, *Poblar la frontera*, 367.

43. Griffen, *Indian Assimilation*, 46; Cramaussel, *Poblar la frontera*, 367.

44. Cramaussel, "The Forced Transfer of Indians," 190–91. Cramaussel, *Poblar la frontera*, 209, asserted (without offering evidence) that the *encomenderos* held the family members of the Native governors hostage to guarantee compliance. She also assumed that the Natives who stayed as permanent salaried workers on

haciendas had to do so because they never were able to pay off their debt to their masters (212).

45. Decree of Governor Lope de Sierra Osorio, 19 January 1678, AHMP-FC. For a simple definition of the Protector of Indians, see Kessell, *Spain in the Southwest*, 424.

46. W. H. Timmons, *El Paso: A Borderlands History* (El Paso: Texas Western Press, 1990), 15, 17.

47. As previously noted, Luján gave the name Otomoacos to the people on the upper reaches of the Conchos and Norte Rivers within the La Junta valley, as well as to the people that the Espejo expedition met for 100 miles beyond San Bernardino as they traveled up the Rio del Norte. At that point the expedition entered territory frequented by a nation that commentators identify with the Sumas. Luján wrote that the Otomoacos and these people were intermarried and had almost the same language. The Juntan boy interpreter Pedro had a Suma grandfather (Hammond and Rey, *The Rediscovery of New Mexico*, 165–68).

48. Imhoff, *The Diary of Juan Domínguez de Mendoza's Expedition*, 139. The biographical information about Father García is from Agustín de Vetancurt, "Menologio Franciscano," 7–8, in *Teatro Mexicano*, 2a ed. facsimilar (México: Editorial Porrúa, 1982).

49. Agustín de Colina to Juan Álvarez, Custos, 13 March 1704, Jémez, in the Biblioteca Nacional de México (BNM) photostat collection (MSS 867) in the Center for Southwest Research and Special Collections, Zimmerman Library, University of New Mexico (UNM), vol. 122B, legajo 5, part 2, no. 5. This study draws heavily upon these BNM photostats at the University of New Mexico, which are henceforth cited as UNM-BNM, followed by the volume number. For Father García's last entry at El Paso, see Alonso de Benavides, *The Memorial of Fray Alonso de Benavides, 1630*, trans. Mrs. Edward E. Ayer, annot. Frederick Webb Hodge and Charles Fletcher Lummis (Albuquerque: Horn and Wallace, 1965), 205. In 1692 Father Sumesta was guardian of the Franciscan convent at San Bartolomé (Griffen, *Culture Change and Shifting Populations*, 43, 44).

50. Morgenthaler, *La Junta de los Rios*, 66.

Chapter 3

1. Missions are understood here as localized efforts by Hispanic Catholic missionaries to convert Indigenous groups to Christianity. This corresponds with the first of the two meanings of the term explained by Guillermo Porras Muñoz: "Puede indicar simplemente una incursion eclesiástica en tierras de infieles o un establecimiento material entre ellos": *Iglesia y Estado en Nueva Vizcaya (1562–1821)* (México: Universidad Nacional Autónoma de México, 1980), 191. Missions do not necessarily imply a set of buildings, the image that comes to most people's

minds. Nor do they necessarily imply support by the colonial government—the "mission institution" classically described by Herbert Eugene Bolton.

2. For studies of Sabeata, see Kelley, "Juan Sabeata"; Elizabeth A. H. John, *Storms Brewed in Other Men's Worlds: The Confrontation of Indians, Spanish, and French in the Southwest, 1540–1795* (College Station: Texas A&M University Press, 1975), 175–94; and Hickerson, *The Jumanos*, 107, 128–43, 182–205.

3. John L. Kessell, *Pueblos, Spaniards, and the Kingdom of New Mexico* (Norman: University of Oklahoma Press, 2008), 97–118.

4. This Concho River in West Texas should not be confused with the Rio Conchos in Nueva Vizcaya that joins the Rio del Norte at La Junta.

5. A report at that time is given in Thomas, *Alonso de Posada Report*, 26, 36–37. For the Apache push into the Edwards Plateau area of south-central Texas, see Thomas A. Britten, *The Lipan Apaches: People of Wind and Lightning* (Albuquerque: University of New Mexico Press, 2009), 60–63.

6. This history is well summarized with a focus upon the Jumanos in Hickerson, *The Jumanos*, 120–26.

7. Jones, *Nueva Vizcaya*, 108; Timmons, *El Paso*, 17–21.

8. Maria F. Wade, *The Native Americans of the Texas Edwards Plateau, 1582–1799* (Austin: University of Texas Press, 2003), 236–37, gives the Sabeata declaration in translation.

9. Domingo Gironza Petris de Cruzate to viceroy, 20 October 1683, El Paso, in Charles Wilson Hackett, ed., *Pichardo's Treatise on the Limits of Louisiana and Texas*, 4 vols. (Austin: University of Texas Press, 1931–1946), vol. 1, 137–39.

10. Juan Agustín Morfi, *History of Texas, 1673–1779*, trans. and ed. Carlos Eduardo Castañeda (Albuquerque: The Quivira Society, 1935), vol. 1, 118; Robert S. Weddle, *Wilderness Manhunt: The Spanish Search for La Salle* (Austin: University of Texas Press, 1973), 12. Neither the 1683 Sabeata notice nor news about La Salle in Texas in early 1685 reached the Council of the Indies in Spain by August 1685, when the king again sent out his 1678 request for information about the geography of the Gulf Coast region and anything to be feared from French proposals (Thomas, *Alonso de Posada Report*, 12–18; Weddle, *Wilderness Manhunt*, 26–27).

11. Wade, *The Native Americans of the Texas Edwards Plateau*, 239–40. The Domínguez expedition that was in response to Sabeata's proposal was actually shown the cross and reverenced it upon arriving in the Jumano lands, but its miraculous origin was debunked (Wade, 98–99).

12. John L. Kessell and Rick Hendricks, eds., *By Force of Arms: The Journals of don Diego de Vargas, New Mexico, 1691–93* (Albuquerque: University of New Mexico Press, 1992), 270n78. López's entry into Franciscan life as a member of the Discalced Franciscans is revealed in Colina to Álvarez, 13 March 1704,

UNM-BNM. For the Discalced in New Spain working only among Hispanics, see Marcela Corvera Poiré, "The Discalced Franciscans in Mexico: Similarities and Differences vis-à-vis the Observant Franciscans in Mexico and the Discalced in the Philippines," in *Francis in the Americas: Essays on the Franciscan Family in North and South America*, ed. John F. Schwaller (Berkeley, CA: Academy of American Franciscan History, 2005), 28, 37–38.

13. "Memorial de Fr. Nicolás López," 24 April 1686, in Cesario Fernández Duro, *Don Diego de Peñalosa y su descubrimiento del reino de Quivira* (Madrid: Manuel Tello, 1882), 68; Angélico Chávez, O.F.M., *Archives of the Archdiocese of Santa Fe, 1678–1900* (Washington, DC: Academy of American Franciscan History, 1957), 11; Eleanor B. Adams and Angelico Chavez, eds., *The Missions of New Mexico, 1776: A Description by Fray Francisco Atanasio Dominguez with Other Contemporary Documents* (Albuquerque: University of New Mexico Press, 1956), 335; Hughes, *The Beginnings of Spanish Settlement*, 327–28.

Vina Walz portrayed Father López as patently dishonest in her dissertation, "History of the El Paso Area, 1680–1692" (University of New Mexico, 1951). Her "evidence" is easily refutable. To make her case she had to assign an undated listing of El Paso missionaries to early 1682, whereas it is demonstrably from 1683 (75–76). She proposed her own interpretation of a passage about the use of timber in 1683 rather than that given by Anne Hughes that she admitted was "allowable" (121–23), and she asserted that López should not have taken credit for what he accomplished in 1683 since much of it was set back by the Manso rebellion of 1684 (122). Regrettably, El Paso historians have repeated Walz's negative characterization: Applegate and Hanselka, *La Junta de los Rios del Norte y Conchos*, 14; C. L. Sonnichsen, *Pass of the North: Four Centuries on the Rio Grande* (El Paso: Texas Western Press, 1968), 54. Morgenthaler, in turn, used Sonnichsen as the primary evidence for his skepticism about the veracity of any positive reports by Franciscans about La Junta (*La Junta de los Rios*, 71–74).

14. López to Viceroy, April 1685, in Hackett, *Pichardo's Treatise*, vol. 2, 349–50, and López to Viceroy [March 1686], in Otto Maas, O.F.M., *Misiones de Nuevo Méjico: Documentos del Archivo General de Indias (Sevilla)* (Madrid: Imprenta Hijos de T. Minuesa de los Ríos, 1929), 117–18 (excerpt). The full March 1686 report is translated in Hackett, *Pichardo's Treatise*, vol. 2, 354–56, and Hackett, *Historical Documents*, vol. 3 (1937), 360–63. The notice of the Tigua aides comes from a recollection of the 1684 uprising at La Junta discussed below. For the employment of converted Natives as models in new missionary efforts, see Philip Wayne Powell, *Soldiers, Indians, and Silver: The Northward Advance of New Spain, 1550–1600* (Berkeley: University of California Press, 1952), 193–97, 213–16 (Tlaxcalan colonists in the north in the 1590s); Kessell, *Spain in the Southwest*, 75 (Native aides brought by the Franciscans to New Mexico in 1598); Gerhard,

The North Frontier of New Spain, 331 (Tlaxcalans in the Coahuila missions in the late 1600s).

15. Imhoff, *The Diary of Juan Domínguez de Mendoza's Expedition*, 2, 23.

16. Griffen, *Indian Assimilation*, 33, pointed out the error, but it has continued to be made.

17. De Marco and Craddock, *Alonso de Posada's Report*, manuscript photocopy, 4. Thomas, *Alonso de Posada Report*, 24 and n33, discusses the different manuscript copies of this report with slightly varying spellings of the nations at La Junta.

18. Kessell, *Spain in the Southwest*, 103.

19. Jim Norris, *After "The Year Eighty": The Demise of Franciscan Power in Spanish New Mexico* (Albuquerque: University of New Mexico Press in cooperation with the Academy of American Franciscan History, 2000), 174 (vow profession); López to Viceroy, [24 March 1686], in Hackett, *Pichardo's Treatise*, vol. 2, 356 (Jumano language); Charles Wilson Hackett, ed., and Charmion Clair Shelby, trans., *Revolt of the Pueblo Indians of New Mexico and Otermin's Attempted Reconquest, 1680–1682* (Albuquerque: University of New Mexico Press, 1942), 59, 116; Chávez, *Archives of the Archdiocese of Santa Fe*, 14, 16, 19–21.

20. Adams and Chavez, *The Missions of New Mexico*, 329; Chávez, *Archives of the Archdiocese of Santa Fe*, 8.

21. Imhoff, *The Diary of Juan Domínguez de Mendoza's Expedition*, 29, 49. Kelley, *Jumano and Patarabueye*, 24, concluded that La Navidad was at the river junction itself; this supposition is strongly supported by Domínguez's original manuscript at this point as described in Imhoff, 5. It is also supported by the Scholes translation in the Center for Southwest Research at the University of New Mexico of a journal that differs in some important ways from the one transcribed by Imhoff (Wade, *The Native Americans of the Texas Edwards Plateau*), 69, 90. As previously noted, the Mexican language was common in the Parral district by the 1620s (Griffen, *Culture Change and Shifting Populations*, 8).

22. López to Viceroy, April 1685, in Hackett, *Pichardo's Treatise*, vol. 2, 350–51. The notice of the 500-plus baptisms and the deaths of children, as well as the four other chapels, is in López to Viceroy [March 1686] in Maas, *Misiones de Nuevo Méjico*, 118 (translated in Hackett's works noted above). Perhaps Domínguez only reported the baptisms that took place during his brief time there, whereas López would have reported those baptized during more than two weeks. López also reported nine nations in the March 1686 document cited above and in the April 1686 "Memorial de Fr. Nicolás Lopez" in Fernández Duro, *Don Diego de Peñalosa*, 69, 71.

23. The April 1685 petition of López notes six *pueblos*, whereas the April 1686 one speaks of nine nations "todas pobladas." The latter phrase probably means that the nine nations were all town dwellers, but not necessarily each having its own

town. That there were six towns is supported by the journal of Domínguez upon his return through La Junta, wherein he stated that the seven (note: not López's nine) nations that declared obedience to the king at that time asked for six priests "since their pueblos are not immediate to each other and have many people" (Imhoff, *The Diary of Juan Domínguez de Mendoza's Expedition*, 137). It is also supported by the fact that Sabeata in El Paso had stated that he was representing six captains at La Junta (see above).

24. Robert E. Wright, "Latino American Religion: Catholics, Colonial Origins," in *Encyclopedia of Religion in America*, vol. 3, eds. Charles H. Lippy and Peter W. Williams, 1174–75 (Washington, DC: CQ Press, 2010).

25. Imhoff, *The Diary of Juan Domínguez de Mendoza's Expedition*, 51, 137–41, 251.

26. Mallouf, "Comments on the Prehistory," 71–73, noted that Plains-type arrow points and pendants found at a nomadic base camp on a high ledge overlooking the Rio del Norte just before it enters the canyons at the bottom end of the La Junta valley might indicate an initial Apache presence there sometime between 1650 and 1690. Apaches were present in central Nueva Vizcaya since the late 1630s, but as slaves, not traders or warriors. Captured or obtained in trade from other Native groups in New Mexico, they were brought down the Camino Real and sold in Parral and further south: Rick Hendricks and Gerald Mandell, "The Apache Slave Trade in Parral, 1637–1679," *Journal of Big Bend Studies* 16 (2004): 59–81; Conrad, *The Apache Diaspora*, 29–33, 47–78.

27. Imhoff, *The Diary of Juan Domínguez de Mendoza's Expedition*, reproduces and transcribes the journal of Domínguez. An English translation was provided by Herbert E. Bolton in his edited collection of documents, *Spanish Exploration in the Southwest, 1542–1706* (New York: Barnes and Noble, 1963), 320–43. But that translation omits the last part of the journal that presents the return trip from La Junta to El Paso through a detour to the south of the Rio del Norte. The Scholes version of the document also accuses Sabeata of being a liar and a cheat but is silent on his expulsion. Wade declared that Sabeata was not expelled, since the Scholes document said there were still some Jumano scouts with the expedition. But the Scholes document also states that out of fear of punishment Sabeata did not accompany the expedition when it turned back toward La Junta and that he sought to have the Spaniards murdered (Wade, *The Native Americans of the Texas Edwards Plateau*, 71, 110, 112–14). A different controversy reported only in the Scholes document was a serious falling out of some of Domínguez's men who fled the expedition (Wade, 100, 112–13).

28. Imhoff, *The Diary of Juan Domínguez de Mendoza's Expedition*, 141–43. Griffen, *Indian Assimilation*, 95–96, posited that the three settlements were Mezquite, Cuchillo Parado, and San Pedro. In 1715 Trasviña Retes calculated about five leagues from the river junction to El Mezquite, twelve leagues to the other side of

the high mountain ridge, five leagues to Cuchillo Parado, and an unspecified distance to San Pedro of the Cholomes. In 1726 Aguirre said that it was twenty-five leagues between San Francisco and Coyame: seven from San Francisco to El Mezquite, an unreported distance to a place on the other side of the high mountain ridge, and seven leagues from there to Coyame. Ydoiaga in 1747 counted four leagues to San Juan Bautista, ten leagues from there to the other side of the mountain ridge, and eleven leagues from there to Coyame. For these reports, see the respective years in the account that follows.

29. For the Franciscans' total presence of eight months at La Junta, see Colina to Álvarez, 13 March 1704, UNM-BNM.

30. Griffen, *Indian Assimilation*, 9–11; Forbes, *Apache, Navaho, and Spaniard*, 181–84, 200–205; Hughes, *The Beginnings of Spanish Settlement*, 334–64 (the most extensive treatment).

31. Griffen, *Indian Assimilation*, 11; Cramaussel, *Poblar la frontera*, 411 (the Salaíces).

32. See the account of the 1715 expedition in the next chapter.

33. Griffen, *Indian Assimilation*, 12–13. Griffen summarized the statement of each witness in his earlier essay about this incident ("A North Mexican Nativistic Movement"). In the early 1600s further south along the colonial frontier, there had been other insurrections whose leaders guaranteed miraculous divine protection for their followers, adopted Christian titles, and mimicked various Christian practices (Deeds, *Defiance and Deference*, 23–24, 30).

34. For the location of the Auchanes, see Griffen, *Indian Assimilation*, 30. It has already been noted that in 1686 Father Posada named several of the nations in the La Junta valley, based upon reports he received about the 1683–1684 Domínguez expedition.

35. Colina to Álvarez, 13 March 1704, UNM-BNM. In 1693 the viceroy's special military inspector, Joseph Francisco Marín, listed the nations that he was told existed "on the other side of La Junta between Texas and New Mexico." In the middle of his list of fifty-four nations came the following cluster: "los humanas [*sic*], los come sibolos, los arcos tirados, los sivolos, los apaches, los mesquites, los cacalotes, los posalmes, los polacmes, los oposmes, los pulicas, los topacolmes" (Marín to Viceroy de Galve, 30 September 1693, in Hackett, *Historical Documents*, vol. 2, 392). Four of the first five are very recognizable as those to the north and east of La Junta; the following seven are the La Junta valley nations, with the very recent move of the Tapacolmes unrecognized (see below). The Conejos of Colina's list appear three places before the Jumanos in Marín's 1693 list.

36. Colina to Álvarez, 13 March 1704, UNM-BNM. Back in 1688 Colina had written the same, stating that the two missionaries departed La Junta "escaping

badly treated and losing the sacred vestments" (Agustín de Colina to Governor Pardiñas, 18 November 1688, in Hackett, *Historical Documents*, vol. 2, 244). Hughes, citing documents immediately after the event that I have not seen, wrote that the La Junta Christians actually conducted the priests all the way to Parral along with the sacred vessels and vestments of their churches (Hughes, *The Beginnings of Spanish Settlement*, 358). The friars did eventually make their way to Parral. They were found there by the new custos Salvador de San Antonio on his way to El Paso, where he arrived in March 1685, bringing the young refugee Acevedo with him (Adams and Chavez, *The Missions of New Mexico*, 261n34).

37. "Carta del P. Fray Silvestre Vélez de Escalante, O.F.M., al P. Morfi, O.F.M., sobre el reino y las misiones del Nuevo Méjico, el Tehuayo y la Gran Quivira," 2 April 1778, in Otto Maas, O.F.M., ed., *Las órdenes religiosas de España y la colonización de América en la segunda parte del siglo XVIII: estadísticas y otros documentos*, vol. 2 (Barcelona: A. G. Belart, 1929), 43.

38. Griffen, *Indian Assimilation*, 9. Sixty years later Father Miguel Menchero mistakenly dated this 1684 uprising at La Junta as occurring in 1670–1671 (probably confusing it with the missionary visit from El Paso at that time). His well-known account about the first mission efforts is similar to Colina's in many respects but has several other mistaken details, besides the wrong dates, that have all found their way into published works to this day. See Miguel Menchero, "Declaración," 10 May 1744, UNM-BNM, vol. 125A, legajo 8, part 1, no. 17. There is a faulty typescript of this document in the H. E. Bolton Collection (C-B 840), Bancroft Library (henceforth Bolton Collection), Part I, no. 447. This Bolton typescript is translated in Hackett, *Historical Documents*, vol. 3, with the La Junta section in pages 407–11. Menchero was the source for Joseph Antonio Villaseñor y Sanchez, *Theatro Americano: descripcion general de los Reynos y Provincias de la Nueva España y sus jurisdicciones*, 2 vols. (Mexico: Imprenta de la Viuda de D. Joseph Bernardo de Hogal, 1746–1748), vol. 2, 424. Villaseñor misread Menchero's 1670 as 1660, further compounding the error in regard to date. Villaseñor in turn was copied by Pedro Alonso O'Crouley, *A Description of the Kingdom of New Spain, 1774*, trans. and ed. Sean Galvin (n.p.: John Howell Books, 1972), 62. Hughes, *The Beginnings of Spanish Settlement*, 330–31, noted the probable discrepancy in Menchero's account, but several modern authors have repeated the mistakes. Morgenthaler, trying to reconcile the varying accounts, jumbled the history between 1670 and 1684 at several points (*La Junta de los Rios*, 55, 68, 169n20).

39. Griffen, "A North Mexican Nativistic Movement," 113. However, some Oposme hacienda workers from La Junta were alleged to have taken part in a multi-nation pillage of a mule train far south between Parral and Durango in 1686 (Griffen, *Culture Change and Shifting Populations*, 36). A Hispanic officer in 1692 alleged

that migrant laborers from the Rio del Norte area often stole animals on their return trip home (ibid., 43); however, the Rio del Norte designation encompassed a broader area than the La Junta district, let alone the La Junta valley itself.

40. "Memorial" of López, 24 April 1686, in Maas, *Misiones de Nuevo México*, 113–15. For the date of the Franciscan meeting in El Paso, see Hughes, *The Beginnings of Spanish Settlement*, 374. The time between the September 1684 decision in El Paso and the May 1685 petition must have been occupied in awaiting a caravan to Mexico City, the months-long journey, and Franciscan consultations in the capital.

41. Lopez to the Viceroy, [24 March 1686], in Hackett, *Historical Documents*, vol. 3, 360–63; Maas, *Misiones de Nuevo Méjico*, 110, 115, 117–18. The king's decree of 2 August 1685 can be found in Fernández Duro, *Don Diego de Peñalosa*, 50–53. In his March memorial López stated that his two brothers in New Spain, inheritors of the Rosario mines discovered by his father, were willing to contribute horses, cattle, and grain to support 100 men that he petitioned the viceroy to obtain from the prisons to settle the promising field of Texas (Maas, *Misiones de Nuevo Méjico*, 117).

42. Barbara De Marco, "Francisco de Ayeta and the 1680 Pueblo Revolt in New Mexico: Preliminaries to a Biography," in Schwaller, *Francis in the Americas*, 183, under IV. "Expediciones misioneras en Indias"; Hackett, *Pichardo's Treatise*, vol. 1, 282.

43. Maas, *Misiones de Nuevo Méjico*, 116.

44. For López as custos and *provisor* of the custody in 1685–1687, see Adams and Chavez, *The Missions of New Mexico*, 335, and López to Viceroy, [24 March 1686], in Hackett, *Historical Documents*, vol. 3, 360–61. In 1776 Father Domínguez noted a document in the archives of the San Pablo Custody that presented the "opinion of the missionary religious of the Junta de los Rios that the said missions could not survive, and a letter of Custos Fray Nicolás López on the same subject" (Adams and Chavez, *The Missions of New Mexico*, 260). Such a document, date unknown, is not listed in Chávez, *Archives of the Archdiocese of Santa Fe*, the calendar of the extant church documents in New Mexico.

45. Colina to Álvarez, 13 March 1704, UNM-BNM.

46. Francisco Antonio de la Rosa Figueroa, *Bezerro General Menologico y Chronologico de todos los Religiosos que ... ha avido en esta Santa Provincia del Santo Evangelio desde su fundación hasta el presente año de 1764*, 390, no. 695, Ayer Collection, Newberry Library, Chicago; Adams and Chavez, *The Missions of New Mexico*, 334; Colina to Álvarez, 13 March 1704, UNM-BNM. Nothing is known about Brother Diego de San Miguel.

47. Colina to Álvarez, 13 March 1704, UNM-BNM. In this 1704 recollection Colina reported having spent one year and eight months at La Junta. His earlier report

stated one year and seven months (Colina to Pardiñas, 18 November 1688, in Hackett, *Historical Documents*, vol. 2, 244). Hinojosa ascended quickly in the leadership of the custody, becoming president of the El Paso district in 1691 and vice-custos in 1692, just prior to the Vargas reconquest of New Mexico. In the latter year he successfully had Vargas deed the chapels and convents of the El Paso missions to the Church: Chávez, *Archives of the Archdiocese of Santa Fe*, 11, 16–18; Kessell and Hendricks, *By Force of Arms*, 239–99, 307–18.

48. Joachin de Hinojosa to Custos Salvador de San Antonio, 23 April 1693, Senecú, Archives of the Archdiocese of Santa Fe, microfilm reel 51, 126–27.

49. Colina to Álvarez, 13 March 1704, UNM-BNM. Studies in the early twentieth century classified the La Junta region as having a frequency of ten desert years out of every twenty (Kelley, "Historic Indian Pueblos," 27 no. 4, 262). For Colina as president of the La Junta missions, see deposition of Colina, 22 November 1688, in Hackett, *Historical Documents*, vol. 2, 240.

50. Colina to Pardiñas, 18 November 1688, in Hackett, *Historical Documents*, vol. 2, 244, 246 (my translation rather than the one given in Hackett, 245, 247).

51. West, *The Mining Community in Northern New Spain*, 72–73.

52. In his classic study of the northern frontier of New Spain up through 1800, Navarro García titled the period from 1680 to 1720 a period of expansion (*Don José de Gálvez*, 25–46). But what he actually described, up until 1715, was a period of frustrated attempts to advance in Nueva Vizcaya, Texas, and Sonora, with the reclamation of lost territory in New Mexico. The only notable advance was that into the peninsula of Baja California.

53. Moorhead, *The Presidio*, 20–22. At this same time the detachment of soldiers at Parral, officially a field company rather than a presidio, was doubled (Jones, *Nueva Vizcaya*, 111).

54. Weber, *The Spanish Frontier in North America*, 141–59.

55. Juan Ysidro de Pardiñas Villar decrees, 2 November 1688, Parral, in Hackett, *Historical Documents*, vol. 2, 248–54. Native reports of Frenchmen in Texas had reached Coahuila by 1686, and search parties had been sent out from there. However, it was not until May 1688 that these Hispanics encountered a Frenchman, and only the following year that they found the destroyed French fort (Hickerson, *The Jumanos*, 179–81).

56. Colina to Pardiñas, 18 November 1688, 244, 246. For Vargas as custos, see Adams and Chavez, *The Missions of New Mexico*, 339.

57. Declarations of Juntans, 21 November 1688, in Hackett, *Historical Documents*, vol. 2, 234–38.

58. In the La Junta documents, as in several other frontier districts of northern New Spain, *ladino* had the basic meaning of "fluency in Spanish." For other frontiers, see Kessell, *Pueblos*, 98 (New Mexico): "Spaniards referred proudly to such

Indian Spanish-speakers as *indios ladinos*"; Cecilia Sheridan, *El "yugo suave del evangelio": las misiones franciscanas de Rio Grande en el periodo colonial* (Saltillo: Centro de Estudios Sociales y Humanísticos, 1999), 51 (Coahuila): "ladino en lengua castellana"; Deeds, *Defiance and Deference*, 116 (Nueva Vizcaya): "All of the Tepehuan mission Indians were ladino, or Spanish speaking." Deeds, 35, also used *ladino* to describe rebel leaders who were Hispanicized or acculturated. Thus, *ladino* in itself signified having learned Hispanic culture, beginning with language, whether one went along with that culture or opposed it.

59. Hackett, *Historical Documents*, vol. 2, 258–60 (governor of the Julime nation); Griffen, *Indian Assimilation*, 15 (governor of the nations of the north), 46 (end of the Eastern Conchería governorship); Griffen, *Culture Change and Shifting Populations*, 45.

60. Fernández de Retana decree, 22 November 1688, and depositions of Colina and Hinojosa, 23 November 1688, in Hackett, *Historical Documents*, vol. 2, 238–42. The text of the order to the Natives mistakenly has "upper" Rio del Norte where it should state "lower."

61. Retana to Pardiñas, 3 March 1689, and depositions by Sabeata and others in Parral, 11 April 1689, in Hackett, *Historical Documents*, vol. 2, 254–80. The ship drawing was sent to Spain, where it is preserved in the Archivo General de Indias. It is illustrated in Kessell, *Spain in the Southwest*, 145.

62. For mentions of Franciscans as still at La Junta by the Sabeata party, see Hackett, *Historical Documents*, vol. 2, 262 and 268. For Hinojosa at El Paso in March 1689, see Adams and Chavez, *The Missions of New Mexico*, 334; for Colina at El Paso in April 1689, see Chávez, *Archives of the Archdiocese of Santa Fe*, 9. Ocaranza, paraphrasing Colina's 1704 document, added that Hinojosa and San Miguel moved from La Junta to a new mission among the Cholomes between La Junta and El Paso: Fernando Ocaranza, *Establecimientos franciscanos en el misterioso Reino de Nuevo México*. México, D.F., 1934), 119.

63. Colina to Álvarez, 13 March 1704, UNM-BNM.

64. Governor Diego de Vargas to Captain Juan Fernández de la Fuente, 29 April 1691, in Maas, *Misiones de Nuevo Méjico*, 129.

65. Hackett, *Historical Documents*, vol. 2, 282–86 (quotations on 286). For Father López's death, see Diego de Vargas to Viceroy, 30 March 1692, in Maas, *Misiones de Nuevo Méjico*, 149, and Kessell and Hendricks, *By Force of Arms*, 270n78. For the beginning of Spanish missionary efforts in East Texas in 1690, see Castañeda, *Our Catholic Heritage in Texas*, vol. 1, 349–54, 359–61.

66. "General Juan de Fernández Retana concerning enemy Indians from the north," 96 (quote), 113 (Fabiata), AGI Guadalajara, box 2, folder 4 (legajo 67-4-11), Spanish and Mexican Manuscript Collection, Catholic Archives of Texas, Austin, Texas. The pagination given is that of the transcript, not of the

original document.

67. Kelley, "Juan Sabeata," 987; Hickerson, *The Jumanos*, 201–8. In 2016 persons claiming Jumano descent organized themselves as the Jumano Indian Nation of Texas; they succeeded in obtaining a resolution honoring their role in Texas history by the Texas legislature in 2019 (House Resolution 1565, Texas House of Representatives, 15 May 2019).

68. "General Juan de Fernández Retana" file, 115, 150–52, 167 (quote).

69. Hackett, *Historical Documents,* vol. 2, 29, 358. James Manly Daniel, "The Advance of the Spanish Frontier and the Despoblado" (PhD thesis, University of Texas at Austin, 1955), 136, cited a decision of the viceroyal council in October 1694 that four missionaries be sent to La Junta and provided with four sets of sacred vessels and vestments. Noting that no further documentation was found, Daniel nevertheless ventured that "it seems probable from later evidence that missionaries were actually sent to La Junta, but after a time gave up their work because of the hostility of the neighboring nations." The only later evidence he gave was the Juntans' 1713 request for missionaries (see the next chapter). Jones, *Nueva Vizcaya*, 92, misinterpreted Hackett's summary in erroneously stating that "after 1693 they [Franciscans] reoccupied seven missions in the Rio Conchos–La Junta de los Rios region." The Durango officials were describing the already existing Franciscan missions in northern Nueva Vizcaya along the Rio Conchos and its tributaries. Jones did not give any history of the La Junta missions in the 1700s.

70. Hackett, *Historical Documents*, vol. 3, 372–78.

71. Susan M. Deeds, "Colonial Chihuahua: Peoples and Frontiers in Flux," in *New Views of Borderlands History*, ed. Robert H. Jackson (Albuquerque: University of New Mexico Press, 1998), 34.

72. Navarro García, *Don José de Gálvez*, 35, 38; Griffen, *Indian Assimilation*, 50.

73. "General Juan de Fernández Retana" file, 91–96 (quote on 95).

74. Ibid., 91, 95–96 (quote), 99, 112–13.

75. Ibid., 110 (first quote), 150 (second quote), 241 (third quote). Daniel, "The Advance of the Spanish Frontier and the Despoblado," 122, mistakenly wrote that the two nations actually settled at Tapacolmes, that he mislocated as "up the Rio Conchos some distance from its mouth."

76. Griffen, *Indian Assimilation*, 68. Griffen reported that the town's governor in 1724 said that there were persons from all the La Junta valley towns, with only Púliques not explicitly mentioned.

77. Luis Aboites Aguilar and Alba Dolores Morales Cosme, eds., *Breve compilación sobre tierras y aguas de Santa Cruz de Tapacolmes, Chihuahua (1713-1927)* (México, D.F.: CIESAS / Comisión Nacional del Agua / Municipio de Rosales / Centro de Información del Estado de Chihuahua, 1998), 66. The editors

commented (p. 13) that this document led the people of Rosales (today's Santa Cruz) to celebrate their founding as in 1698. Actually, "more than twenty-five years" before 1723 would make the date earlier than 1698.

78. Joseph de Miguelena testimony, 4 September 1715, Parral, in the "Los labradores" file, AHMP-FC, frame 25 in the more recent numbering.

79. Griffen, *Culture Change and Shifting Populations*, 56, 93. By 1713 the Suninoliglas consisted of only sixteen warriors.

80. Griffen, *Indian Assimilation*, 50.

81. Ibid., 15. The Retana campaign journal in 1793 noted "la Sienega [marshland] de los Cholomes" along the western route from the Hormigas hacienda to the Cuesta Grande, describing the place as "the springs where the Cholomes under Don Marcos lived": "General Juan de Fernández Retana" file, 93–94.

82. "General Juan de Fernández Retana" file, 151.

83. For example, see Conrad, *The Apache Diaspora*, 71, 309n42.

84. Griffen, *Indian Assimilation*, 59. During the 1686–1704 period, baptisms at San Bartolomé were counted by Griffen only for 1697–1699, probably due to the disappearance of records for the other years. The Sonorans were way ahead of the rest, with twenty-five. Next came the Julimes with six and the Polacmes with four. There were six marriages for Julime people between 1686 and 1701, and four Tapacolme marriages in 1700–1704.

85. Weber, *The Spanish Frontier in North America*, 156–58; Castañeda, *Our Catholic Heritage in Texas*, vol. 2, 20–21.

86. Guillaume Delisle's 1702 "Carte du Canada et du Mississipi" [*sic*] is reproduced in Carl I. Wheat, *Mapping the Transmississippi West*, vol. 1: *The Spanish Entrada to the Louisiana Purchase, 1540–1804* (San Francisco: The Institute of Historical Cartography, 1957), facing page 49. A section of Delisle's 1703 map, "Carte du Mexique et de la Floride," is reproduced here from the original at the Museum of the Big Bend. Both show the importance of "S. Christoval" at La Junta at this time by naming it at its proper place. Also indicated near the river junction are five other settlements with mostly French versions of their names: "S. George" and "La Conception" above San Cristóbal on the north side of the Rio del Norte, "Assomption" where San Francisco would subsequently be identified at the river junction, "S. Pablo" below San Cristóbal on the same side of the Rio del Norte, and "Corpus Christi" above "Assomption" along the Rio Conchos. Could these have been the names given to the other La Junta towns by the Franciscans in the 1680s? Wheat stated that the 1701 map (not reproduced by him) was based on information that came from the French entries along the Gulf Coast and depicted the routes of Spaniards to La Salle's ill-fated fort on the Texas coast (Wheat, 56–58). The 1702 and 1703 Delisle maps do not show the Spanish travel routes.

87. Luis Céspedes to Commissary General, 14 January 1712, Convento de San

Francisco, UNM-BNM, 123C, legajo 6, part 3, no. 9, 265.

Chapter 4

1. Jones, *Nueva Vizcaya*, 118–21.
2. Reginald G. Reindorp, trans., *The Founding of Missions at La Junta de los Rios*, Supplementary Studies of the Texas Catholic Historical Society (Austin: St. Edward's University, 1938), 14–15. Reindorp's translation has been reprinted twice in documentary collections. A facsímile reprint is in Arthur R. Gómez, ed., *Documentary Evidence for the Spanish Missions of Texas* (New York: Garland Publishing, 1991), 243–68. A repaginated version is in Jesús F. de la Teja, ed., *New Foundations*, Preliminary Studies of the Texas Catholic Historical Society III (Austin: Texas Catholic Historical Society, 2000), 159–83. That Father Ramírez was one of the two missionaries at Santa Cruz is noted in Aboites Aguilar and Morales Cosme, *Breve compilación*, 40.
3. Menchero, "Declaración" (my translation).
4. Castañeda, *Our Catholic Heritage in Texas*, vol. 2 (1936), 28–32. The expeditions of St. Denis led to the Spanish occupation of East Texas in 1716 and subsequently the formation of the Spanish province of Texas.
5. Viceroy Duque de Linares to Governor San Juan de Santa Cruz, 24 October 1714, Ciudad de Mexico, AHMP-FC, Gobierno y administración, Peticiones, AHMP.FC.A20.003.048.
6. For most of the documents relating to the 1715 expedition, I principally cite Reindorp's translation, *The Founding of Missions at La Junta*, based upon one of the later manuscripts in the Archivo Franciscano at the Biblioteca Nacional de México. I cite Reindorp since his translation is well known and the only account in print in English. The original Spanish manuscript was sent to the viceroy. The Archivo Franciscano has the contemporaneous copy of that manuscript made for the Franciscans, certified on 12 July 1715, with original signatures. I cite it as the 1715 Franciscan copy, from photostats at UNM-BNM, vol. 123D, legajo 6, part 4, doc. 19, 165–203. In various places I modify the Reindorp translation by reference to this 1715 copy, since Reindorp's translation is from one of two later copies also in the Archivo Franciscano. The 1792 copy was transcribed in the *Documentos para la historia eclesiástica y civil de la Nueva Vizcaya* (1857), 141–72, that was in turn republished in 2009 in *La Historia eclesiástica y civil de la Nueva Vizcaya, 1554–1831*, 155–84 (both editions are cited above, chapter 2, no. 22). A complementary journal from the expedition that I will also utilize is that of Captain Beasoain (see below).
7. This is a theme classically covered in Philip Wayne Powell's *Soldiers, Indians, and Silver*.
8. Robert E. Wright, "Spanish Missions," in *The Handbook of Texas Online*, Texas

State Historical Association, https://tshaonline.org/handbook/online/articles/
its02 (accessed 22 November 2018).

9. For the ministry of the Zacatecan friars in northeastern Nueva Vizcaya, see
Gerhard, *The North Frontier of New Spain*, 198–99.

10. Joseph de Arranegui to Governor San Juan de Santa Cruz, 26 March 1715, Parral,
AHMP-FC, Gobierno y administración, Peticiones, AHMP.FC.A20.003.048.
The date of the governor's receipt of the viceroy's note is on the reverse side of
[Viceroy] Duke of Linares to Governor of Nueva Vizcaya, 24 October 1714, the
first document in this file.

11. Trasviña Retes journal, 1715 Franciscan copy. The later copies and Reindorp
give a different date and misspell Retes as Retis.

12. Cheryl English Martin, *Governance and Society in Colonial Mexico: Chihuahua
in the Eighteenth Century* (Stanford: Stanford University Press, 1996), 34, 201.
The age of Trasviña Retes is from Reindorp, *The Founding of Missions*, 26.

13. Porras Muñoz, *Iglesia y Estado en Nueva Vizcaya*, 299–301. The author called
this an inventory, but it was probably a list of items to be provided. He cited it
from the report of the viceroy to the king on February 19, 1716.

14. Reindorp, *The Founding of Missions*, 5–8, 19.

15. Ibid., 6, 8, 22–23.

16. The kinship-based structure with extended family units of Native American
societies has been well brought out by studies such as those by Juliana Barr and
Paul Conrad. For Barr, who insists that "kinship provided the foundation for
every institution of [Native] societies," see, for example, *Peace Came in the Form
of a Woman*, 2 (quote), 113, 115, 127–28, 131–34. For Conrad, see chapter 4 in
his *Apache Diaspora*, 113–40.

17. Griffen, *Indian Assimilation*, 31.

18. Reindorp, *The Founding of Missions*, 10–11, with modifications from the 1715
Franciscan copy. Reindorp does not have the phrase describing El Torito as fluent
in Spanish, given in the 1715 Franciscan copy as "ladino en lengua castellana"
and in *Historia Eclesiástica*, 163, as "ladino con lengua castellana." Nor does he
have the 1715 Franciscan copy's designation of Juan Cortés as the master (*amo*)
of Andrés Coyame.

19. Ortelli, *Trama de una guerra conveniente*, 46–47. For the Coyame valley in the
early 1750s, see chapter 7.

20. Reindorp, *The Founding of Missions*, 10–11; Captain Joseph de Beasoian journal,
20 May–14 June 1715, in "Los labradores" file (see chapter 2, n35), 44r/42r (in citing this journal I give the two-page numberings in the document). Reindorp misinterpreted "que son los mas cristianos" (1715 Franciscan copy, as also *Historia
Eclesiástica*, 163) as "they are the most Christianized"; it should be "most are
Christian." I also follow the 1715 Franciscan copy in differing in some details

from Reindorp's rendering of the crops at San Pedro and clarifying that El Torito said he would ask both his Cholome general and the Hispanic *hacendado* to seek priests.

21. Reindorp, *The Founding of Missions*, 11, 18; Beasoian journal. The fact that it was Fr. Ramírez who said that the inhabitants were from the eight pueblos of the La Junta valley as well as the description of the town are taken from the 1715 Franciscan copy of the Trasviña Retes journal, confirmed by the later copy in *Historia Eclesiástica*, 164. Reindorp mistranslated both passages.

22. Reindorp, *The Founding of Missions*, 11–13. The title of Our Lady of Loreto to Mezquite is from the 1715 Franciscan copy; the Reindorp translation is less accurate. The Beasoain journal, 45v/43v–46r/44r, is the source for the more detailed description of the house construction in both El Mezquite and San Juan Bautista, as also for the distance from San Juan Bautista to San Francisco and the naming of the latter town.

23. Reindorp, *The Founding of Missions*, 13, 15–17 (quotes on 15–16, with my translation of *política*, rather than Reindorp's "polite"). A government official had already declared in 1671 that "cloth is the money that circulates among the Indians": Cynthia Radding, *Wandering Peoples: Colonialism, Ethnic Spaces, and Ecological Frontiers in Northwestern Mexico, 1700–1830* (Durham, NC: Duke University Press, 1997), 36. The same love of European clothes was noted among the Yaquis and Ópatas in Sonora in the first half of the 1700s who traveled as far as Chihuahua for work to be able to buy them: José Refugio de la Torre Curiel, *Twilight of the Mission Frontier: Shifting Interethnic Alliances and Social Organization in Sonora, 1768–1855* (Stanford: Stanford University Press / Berkeley: Academy of American Franciscan History, 2012), 11, 18.

24. Reindorp, *The Founding of Missions*, 5 (gifts to all the natives), 6, 13–17; Beasoian journal, 46v/44v, 48rv/46rv (quote). Reindorp misinterpreted who spoke and who translated; this has been corrected based upon the 1715 Franciscan copy. Another correction is the translation of 400 pesos' worth of clothes and tobacco (*pesos en ropa y Tabaco*), rather than "four hundred yards of cloth and some tobacco" in Reindorp, 15. For the Oposmes as the people of San Francisco, see Reindorp, *The Founding of Missions*, 26.

25. Reindorp, *The Founding of Missions*, 16, 20 (quotation). Reindorp's ten "or less" for the age of the boys to be sent to the convent has been changed to ten "more or less," as in the 1715 Franciscan copy and *Historia eclesiástica*, 174. From the first decades of evangelization in New Spain, Franciscans adopted the strategy of bringing some boys under their closer direction in order to turn them into Hispanic Christian aides. See Lino Gómez Canedo, "La primitiva evangelización de México: objetivos, problemas y métodos," in *Evangelización, cultura y promoción social: ensayos y estudios críticos sobre la contribución franciscana a los orígenes*

cristianos de México (siglos XVI–XVIII), ed. José Luis Soto Pérez (México, D.F.: Porrúa, 1993), 287–88. For examples of the same approach elsewhere on the northern frontier by Franciscans and Jesuits, see Kessell, *Pueblos, Spaniards, and the Kingdom of New Mexico*, 99–100 (New Mexico); Hughes, *The Beginnings of Spanish Settlement*, 308–9 (boys and girls at El Paso); Peter Masten Dunne, S.J., *Pioneer Black Robes on the West Coast* (Berkeley: University of California Press, 1940), 73–74 (Sinaloa); Deeds, *Defiance and Deference*, 28, 90 (Nueva Vizcaya).

26. Reindorp, *The Founding of Missions*, 17. The translation in the block quotation is mine from the 1715 Franciscan copy, especially in order to replace Reindorp's vague translation of "y alsarse con ellos a las sierras" as "to go with them up into the mountains." Griffen, *Culture Change and Shifting Populations*, 17, noted that in the mid-1600s Native groups in this region who would not join in an uprising would often be attacked by the rebels. The basic meaning of the Nahuatl *tlatole/ tlazole* is a deliberative meeting among elders: "consultations among Indian elders, often associated with a call to arms or dealing with encroachments by outsiders" (Deeds, *Defiance and Deference*, 167). The Beasoain journal spoke of conversing with the Juntan leaders at San Francisco with "different questions and *parlamentos* [parlays] *y tzatoles* [*sic*] in their customary way." So did Arranegui (*tlazoles*) in the 1715 Franciscan copy of his post-expedition certification of Trasviña Retes's achievements that was included in the expedition documents. Beasoian, 48v/46v, mistakenly wrote that the expedition crossed the Rio del Norte to reach the Guadalupe town.

27. Reindorp, *The Founding of Missions*, 12. I changed Reindorp's "fenced" for "enclosed" (*cercado* in the 1715 Franciscan copy) in the descriptions of El Mezquite and San Juan Bautista. Beasoian made this clear by describing these two towns as "in the form of barracks (*cuarteles*) with their plazas in the middle" (Beasoian journal, 45v/43v).

28. Reindorp, *The Founding of Missions*, 13, 17–18. For the three towns below Guadalupe the 1715 Franciscan copy reads: "y mas abajo como una legua a las orillas de los dos rrios [*sic*] juntos están tres pueblos." Reindorp read this as the three towns being "close together," whereas the adjective "juntos" is about the rivers, not the towns. Expeditions in 1747 did have San Cristóbal about a league below Guadalupe, but on the opposite side of the river, Púliques three "short leagues" below Guadalupe and thus two leagues below San Cristóbal, and San Antonio de Padua no longer noted (see the reports on the 1747 expeditions in chapter 6). Beasoian, whose account parallels that of Trasviña Retes so much that one may conclude that one was used as the basis for the other, wrote that the towns were "muy immediatos" (49v/47v). The interpretation all depends on whether one considers two leagues (five miles) and even further as very close together. Given this geographical question and the almost complete

lack of description of the three downriver towns and of travel between them, it is doubtful that the expedition visited them.

29. Reindorp, *The Founding of Missions*, 18; Hammond and Rey, *The Rediscovery of New Mexico*, 75, 163–64. That the eighty persons noted as absent migrants in 1715 counted only the men, and not the families accompanying them, is known from a lawyer's brief on those migrants. See note 61 below.

30. The lesser toll of epidemics after prolonged contact with Hispanics was a general phenomenon in Spanish America: David J. Weber, *Bárbaros: Spaniards and Their Savages in the Age of Enlightenment* (New Haven: Yale University Press, 2005), 95.

31. Reindorp, *The Founding of Missions*, 19, 24. What is stated here, based on the 1715 Franciscan copy, corrects Reindorp's version that has been followed by recent scholars, where he wrote that the Apache band was already living "above and below" La Junta. The 1715 Franciscan copy states that the Apache *promised* that his group would live "immediately downriver or upriver" from La Junta. Also, Reindorp did not read properly that the Apache was named after his godfather.

32. Beasoian journal, 50v/48v.

33. Anderson, *The Indian Southwest, 1580–1830*, 114. This had been an Apache stratagem for decades. Posada noted as early as the 1680s that while the Apaches had been constantly raiding the Pueblos of New Mexico and stealing the Hispanics' horses there, those to the east—such as near La Junta—were careful to maintain peace with the Hispanics in order to trade their buffalo hides and deerskins (Thomas, *Alonso de Posada Report*, 41).

34. Griffen, *Indian Assimilation*, 16.

35. Salvador Álvarez, "Manuel San Juan de Santa Cruz: gobernador, latifundista y capitán de guerra de la frontera norte," *Revista de Indias* LXX, núm. 248 (2010), 109, citing San Juan's decree on March 5, 1715.

36. Reindorp, *The Founding of Missions*, 18. The quoted statements are translations from the 1715 Franciscan copy, as more precise than the Reindorp translations in such an important matter.

37. Reindorp, *The Founding of Missions*, 20–21, 23. Corrections based upon the 1715 Franciscan copy include the notice of the lack of any sheep (not just cattle) at La Junta, the giving of fifty pounds (*un tercio de seis arrobas*) of meat (rather than 150 as in Reindorp) at Cuchillo Parado, and the date of the arrival of Trasviña Retes back in Chihuahua.

38. Andrés Ramírez to Commissary General, 11 June 1715, San Antonio de Julimes, UNM-BNM, vol. 123 D, no. 21, 208.

39. Joseph de Arranegui to Commissary General, 18 July 1715, Chihuahua, UNM-BNM, vol. 123D, no. 21, 205-7.

40. Joseph de Beasoain to Franciscan Commissary General, 26 June 1715, San

Francisco de Conchos, UNM-BNM, vol. 123D, no. 18.

41. Gregorio Osorio to Trasviña Retes, 17 June 1715, San Francisco de la Junta, in Reindorp, *The Founding of Missions*, 27–28.

42. Juan Cortés to Trasviña Retes, 1 July 1715, Hacienda de N. S. del Pilar, in Reindorp, *The Founding of Missions*, 26–27; see also 22–23 for the account by Trasviña Retes. Reindorp had Cortés calling Coyame "a bad man." This is an over-interpretation of the text, since Cortés actually wrote more generically that he "desired that everyone lacking the light of the Gospel (even if a bad man) would enjoy it."

43. Juan Cortés to Governor San Juan, 26 July 1715, N. S. del Pilar, and meeting of the governor and Andrés Coyame, 27 July 1715, Parral, in "Los labradores" file, 55v/53v-58v/56v.

44. Reindorp, *The Founding of Missions*, 22–23.

45. Ibid., 22. The translation of "todos frutos" in the 1715 Franciscan copy alters Reindorp's "fruit" to the italicized text.

46. Reindorp, *The Founding of Missions*, 21–22.

47. Ibid., 25–26, correcting the money measurement from grains to pesos.

48. Trasviña Retes to Governor San Juan, 20 June 1715, San Francisco de Cuellar, in "Los labradores" file (see chapter 2, note 35), 54r/52r.

49. My own translation of the 1715 Franciscan copy, since Reindorp, *The Founding of Missions*, 24, misread the proposal about the governor's action. This statement demonstrates that the labor arrangements of the Juntans (and the Cholomes) were still subject to the governor's directives, as in the 1640s.

50. Algier, "Feudalism on New Spain's Northern Frontier," 77. The hacienda's head-quarters were at today's Valle de Zaragoza: Francisco R. Almada, *Resumen de historia del Estado de Chihuahua* (México, D.F.: Libros Mexicanos, 1955), 78. Other Cortés del Rey haciendas were to the north of this along the lower Santa Isabel River to the west of San Pedro de los Conchos, and thus within the larger San Pedro River–Chihuahua área (Ortelli, *Trama de una guerra conveniente*, 47).

51. The wealth and resources of Juan Cortés's father, the Spaniard Valerio Cortés del Rey, had given him access to governors and to *audiencia* (high court) officials in Guadalajara, leading him to boast that he was the key to the kingdom of Nueva Vizcaya. Economic reversals in central Nueva Vizcaya between 1696 and 1707 severely impacted many landowners, including Valerio's heir Juan (Deeds, "Rural Work in Nueva Vizcaya," 438, 440; Deeds, "Colonial Chihuahua," 29; Deeds, *Defiance and Deference*, 73–74, 80, 141). But Juan Cortés was not a person to be messed with. He had actually been Governor San Juan's predecessor as governor, having served as lieutenant governor in 1712–1714 and interim governor in 1714 until San Juan y Santa Cruz arrived (Almada, *Resumen de historia*, 93).

52. Catherine Tracy Goode, "Corrupting the Governor: Manuel San Juan de Santa

Cruz and Power in Early Eighteenth-Century Nueva Vizcaya" (MA thesis, Northern Arizona University, 2000), 34–42, 51–52, 61–63. Álvarez, "Manuel San Juan," disputed Goode's characterization of San Juan, criticizing her as "going too far" (109) by ignoring his continued "audacious" role (110) as a military commander and his significant patronage of local religious projects (108–11). Álvarez preferred to describe San Juan as "discreet" (111) in hiding his illegal business affairs while governor.

53. Martin, *Governance and Society*, 50–51. A later chronicle stated that San Juan mined 500 pounds of silver every week for three straight years (Arlegui, *Crónica de la Provincia*, 91–92).

54. Governor San Juan to Alcalde Mayor of the San Bartolomé Valley, 9 August 1715, in "Los labradores" file, AHMP-FC. Goode made the same point about the governor's motives, but seriously misinterpreted the founding of missions at La Junta at this time ("Corrupting the Governor," 76).

55. The inclusion of Bartolomé de Porraz among the growers is interesting, since, as will be noted below, the *lobo* (predominantly Black and Indian mixture) lieutenant general of the Juntans in 1750 bore the same name, and in 1759 he was one of the Hispanophile Juntans living in Chihuahua who played an important role in the establishment of a presidio at La Junta. This later Bartolomé de Porraz may have been the godson of the San Bartolomé grower, taking the latter's Christian name at his baptism. Or he may have taken the grower's name wanting to emulate his prestige and power, as in other documented cases (Deeds, *Defiance and Deference*, 64).

56. San Bartolomé growers to Governor San Juan, [August 1715], in "Los labradores" file, AHMP-FC. In his excellent summary of the Tarahumara history during the colonial period, Spicer noted how the Natives of the Lower Tarahumara country near Parral continued to assimilate into Spanish culture, while those of the Upper Tarahumara followed a different pattern of passive resistance or withdrawal into the mountains in response to the continued efforts of Hispanics, especially in the Chihuahua district after 1710, to force them into laboring for them (*Cycles of Conquest*, 36).

57. Governor San Juan order, 27 August 1715, and Cervantes declaration [no date, but entered in the file on 2 September 1715] in "Los labradores" file.

58. Pedro de Ortega statement, 2 September 1715, San Bartolomé, in "Los labradores" file.

59. Francisco Cupula statement, 18 September 1715, San Bartolomé, in "Los labradores" file.

60. Joseph de Miguelena response, [n.d., added to file on November 14], in "Los labradores" file, folio 34 in the more recent numbering.

61. Joseph de Miguelena testimony, 4 September 1715, Parral, in "Los labradores"

file, folio 25. Miguelena's numbers clarify that when Trasviña Retes was told in La Junta that eighty persons were absent from the valley, that number referred only to the adult men, not their accompanying wives and children.

62. Gregorio Osorio and Juan Antonio García to Governor San Juan, 28 September 1715, San Francisco de Cuellar [Chihuahua], in "Los labradores" file, folios 36–37.

63. "Información por mandato de Manuel de Santa Cruz, sobre la averiguación hacia algunos gobernadores, por la repartición de trabajadores a las haciendas de la jurisdicción de San Francisco de Cuéllar," AHMP-FC, Gobierno y administración, serie encomiendas y repartimientos, AHMP.FC.A05.001.019 [henceforth "Información por mandato"] (accessed 22 March 2022), folios 1–3. For the history of the Tabalaopa hacienda, see Álvarez, "Manuel San Juan," 105, 114.

64. "Información por mandato" file, 1–12 (quotes 8v, 9r, 10r).

65. "Información por mandato" file, 8r; María de Apressa Ybarra to Governor San Juan, n.d., and Governor San Juan decree, 3 June 1716, Parral, in "Los labradores" file, 38–39.

66. Thus the La Junta case does not fit the argument of Cramaussel, "The Forced Transfer of Indians," 188, that in Nueva Vizcaya in the eighteenth century "Indian transfers were forced and had little to do with movements of free Indian workers." Cramaussel's conclusions are based on the sacramental registers of the parishes of Parral and Chihuahua. The transfer of the Juntans' labor to the Chihuahua vicinity rather than the Valley of San Bartolomé may or may not have been their choice, at least initially, but their labor itself was not forced.

67. Andrés Varo informe to provincial, 29 January 1749, Hospicio de Santa Bárbara extramuros de México, UNM-BNM, 125B, legajo 8, no. 57, pages 23, 30–31. The founding of these missions by expeditions from Chihuahua, not El Paso, and the increasing migration of Juntans to Nueva Vizcaya solidified the claim of that province to the La Junta district. By 1726 Las Boquillas, about 125 miles north of Chihuahua on the road to El Paso, was recognized as the boundary between New Mexico and Nueva Vizcaya (Jones, *Nueva Vizcaya*, 128–29). Gerhard, *The North Frontier of New Spain*, 198, interpreted Porraz Muñoz as locating the Boquillas dividing line on the Rio del Norte.

68. Gonzalo de Sobenes y Barreda, custos, to the La Junta missionaries, 11 November 1718, San Francisco de la Junta, Archives of the Archdiocese of Santa Fe, microfilm 51, 904–6.

69. [Varo] to Provincial Joseph Jimeno, undated [1749–1750], UNM-BNM, vol. 126A, legajo 9, no. 10, 2930–2932. Menchero, "Declaración," mistakenly had all six missionaries arriving in 1716. Most subsequent authors have repeated this mistake.

70. Varo's year of birth and year of entry into the Franciscans are from a Franciscan investigation in Mexico City in 1748 at which he was a witness (UNM-BNM,

vol. 125A, legajo 8, no. 38, Convent of San Francisco, 24 octubre–6 noviembre 1748). Information about his ministry in the Custody of San Pablo can be found in Chávez, *Archives of the Archdiocese of Santa Fe*, 38, 160–63, 257, and Adams and Chavez, *The Missions of New Mexico*, 339–40 (with an erroneous birth year).

71. Eleanor B. Adams, ed., *Bishop Tamarón's Visitation of New Mexico, 1760* (Albuquerque: Historical Society of New Mexico, 1954), 15–18, 95, 100–106; Norris, *After "The Year Eighty,"* 76–78, 81, 123–24. The portrait of Varo by Norris is more nuanced than that of Adams.

72. For Lepiane's age, one and a half years' ministry at La Junta, and claim of four and a half years as custos, see Francisco Lepiane affidavit, 28 July 1739, Colegio de Tlatelolco, UNM-BNM, vol. 124D, legajo 7, no. 75, 345.

73. Martínez Clemente stated that he served for eleven years, eleven months in the San Pablo Custody: Luis Martínez Clemente affidavit, 28 July 1739, Colegio de Tlatelolco, UNM-BNM, vol. 124D, legajo 7, no. 75, 347. His name does not appear as a resident minister in any of the upper New Mexico missions in Chávez, *Archives of the Archdiocese of Santa Fe*. After La Junta he must have been in the El Paso district. The Aparicio information comes from Kessell, *Kiva, Cross, and Crown*, 318, 499.

74. Andrés Varo to Governor López de Carbajal, 30 May 1724, Santiago de la Redonda, in "Autos sobre providencias en orden a impedir sublevación inttentada por los Indios de los Pueblos de las Misiones de la Junta de los Rios del Norte" (henceforth "Autos sobre impedir sublevación"), AHMP-FC, Milicia y Guerra, sección sediciones, AHMP.FC.C11.018.190. For Martin de Alday as governor in 1720–1723, see Jones, *Nueva Vizcaya*, 239.

75. Pedro Ruiz de Azua affidavit, 3 January 1728, in "Testimonio de los autos . . . sobre el alzamiento de los Yndios Sumas de la Mission de Santiago del Coyame," Biblioteca Nacional de México, Archivo Franciscano [henceforth BNM-AF], caja 14, no. 241, 100.

76. Varo to López de Carbajal, 30 May 1724, in "Autos sobre impedir sublevación" file. Varo's sentence construction leaves it unclear whether crops were harvested in July or August, or the two rivers were swollen in July or August, or both of these occurred in July or August. Berroterán stated almost three decades after the event (see below) that the uprising was in September.

77. Andrés Varo, "Informe al Virrey," March 1749, BNM-AF, caja 15, no. 268, 1–2.

78. Luis Caburraja testimony, 21 July 1724, San Bartolomé, in "Autos sobre impedir sublevación" file.

79. Joseph de Berroterán, Mexico, to Viceroy, 17 April 1748, in Diana Hadley, Thomas H. Naylor, and Mardith K. Schuetz-Miller, eds., *The Presidio and Militia on the Northern Frontier of New Spain: A Documentary History*, vol. 2 part 2, *The Central Corridor and the Texas Corridor, 1700–1765* (Tucson: University

of Arizona Press, 1997), 210–11 (English translation on 182–83). Berroterán's timing of this incident in September 1720 corresponds well with the one and a half years that Lepiane is known to have been in the La Junta missions. For Berroterán at Mapimí, see Jones, *Nueva Vizcaya*, 130.

80. Menchero, "Declaración"; English translation in Hackett, *Historical Documents*, vol. 3, 408–9. Menchero did not enter the San Pablo Custody until a decade after these events and thus relied upon others' stories. He correctly wrote of an initial (almost) two peaceful years after the founding of the missions, but he mistakenly dated the founding of all six to 1716. Several scholars have consequently misdated this uprising to 1718.

81. Pedro de Arizaga certifications, 6 February 1721, and Gras to Sousa, 21 July 1721, BNM-AF, caja 13, no. 236.1-3. How much longer Gras remained in the La Junta district is unknown.

82. Varo, "Informe al Virrey," 2–2v.

83. Almada, *Resumen de historia*, 94.

Chapter 5

1. Menchero, "Declaración," 410; Castañeda, *Our Catholic Heritage in Texas*, vol. 3, 212; Daniel, "La Junta de los Rios," 106–7; Kelley, "Historic Indian Pueblos," vol. 27, no. 4, 270; Kelley, *Jumano and Patarabueye*, 64; Griffen, *Indian Assimilation*, 54, 95–97; Folsom, "Spanish La Junta de los Rios," 79–80, 81; Morgenthaler, *La Junta de los Rios*, 97–98.

2. Cramaussel, *Poblar la frontera*, 229, 231–33. The closest Native place to La Junta whose people were participating in the *repartimientos* assigned by the governor was Julimes. But events in 1724, discussed below, confirm that the people of the La Junta district were still engaged in migrant labor. Cramaussel demonstrated that less than half of the haciendas in the San Bartolomé Valley received *repartimiento* Natives during this time, and they were not the most productive enterprises. Her conclusion was that the owners had mostly permanent laborers, and that in contrast temporary workers who continued to be tied to their original communities were completely alien to colonial society in the province. Whether or not that was true for the San Bartolomé Valley, it was certainly not true for the people residing in the La Junta district, who were still autonomous yet far from alien to colonial society. In fact, Cramaussel did not discuss the area between the San Pedro River and Chihuahua where most Juntans were then laboring.

3. Griffen, *Indian Assimilation*, 68. The only Juntan groups not named were the Púliques and Conchos, noted in 1715 as at the lower end of the La Junta valley.

4. Cramaussel, *Poblar la frontera*, 229, 231–32.

5. Aboites Aguilar and Morales Cosme, *Breve compilación*, 53–58.

6. The identification of "Santa Cruz de nación Tapacolmes" is on p. 41.

7. Aboites Aguilar and Morales Cosme, *Breve compilación*, 61–68, 75–76. The documents cited did not include any response from the Zacatecan Franciscans; presumably there was one. The shifting labor system, with the increasing presence of Hispanics, is evident by the fact that in 1746 the Franciscans along the lower San Pedro River began paying the Native "peones" for their work in the fields still allotted to the missionary, while many Natives worked in the local haciendas: Luis Aboites Aguilar, *Demografía histórica y conflictos por el agua: Dos estudios sobre 40 kilómetros de historia del río San Pedro, Chihuahua* (México, D.F.: Centro de Investigaciones y Estudios Superiores en Antropología Social, 2000), 34.

8. Francisco Lepiane to the missionaries of the custody, 2 November 1723, Santa Fe, Archives of the Archdiocese of Santa Fe, microfilm 51, 948.

9. Varo to López de Carbajal, 30 May 1724, folio 5–5v, in "Autos sobre impedir sublevación" file (see chapter 4, no. 74). Varo's statement about the Venado captain "as well as the other (*los demás*) Cholomes" might seem to identify him as a Cholome. However, it might also be interpreted as distinguishing the Cholomes at Coyame from those on the upper Rio del Norte ("the other Cholomes"). Griffen, *Indian Assimilation*, 36, "Venados," cited a report that placed the Venados twelve leagues above La Junta along the Rio del Norte in 1726 (see below) without trying to identify them ethnically.

10. Hispanic settlement in Coahuila along the Rio Grande or Rio Bravo (the river's name below the La Junta district) and to its west began in 1701 with the presidio of San Juan Bautista and spread from there (Gerhard, *The North Frontier of New Spain*, 329–30, 332).

11. For the general Cholome territory, see Griffen, *Indian Assimilation*, 31–32. In this period there are examples of a Hispanic confusion or connection of Cholome and Cíbolo for some Natives. Griffen cited a case of an individual being called both a Cholome and a Cíbolo, stated that the two groups were both considered very civilized, and noted that "Cholome" was sometimes used more generically for other nearby groups. Varo wrote that "Cholome Cíbolos" were part of the 1726 uprising (see below). The 1726 documents reveal that Juan Cíbolo's people lived to the east of La Junta, part of the traditional Cíbolo territory.

12. For Varo's 1726 comments, see the section on the 1726 uprising below. In the 1740s the Venados were again distinguished from Apaches, and possibly even from Cholomes. See the discussion on hostilities in 1743 near the end of this chapter.

13. Missionaries in previous times and places had noticed the same careful Indigenous strategy of guaranteeing food supplies before engaging in premeditated warfare (Deeds, *Defiance and Deference*, 37).

14. Governor López de Carbajal decree, 4 July 1724, El Pasaje; Father Pedro Sanches

interview, 16 July 1724, San Bartolomé; Carbajal decree, 17 July 1724, San Bartolomé: all in "Autos sobre impedir sublevación" file.

15. Testimonies of Diego Moreno, Martín de Juangorena, Diego de Acosta, and Joseph Del Hierro, 17–18 July 1724, San Bartolomé, in "Autos sobre impedir sublevación" file. The quoted phrase is from Del Hierro.

16. Caburraja and Talamantes testimonies, 21 July 1724, San Bartolomé, in "Autos sobre impedir sublevación" file.

17. Salvador de Acosta to Governor Carbajal, 31 August 1724, San Pedro, in "Autos sobre impedir sublevación" file.

18. Governor Carbajal document, 19 September 1724, Chihuahua, in "Autos sobre impedir sublevación" file.

19. Andrés Varo to Governor Carbajal, 14 October 1724, Nombre de Dios, in "Autos sobre impedir sublevación" file. Fray Diego Arias de Espinosa de los Monteros appears in the extant church records of upper New Mexico in February–June 1723 and then again in 1731–1737 (Chávez, *Archives of the Archdiocese of Santa Fe*, 242). So he possibly arrived in the La Junta district in later 1723. For his presence at La Junta in early 1726, see below.

20. Governor Carbajal consultation of Chihuahuan leaders, 21 October 1724, Chihuahua, in "Autos sobre impedir sublevación" file.

21. Varo, "Informe al Virrey," 2v. In several later Franciscan documents, even as early as 1728, this uprising was dated in 1725, and this dating has been followed by several modern historians. But the year 1726 is clearly the accurate one, as demonstrated by this Varo report and especially by the reports of the rescue party that follow.

22. For Suma missions and Suma hostilities, see Timmons, *El Paso*, 17–39 passim. Varo probably erred in this much later account when he included the people from Cuchillo Parado among the insurgents. Nowhere else were they noted as such; in fact, some of them were credited rather with aiding the counterinsurgency. More puzzling is the reference to the "interior missions" of the Cholome Cíbolos. There were no missions deeper inland (the meaning of "interior" territory in New Spain) in the Cíbolo area to north and east of La Junta (for the Cíbolo area, see Griffen, *Indian Assimilation*, 32). Perhaps, writing twenty years later, Varo was confusing them with the Cholomes who lived upriver from La Junta along the Rio del Norte. See n11 (above) about the confusion or connection between Cholome and Cíbolo. Two decades later Berroterán wrote that the March 1726 uprising included Apaches and Cholomes and other Indians along the Rio del Norte all the way from the Pecos (*Puerco*) River to El Paso (Berroterán to Viceroy, in Hadley, Naylor, and Schuetz-Miller, *The Presidio and Militia*, 214). That would include the Cíbolos downriver from La Junta.

23. The following account is from "Testimonio de los autos" (see chapter 4, note

75), 1–8v, 22v–30v, 39–49v, 55–75, 108v–109v, unless otherwise noted. There is also a transcript of the Aguirre documents with an attached memorial by the Franciscan procurator general of the Indies in AGI, Aud. de Guad. 67-3-12, Dunn Transcripts vol. 23 (1710–1738), University of Texas at Austin, Briscoe Center for American History (henceforth UT-BCAH). For a much later summary account, see Berroterán to Viceroy, 214–15. Menchero's 1744 "Declaración" once again gave a wrong date, 1725, a mistake repeated in the "Informe del R. P. Provincial de Nueva Mexico al Exmo. Sor. Virrey," March 1750 [henceforth "Informe del Provincial, March 1750"], Bolton Collection, Part I, no. 451, 21. Menchero, but not Berroterán, credited the Hispanics alone for rescuing the friars, completely ignoring the heroic actions of the Juntans themselves.

24. Salvador Álvarez, "Agricultural Colonization and Mining Colonization: The Area of Chihuahua During the First Half of the Eighteenth Century," in *In Quest of Mineral Wealth: Aboriginal and Colonial Mining and Metallurgy in Spanish America*, ed. Alan K. Craig and Robert C. West (Baton Rouge: Department of Geography and Anthropology, Louisiana State University, 1994), 195, 202n14.

25. Important Native leaders often took or were given the surnames of important Hispanic persons. Governor López Carbajal was governor of Nueva Vizcaya in 1723–1727 (Jones, *Nueva Vizcaya*, 239).

26. For the general meaning of cacique and its use in New Mexico, see Kessell, *Spain in the Southwest*, 421. For a vivid account of the opposition between them and the early missionaries in New Mexico, see Benavides, *The Memorial of Fray Alonso de Benavides*, in which the Native religious leaders are called *hechiceros* (sorcerers) by Benavides.

27. See the next chapter.

28. Could this be the origin of the Cholomes identified as one of the groups at San Juan Bautista in 1747? (See the next chapter.)

29. Berroterán to Viceroy, 215.

30. "Testimonio de los autos," 7, 61v, 63.

31. Arlegui, *Crónica de la Provincia*, 90–91, 100. Griffen, *Indian Assimilation*, 17, 80, alerted me to this information about Don Pedro Coyame. However, he misinterpreted Pedro Coyame's people as having been initially among the rebels.

32. Varo, "Informe al Virrey," 3; Menchero, "Declaración," English translation in Hackett, *Historical Documents*, vol. 3, 409.

33. For Rivera's recommendation, see Hackett, *Pichardo's Treatise*, vol. 3 (1941), 237–38. On a note attached to a March 1727 list of the missionary placements in the custody, there is written "Fr. Andrés Varo in La Junta, Fr. Antonio de Aparicio ----- these are in La Junta de los Rios" ("Misiones que componen la Custodia," 7 March 1727, UNM-BNM, vol. 124C, legajo 7, no. 10, 3). But this was their anticipated assignment, that fell through with the final decision not

to establish the presidio at that time.

34. Thomas H. Naylor and Charles W. Polzer, S.J., eds., *Pedro de Rivera and the Military Regulations for Northern New Spain, 1724–1729: A Documentary History of his Frontier Inspection and the Reglamento de 1729* (Tucson: University of Arizona Press, 1988), 100 (quotation), 176; Berroterán to Viceroy, 215; Morgenthaler, *La Junta de los Ríos*, 95–96.

35. Varo, "Informe al Virrey," 3–3v.

36. Documents from 7 July 1727 through 8 January 1728, "Testimonio de los autos," 76–108.

37. Francisco de Lepiane, "En la Custodia de la Conversion de San Pablo," 1728, UNM-BNM, vol. 124C, legajo 7, part 3, no. 14, pages 2–3 and 8. For the Franciscan response to the 1748 Ornedal report, see chapter 6.

38. Luis Martínez Clemente visita de la Custodia de Nuevo México año de 1728, UNM-BNM, vol. 124C, legajo 7, no. 16, 20.

39. "Tabula Capituli Provincialis Provinciae Sancti Evangelii," 8 January 1729, México, UNM-BNM, vol. 124D, legajo 7, no. 22, 1046; "Nómina de los padres custodios y procuradores de Nuevo México, 1623–1759," UNM-BNM, vol. 126A, legajo 9, no. 8. This latter document also, by exception, gave all the mission assignments for the San Pablo Custody listed at the January 1729 chapter. There is no indication that any of the other men listed for the La Junta district ever served there. In a July 1739 affidavit Menchero gave his age as 44 (UNM-BNM, vol. 124D, legajo 7, no. 75, 349).

40. Adams, *Bishop Tamarón's Visitation*, 99.

41. Griffen noted the presence of Juntans in the haciendas of Nueva Vizcaya until at least 1755 (*Indian Assimilation*, 48, 59).

42. This assessment disagrees substantially with Weber, *The Spanish Frontier in North America*, 214, and Kessell, *Spain in the Southwest*, 221, who deemed the impact as very minor. For a more thorough and critical assessment of the effect in Texas, see Castañeda, *Our Catholic Heritage in Texas*, vol. 2, 212–43.

43. Naylor and Polzer, *Pedro de Rivera*, 240–44. For the strong negative impact of Rivera's recommendations in Nueva Vizcaya, see Jones, *Nueva Vizcaya*, 127–37. Additionally, Rivera's recommendation that the governor's fund for Indian affairs in Nueva Vizcaya be drastically cut from 6,000 to 2,000 pesos was also implemented (Berroterán to Viceroy, 218). See also Moorhead on the *Reglamento*: "the economies which it instituted so reduced the military effectiveness of the presidios that Indian depredations in Nueva Vizcaya and Sonora reached proportions reminiscent of the Great Northern Revolt" (*The Presidio*, 47).

44. For Menchero's appointment as "Commissary Visitor General" on January 13, 1731, in Mexico City, and his announcement from El Paso of that appointment to the friars in upper New Mexico on July 3 of that year, see Chávez, *Archives of*

the Archdiocese of Santa Fe, 32, 1731 no. 1.

45. Petition of Juntan leaders, undated, in "Diligencias que se han formado para que los Religiosos de Nuestro Padre San Francisco entran a los Pueblos de los Rios del Norte y Conchos a catequizar a los Indios" (henceforth "Diligencias para que los Religiosos"), AHMP-FC, Iglesia, sección misiones, AHMP.FC.F10.001.002.

46. Kessell, *Kiva, Cross and Crown*, 329; Norris, *After "The Year Eighty,"* 99–100, 107.

47. Miguel Menchero document, 25 May 1731, Chihuahua, in "Diligencias para que los Religiosos" file, AHMP-FC.

48. Governor Barrutia decree, 29 May 1731; Menchero to Barrutia, no date; certification of La Junta Franciscans, 8 June 1731; all in Chihuahua, in "Diligencias para que los Religiosos" file, AHMP-FC.

49. Joachín de Amestigui receipt, 7 May 1731, Chihuahua, UNM-BNM, vol. 124F, legajo 7, no. 56, 167–68.

50. Inventories of the Guadalupe and San Francisco missions, 1 June and 18 October 1731, BNM-AF, caja 27, no. 515, 1–3.

51. Lorenzo de Saavedra receipts, 11–12 June 1731, Chihuahua, UNM-BNM, vol. 124F, legajo 7, no. 56, 187–89.

52. Menchero, "Declaración"; English translation in Hackett, *Historical Documents*, vol. 3, 410. The previous two mission foundings were in 1683 and 1715.

53. Fray Lorenzo Saavedra to Comisario General Fernando Alonso González, San Francisco de la Junta de los Rios, 18 July 1731, BNM-AF, caja 27, no. 517.

54. Juan Miguel Menchero visita a la Custodia de Nuevo México, 1731, BNM-AF, caja 27, no. 519, 18–20.

55. Joaquin Antonio Amesti to Father Visitor Menchero, 19 October 1731; doctor's certification, 21 October 1731; Menchero authorization, 23 October 1731—all written in Chihuahua. UNM-BNM, vol. 124F, legajo 7, no. 56, 164–66.

56. Menchero, "Declaración."

57. Raymundo Gras affidavit, 23 October 1731, Chihuahua, UNM-BNM, vol. 124F, legajo 7, no. 56, 194. Four days earlier Gras had his official interview with Menchero as Visitor of the Custody (Menchero visita 1731, 19).

58. Miguel Menchero to Governor Barrutia, no date, and Governor Barrutia declaration, 26 October 1731, both written in Chihuahua, in "Diligencias para que los Religiosos" file, AHMP-FC.

59. Inventory of the Guadalupe Mission, 18 October 1731 (see note 50 above).

60. Joseph Manuel de Eguia to Menchero, Chihuahua, no date, in BNM-AF, caja 23, no. 468, 3; Chávez, *Archives of the Archdiocese of Santa Fe*, 246 (Santa Cruz).

61. Menchero, "Declaración," 22.

62. "Los religiosos que se hallan en las misiones de esta Santa Custodia," UNM-BNM, 126A, legajo 9, no. 7, 2822–23. Father Saavedra was not listed anywhere in the custody. This undated list can be traced to 1736 by comparing it with the

assignments listed for each missionary in Chávez, *Archives of the Archdiocese of Santa Fe*, 241–58.

63. Griffen, *Indian Assimilation*, 16, citing the Berroterán report of 1748 and Menchero's 1744 account, stated that this practice of impermanent residency was adopted "in 1720 or shortly thereafter." From the information presented up to this point, the more accurate date is sometime after 1731.

64. Juan García to Comisario General Pedro Navarrete, Chihuahua, 28 January 1738, BNM-AF, caja 28, no. 524.4. In the chronicle of the Zacatecan Province published in 1737, José Arlegui, writing in Zacatecas, stated that "various nations are being discovered toward the North in La Junta de los Ríos, [nations] that have given obedience to the Church and the King in three distinct missions" (*Crónica de la Provincia*, 99). This comment shows the fluctuating sense of a Franciscan presence at La Junta at the time and the possibility that a new province of Franciscans might provide that presence. In a letter that he wrote to the Franciscan Commissary General in Mexico City after his visit to New Mexico including El Paso in 1737, Bishop Elizacoechea made no mention of La Junta: Bishop Martín de Elizacoechea to Commissary General Pedro Navarrete, Durango, 17 March 1738 (UNM-BNM, vol. 124F, legajo 7, no. 69, 323–27).

65. Antonio de Esquivel to Comisario General Pedro Navarrete, Chihuahua, 13 October 1737, BNM-AF, caja 28, no. 524.2. Francisco Manuel Bravo Lerchundi was a native of Puebla and made his first profession as a Franciscan there in 1700 at the age of 16 (Norris, *After "The Year Eighty,"* 166). For his previous ministry in New Mexico, see Chávez, *Archives of the Archdiocese of Santa Fe*, 243.

66. Antonio de Esquivel to Comisario General Pedro Navarrete, Chihuahua, 19 January 1738, BNM-AF, caja 28, no. 524.3, and García to Navarrete, 4v. Norris, *After "The Year Eighty,"* 173, lists Tejada as in the missions of upper New Mexico from 1738 to 1752. But neither of the two references that Norris cites in relation to Tejada (Adams and Chavez, *The Missions of New Mexico*, 328–40; Kessell, *Kiva, Cross, and Crown*, 496–503) mentions the friar at all. The only note of him in Chávez, *Archives of the Archdiocese of Santa Fe*, is in August 1749 at Albuquerque (257).

67. Deeds, "Colonial Chihuahua," 33, 37.

68. For the 1715 statistics, see Reindorp, *The Founding of Missions*, 18. For those in 1747, see Enrique Rede Madrid, trans., *Expedition to La Junta de los Ríos, 1747–1748: Captain Commander Joseph de Ydoiaga's Report to the Viceroy of New Spain.* Austin: Texas Historical Commission, 1992. For the latter I have calculated slightly different totals for two towns in the next chapter, since Madrid's totals do not always correspond to the number of persons listed.

69. Menchero, "Declaración."

70. Above it was noted that in 1726 El Pescado's usual encampment was reported

to be upriver from La Junta. Before 1747, however, the Pescados had been living at the Tapacolmes site, as reported by the Ydoiaga expedition. See Robert E. Wright, "The Native Mission Site at Polvo," *Journal of Big Bend Studies* 31 (2019), 167–77, that comes to different conclusions than Enrique R. Madrid, "The Lost Mission of El Polvo: Searching for the History of a State Archeological Landmark," *Journal of Big Bend Studies* 15 (2003): 55–68. To my 2019 essay may be added that the very brief existence of a mission is supported by the lack of extensive mission-period artifacts found there by archaeologists (Kelley, "Historic Indian Pueblos," 42). A further indication of a mission in the late 1730s is the fact that only 9 percent of the "modest" number of ceramic sherds recovered in 1994 from the entire area were from near the presumed chapel site; only one-sixth of those from the chapel site were Mexican-style (possibly indicating missionary presence), and the earliest Mexican-style piece anywhere was from the mid-1700s: William A. Cloud, Robert J. Mallouf, Patricia A. Mercado-Allinger, Cathryn A. Hoyt, Nancy A. Kenmotsu, Joseph M. Sánchez, Enrique R. Madrid, *Archaeological Testing at the Polvo Site, Presidio County, Texas*, Office of the State Archaeologist Report 19 (Austin: Texas Historical Commission and U.S. Department of Agriculture, Soil Conservation Service, 1994), 102.

71. Cristóbal Iraeta, custos, to Commissary General Navarrete, 10 September 1741, El Paso, UNM-BNM, vol. 125A, legajo 8, no. 2, 447.

72. Berroterán to Viceroy, 217; Madrid, *Expedition to La Junta de los Ríos* 36.

73. Spicer, *Cycles of Conquest*, 51–53, provides a good summary but does not mention the involvement of military contingents from Nueva Vizcaya.

74. Frederic J. Athearn, *A Forgotten Kingdom: The Spanish Frontier in Colorado and New Mexico 1540–1821*, Cultural Resource Series no. 29 (Denver: Bureau of Land Management, 1989), 50.

75. Lorenzo de Saavedra, "Breve noticia," filed together with his "Memoria de los Religiosos Misioneros existentes en la Custodia de la Nueva Mexico," BNM-AF, caja 7, no. 14, pages 5–6. Both of these are undated, but the friars listed as serving in the custody were only verifiably present there simultaneously in 1740–1741 (from their dates of service given in Chávez, *Archives of the Archdiocese of Santa Fe*, 241–58), and one of them, Father Lerchundi, died on 5 July 1741, in Chihuahua, as noted above. In view of later charges by royal officials regarding missionary personnel at La Junta, I note here that Saavedra listed thirty-five Franciscans, including the procurator (Menchero) and a lay Brother surgeon, and added that "there is one more than the royal permission" (*sobra uno segun el Real permiso*).

76. Adams and Chavez, *The Missions of New Mexico*, 333. This source also notes that García was the recording secretary for Menchero's visitation of the custody in 1743. This would have taken him away from his regular assignment for several

months. García was born in Murcia, Spain, and made his first religious profession in the mother convent of San Francisco in Mexico City in February 1728 at the age of 24: Francisco Morales, O.F.M., *Inventario del Fondo Franciscano del Museo de Antropología e Historia de México*, vol. 1 (Washington, DC: Academy of American Franciscan History, 1978), 288.

77. "Segunda visita pastoral del Obispo Dn. Martín de Elizacoechea, Año 1742," Archivo Eclesiástico de la Catedral de Durango, microfilm roll 9, Libro 48, frames 499 and 513, in Special Collections, University of Texas at El Paso Library (henceforth AECD-UTEP). I owe notice of this visitation to Norris, *After "The Year Eighty,"* 187n41, who, however, gave a much lower number of confirmations and did not mention the missionaries. Dennis Daily at New Mexico State University located the document for me, since the repository was mistakenly identified in Norris's volume.

78. Madrid, *Expedition to La Junta de los Ríos*, 53 (the report of the Juntans in 1747). The Madrid translation of this incident has been corrected according to the Spanish transcript of the passage, graciously provided by Madrid in a telephone conversation on 22 June 2021. Madrid agreed that "como lo habian hecho ahora [in 1747] cuatro años" should be translated "as they had done four years ago," rather than "as they had done now for four years." Berroterán also wrote that everything had been quiet on his frontier since 1743 (Berroterán to Viceroy, in Hadley, Naylor, and Schuetz-Miller, *The Presidio and Militia*, 222).

79. Menchero, "Declaración" (my translation).

80. Informaciones, 30 August–3 September 1745, Chihuahua, and Francisco Benites Murillo, 2 October 1745, Villa de Leon, UT-BCAH, AGI Mexico, box 2Q147, file 87, 199, 221–22, 228, 256.

81. Juan Antonio de Ornedal y Maza to the Viceroy, 26 July 1749, El Paso, UNM-BNM, vol. 125B, legajo 8, no. 56, sections 13–14.

82. González was not present in La Junta during the several months of the 1747–1748 military expeditions there (see below). And in a judicial process in Mexico City in October 1748 exonerating him of false accusations, he was stated to have been in New Mexico from 1744 to early 1748 (testimony of Joseph Irigoyen and Juan Joseph Oronzoro, 24 and 26 October 1748, in investigation of González, 24 October–6 November 1748, Mexico City, UNM-BNM, vol. 125A, legajo 8, no. 38, 2008–28).

83. Scholars have been led astray, positing another raid on La Junta in 1745 or 1746, by a malicious secret investigation into the conduct of Captain Berroterán in 1746. The captain was accused of failing to prevent an attack on the La Junta missions by Apaches and Sumas, resulting in the flight of the Franciscans there (Joseph Velarde Cosio to the Conde de Fuenclara, 21 April 1746, UT-BCAH, AGI Guadalajara, box 2Q138, file 32, 4). Daniel and others have interpreted the

documents as placing this attack in June 1745: Daniel, "La Junta de los Rios and the Despoblado," 105–6 (followed by Folsom, "Spanish La Junta de los Rios," 92); Daniel, "The Advance of the Spanish Frontier," 185; Ortelli, *Trama de una guerra conveniente*, 36, 48. Similarly, Griffen wrote that the La Junta pueblos were attacked in 1746 (*Culture Change*, 74), but gave no more information. But a careful reading of the prior documents in this investigation points to the fact that the raid in question was the 1743 one, that did not result in the flight of the Franciscans. The actual case was that since at least the end of 1744 Diego González de la Herrán, the owner of the Hormigas hacienda between Chihuahua and La Junta, was asking for a squad of soldiers to assist the Juntans in an expedition against the Apaches and Sumas far upriver from La Junta, who had previously raided La Junta and were raiding the *hacendado*'s lands (Joan Joseph de Arezpacochaga to Joseph de Ydoyaga, 3 February 1745, and mandamiento of Joseph de Cosio y Campa Marques de Torre Campo, 25 June 1745, UT-BCAH, AGI Guadalajara, box 2Q138, file 32, 68, 71).

84. Juan Miguel Menchero to Viceroy [Fuenclara], Chihuahua, 28 March 1746, and Marqués de Altamira dictamen and viceroyal decree, 28 June 1746, UT-BCAH, AGI Mexico, box 2Q147, file 88, 1–4, 7–12.

85. Juan Miguel Menchero to Viceroy [Güemes y Horcasitas], n.d., UT-BCAH, AGI Mexico, box 2Q147, file 88, 12–13. Regrettably, there is not a copy of the Sánchez documents in this file. For Sánchez as visitor in early 1745, see Chávez, *Archives of the Archdiocese of Santa Fe*, 33, 161, 162, 195.

86. The lower half of the map is reproduced here. A full-page reproduction is in Marc Simmons, "History of Pueblo-Spanish Relations to 1821," in *Southwest*, edited by Alfonso Ortiz, Handbook of North American Indians, vol. 9 (Washington, DC: Smithsonian Institution, 1979), 188. The map is undated, but the name of the viceroy, who arrived in 1746, and Menchero's self-identification as Visitor places it in 1746 or 1747. The map named Guadalupe, San Pedro, San Juan, San Cristóbal, and San Francisco near the junction of the Rios del Norte and Conchos but located all of them in the wrong places. Menchero had obviously never actually been in the La Junta district.

87. Berroterán to Viceroy, 211.

88. "Informe del Provincial, March 1750," 21.

Chapter 6

1. Menchero to the Viceroy, 27 May 1747, and the deliberations of the viceregal administration in June 1747, in Hadley, Naylor, and Schuetz-Miller, *The Presidio and Militia*, 162–66 (Spanish), 156–62 (English). The quotation is on page 166 (Spanish, my translation), 161 (a somewhat faulty English translation). Altamira's list of missions was what he found on record in Mexico City, not the actual

situation at La Junta.

2. Madrid, *Expedition to La Junta de los Ríos*, 26–31.

3. Madrid, *Expedition to La Junta de los Ríos*, 32, 107–8 (quotes on 107); Domingo Antonio García diario y derrotero, 11 November 1747–20 January 1748, AGI Guadalajara 136, 67-3-30, UT-BCAH, box 2Q138, file 33, 5–7.

4. The apparent discrepancy between García and Ydoiaga in regard to when the people left Coyame and Cuchillo Parado—years ago or the past June—may be due to a distinction between the partial and total abandonment of those places.

5. Madrid, *Expedition to La Junta de los Ríos*, 34–36, 98; Saavedra to Ydoiaga, 10 January 1748, UNM-BNM, vol. 125B, legajo 8, no. 46. Saavedra wrote that it was Francisco Conchero who carried his note to Ydoiaga, whereas Ydoiaga wrote that it was Pedro el Mulato. For the expedition numbers, see Madrid, *Expedition to La Junta de los Ríos*, 19–25, 33. The chaplain of the San Bartolomé troops, Joseph Joachín de Orrantía, accompanied the expedition until he departed on January 15, having contracted a serious urinary illness (Madrid, *Expedition*, 103).

6. Madrid, *Expedition to La Junta de los Ríos*, 36–41. Madrid's total of 156 Cacalotes at San Juan Bautista apparently included a non-indicated wife (transcription error?) within the listing of married couples.

7. Madrid, *Expedition to La Junta de los Ríos*, 42–48 (quote on 47), 106. Madrid gave the Guadalupe total as 171, but there are actually 172 listed.

8. Sánchez must have been at either La Junta or El Paso after early 1745, since other than as Visitor in 1745 his name does not appear in Chávez, *Archives of the Archdiocese of Santa Fe*, that deals only with upper New Mexico. He is named in all the documents of the 1747–1748 expeditions, and his autograph certification of the participation of the troops of Governor Rábago y Teran of Coahuila is an original document, with his own signature and rubric (Francisco Sánchez certification, Guadalupe mission, 28 December 1747, Center for Southwest Research and Special Collections, Zimmerman Library, University of New Mexico, MSS 867, AGN Historia (henceforth UNM-AGN), vol. 37A, expediente 6, 1651). Father Francisco de la Concepción González, whom Ornedal mistakenly placed at La Junta since 1746, was secretary for Sánchez during the latter's 1745 visitation of the custody (Chávez, *Archives of the Archdiocese of Santa Fe*, 34, 1743 no. 2). Perhaps the two friars were closely linked together in the minds of many. I thank Bernadette Lucero, archivist for the Archdiocese of Santa Fe, for sending me a copy of the 1745 document signed by both Sánchez and González.

9. Alonso Victores Rubín de Celís journal, in "Testimonio de los autos del reconocimiento fecho, Rio avajo de el Norte, desde el expresado Rio hasta las Misiones de la Junta de dicho Rio, y el de Conchos, por el Capitan del Real Presidio del Paso," typescript at UT-BCAH, box 2Q138, vol. 33 (cuaderno 5, 136-67-3-30), 22.

10. Madrid, *Expedition to La Junta de los Ríos*, 50–51, 54–56 (quote on 50). Madrid gave totals of 110 Púliques, nintety-three Cíbolos, and sixty Pescados, but 115 Púliques are actually listed.
11. Madrid, *Expedition to La Junta de los Ríos*, 57.
12. Ibid., 53, 63–65. The Cíbolo general and a few Native guides led Ydoiago and a few of his officers to inspect the former Cíbolo site in the mountains once the party reached San Cristóbal on its return trip up the Rio del Norte.
13. Madrid, *Expedition to La Junta de los Ríos*, 59–63 (quotes on 60–61), 97 (Saavedra quote). The people in Madrid's list for San Cristóbal actually total 158, not Madrid's 157. Kenmotsu, "Jornada Connections," 199, unaware of these notices of heritable land tenure, nevertheless concluded that such was the case based upon the successive pattern of housing evident at La Junta.
14. Madrid, *Expedition to La Junta de los Ríos*, 60–61.
15. García diario y derrotero, 10. García's inclusion of Tapacolmes Natives was probably a mistake, occasioned by the mention of them as former inhabitants. His total of families for the five nations was 137, whereas the total given by Madrid from Ydoiaga's census adds up to only 107 families. But Madrid did not include as families those listed without spouse or child by Ydoiaga. If those are added, Ydoiaga's list yields 136 families at Púliques and San Cristóbal, practically identical to García's count.
16. Madrid, *Expedition to La Junta de los Ríos*, 97, 105.
17. Ibid., 51–52 (quote on 51), 112–13. The age of El Lijero was given by Vidaurre's expedition, the last to arrive. They encountered his group in the mountains southeast of La Junta and estimated their number as about 250. That number seems low, given that El Lijero later reported 150 families to Ydoiaga. Perhaps in the earlier encounter with Vidaurre some of Lijero's people were away hunting or had remained hidden out of caution. Through sign language, El Lijero indicated that his group was being bothered by the Natagés, whom he described similarly as he later did to Ydoiaga (Daniel, "La Junta de los Rios and the Despoblado," 168–69).
18. Madrid, *Expedition to La Junta de los Ríos*, 51–52, 113.
19. Ibid., 52, 57–58, 60 (quote). Vidaurre's troops were visited by Don Pascual on January 26 as they drew near the La Junta valley from the southeast. Don Pascual carried the Spanish baton of authority, and he told Vidaurre that he, his wife, and his children had been baptized and that he ruled over five *rancherías* of thirty families (Daniel, "La Junta de los Rios and the Despoblado," 171–72).
20. Pedro de Rábago y Terán, "Derrotero," 1747–1748, UNM-AGN, vol. 37A, expediente 6, 23r–24r.
21. Ibid., 24v.
22. Madrid, *Expedition to La Junta de los Ríos*, 53, 68. Basing himself on the report

by Ydoiaga, Kelley considered the band of El Venado to be Apaches ("Factors Involved in the Abandonment," 377), but the accumulated evidence discussed previously does not warrant such a conclusion.

23. Madrid, *Expedition to La Junta de los Ríos*, 66–69, 76–77. Today a settlement called Ruidosa is about the same distance from the river junction as that given by Ydoiaga for the first place he called by that name.

24. Madrid, *Expedition to La Junta de los Ríos*, 37, 41–42, 46, 49–51, 57, 60–61, 66–67, 80.

25. Ibid., 42, 89–90; Rábago y Terán, "Derrotero," 25.

26. Rábago y Terán to the Viceroy, 12 February 1748, Monclova, UNM-AGN, vol. 37A, expediente 6, 1667.

27. Rábago y Terán, "Derrotero," 23v.

28. Ibid., 24r, 25v (quotes).

29. Ibid., 26.

30. Madrid, *Expedition to La Junta de los Ríos*, 83–84, 88–92 (quote on 91).

31. Ibid., 96, 98 (quote), 100–101.

32. Ibid., 99; see also 95. For the trade in captives among Natives and with Hispanics in upper New Mexico, see Brooks, *Captives and Cousins*.

33. Madrid, *Expedition to La Junta de los Ríos*, 106–7.

34. Ibid., 107, 113. Morgenthaler seized upon Sánchez's remark to return to his thesis of Juntan negativity toward the friars (*La Junta de los Ríos*, 112; see also 134–35).

35. Madrid, *Expedition to La Junta de los Ríos*, 93–94.

36. Ibid., 46, 76, 95.

37. Ibid., 97–98; see also 99. My translation of the quoted sentence in the original manuscript: "el día de hoy se hallarán los *pocos* [pueblos], que han quedado, con quarenta o sinquenta familias, *pocas* [familias] mas, o menos con bastantes niños, y niñas de doctrina qotidiana" (Saavedra to Ydoiaga, 10 January 1748). Madrid's translation (97) gave a different sense, possibly relying upon a faulty transcription of *pocas* as *pocos*. The Madrid text also differs from the original in having the increase by procreation occurring only through the gentiles and not also through the already existing Juntan families.

38. Madrid, *Expedition to La Junta de los Ríos*, 97. The census placed the Cíbolos at Puliques; here Saavedra placed them at San Cristóbal. But all these groups below the river junction were reported to be very united, almost as one.

39. Madrid, *Expedition to La Junta de los Ríos*, 106–7.

40. Ibid., 112, 114. Madrid's publication ends at this point, since this is where the first Ydoiaga report ends. For Vidaurre, see Fermín de Vidaurre diario y derrotero, UNM-AGN, vol. 37B, expediente 8.

41. Ydoiaga return trip documents, April 1748, UNM-AGN, vol. 37B, expediente 7.

42. Ornedal, writing from El Paso in July 1749, had Saavedra still at La Junta

(Ornedal y Maza to the Viceroy, 26 July 1749, section 13).

43. Varo report to provincial, 29 January 1749 (see chapter 4, no. 67), 26–27.

44. Varo to Jimeno [1749–1750] (see chapter 4, no. 69), 2930–32.

45. Consulta del Theniente de Governador Joseph Velarde Cosio al Virrey Conde de Fuenclara, San Phelipe el Real, 21 April 1746; El Marqués de Altamira al Virrey, 21 June 1746; defense by presidial captains, San Francisco de Conchos, 21 October 1746, UT-BCAH, AGI Guadalajara, box 2Q138, file 32 (1746–1751), 4, 24 (quote), 38, 41–43.

46. Berroterán to Viceroy, in Hadley, Naylor, and Schuetz-Miller, *The Presidio and Militia*, 205, 225–26. The English translation of this document on pages 175–204 is unreliable at several important points, as demonstrable from the accompanying Spanish transcription. For Berroterán's history, see the editors' introduction to this document on pages 167–74.

47. Berroterán to Viceroy, 216 (quotation), 218, 222.

48. Ibid., 219. In Roman Catholicism, a canonized saint is one officially recognized by the Church for heroic virtues, since medieval times usually demonstrated by miraculous cures. The beatification of a deceased person is the first step in this process, recognizing a virtuous life, but referring to them as "blessed" rather than "saint."

49. Berroterán to Viceroy, 222–26. The translation in Hadley, Naylor, and Schuetz-Miller, *The Presidio and Militia*, 203, mistakenly has Berroterán advocating the move of the two presidios. Sara Ortelli's *Trama de una guerra conveniente* advanced the provocative thesis that the declarations of an "Apache" threat since 1748 by Berroterán and the Nueva Vizcayan elite, and accepted by historians ever since, were spurred primarily by those elites' efforts to protect the lucrative system of military posts from government reductions, to maintain their avoidance of taxes by pleading losses due to Apache raids, and to continue to capture workers and justify forced labor (19). But her effort to minimize the impact of hostilities does not hold up. Noting that the non-Native population of Nueva Vizcaya almost doubled between 1750 and 1800, she lamely stated that the population of Santa Eulalia, close by Chihuahua, "did not experience a strong demographic collapse" (without giving the numbers) and that in the Chihuahua district, including the San Pedro River and extending all the way to the Rio del Norte, it only "decreased lightly," whereas some of the figures that she cited argue differently (100).

50. John, *Storms Brewed in Other Men's Worlds*, 241–73. For the 1748 marker, see also Moorhead, *The Presidio*, 48, and Navarro García, *Don José de Gálvez*, 78. Ortelli noted this canonization of the Berroterán report but argued that the Apaches did not wage war on Hispanics in Nueva Vizcaya for territorial dominance, rather that they raided principally to obtain horses and mules (*Trama de*

una guerra conveniente, 18). This may have been true in many cases, but not at La Junta, as events in 1759–1760 will clearly show. Furthermore, the destructive impact was basically the same in either case.

51. Morfi, *History of Texas*, 266.
52. Weber, *Bárbaros*, 104 (quote)–107; Osante, *Orígenes del Nuevo Santander (1748–1772)*, 103–8, 125. Weber noted that this "radical experiment" was quite successful in terms of Hispanic colonization yet never repeated in Spanish America. It contravened the laws that protected Indians from being exterminated if non-cooperative and was very detrimental to conversion efforts. Franciscans were recruited and subsidized by the government as missionaries to the Natives but found themselves actually functioning as pastors to the civilian settlements without any support for their mission efforts—in fact, denied the means to accomplish that end.
53. See the following chapter.
54. The full report is Varo informe to the Provincial, 29 January 1749 (see chapter 4, no. 67). This report is briefly summarized in Norris, *After "The Year Eighty,"* 117–19. Norris inexplicably wrote that Varo stated that only one missionary was in the La Junta district at the time, since flooding had forced the temporary abandonment of the other missions. There is no such statement in the University of New Mexico photocopy of the manuscript copy at the Biblioteca Nacional that both Norris and I viewed.
55. For the controversies that occasioned the two banishments of González from New Mexico, see Norris, *After "The Year Eighty,"* 102, 114, 115–16, and Kessell, *Kiva, Cross, and Crown*, 335. Norris gives the more accurate report, but he also has some misinterpretations.
56. Ornedal y Maza to the Viceroy, 26 July 1749, section 14. The Franciscan provincial reported that as soon as Vélez Cachupín was appointed interim governor of New Mexico González fled to his protection, in order to protest, among other things, his transfer from Nambé to La Junta, and that the governor barred the Franciscans from having González sent to the provincial in Mexico City to answer for his disobedience ("Informe del Provincial, March 1750," 8, 10–11, 22–23). Vélez Cachupín became governor in April 1749 (Norris, *After "The Year Eighty,"* 120). Later in 1749 the viceroy reprimanded the governor for interfering in the Franciscans' clergy assignments (BNM-AF, caja 23, no. 471.2). In August 1749 González began sacramental entries in Pecos, where he remained for only a year (Chávez, *Archives of the Archdiocese of Santa Fe*, 247).
57. Certification of the ministry of Fray Francisco Guzmán, 5 November 1748, Nra. Sra. de Guadalupe del Paso, UNM-BNM, vol. 125A, legajo 8, no. 29, 1936–1937.
58. Chávez, *Archives of the Archdiocese of Santa Fe*, 246.
59. Juan Miguel Menchero, "Nómina de los Religiosos Misioneros que servieron el

año de quarenta y ocho," 15 May 1751, Sandía, copied in a certified document by Joseph Gorraenz, 29 November 1752, Mexico City, UNM-BNM, vol. 126B, legajo 9, part 2, no. 23, 3133–41. For two years the Franciscans were unable to get the 1748 missionary list certified by the New Mexico governors; Menchero finally succeeded in 1751, thus the later date.

60. Varo stated in the earlier part of his report that the Crown was supporting "thirty-seven ministers [priests], including the procurator, the four missionaries who are destined for the Navajo foundation, and a lay Brother teacher." Serving without government support were a missionary in the new mission of Sandía, an "almost unserviceable" old priest helping in Albuquerque, and another lay Brother (in El Paso). If one does not count the mostly inactive old priest in Albuquerque, this agreed with Varo's comment toward the end of his report that there were thirty-eight priests in the custody including the Father Procurator (still Menchero) and two lay Brothers, for a total of forty Franciscans.

Chapter 7

1. Chávez, *Archives of the Archdiocese of Santa Fe*, 34, 35, 162.
2. Varo, "Informe al Virrey," March 1749, BNM-AF, caja 15, no. 268, 3v-4.
3. Varo, "Informe al Virrey," 4-4v. The interest in mining to the north of La Junta was not misplaced. Kelley noted that rich silver deposits were discovered and mined there in the following century (introduction to Madrid, *Expedition to La Junta de los Ríos*, xv).
4. Norris, *After "The Year Eighty,"* 117, 119–20, 126–28. The characterizations of Varo and Vélez Cachupín are by Kessell, *Kiva, Cross, and Crown*, 334, 378. Norris, 119, described Vélez Cachupín as uncompromising and domineering.
5. Ornedal to Viceroy, 26 July 1749 (see chapter 5, note 81).
6. Norris, *After "The Year Eighty,"* dealt only with the central and northern area (what he termed the Santa Fe district) of New Mexico, with only occasional summary notes on La Junta and almost nothing on the El Paso district. Its value to this study is in assessing comprehensively the power dynamics between Franciscans and governors.
7. Norris, *After "The Year Eighty,"* 23, 67, 93–126.
8. Of fifteen new arrivals in upper New Mexico in 1731–1736 noted by Norris, at least five were in their mid-20s and/or recently ordained; another seven were 30–40 years old, having been ordained at least five years, with no known frontier experience (Norris, *After "The Year Eighty,"* 93–94). Of the twelve new arrivals in 1737–1749 whose background is known, three were in their 20s, one 31, and three more in their 30s (108–9).
9. Norris, *After "The Year Eighty,"* 103–8, 125. Norris's own conclusions about the Franciscan efforts conflict with each other. Throughout most of his text

they were negative (4, 68). Only in his final comments did he acknowledge that a significant factor in the Puebloans' ability to retain their cultural autonomy was the accommodation accepted by the Franciscans after the 1680 and 1696 uprisings (164). He also stated that "as to teaching the Puebloans Spanish, the Franciscans probably deserved more credit than they officially received" and that "the Puebloan people partially defended themselves with a linguistic shield" (162–63). The linguistic defense of most Pueblo groups has endured to this day.

10. Norris, *After "The Year Eighty,"* 126 (quote), 128–29.

11. Ornedal to Viceroy, sections 13–14.

12. Navarro García, *Don José de Gálvez*, 110.

13. María del Carmen Velázquez, *El Marqués de Altamira y las provincias internas de Nueva España* (México, D.F.: Colegio de México, 1976), 109–31, https://www.jstor.org/stable/j.ctv2868cb.

14. Velázquez, *El Marqués de Altamira*, 125–26.

15. Ortelli, *Trama de una guerra conveniente*, 182. This is the major thesis of Ortelli's study.

16. Varo to Jimeno [1749–1750]. A sidebar by the same later writer added that "by exception" four more subsidies were added in 1746, 1747, and 1748 [only] for the new missionary effort among the Navajos.

17. "Puntos que podrán servir para la dirección," UNM-BNM, vol. 126C, legajo 9, no. 54, 3706–12, and "Informe del Provincial, Marzo 1750," 21–22, 24. The Bandelier transcription of a copy of this report in AGN Historia, vol. 25, is translated in Hackett, *Historical Documents*, vol. 3, 438–59. The provincial's statements about La Junta were obviously based upon Varo to Jimeno [1749–1750], which it followed fairly closely. For the provincial's statements about Fr. González, see chapter 6, note 56.

18. José Berroterán certification to custodio Varo, 14 April 1750, Chihuahua, BNM-AF, caja 29, no 559.3. Páez, just as Varo, evidently served mostly in the El Paso district. He arrived in the San Pablo Custody by 1735 (August entries in Albuquerque) and served the following year as Varo's secretary in Senecú in the El Paso district (Chávez, *Archives of the Archdiocese of Santa Fe*, 253, 160). As stated above, in November 1748 he was serving as the president or leader of the missions in the El Paso district.

19. Antonio Gutierrez y Noriega certification to the Viceroy and the Franciscan Commisary General, 5 February 1751, Chihuahua, BNM-AF, caja 29, no. 573.2.

20. Alonso de Gastessi to the Viceroy and to the Franciscan Commissary General, 8 February 1751, Chihuahua, UNM-BNM, vol. 125C, legajo 8, no. 76, 2466–67.

21. Velázquez, *El Marqués de Altamira*, 154–56. This order was transmitted through the governor of Nueva Vizcaya to all the presidio captains on the Camino Real below Chihuahua, commanding them to "obligate the 400 Apaches led by

Captain Pascual to settle themselves in some town or towns" (Ortelli, *Trama de una guerra conveniente*, 36n56). In this communication Pascual was incorrectly made the leader of all the Apache groups.

22. Marqués de Altamira to Viceroy, 22 April 1752, UNM-BNM, vol. 126B, legajo 9, part 2, no. 19, 3102.
23. Velázquez, *El Marqués de Altamira*, 132–34. Velázquez transcribed the entire 1751 document.
24. Ibid., 137–48.
25. Ibid., 149–50, 165 (quote)–166.
26. Marqués de Altamira to Viceroy, 22 April 1752. Locating Coyame only fourteen leagues from Guadalupe was an obvious error; perhaps this was a transcriber's mistake for twenty-four leagues.
27. Velázquez, *El Marqués de Altamira*, 156.
28. Marqués de Altamira to Viceroy, 22 April 1752, 3102–3.
29. Census of San Pablo Custody in 1750, UNM-BNM, vol. 125D, legajo 8, part 4, no. 81, 2747–59. For a transcription of and detailed commentary upon the La Junta section of this census, see Robert E. Wright, "The People of La Junta in 1750: A Census," *Journal of Big Bend Studies* 29 (2017): 21–38. There was no indication why the towns of San Cristóbal and Púliques were not included. Either Páez did not count them or those records were lost. In my 2017 essay I incorrectly assumed that the Venados were Apaches; subsequent research detailed above argues otherwise.
30. See, for example, John Francis Bannon, S.J. *The Mission Frontier in Sonora, 1620–1687* (New York: United States Catholic Historical Society, 1955), 94, who noted that the Jesuit missionary at Ures "had been able to complete his church, care for some 350 *muchachos y muchachas de doctrina*, and reach out to new fields."
31. Steven W. Hackel, *Children of Coyote, Missionaries of St. Francis: Indian-Spanish Relations in Colonial California, 1769–1850* (Chapel Hill: University of North Carolina Press for the Omohundro Institute of Early American History and Culture, 2005), 202.
32. There are several variables that make such a comparison conjectural. The assumption is that the 1750 San Juan census included the Mezquites and Conejos. See Wright, "The People of La Junta," 25–28.
33. In December 1751 the bishop of Durango wrote about a three-year drought in the region just abating (Daniel, "The Advance of the Spanish Frontier," 208). For the continuing migrant work, see "Carta del Padre Trigo," 23 July 1754, Ixtacalco, in Bolton Collection, Part I, no. 453, 14, translated in Hackett, *Historical Documents*, vol. 3, 468.
34. Carlos Delgado to Provincial Jimeno, 27 March 1750, Hospice of Santa Barbara

Tlaltelolco, in Hackett, *Historical Documents*, vol. 3, 428–29.

35. Rubín de Celís journal, 1–14 (see chapter 6, note 9). For a map of this area, see Álvarez, "Manuel San Juan," 119.

36. Rubín de Celís journal, 14–16.

37. Ibid., 16–20. "Coyotes" were the mixed-blood descendants of mestizo and mulatto (Kessell, *Spain in the Southwest*, 422). Typical visual indicators of race were such things as skin color, hair type, eye color, and even clothing, but most of these could be disguised when engaged in raids (Ortelli, *Trama de una guerra conveniente*, 132–33).

38. Rubín de Celís journal, 19. The multiple-mixed-race situation developing in the Coyame valley is a textbook case of people whom Hispanic *gente decente* (decent people) looked down upon as marginal to their societal construct and whom they feared when not strictly controlled. An excellent synthesis of this dimension of colonial society is Peter Stern, "Marginals and Acculturation in Frontier Society," in *New Views of Borderlands History*, ed. Robert H. Jackson (Albuquerque: University of New Mexico Press, 1998), 157–88; Ortelli, *Trama de una guerra conveniente* (18, 57, and chapter 4) discovered that reports of mixed-ethnicity outlaws were not common in Nueva Vizcaya until the 1770s. But she argued that this was actually the case in several situations before that time when hostilities were simply attributed to the "Apaches" (93, 114). Most of the many towns accused of complicity with "Apache" raids in the 1770s and 1780s (123n43) were in the Tarahumara country, but they also included Santa Cruz de Tapacolmes (with a strong Tarahumara population by then: see Griffen, *Indian Assimilation*, 68) and one named San Pedro.

39. A traditional Hispanic Catholic greeting until recent times was "Ave María purísima" (Hail most pure Mary), to which the response was "sin pecado concebida" (conceived without sin).

40. Could this have been the "old general" Bernardo at San Cristóbal in the 1747 census? In that census he was the only one named Bernardo in any of the towns.

41. Rubín de Celís journal, 20–24. The red banner with white cross was apparently what Hispanics gave those Native groups who agreed to be their allies. Back in 1653 a group of Hispanic allies led by the Salineros entered Parral with such a flag (Griffen, *Culture Change and Shifting Populations*, 24). This was presumably the type of banner sent or given by Hispanic officials to other native groups with whom they were seeking to establish peace in the 1690s (*Culture Change*, 42, 44).

42. Rubín de Celís journal, 24–27.

43. Ibid., 27–34.

44. Joseph Páez to Andres Varo, 11 December 1750, San Francisco de la Junta, UNM-BNM, vol. 125C, legajo 8, part 3, doc. 77. So Páez located the camp of Rubín de Celís three leagues upriver from San Francisco, whereas the captain

placed it at two leagues.

45. Rubín de Celís journal, 27 (Guadalupe), 24 (San Juan).

46. Fray Jacobo de Castro to provincial, 31 January 1753, El Paso, BNM-AF, caja 15, no. 275, 10. This document was printed in *Documentos para la historia eclesiástica y civil de la Nueva-Vizcaya*, 139–41, and in the republication of that volume in 2009, *La historia eclesiástica*, 153–55.

47. Rubín de Celís to the Viceroy, 24 December 1750, in "Testimonio de los autos del reconocimiento fecho ... por el Capitan del Real Presidio del Paso," 35–38.

48. In upper New Mexico, Vélez Cachupín skillfully brought about peaceful relations with all the neighboring Native nations by the end of 1752 (John, *Storms Brewed in Other Men's Worlds*, 321–29).

49. Vélez Cachupín to the Viceroy, 29 March 1751, in "Testimonio de los autos del reconocimiento fecho ... por el Capitan del Real Presidio del Paso," 43–45.

50. Marqués de Altamira opinion and Viceroy's order, 19 and 23 June 1751, in "Testimonio de los autos del reconocimiento fecho ... por el Capitan del Real Presidio del Paso," 53–57.

51. Wanting Varo's defense to reach the viceroy and king a decade later, but in a less acerbic tone, Father Figueroa produced a much more extensive version, altering various heated passages but also adding seventeen leaves of information from the archives and forging Varo's signature at the end. A copy of this massive document by Figueroa is in UNM-BNM, vol. 126C, legajo 9, no. 53 (3592–3698). To prompt the viceroy at that later date to ask for the revised and expanded report, subsequently curtailed due to its huge size, Figueroa in his ghost-writing of provincial Serrano's report in 1761 (see chapter 9) made note of the Varo report as very worthy of being read: Fr. Francisco Antonio de la Rosa Figueroa, "Nota especialissima," UNM-BNM, vol. 126A, legajo 9, no. 17, 3007; Adams, *Bishop Tamarón's Visitation*, 24–25.

52. Andrés Varo to Provincial Jimeno, 29 January 1751, El Paso, UNM-BNM, vol. 126A, legajo 9, no. 17. The biblical passage is from I Kings 18:17. Norris, *After "The Year Eighty,"* 124, noted that Varo's report was "so incendiary" that it was not included in the documents sent in rebuttal at this time by the provincial.

53. Navarro García, *Don José de Gálvez*, 111–12. As Moorhead, *The Presidio*, 50n4, pointed out, there is a typographical error in the text of Navarro García, giving the year as 1755 rather than 1751, whereas his footnotes correctly indicate 1751.

54. Navarro García, *Don José de Gálvez*, 112–13; Moorhead, *The Presidio*, 50n5. The ravages of the 1750s and 1760s in northeastern Nueva Vizcaya, including the lower San Pedro River district, are documented in Moorhead, *The Presidio*, 49 (Lafora); Ocaranza, *Crónica de las Provincias Internas*, 187–91 (Oconor); Griffen, *Indian Assimilation*, 69; Aboites Aguilar, *Demografía histórica*, 45–46.

55. Antonio Gutiérrez de Noriega certification, 1 September 1752, Chihuahua,

UNM-BNM, vol. 126B, legajo 9, part 2, no. 21.

56. Adams and Chavez, *The Missions of New Mexico*, 80, 338. The estimate of this occurring in 1752 is drawn from the account of the years of Rojo's service in the custody given by Domínguez and his known assignments in upper New Mexico, where there is a six-month gap between March and October 1752.

57. Castro to provincial, 31 January 1753, 10-10v.

58. Conde de Revillagigedo to Comisario General Fray Juan Antonio Abasolo, 14 September 1753, BNM-AF, caja 15, no. 275, 1. This was printed in *Documentos... de la Nueva-Vizcaya*, 132–33, and republished in *Historia eclesiástica*, 145–46.

59. Joseph de Gorraez, "Párrafo del dictamen del Señor Auditor Gral. de la Guerra," 7 September 1753, BNM-AF, caja 15, no. 275, 3. It seems very odd to have missionaries shared by San Cristóbal, on the Rio del Norte below the river junction, and the missions on the other side of the Cuesta Grande thirty leagues distant. Was this itemization possibly going back to the 1720s, when Varo, the designated missionary for San Cristóbal, was actually at Coyame and another Franciscan at San Pedro when the 1726 uprising broke out?

60. Juan Antonio Abasolo to Viceroy Revillagigedo, 22 September 1753, BNM-AF, caja 15, no. 275, 6v-9. This was printed in *Documentos... de la Nueva-Vizcaya*, 134–38, and republished in *Historia eclesiástica*, 147–51.

61. Manuel de San Juan Nepumoceno y Trigo to Procurado General Joseph Miguel de los Rios, Ixtacalco, 23 July 1754, UNM-BNM, vol. 126B, legajo 9, no. 30, 3229–30. Transcript in Bolton Collection, Part I, no. 453, 14. An English translation of this Bolton copy is in Hackett, *Historical Documents*, vol. 3, 468. Trigo had been in New Mexico at least in 1749–1752 and was actually appointed vice-custos in 1750: Chávez, *Archives of the Archdiocese of Santa Fe*, 162 (28 June 1750), 257 (1749–1752).

62. Although Jones, *Nueva Vizcaya*, 240, has Mendoza as governor as early as 1750, Mendoza himself clearly stated that he took possession of his governorship on December 10, 1753: Mendoza to Viceroy Arriaga, 17 July 1760, La Junta Presidio Collection (henceforth LJPC), box 1, folder 1, Archives of the Big Bend, Sul Ross State University, Alpine, Texas.

63. "Testimonio de la Real Junta de Guerra y Hazienda ... sobre que el Presidio mandado cituar en el parage nombrado los Pilares se extablesca en los Pueblos de la Junta de los Rios del norte y Conchos," 31 julio 1757, AGI Guadalajara, 67-3-31, UT-BCAH, box 139, file 35, 17–22, 31–32, 37. Besides this typewritten transcription in Austin, there is a photostat copy of a 1760 certified manuscript copy of this lengthy document in LJPC, box 1, folder 17. Mendoza's 1759 extract of what he presented as Rubín de Celís's opinion in 1754 is in LJPC, box 1, folder 24, 510–13.

64. Juan Sanz de Lezáun, "Noticias lamentables acaecidas en la Nueva Mexico," 4

November 1760, UNM-BNM, vol. 126C, legajo 9, no. 46 (a copy by Lezáun). I cite the transcription in the Bolton Collection, Part I, no. 454, 14–16, translated in Hackett, *Historical Documents*, vol. 3, 477–78. Almada, *Resumen de historia*, 111–12, wrote that before 1758 Governor Mendoza sent a military detachment led by Captain Berroterán to reestablish the missions at La Junta that had been temporarily abandoned by the Franciscans due to disturbances there. Almada did not cite his sources, and nothing more is known about this nor how to interpret it.

65. "Memoria de los R.R.s que existieron en la Custodia . . . el año pasado de 1757," UNM-BNM, vol. 126B, legajo 9, no. 38, 3451–52.

Chapter 8

1. Castro to Mendoza, 15 February 1759, LJPC (see chapter 7, note 62), box 1, folder 21, 397.
2. For the San Saba debacle, see Castañeda, *Our Catholic Heritage in Texas*, vol. 3, 408; vol. 4, 102–8, 127–30; and Weber, *The Spanish Frontier in North America*, 188–89.
3. Mendoza to Castro, 25 March 1759; decree of Mendoza, 15 May 1759; "Razón," 15 May 1759—all in LJPC, box 1, folder 21, 399b–403.
4. Mendoza to Páez, 26 May 1759, LJPC, box 1, folder 21, 403–7.
5. Juan Sanz de Lezáun, "Noticias funestas," 8 May 1760, UNM-BNM, vol. 126C, legajo 9, part 3, no. 45.
6. Jones, *Nueva Vizcaya*, 155–57, seriously misinterprets the Mendoza documents on the presidio founding. Besides minor errors, Father Páez is described as anti-presidio, and nothing is said about the strong Native reaction. Morgenthaler's more extensive account in his *La Junta de los Rios*, 115–24, repeats the errors of Jones but, using the same set of Mendoza documents, continues the story beyond the presidio founding. Neither Jones nor Morgenthaler was aware of Sanz de Lezáun's more comprehensive report. But Morgenthaler did refer to a brief contrasting description by Sanz de Lezáun quoted by another Franciscan in Hackett's *Historical Documents*. Already disposed to be anti-missionary, Morgenthaler accepted the self-serving adulterated account of the Mendoza documents. He also introduced several mistakes, the principal one being identifying the Juntan general Arroyo and his followers as nomadic Cholomes. This made the Cholomes, not the Juntans, the main Native actors in the drama. He also wrote that the Spanish commander considered his troops "a peaceful Spanish delegation" (119) inappropriately viewed as hostile by General Arroyo!
7. Derrotero de Alférez Juan Ydalgo, 31 mayo–31 julio 1759, LJPC, box 1, folder 22, 422–24. Sanz de Lezáun wrote that they arrived on Holy Trinity Sunday, without specifying the date or the town.

8. Derrotero de Alférez Juan Ydalgo, 424–25.
9. Páez to Mendoza, 20 June 1759, Nuestra Señora de Guadalupe, LJPC, box 1, folder 21, 408–14.
10. This group of more belligerent Apaches' exclusive use of guns goes against the assertion of Babcock that bows, arrows, and lances remained more important weapons than firearms for Apaches in the colonial era (Matthew Babcock, *Apache Adaptation to Hispanic Rule* (New York: Cambridge University Press, 2016), 30–31). Whereas Domínguez in 1684 had written about Salineros as "cosarios" from Nueva Vizcaya distinct from Apaches (Imhoff, *The Diary of Juan Domínguez de Mendoza's Expedition*, 111–13), here Hidalgo included them as an Apache group. Babcock (61, 95n1) accepts Willem De Reuse's identification of Salineros in 1745 as a Mescalero band from the Pecos River.
11. Derrotero de Ydalgo, 425–28. Hidalgo wrote of Apache arrivals beginning June 21, whereas Páez wrote of a group arriving by June 20. The Apache captain's statement that he knew all the soldiers as from El Paso demonstrates that he had been in that place several years previously, before the military company of Rubín de Celís was transferred from there. Anderson quoted a Franciscan in San Antonio in 1745 who considered the Natagés more "proud and domineering" than the other Apaches. The Apache leader El Ligero had made the same comment in 1747 (*The Indian Southwest, 1580–1830*, 112, 116). Ortelli, *Trama de una guerra conveniente*, 211, noted that mules were prized more highly than horses by Hispanics since they were usually bred selectively, were more difficult to tame, hardier, had a longer serviceable life span, and could digest coarser and thus cheaper food. The Apaches' preference for horses, on the other hand, was most probably due to their greater speed and tractability and the fact that Apaches engaged much less in agriculture and trade caravans. The Apache mules probably originated as stolen animals, precisely for the purpose of trade as well as for a source of meat.
12. Derrotero de Ydalgo, 428–30. El Pueblito is identified as next to Cuchillo Parado in Decreto de Mendoza, 9 October 1759, LJPC, box 1, folder 24, 507 (see below).
13. Sanz de Lezáun, "Noticias funestas."
14. Decree of Mendoza, 19 July 1759, LJPC, box 1, folder 21, 414–15. Jones, *Nueva Vizcaya*, 156–57, followed by Morgenthaler, *La Junta de los Rios*, 115, erred in asserting that Páez ordered Hidalgo's squad to leave La Junta because the friar "objected strongly to the presence of soldiers and the establishment of any new presidio in his jurisdiction." These authors failed to distinguish between the Franciscans' strong advocacy for a presidio in the La Junta *vicinity* and their objection to its being placed *within* the La Junta towns themselves.
15. Mendoza to Arroyo et al., 24 July 1759, LJPC, box 1, folder 21, 418–19.
16. Rubín de Celís to Mendoza, Chihuahua, 6 August 1759, LJPC, box 1, folder

22, 432–35.

17. Páez to Mendoza, 9 August 1759, LJPC, box 1, folder 22, 439–45.

18. Decree of Mendoza, 13 August 1759, and the Razón immediately following, LJPC, box 1, folder 23, 447.

19. Sanz de Lezáun, "Noticias funestas."

20. Sanz de Lezáun made no mention in his memoir of this trip to La Junta by Páez.

21. Decree of Mendoza, 27 September 1759, LJPC, box 1, folder 23, 454–57.

22. Páez to Mendoza, 26 September 1759, LJPC, box 1, folder 23, 447–52.

23. Decree of Mendoza, 27 September 1759, LJPC, box 1, folder 23, 457–58; Mendoza to Castro, 29 September 1759, LJPC, box 1, folder 24, 489–90.

24. Sanz de Lezáun, "Noticias funestas."

25. Diligencia matrimonial of Manuel Muñoz and Gertrudis de San Ciprián, 15 July 1773, Chihuahua, AHAD-25, frames 208–14.

26. "Razón," 3 October 1759, and Mendoza to Páez, 29 September 1759, in LJPC, box 1, folder 24, 499, 487–89 (quote on 488–89).

27. Decree of Mendoza, 9 October 1759, LJPC, box 1, folder 24, 507.

28. Decree of Mendoza, 10 October 1759, LJPC, box 1, folder 24, 508, and Rubín de Celís to Mendoza, 27 August 1754, as copied 10 October 1759, LJPC, box 1, folder 24, 510–13.

29. Mendoza to Viceroy Marques de Amarillas, 13 October 1759, LJPC, box 1, folder 24, 518.

30. Sanz de Lezáun, "Noticias funestas." Unaware of Sanz de Lezáun's much more contemporaneous and informed account, Castañeda (*Our Catholic Heritage in Texas*, vol. 3, 229–30) and Morgenthaler (*La Junta de los Rios*, 117) were misled by another participant, Narciso Tapia, whose undated note (see next chapter), written no earlier than 1761 and probably even later, conflated this occasion with the later standoff in December at the canyon mouth.

31. Sanz de Lezáun, "Noticias funestas." Again misled by Tapia's later account, Castañeda, *Our Catholic Heritage in Texas*, vol. 3, 229, and Morgenthaler, *La Junta de los Rios*, 117, wrote that two Franciscans went on to La Junta on this second trip to calm the people.

32. Sanz de Lezáun, "Noticias funestas."

33. The following account of everything that occurred until Pedro el Mulato and some others went from La Junta to Coyame to talk to Captains Leizaola and Muñoz is taken from Sanz de Lezáun, "Noticias funestas."

34. This gendered response of the Juntans—the males in battle posture and the women with intermediary gestures—is a theme pursued for the Natives of the Spanish province of Texas by Juliana Barr in her *Peace Came in the Form of a Woman*.

35. Leizaola auto y diligencias, 19 December 1759, LJPC, box 3, folder 47, 1103–6.

36. Sanz de Lezáun, "Noticias funestas."
37. Leizaola diligencia, 20 December 1759, LJPC, box 3, folder 47, 1106–11.
38. Sanz de Lezáun, "Noticias funestas." For a synthesis of Muñoz's predictably self-serving account that made no mention of the friars' mediation and reported that he was merely resting his troops to explain the week spent at Coyame, see Morgenthaler, *La Junta de los Rios*, 117–19.
39. Sanz de Lezáun, "Noticias funestas." The manuscript actually has "una bez dentro del pressidio se alsarían," which I take to be a writer's slip for "una vez dentro el presidio."
40. Leizaola diary, 22 December 1759, LJPC, box 3, folder 48, 1111–15. The lack of punctuation makes it unclear whether General Arroyo was governor or former governor. Jones, *Nueva Vizcaya*, 157, and "Settlements and Settlers at La Junta de los Rios," 52, 68n27, followed by Morgenthaler, *La Junta de los Rios*, 174n59, mistook the lists of the two Juntan delegations as being a census of the La Junta villages.
41. Sanz de Lezáun, "Noticias funestas."
42. Ibid. This description of the site of the presidio rules out Morgenthaler's interpretation of "three *quadras*" in a different document of Sanz de Lezáun as meaning "two miles" in his *La Junta de los Rios*, 119, explained by him on 173n54. So does the description of the site by Leizaola to be discussed below.
43. The diminutive "gobernadorcillo" should not be taken as patronizing or demeaning. It was used in Nueva Vizcaya (since 1677) and New Mexico, if not elsewhere, as a way of distinguishing the head of an Indigenous community from the Spanish governor of a province. See Almada, *Resumen de historia*, 75, and Simmons, "History of Pueblo-Spanish Relations," 183.
44. Leizaola report for 26 December 1759, LJPC, box 3, folder 48, 1118–19.
45. Ibid., 1122–24.
46. Ibid., 1126–28, 1130.
47. For New Mexico, see Kessell, *Kiva, Cross, and Crown*, 320: "To hear the missionaries tell it, the governors were avaricious, cruel, tyrannical brutes utterly devoid of scruples or a sense of duty. . . . To hear the governors tell it, the missionaries were the ones who forced the Indians to labor without pay, who appropriated their maize, and who entered into trading ventures while neglecting their spiritual obligations."
48. Leizaola report for 28 December 1759, LJPC, box 3, folder 48, 1130–36. The plan for the presidio drawn up at this time can be seen in Navarro García, *Don José de Gálvez*, plate no. 59, and described on page 533, and Jones, *Nueva Vizcaya*, 46–47. Courtesy of the Archivo General de Indias, Sevilla, Spain, Mapas y Planos, México 621.

Chapter 9

1. Leizaola memorandum, 28 December 1759, LJPC, box 3, folder 49, 1141–43. The inclusion of Santa Cruz among the opponents is puzzling. Sanz de Lezáun had identified the same nations as having withdrawn from La Junta, but rather than Santa Cruz he spoke of a settlement next to San Francisco, probably the Tecolotes. Leizaola or the transcriber of his memo may have inadvertently given the wrong name, having in mind the Tecolotes. This possibility is heightened by the fact that the Hispanics knew about the settlement of Santa Cruz on the other side of the Cuesta Grande to which the Cholomes and some Tecolotes had moved in 1747. And Muñoz in his reports said that when he first arrived at Coyame some people from Santa Cruz and Cuchillo Parado came to greet him: Cuaderno tercero, AGI Guadalajara 511 (104-6-13), LJPC, box 3, folder 52, 9.

2. See above, chapter 6.

3. Decree of Mendoza, 3 January 1760, LJPC, box 3, folder 49, 1138.

4. "Informe del Padre Rdo. Provincial Fr. Pedro Serrano," July 1761, UNM-BNM, vol. 126C, legajo 9, no. 49, 3538–57 (original copy). I cite the transcription in Bolton Collection, Part I, no. 456, 33; translated in Hackett, *Historical Documents*, vol. 3, 499–500. This 1761 "Serrano" report was actually ghostwritten by the provincial archivist, Francisco Antonio de la Rosa Figueroa: see his "Nota especialissima," UNM-BNM, vol. 126A, legajo 9, no. 17, 3007. Figueroa explained why and how he composed the report with all its supportive documentation in a lengthy note (3558–63) following the original copy.

5. Mendoza to the Viceroy, 14 January 1760, LJPC, box 3, folder 50, 1166–69.

6. Muñoz to Mendoza, 12 January 1760, LJPC, box 3, folder 52, 10.

7. Sanz de Lezáun, "Noticias funestas."

8. Juan Sanz Lezáun, 15 January 1760, as quoted in "Informe del Padre Rdo. Provincial Fr. Pedro Serrano" (1761), 32 (my translation); also in Hackett, *Historical Documents*, vol. 3, 499 (mistranslated). Kelley, *Jumano and Patarabueye*, 65, erred in placing six missions and five missionaries at La Junta at this time. He did not notice that this 1761 document upon which he was relying was citing an early 1751 document. Furthermore, the translation he utilized is faulty at this point; it should read five ministers at El Paso, not at La Junta: see the Bolton transcription, 21, (mis)translated in Hackett, *Historical Documents*, vol. 3, 492. Anderson, *The Indian Southwest, 1580-1830*, 79, also misapplied a New Mexico description in this document to La Junta.

9. Sanz de Lezáun, "Noticias funestas."

10. Muñoz to Mendoza, 21 February 1760, and Mendoza proclamation, 29 February 1760, LJPC, box 3, folder 52, 11–15. Morgenthaler, *La Junta de los Rios*, 120–22, summarizes the ensuing exchange of messages between Muñoz and the insurgents led by Arroyo between March and July but continues to misidentify them

all as Cholomes.

11. "Informe del Padre Rdo. Provincial Fr. Pedro Serrano" (1761), 32–33; also in Hackett, *Historical Documents*, vol. 3, 499.

12. Elizabeth Howard West, "The Right of Asylum in New Mexico in the Seventeenth and Eighteenth Centuries," *New Mexico Historical Review* 41, no. 2 (April 1966), 144–45.

13. Sanz de Lezáun, "Noticias funestas." No documents have surfaced as to how this attempted usurpation of mission jurisdiction by Mendoza was resolved politically. It probably ceased to be an issue for La Junta when Mendoza was appointed interim governor of New Mexico that fall (Adams, *Bishop Tamarón's Visitation*, 30n53). The Holy Gospel friars did return to La Junta, as noted in what follows.

14. Muñoz to Mendoza, 11 July 1760, LJPC, box 3, folder 52, 30–32.

15. Peter Masten Dunne, S.J., *Early Jesuit Missions in Tarahumara* (Berkeley: University of California Press, 1948), 224–27, 237.

16. Narciso Tapia, "Noticia de la entrada ultima a la Junta de los Rios," UNM-BNM, vol. 128, legajo 37, expediente 5, stated that the presidio walls were completed by July 22; he did not give the number of priests. Tapia's account is especially valuable for events that happened in 1760. His recollections were written more than a year later, by which time he was a lieutenant. Morgenthaler's misidentification of Arroyo as the Cholome general mistakenly had him returning to La Junta on July 11, eleven days before the attack on the presidio (*La Junta de los Rios*, 122).

17. Muñoz to Mendoza, 22–24 July 1760, LJPC, box 3, folder 52, 36.

18. Morgenthaler, *La Junta de los Rios*, 123–24. Morgenthaler's very brief summary of this campaign mistakenly identified all the insurgents as Cholomes and confused the dates and events.

19. "Derrotero y diario de campaña," 6–24 September 1760, LJPC, box 3, 67–73; Tapia, "Noticia de la entrada ultima."

20. Lino Gómez Canedo, "Misiones del Colegio de Pachuca en el Obispado del Nuevo Reino de León," in *Estudios de Historia del Noreste* (Monterrey: Editorial Alfonso Reyes, 1972), 132, 140, 147, 165n8; Sheridan, *El "yugo suave del evangelio,"* 61–63. The map from the 1750s that is reproduced here is map M973 1750 from the Benson Latin American Collection, LLILAS Benson Latin American Studies and Collections, University of Texas at Austin. The combined Peyotes and Vizarrón along with the nearby town of Gigedo are now named Villa Unión.

21. This account is pieced together from Anderson, *The Indian Southwest, 1580–1830*, 114, and William E. Dunn, "Missionary Activities among the Eastern Apaches Previous to the Founding of the San Sabá Mission," *Quarterly of the Texas State Historical Association* 15, no. 3 (January 1912), 197–200. Both are based on the

Bolton Papers at the Bancroft Library, University of California, Berkeley.

22. "Derrotero y diario de campaña," 73–86. The numbers are approximations since some of the entries are partially or entirely illegible. Morgenthaler, *La Junta de los Rios*, 123, counted only 406 people.

23. "Visita pastoral del Obispo Dn. Pedro Tamarón y Romeral," roll 10, Libro LIII, AECD-UTEP. The bishop wrote to the viceroy on September 28 with the news of the Spanish victory: Bishop Tamarón to Viceroy el Marques de Cruillas, 7 January 1761, Real de Oro de Agua Caliente, LJPC, box 3, folder 52, 121–22.

24. Tamarón to Viceroy Cruillas, 7 January 1761, 123–24.

25. Adams, *Bishop Tamarón's Visitation*, 20.

26. Pedro Tamarón y Romeral, "Viajes pastorales y descripción de la Diócesis de Nueva Vizcaya," ed. Mario Hernández y Sánchez-Barba, in *Viajes por Norteamérica*, ed. Manuel Ballesteros Gaibrois (Madrid: Aguilar, 1958), 986; "Libro II de la visita del Señor [*sic*] Pedro Tamarón y Romeral," roll 7, Libro XXXVI, 9r, AECD-UTEP.

27. Tamarón to Viceroy Cruillas, 7 January 1761, 123.

28. Tamarón y Romeral, "Viajes pastorales," 986–87.

29. Esteban L. Portillo, *Apuntes para la historia Antigua de Coahuila y Texas* (Saltillo: Biblioteca de la Universidad Autónoma de Coahuila, 1984), 241, 335–37; Conde de Revilla Gigedo, *Informe sobre las Misiones, 1793, e Instrucción reservada al Marqués de Branciforte, 1794*, ed. José Bravo Ugarte (México, D.F.: Editorial Jus, 1966), 61. If the description of the land grant is interpreted as half *sitios de ganado mayor* and half *sitios de ganado menor*, its area was 245 square miles, or about 15.6 miles by 15.6 miles.

30. Griffen, *Indian Assimilation*, 33 ("Julimeños"), even though confused on certain points, first alerted me to these former Juntans in Coahuila. On his page 18 he misinterpreted Portillo in having them arrive in Coahuila in 1754.

31. Griffen, *Indian Assimilation*, 70–71.

32. Ibid.

33. Tamarón y Romeral, "Viajes pastorales," 979.

34. Lawrence Kinnaird, *The Frontiers of New Spain: Nicolás de la Fora's Description* (Berkeley: Quivira Society, 1958), 188: at El Carrizo near the Vizarrón mission "many of the Julimeños who fled from Julimes in Nueva Vizcaya have gathered." They served as scouts for the Rubí expedition even as far as San Saba on the border of the province of Texas (151). La Fora also described "Julimes" as well acquainted with the country between La Junta and Santa Rosa in Coahuila (159). In that case he was probably referring to the Natives still at Julimes on the Rio Conchos. For another 1767 reference to the Julimeños on the Vizarrón mission lands in Coahuila, see Jack Jackson and William C. Foster, eds. *Imaginary Kingdom: Texas as Seen by the Rivera and Rubí Military Expeditions, 1727 and*

1767 (Austin: Texas State Historical Association, 1995), 165.

35. Juan Agustín de Morfi, *Viaje de Indios y Diario del Nuevo México*, ed. Vito Alessio Robles (México, D.F.: Manuel Porrúa, 1980), 309. The map is from "Autos hechos . . . sobre haberse descubierto en el cerro del Dulcísimo Nombre de Jesús un mineral muy opulento, 1739," Archivo General de la Nación, Ciudad de México, Provincias Internas, tomo 30, expediente 3, Coahuila 1738–43, as reproduced in Alessio Robles, *Coahuila y Texas en la época colonial*, 539.

36. Tamarón y Romeral, "Viajes pastorales," 986–87.

37. Adams and Chavez, *The Missions of New Mexico*, 169 (quotation), 329. Their sources date Abadiano's birth year as 1713 or 1721. He began his theological studies as an older presbyteral candidate for the Missionary College of Santa Cruz de Querétaro in 1750, a later age than usual. Upon the completion of two years of theology there, he apparently applied to join the Santo Evangelio Province: Francisco Morales, O.F.M., *Inventario del Fondo Franciscano del Archivo Histórico de la Bibliotéca Nacional de Antropología e Historia*, vol. 2 (Washington, DC: Academy of American Franciscan History, 2008), no. 4500. He must have been ordained only a few years when he was sent north. Abadiano's subsequent ministry after leaving La Junta was in central and northern New Mexico. He died at Santa Ana in January 1777 (*Missions*, 169).

38. Ortelli, *Trama de una guerra conveniente*, 63n62.

39. Marqués de Rubí to Viceroy Croix, 10 April 1768, AGI, Guadalajara, 104-6-13, UT-BCAH, box 2Q140, file 46, 24.

40. Navarro García, *Don José de Gálvez*, 113, 132; Kinnaird, *The Frontiers of New Spain*, 12, 72–73. Navarro García did not report whether the 1762 inspection was carried out.

41. Rubí to Croix, 10 April 1768, 23–24.

42. Ocaranza, *Establecimientos franciscanos*, 195–97 (San Pablo Custody); Revilla Gigedo, *Informe*, 47 (Julimes).

43. Kessell, *Spain in the Southwest*, 253–70. The information about the four companies of *dragones* in Nueva Vizcaya comes from Moorhead, *The Presidio*, 61.

44. Informe de Oconor al Virrey Croix, 20 July 1777, AGI Guadalajara 104-6-18, UT-BCAH, box 2Q141, vol. 49, nn. 28 and 48; published in Enrique González Flores and Francisco R. Almada, eds., *Informe de Hugo de O'Conor sobre el estado de las Provincias Internas del Norte, 1771–76* (México, D.F.: Editorial Cultura, 1952), 31, 40–41. In 1770 "a detachment of Norteño Indians, not without having to battle and experience losses," recovered 800 of the more than 1,000 mules and horses stolen on the feast of San Lorenzo (Navarro García, *Don José de Gálvez*, 192).

45. Sidney B. Brinkerhoff and Odie B. Faulk, *Lancers for the King: A Study of the Frontier Military System of Northern New Spain, with a Translation of the Royal*

Regulations of 1772 (Phoenix: Arizona Historical Foundation, 1965), 54.

46. Viceroy Bucareli to Baylio Fr. D. Julian de Arriaga, 27 October 1772, AGI Guadalajara 104-3-2, UT-BCAH, box 2Q140, file 46, 116.

47. Navarro García, *Don José de Gálvez*, 214.

48. Fray José Ignacio María Alegre y Capetillo, "Itinerario del Teniente Coronel don Hugo O'Conor, de la ciudad de Mexico a la villa de Chihuahua," transcrito por J. Ignacio Rubio Mañe, *Boletín del Archivo General de la Nación* 30, no. 3 (julio–septiembre 1959), 457–60.

49. Navarro García, *Don José de Gálvez*, 223–24, 233–34. I thank Mark Santiago for the copy of Oconor's diary from which I quote the description of the refounding of the presidio: Hugo Oconor, "Diario de la marcha que el dia 19 de octubre de 1773 emprendí de la Villa de Chihuahua," 1 November 1773, Real Presidio de las Juntas de los Rios grande del Norte y Conchos, AGI Guadalajara, ramo 512 (104-8-14), Bancroft Library microfilm. For the campaign against the Apaches, see Mark Santiago, "'An Illustrious Victory': Hugo O'Conor's Battle with the Apaches in the Davis Mountains," *Journal of Big Bend Studies* 30 (2018): 103–19.

50. Most writers, with the notable exceptions of Kelley, Gerhard, and Morgenthaler, err in stating that there were still missions at La Junta as late as the 1790s. Several were misled by a typographical error in Kelley, *Jumano and Patarabueye*, 64, where 1794 should read 1754. Others mistook the 1790s missions of Julimes and Tapacolmes (see Revilla Gigedo, *Informe*, 47) as missions of La Junta, whereas this study has discussed their history in the San Pedro River district. In Oconor's overview of the missions on the northern frontier in 1777, he made no mention of any at La Junta: Ocaranza, *Crónica de las Provincias Internas*, 210.

51. Besides Morgenthaler's *La Junta de los Rios*, see Moorhead, *The Presidio*, 245–57, and John, "Spanish-Indian Relations." In 1780 Teodoro de Croix wrote about "repopulating the ancient pueblos that were abandoned in 1767" (Morgenthaler, *La Junta de los Rios*, 131). The Apache reservations on the northern frontier are the major focus of Babcock's *Apache Adaptation*. He called the one at La Junta "the most enduring" of all (62), but only after an initial unsuccessful beginning. For his discussion of La Junta / Presidio del Norte, see his pages 63–65, 87–93, 105, 117–21, 162, 192–93, 197–99, 204.

52. Alfred Barnaby Thomas, trans. and ed., *Teodoro de Croix and the Northern Frontier of New Spain, 1776–1783* (Norman: University of Oklahoma Press, 1941), 125.

53. The extant sacramental records of the presidio at La Junta begin with baptisms in 1775; the first marriage records begin in 1785: Michael F. Fry, "Collection Summary of the La Junta Church Records, 1775–1857," Archives of the Big Bend, Sul Ross State University. Of the sixty-three baptisms conducted in 1775–1780, apparently only one, on 6 November 1779, clearly had a Native

parent from La Junta, but perhaps from across the Cuesta Grande. Her mother was an "Yndia de estos pueblos" named Maria Cholome, while her father was an "Yndio" soldier from Julimes. There were a few other parents identified only as "Yndios" without further specification. It was not until 1790 that a marriage request involved a citizen (*vecina*) of the town who was a daughter of "Yndios Norteños" of the garrison (Jones, "Settlements and Settlers," 53–54, 60–65). By that time it is uncertain who were being called Norteños, although this may well have been one of the Juntan auxiliary soldiers. Even though only able to provide these very sparse—one may say almost nonexistent—indications of continued presence of aboriginal Juntans in the Junta valley, Jones nevertheless asserted that they remained there and gradually assimilated into the Hispanic society. This study arrives at very different conclusions.

54. However, in the nearby village of San Pablo the governor was an 85-year-old Julime. There were six other families in which at least one spouse was Julime, and also a Julime single man. The two absent military-auxiliary families were Julime, the husband in one of them being a Tarahumara. Intriguingly, whereas in San Pablo the Natives retained the control of most of their lands, in Julimes the local governmental administrator (*teniente de partido*) had taken over the leasing to Hispanics of all but individual Native plots, with no return being given to the Natives (Aboites Aguilar and Morales Cosme, *Breve compilación*, 82–87). These contrasting land-management situations are yet one more indication of Juntan/Julime insistence on autonomy. According to Gerhard, there was a *compañía volante* (light cavalry company) headquartered at San Pablo from 1773, the same year that the garrison at Julimes was moved back to La Junta (*The North Frontier of New Spain*, 200, but no reference given). This would be another factor to take into consideration. Griffen (*Indian Assimilation*, 71) noted documents from 1789 onwards classifying Natives at Julimes as either Tarahumaras or "Julimeños," a term that he interpreted to mean the "conglomeration" of non-Tarahumara Natives in the town. He was very mistaken, however, when he commented that "many persons from La Junta had now migrated into the town." He was evidently not aware of the 1778 census.

55. For the Toboso activity and elimination, see Griffen, *Indian Assimilation*, 14. For the Apaches in the 1760s, see Kinnaird, *The Frontiers of New Spain*, 76–77, 141–59; Jackson and Foster, *Imaginary Kingdom*, 102, 107–8, 165–68.

56. Max L. Moorhead. *The Apache Frontier: Jacobo Ugarte and Spanish-Indian Relations in Northern New Spain, 1769–1791* (Norman: University of Oklahoma Press, 1968), 23–24, 29–30 (quotes on 29). Moorhead accepted Ugarte's characterization of the Julimeños as "disloyal," although he judged the governor's solution to be rash (29, 51).

57. Flores and Almada, *Informe de Hugo de O'Conor*, 106.

58. Barr, *Peace Came in the Form of a Woman*, 271. The quotation is from Governor Cabello to Croix, 14 May 1779.
59. Morfi, *Viaje de Indios*, 310.
60. Roberto Moreno, "Viajes de Fray Juan Agustín de Morfi," in *Anuario de Historia* (UNAM, Mexico), años VI–VII (1966–67), 191–92.
61. José David García, "Estado actual de las misiones de la Provincia de Coahuila y Rio Grande de la misma jurisdicción. Año de 1786," 3 marzo 1786, in *Estudios de Historia del Noreste* (Monterrey: Editorial Alfonso Reyes, 1972), 141–42.
62. Revilla Gigedo, *Informe*, 61–62. Leaving the story of the Juntans/Julimeños at this point, there remains a great curiosity as to their future history in Coahuila. Perhaps someone will take up the thread!

Appendix

1. Also for the sake of brevity, the endnotes in this section are abridged, leaving the full reference to be found in the bibliography section of this work. Spicer summed up the situation in Sonora: the country of the lower Pimas "was penetrated by small groups of Spaniards very early," and among the Opatas "Spanish settler intrusion into the missionized areas was even more intensive than it was among the Tarahumaras" (*Cycles of Conquest*, 89, 96). Robert West was as succinct as he was comprehensive: "There was probably no other area of colonial Spanish America in which mines and missions were in such close proximity as in Sonora" (*Sonora*, 60). The author would be happy to explain his assessment of the Pimeria Alta district of Sonora with anyone interested.
2. Decorme, *La obra de los Jesuitas mexicanos durante la época colonial, 1572–1767*, tomo II: *Las misiones*, 448–51; Navarro García, *Don José de Gálvez*, 84–85.
3. Deeds, *Defiance and Deference*.
4. The priest at the northernmost mission center was killed along with two Hispanics living with him: Dunne, *Early Jesuit Missions in Tarahumara*, 167. See also Sheridan and Naylor, *Rarámuri*, 39, 41–42. Helpful for the distances between mission centers and Hispanic settlements are Tamarón y Romeral, "Viajes pastorales," 981–84 (with some directions reversed), and Guendulain in *Historia Eclesiástica*, 33–43.
5. For the specific location of Hispanics and the length of time that Jesuits were present in the various missions, Gerhard, *The North Frontier of New Spain*, 181–83, 185–91, is invaluable. Spicer, *Cycles of Conquest*, 25–39, gives an excellent summary of the Tarahumara history for this period; however, he erred in stating that there were no regular clergy in the Alta Tarahumara after 1767. A good assessment of Hispanic-Tarahumara relations, especially in regard to Christianization, is Merrill, "Conversion and Colonialism in Northern Mexico."
6. A Hispanic near Caríchic was encroaching upon Native lands in 1732 (Sheridan

and Naylor, *Rarámuri*, 92–93). For another case near Papigóchic, see Dunne, *Early Jesuit Missions in Tarahumara*, 213. Hispanics other than Jesuits began to reside in some mission centers, such as a storeowner and his wife in Papigóchic in 1734 (Deeds, *Defiance and Deference*, 125). The missionary in Teméchic, upriver from the Hispanic settlements in the Papigóchic valley and not that far from the mines at Cusihuiriáchic, remarked in 1730 that the Tarahumaras acted as they pleased with the missionaries and that without them there would be no silver produced and that Hispanic intercourse with the women was resulting in a whitening of the people (Sheridan and Naylor, 74–75; Deeds, 242n56, corrects the mission identification). That same year the Jesuit at Sisoguíchic, the most isolated of the mission centers, defended the practice of the Natives keeping for themselves whatever they mined beyond their assigned quota (Deeds, 120). In 1744 the priest at Caríchic, also fairly close to the Cusihuiriáchic mines, complained about regional officials requiring illegally excessive work levies (Sheridan and Naylor, 82–83). These Jesuits advocated stationing soldiers at the missions as the only remedy to instill obedience. In 1744 the governor reported that more than eighty families had fled from Tomóchic into the mountain canyons to avoid the labor drafts. Three years later they did not escape in time: a squad of military and civilians from Papigóchic forcibly removed neophytes from the Tomóchic district into their own (Dunne, *Early Jesuit Missions in Tarahumara*, 212–13). Even in Tutuaca, the most remote station sometimes visited by the Jesuits, but not a mission center, at the western mountainous extremity of the Alta Tarahumara, the Natives complained in 1764 about the outside overseer of mission property who was brought in by liberalizing government reformers of mission management (Dunne, *Early Jesuit Missions*, 186). Pennington, "Tarahumara," in *Handbook of North American Indians*, vol. 10: *Southwest*, ed. Alfonso Ortiz, 276–77, provides a map of all the Tarahumara territory that shows how those Natives who did not merge into the mestizo world after the stamped-out uprisings in the 1640s (southern area) and 1690s (northern area) moved to the southwest and west across the Sierra Madre where there were no mission centers.

7.   Hodge, Hammond, and Rey, eds., *Fray Alonso de Benavides' Revised Memorial of 1634*, 74–80, 212–21, 291–93, 298–302; Brew, "The History of Awatovi," and Montgomery, "San Bernardo de Aguatubi," in *Franciscan Awatovi*, by Montgomery, Smith, and Brew (1949), 1–43, 111–288. Besides the years noted in the above works, the presence of a priest at Zuñi in 1675 is indicated by Hackett and Shelby, *Revolt of the Pueblo Indians* (1942), vol. 2, 289.

8.   The only notices of a Hispanic in the La Junta missions were the one killed in the 1726 uprising at Coyame and one brief case of a Hispanic living several miles upriver from the Juntans.

9. Brew, "Hopi Prehistory and History to 1850," in *Southwest*, ed. Alfonso Ortiz, Handbook of North American Indians, vol. 9, 522.

10. Sheridan, Koyiyumptewa, Daughters, Brenneman, Ferguson, Kumanwisiwma, and Lomayestewa, eds., *Moquis and Kastiilam*, vol 1, 122. Several researchers for this Hopi project found almost no new records in Spain, Mexico City, and major US collections beyond what had already been published by 1950 (Sheridan et al., 14–15).

11. Some soldiers were at least initially left as guards in both the Zuñi and the Hopi districts at the founding of the missions, unlike at La Junta (Hodge, Hammond, and Rey, *Fray Alonso de Benavides*, 215–18). In 1659 a Hispanic was penalized by being sent to the Hopi area. Frances V. Scholes explained: "From time to time [*encomenderos*] were called upon for special guard duty in frontier areas such as Taos, Jémez, and the Zuñi-Hopi district. . . . [T]he governors sometimes used assignments to guard duty in these areas as a form of discipline, or as a means of temporarily ridding the province of insubordinate characters or notorious offenders" (*Troublous Times in New Mexico, 1659-1670* (Albuquerque: University of New Mexico Press, 1942), 43). In 1662 another person was sent to the Hopi district (Sheridan et al., *Moquis and Kastiilam*, 218). The friar at Zuñi in 1672 wrote of his difficulty in providing sufficient supplies for maintaining the soldiers as well as the Zuñis (Adams and Chavez, *The Missions of New Mexico*, 197n2). When the Great Revolt broke out in 1680, some Hispanic citizen-soldiers were at Zuñi and were all reported killed (Hackett and Shelby, *Revolt of the Pueblo Indians*, vol. 1, lxix, 78, 113). A Hopi interviewed in 2012 related a Hopi tradition describing the pre-Revolt period as a time when soldiers were usually in the Hopi towns (Sheridan et al., 172–77).

12. Sheridan et al., *Moquis and Kastiilam*, 215, 217. Spicer, *Cycles of Conquest*, 187, 190, stated that the Zuñis and the Hopis remained exempt from giving tribute after 1621. He was probably following Hodge, but the quotation in Hodge declared that they were deemed exempt *in* 1621 since they "are said actually to be Gentile and to whom no spiritual aid or doctrine is being given" (Hodge, *History of Hawikuh*, 78). That situation changed once they received missionaries with their military escorts.

13. Frances V. Scholes, *Church and State in New Mexico, 1610-1650* (Albuquerque: University of New Mexico Press, 1937), 180.

14. Simmons, *Spanish Government in New Mexico*, 166–67.

15. Ibid., 175.

16. Scholes, *Troublous Times*, 68.

17. Brew, "The History of Awatovi," in *Franciscan Awatovi*, 19–40; John, *Storms Brewed in Other Men's Worlds*, 146–48, taken from Frank D. Reeve, "Navaho-Spanish Wars, 1680–1720," *NMHR* 33 (1958), 213–14.

18. John, *Storms Brewed in Other Men's Worlds*, 126, 134, 146, 148. Bancroft, *History of Arizona and New Mexico, 1530–1888*, 225–26, reported that a garrison of twenty men was sent to Zuñi in early 1702 but then reduced by the next year.

19. Hackett, *Historical Documents*, vol. III, 376–77.

20. In April 1706 a nine-man squad was sent to Zuñi and reinforced later that year (Bancroft, *History of Arizona*, 229). Bancroft stated that the Zuñis "presently" asked to have their *escolta* removed due to Hopi pressure, and that in April 1707 it was decided to remove the frontier squads so that their horses could recuperate. A few soldiers accompanied by citizen-levies were stationed there during the summer of 1708 (Simmons, *Spanish Government*, 125). In 1714 the governor decreed that selling weapons to the Pueblos would be punished by four years' duty on the Zuñi frontier (Kessell, *Kiva, Cross, and Crown*, 317). The following year twenty-five men were deployed there due to worsening Apache raids (John, *Storms Brewed in Other Men's Worlds*, 236). Citing entries in Ralph E. Twitchell's *The Spanish Archives of New Mexico*, Caywood wrote, without giving specific references, that "there appeared to have been soldiers continuously stationed at Zuñi from 1701 to 1715" (Caywood, *The Restored Mission of Nuestra Senora de Guadalupe de Zuni*, 11). Thus, Spicer's statement (*Cycles of Conquest*, 188) that the Zuñis "remained in considerable isolation from the Spaniards during the whole of the 1700's" needs correcting.

21. Chávez, *Archives of the Archdiocese of Santa Fe*, 240.

22. This information is gleaned from the church records annotated in Chávez, *Archives of the Archdiocese of Santa Fe*, 219, 229–30, 239–58.

23. For the post-1776 situation, see Delaney and Jenkins, *Guide to the 'Lost' Records*, 11 (quote). In 1732 the governor banished a man to Zuñi for two years (Cutter, *The Protector de Indios*, 78–79). In 1734 a friar complained that there were no soldiers as provided in earlier years (Chávez, *Archives of the Archdiocese of Santa Fe*, 229). For a "lieutenant and *alcalde mayor*" in 1750, see Hackett, *Historical Documents*, vol. 3, 436–37. For a different "lieutenant-alcalde" in 1754 and the *alcalde* in 1779, see Thomas, trans. and ed., *Forgotten Frontiers*, 156, 166–68.

24. Gerhard, *The North Frontier of New Spain*, 264–69; Radding, *Wandering Peoples*, 36; Radding, "Colonial Spaces," 118 (map), 136–39.

25. Pérez de Ribas, *Historia de los Triunfos de N.S. Fe*, vol. 2, 112–13, 127 (quotation). Cramaussel, "The Forced Transfer of Indians," 184–207, marshalled every possible hypothesis to assert that Yaquis and other Natives did not voluntarily engage in mining labor, just as she also tried to make almost all "free workers" and "wage workers" involuntary. When she had to admit that some were probably voluntary, she attributed this to Natives "fleeing" their missions. Her hypotheses far outweigh her facts.

26. Spicer, *The Yaquis*, 20. In his works, including the classic *Cycles of Conquest*,

Spicer never addressed the people of La Junta.

27. Spicer, *The Yaquis*, 16.

28. Pérez de Ribas, *Historia de los Triunfos*, 119–20.

29. Ibid., 68–77, 109, 112, 115 (quotation), 121.

30. Libro V (63–145) in vol. 2 of Pérez de Ribas is *the* source on the early Yaqui missions; it was first published in Madrid in 1645, during his lifetime. He reported almost nothing after 1626 beyond very general statements about mission improvements. Scholars have almost nothing to say beyond that volume until the 1680s, when Hispanics moved much closer to the Yaquis. Hu-DeHart, *Missionaries, Miners and Indians*, 45–48, described the unsuccessful litigation in 1672–1674 by miners seeking unfettered access to the Yaqui workers and other nations that had Jesuit missionaries. In 1678 a Jesuit inspector reported that some Yaqui towns were completely ruined due to the absence of many of them in the mines; he said that some who remained had become very fluent in Spanish (Hu-DeHart, 52). Spicer, *Cycles of Conquest*, 51, took no note of migration by Yaquis until after 1684 and downplayed it. He did not report missionary disputes with miners until the 1730s (55). Unaware of the mining camps started after 1675, he stated that before 1683 there was no Hispanic town or mine closer than El Fuerte (49). He did note, however, that a port was opened at the mouth of the Yaqui River around 1680 that shipped wheat and livestock to the beginning mission effort in Lower California (51). One would assume that at least a few Hispanics resided at that port.

Works Cited

Manuscript Collections

ACHP-FC. Archivo Histórico Municipal de Parral, Fondo Colonial. Rootspoint, Fondo Colonial Collection Archival Records, 1611–1821, http://www.rootspoint.com/fondo-colonial.

AECD-UTEP. Archivo Eclesiástico de la Catedral de Durango, microfilm, University of Texas at El Paso.

AHAD. Archivos Históricos del Arzobispado de Durango, microfilm, Special Collections, New Mexico State University Library.

Archives of the Archdiocese of Santa Fe, Santa Fe, New Mexico.

BNM-AF. Biblioteca Nacional de México, Archivo Franciscano, Ciudad de México.

Bolton Collection. H. E. Bolton Collection typescripts (C-B 840), Bancroft Library, University of California, Berkeley.

Catholic Archives of Texas, Austin, Texas.

LJPC. La Junta Presidio Collection, Archives of the Big Bend, Sul Ross State University, Alpine, Texas. Page citations are to the archival accession numbering.

New Mexico State Library, Southwest Collection, Santa Fe, New Mexico.

Newberry Library, Chicago.

UNM-AGI. University of New Mexico (Albuquerque) photostats of Archivo General de las Indias documents, Zimmerman Library, Center for Southwest Research and Special Collections, MSS 841.

UNM-AGN. University of New Mexico (Albuquerque) photostats of Archivo General de la Nación documents, Zimmerman Library, Center for Southwest Research and Special Collections, MSS 867.

UNM-BNM. University of New Mexico (Albuquerque) photostats of Biblioteca Nacional de México documents, Zimmerman Library, Center for Southwest Research and Special Collections, MSS 867.

UT-BCAH. University of Texas at Austin, Briscoe Center for American History. Archivo General de Indias (AGI) Audiencia de Guadalajara transcripts.

Publications

Aboites Aguilar, Luis. *Demografía histórica y conflictos por el agua: Dos estudios sobre 40 kilómetros de historia del río San Pedro, Chihuahua.* México, D.F.: Centro de

Investigaciones y Estudios Superiores en Antropología Social, 2000.

Aboites Aguilar, Luis, and Alba Dolores Morales Cosme, eds. *Breve compilación sobre tierras y aguas de Santa Cruz de Tapacolmes, Chihuahua (1713–1927).* México, D.F.: Ayuntamiento de Rosales / Centro de Información del Estado de Chihuahua / CIESAS / Comisión Nacional del Agua, 1998.

Adams, Eleanor B., ed. *Bishop Tamarón's Visitation of New Mexico, 1760.* Albuquerque: Historical Society of New Mexico, 1954.

Adams, Eleanor B., and Angelico Chavez, eds. *The Missions of New Mexico, 1776: A Description by Fray Francisco Atanasio Dominguez with Other Contemporary Documents.* Albuquerque: University of New Mexico Press, 1956.

Alegre, Francisco Javier, S.J. *Historia de la Provincia de la Compañía de Jesús de Nueva España.* Roma: Institutum Historicum S.J., 1959.

Alegre y Capetillo, Fray José Ignacio María. "Itinerario del Teniente Coronel don Hugo O'Conor, de la ciudad de Mexico a la villa de Chihuahua." Transcribido por J. Ignacio Rubio Mañe. *Boletín del Archivo General de la Nación* 30, no. 3 (julio–septiembre 1959): 393–471.

Alessio Robles, Vito. *Coahuila y Texas en la época colonial.* 2a ed. México, D.F.: Editorial Porrúa, 1978.

Algier, Keith Wayne. "Feudalism on New Spain's Northern Frontier: Valle de San Bartolomé, a Case Study." PhD diss., University of New Mexico, 1966.

Almada, Francisco R. *Diccionario de historia, geografía y biografía chihuahuenses.* 2a ed. Ciudad Juárez: Universidad de Chihuahua, Departamento de Investigaciones Sociales, 1968.

———. *Resumen de historia del Estado de Chihuahua.* México, D.F.: Libros Mexicanos, 1955.

Álvarez, Salvador. "Agricultural Colonization and Mining Colonization: The Area of Chihuahua During the First Half of the Eighteenth Century." In *In Quest of Mineral Wealth: Aboriginal and Colonial Mining and Metallurgy in Spanish America,* edited by Alan K. Craig and Robert C. West, 171–204. Baton Rouge: Department of Geography and Anthropology, Louisiana State University, 1994.

———. "Manuel San Juan de Santa Cruz: gobernador, latifundista y capitán de guerra de la frontera norte." *Revista de Indias* LXX, núm. 248 (2010): 101–26.

Anderson, Gary Clayton. *The Indian Southwest, 1580–1830: Ethnogenesis and Reinvention.* Norman: University of Oklahoma Press, 1999.

Applegate, Howard G., and C. Wayne Hanselka. *La Junta de los Rios del Norte y Conchos.* El Paso: Texas Western Press, 1974.

Archibald, Robert. *The Economic Aspects of the California Missions.* Washington, DC: Academy of American Franciscan History, 1978.

Arlegui, José. *Crónica de la Provincia de N.S.P.S. Francisco de Zacatecas.* México: Cumplido, 1851.

Athearn, Frederic J. *A Forgotten Kingdom: The Spanish Frontier in Colorado and New Mexico, 1540–1821*. Cultural Resource Series no. 29. Denver: Bureau of Land Management, 1989.

Babcock, Matthew. *Apache Adaptation to Hispanic Rule*. New York: Cambridge University Press, 2016.

Bancroft, Hubert Howe. *History of Arizona and New Mexico, 1530–1888*. San Francisco: History Co., 1889.

Bannon, John Francis, S.J. *The Mission Frontier in Sonora, 1620–1687*. New York: United States Catholic Historical Society, 1955.

Barr, Juliana. *Peace Came in the Form of a Woman: Indians and Spaniards in the Texas Borderlands*. Chapel Hill: University of North Carolina Press, 2007.

Benavides, Alonso de. *The Memorial of Fray Alonso de Benavides, 1630*. Translated by Mrs. Edward E. Ayer, annotated by Frederick Webb Hodge and Charles Fletcher Lummis. Albuquerque: Horn and Wallace, 1965.

Bolton, Herbert Eugene. *Rim of Christendom: A Biography of Eusebio Francisco Kino, Pacific Coast Pioneer*. New York: Russell and Russell, 1960; 1st ed. Macmillan, 1936.

———. ed. *Spanish Exploration in the Southwest, 1542–1706*. New York: Barnes and Noble, 1963.

Brew, J. O. "The History of Awatovi." In *Franciscan Awatovi: The Excavation and Conjectural Reconstruction of a 17-Century Spanish Mission Establishment at a Hopi Indian Town in Northeastern Arizona*, by Ross Gordon Montgomery, Watson Smith, and John Otis Brew, 1–43. Papers of the Peabody Museum of American Archaeology and Ethnology, Harvard University, vol. XXXVI. Cambridge: Peabody Museum of American Archaeology and Ethnology, 1949.

———. "Hopi Prehistory and History to 1850." In *Southwest*, edited by Alfonso Ortiz, 514–23. Handbook of North American Indians, vol. 9. Washington, DC: Smithsonian Institution, 1979.

Brinkerhoff, Sidney B., and Odie B. Faulk. *Lancers for the King: A Study of the Frontier Military System of Northern New Spain, with a Translation of the Royal Regulations of 1772*. Phoenix: Arizona Historical Foundation, 1965.

Britten, Thomas A. *The Lipan Apaches: People of Wind and Lightning*. Albuquerque: University of New Mexico Press, 2009.

Brooks, James F. *Captives and Cousins: Slavery, Kinship, and Community in the Southwest Borderlands*. Chapel Hill: University of North Carolina Press for the Omohundro Institute of Early American History & Culture, 2002.

Castañeda, Carlos E. *Our Catholic Heritage in Texas*. 7 vols. Austin: Von Boeckmann-Jones, 1936–1958.

Caywood, Louis R. *The Restored Mission of Nuestra Senora de Guadalupe de Zuni, Zuni, New Mexico*. St. Michael's, AZ: St. Michael's Press, 1972.

Chávez, Angélico, O.F.M. *Archives of the Archdiocese of Santa Fe, 1678–1900*. Washington, DC: Academy of American Franciscan History, 1957.

Chipman, Donald E. "In Search of Cabeza de Vaca's Route across Texas: An Historiographical Survey." *Southwestern Historical Quarterly* 91, no. 2 (October 1987): 127–48.

———. *Spanish Texas, 1519–1821*. Austin: University of Texas Press, 1992.

Cloud, William A., Robert J. Mallouf, Patricia A. Mercado-Allinger, Cathryn A. Hoyt, Nancy A. Kenmotsu, Joseph M. Sánchez, Enrique R. Madrid. *Archaeological Testing at the Polvo Site, Presidio County, Texas*. Office of the State Archaeologist Report 19. Austin: Texas Historical Commission and U.S. Department of Agriculture, Soil Conservation Service, 1994.

Conrad, Paul. *The Apache Diaspora: Four Centuries of Displacement and Survival*. Philadelphia: University of Pennsylvania Press, 2021.

Corvera Poiré, Marcela. "The Discalced Franciscans in Mexico: Similarities and Differences vis-à-vis the Observant Franciscans in Mexico and the Discalced in the Philippines." In *Francis in the Americas: Essays on the Franciscan Family in North and South America*, edited by John F. Schwaller, 27–44. Berkeley, CA: Academy of American Franciscan History, 2005.

Craddock, Jerry R., ed. "Antonio de Espejo's Report on His Expedition to New Mexico 1682–1683 with Associated Documents." Berkeley: Cíbola Project, Research Center for Romance Studies, Institute of International Studies, University of California, 2017.

Cramaussel, Chantal. *Diego Pérez de Luján: Las desventuras de un cazador de esclavos arrepentido*. Ciudad Juárez: Gobierno del Estado / Universidad Autónoma de Ciudad Juárez, 1991.

———. "The Forced Transfer of Indians in Nueva Vizcaya and Sinaloa: A Hispanic Method of Colonization." In *Contested Spaces of Early America*, edited by Juliana Barr and Edward Countryman, 184–207. Philadelphia: University of Pennsylvania Press, 2014.

———. "El mapa de Miera y Pacheco de 1758 y la cartografía temprana del sur del Nuevo México." *Estudios de Historia Novohispana* 13, no. 13 (Octubre 1993): 73–92.

———. "Mestizaje y familias pluriétnicas en la villa de San Felipe El Real de Chihuahua y multiplicación de los mulatos en el septentrión novohispano durante el siglo XVIII." En *Familias pluriétnicas y mestizaje en la Nueva España y el Río de la Plata*, coordinado por David Carbajal López, 17–45. Guadalajara: Centro Universitario de Ciencias Sociales y Humanidades, Universidad de Guadalajara, 2014.

———. *Poblar la frontera: La provincia de Santa Barbara en Nueva Vizcaya durante los siglos XVI y XVII*. Zamora: El Colegio de Michoacán, 2006.

———. *La Provincia de Santa Barbara, 1563–1631*. Chihuahua: Secretaría de Educación y Cultura, Gobierno del Estado de Chihuahua, 2004.

Crosby, Harry W. *Antigua California: Mission and Colony on the Peninsular Frontier, 1697–1768*. Albuquerque: University of New Mexico Press in cooperation with the University of Arizona Southwest Center and the Southwest Mission Research Center, 1994.

Cutter, Charles R. *The Protector de Indios in Colonial New Mexico, 1659–1821*. Albuquerque: University of New Mexico Press, 1986.

Daniel, James Manly. "The Advance of the Spanish Frontier and the Despoblado." PhD diss., University of Texas at Austin, 1955.

———. "La Junta de los Rios and the Despoblado, 1680–1760." MA thesis, University of Texas at Austin, 1948.

Decorme, Gerard, S.J. *La obra de los Jesuitas mexicanos durante la época colonial, 1572–1767*, tomo II: *Las misiones*. México: Antigua Librería Robredo de José Porrúa e Hijos, 1941.

Deeds, Susan M. "Colonial Chihuahua: Peoples and Frontiers in Flux." In *New Views of Borderlands History*, edited by Robert H. Jackson, 21–40. Albuquerque: University of New Mexico Press, 1998.

———. *Defiance and Deference in Mexico's Colonial North: Indians under Spanish Rule in Nueva Vizcaya*. Austin: University of Texas Press, 2003.

———. "Mission Villages and Agrarian Patterns in a Nueva Vizcayan Heartland, 1600–1750." *Journal of the Southwest* 33, no. 3 (Autumn 1991): 345–65.

———. "Rural Work in Nueva Vizcaya: Forms of Labor Coercion on the Periphery." *Hispanic American Historical Review* 69, no. 3 (August 1989): 425–49.

Delaney, Robert W., and Myra Ellen Jenkins, *Guide to the "Lost" Records of the Mission of Nuestra Señora de Guadalupe de Zuni, 1775–1858*. Santa Fe: New Mexico State Records Center and Archives, 1988.

de la Teja, Jesús F., ed. *New Foundations*. Preliminary Studies of the Texas Catholic Historical Society III. Austin: Texas Catholic Historical Society, 2000.

de la Torre Curiel, José Refugio. *Twilight of the Mission Frontier: Shifting Interethnic Alliances and Social Organization in Sonora, 1768–1855*. Stanford: Stanford University / Berkeley: Academy of American Franciscan History, 2012.

Del Rio, Ignacio. *Guia del Archivo Franciscano de la Biblioteca Nacional de México*. México: Universidad Nacional Autónoma de México / Washington, DC: Academy of American Franciscan History, 1975.

De Marco, Barbara, and Jerry R. Craddock, eds. *Alonso de Posada's Report on the Geography of North America, 14 March 1686*. Berkeley: Research Center for Romance Studies, University of California, 2021. https://escholarship.org/uc/item/6gx2x5gd.

———. *Relación de Hernán Gallegos sobre la expedición del padre Agustín Rodríguez y el Capitán Francisco Sánchez Chamuscado a Nuevo México, 1581–1582*. Berkeley: Research Center for Romance Studies, University of California, 2013. https:// escholarship.org/uc/item/4sv5h1gz.

Documentos para la historia eclesiástica y civil de la Nueva-Vizcaya. Documentos para la historia de México, Cuarta Série, Tomo IV. México: Imprenta de Vicente García Torres, 1857.

Donohue, John Augustine, S.J. *After Kino: Jesuit Missions in Northwestern New Spain, 1711–1767*. St. Louis: Jesuit Historical Institute, St. Louis University, 1969.

Dunn, William E. "Missionary Activities among the Eastern Apaches Previous to the Founding of the San Sabá Mission." *Quarterly of the Texas State Historical Association* 15, no. 3 (January 1912): 186–200.

Dunne, Peter Masten, S.J. *Early Jesuit Missions in Tarahumara*. Berkeley: University of California Press, 1948.

———. *Pioneer Black Robes on the West Coast*. Berkeley: University of California Press, 1940.

Engelhardt, Zephyrin, O.F.M. *The Missions and Missionaries of California, vol. 1: Lower California*. San Francisco: James H. Barry Co., 1908.

Esparza Terrazas, Eduardo. *Santa Cruz, antigua región de los tapalcomes: Historia de la Villa de Rosales*. Chihuahua: Instituto Chihuahense de la Cultura, 2004.

Espejo, Antonio. "Account of the Journey to the Provinces and Settlements of New Mexico, 1583." In *Spanish Exploration in the Southwest, 1542–1706*, edited by Herbert Eugene Bolton, 168–94. New York: Charles Scribner's Sons, 1908.

Favata, Martin A., and José B. Fernández, trans. *The Account: Álvar Núñez Cabeza de Vaca's Relación*. Houston: Arte Publico Press, 1993.

Fernández Duro, Cesáreo. *Don Diego de Peñalosa y su descubrimiento del reino de Quivira*. Madrid: Manuel Tello, 1882.

Folsom, Bradley. "Spanish La Junta de los Rios: The Institutional Hispanicization of an Indian Community along New Spain's Northern Frontier, 1535–1821." MA thesis, University of North Texas, 2008.

Forbes, Jack D. *Apache, Navaho, and Spaniard*. Norman: University of Oklahoma Press, 1960.

Frank, Ross. *From Settler to Citizen: New Mexico Economic Development and the Creation of Vecino Society, 1750–1820*. Berkeley: University of California Press, 2007.

Gallegos C., José Ignacio. *Historia de la Iglesia en Durango*. México: Editorial Jus, 1969.

García, José David. "Estado actual de las misiones de la Provincia de Coahuila y Rio Grande de la misma jurisdicción. Año de 1786," 3 marzo 1786, in *Estudios de Historia del Noreste*, 126–45. Monterrey: Editorial Alfonso Reyes, 1972.

Gerhard, Peter. *The North Frontier of New Spain*. Rev. ed. Norman: University of Oklahoma Press, 1993.

Gómez, Arthur R., ed. *Documentary Evidence for the Spanish Missions of Texas*. New York: Garland Publishing, 1991.

Gómez Canedo, Lino. "Misiones del Colegio de Pachuca en el Obispado del Nuevo Reino de León." In *Estudios de Historia del Noreste*, 117–68. Monterrey: Editorial Alfonso Reyes, 1972.

———. "La primitiva evangelización de México: objetivos, problemas y métodos." In *Evangelización, cultura y promoción social: ensayos y estudios críticos sobre la contribución franciscana a los orígenes cristianos de México (siglos XVI–XVIII)*, edited by José Luis Soto Pérez, 269–308. México, D.F.: Porrúa, 1993.

González Flores, Enrique, and Francisco R. Almada, eds. *Informe de Hugo de O'Conor sobre el estado de las Provincias Internas del Norte, 1771–76*. México, D.F.: Editorial Cultura, 1952.

González Salas, Carlos. *La evangelización en Tamaulipas*, tomo II: *Las misiones novohispanas en la costa del Seno Mexicano (1757–1833)*. Ciudad Victoria: Universidad Autónoma de Tamaulipas / Instituto de Investigaciones Históricas, 2003.

Goode, Catherine Tracy. "Corrupting the Governor: Manuel San Juan de Santa Cruz and Power in Early Eighteenth-Century Nueva Vizcaya." MA thesis, Northern Arizona University, 2000.

Greenleaf, Richard E. "The Inquisition in Eighteenth-Century New Mexico." *New Mexico Historical Review* 60, no. 1 (January 1985): 29–60.

Griffen, William B. *Culture Change and Shifting Populations in Central Northern Mexico*. Tucson: University of Arizona Press, 1969.

———. *Indian Assimilation in the Franciscan Area of Nueva Vizcaya*. Tucson: University of Arizona Press, 1979.

———. "A North Mexican Nativistic Movement, 1684." *Ethnohistory* 17, nos. 3–4 (Summer–Fall 1970): 95–116.

———. "Southern Periphery: East." In *Southwest*, edited by Alfonso Ortiz, 329–42. *Handbook of Northern American Indians*, vol. 10. Washington, DC: Smithsonian Institution, 1983.

Gutiérrez, Ramón A. *When Jesus Came, the Corn Mothers Went Away: Marriage, Sexuality, and Power in New Mexico, 1500–1846*. Stanford: Stanford University Press, 1991.

Guy, Donna J., and Thomas E. Sheridan. "On Frontiers: The Northern and Southern Edges of the Spanish Empire in the Americas." In *Contested Grounds: Comparative Frontiers on the Northern and Southern Edges of the Spanish Empire*, edited by Donna J. Guy and Thomas E. Sheridan, 3–15. Tucson: University of Arizona Press, 1998.

Hackel, Steven W. *Children of Coyote, Missionaries of St. Francis: Indian-Spanish Relations in Colonial California, 1769–1850*. Chapel Hill: University of North Carolina Press for the Omohundro Institute of Early American History and Culture, 2005.

Hackett, Charles Wilson, ed. *Historical Documents relating to New Mexico, Nueva Vizcaya, and Approaches Thereto, to 1773*. 3 vols. Washington, DC: Carnegie Institution, 1923–1937.

———. ed. *Pichardo's Treatise on the Limits of Louisiana and Texas*. 4 vols. Austin: University of Texas Press, 1931–1946.

Hackett, Charles Wilson, ed., and Charmion Clair Shelby, trans. *Revolt of the Pueblo Indians of New Mexico and Otermin's Attempted Reconquest, 1680–1682*. 2 vols. Albuquerque: University of New Mexico Press, 1942.

Hadley, Diana, Thomas H. Naylor, and Mardith K. Schuetz-Miller, eds. *The Presidio and Militia on the Northern Frontier of New Spain: A Documentary History*. Vol. 2, part 2: *The Central Corridor and the Texas Corridor, 1700–1765*. Tucson: University of Arizona Press, 1997.

Hammond, George P., and Agapito Rey, ed. and trans. *Obregón's History of 16th Century Explorations in Western America*. Los Angeles: Wetzel Publishing Company, 1928.

———. *The Rediscovery of New Mexico, 1580–1594: The Explorations of Chamuscado, Espejo, Castaño de Sosa, Morlete, and Leyva de Bonilla and Humaña*. Albuquerque: University of New Mexico Press, 1966.

Hedrick, Basil C., and Carroll L. Riley, eds. *The Journey of the Vaca Party: The Account of the Narváez Expedition, 1528–1536, as related by Gonzalo Fernández de Oviedo y Valdés*. Carbondale, IL: University Museum, Southern Illinois University, 1974.

Hendricks, Rick, and Gerald Mandell. "The Apache Slave Trade in Parral, 1637–1679." *Journal of Big Bend Studies* 16 (2004): 59–81.

Hickerson, Nancy Parrott. *The Jumanos: Hunters and Traders of the South Plains*. Austin: University of Texas Press, 1994.

Hodge, Frederick Webb. *History of Hawikuh, New Mexico: One of the So-Called Cities of Cíbola*. Los Angeles: The Southwest Museum, 1937.

Hodge, Frederick Webb, George P. Hammond, and Agapito Rey, eds. *Fray Alonso de Benavides' Revised Memorial of 1634, with Numerous Supplementary Documents Elaborately Annotated*. Albuquerque: University of New Mexico Press, 1945.

Hodge, Frederick Webb, and Charles Fletcher Lummis, eds. *The Memorial of Fray Alonso de Benavides, 1630*. Trans. Mrs. Edward E. Ayer. Albuquerque: Horn and Wallace, 1965.

Hu-DeHart, Evelyn. *Missionaries, Miners and Indians: Spanish Contact with the*

Yaqui Nation of Northwestern New Spain, 1533–1820. Tucson: University of Arizona Press, 1981.

Hughes, Anne E. *The Beginnings of Spanish Settlement in the El Paso District.* Berkeley: University of California Press, 1914.

Imhoff, Brian, ed. *The Diary of Juan Domínguez de Mendoza's Expedition into Texas (1683–1684): A Critical Edition of the Spanish Text with Facsimile Reproductions.* Dallas: William P. Clements Center for Southwest Studies, Southern Methodist University, 2002.

Ing, J. David, and Sheron Smith-Savage. "Culture History." In *Archaeological Reconaissance on Big Bend Ranch State Park, Presidio and Brewster Counties, Texas, 1988–1994,* by J. David Ing, Sheron Smith-Savage, William A. Cloud, and Robert J. Mallouf (Alpine, TX: Center for Big Bend Studies, Sul Ross State University, 1996), 25–72.

Jackson, Jack, and William C. Foster, eds. *Imaginary Kingdom: Texas as Seen by the Rivera and Rubí Military Expeditions, 1727 and 1767.* Austin: Texas State Historical Association, 1995.

Jackson, Robert H., and Edward Castillo. *Indians, Franciscans, and Spanish Colonization: The Impact of the Mission System on California Indians.* Albuquerque: University of New Mexico Press, 1995.

John, Elizabeth A. H. "Spanish-Indian Relations in the Big Bend Region during the Eighteenth and Early Nineteenth Centuries." *Journal of Big Bend Studies* 3 (1991): 71–80.

———. *Storms Brewed in Other Men's Worlds: The Confrontation of Indians, Spanish, and French in the Southwest, 1540–1793.* College Station: Texas A&M University Press, 1975.

Jones, Oakah L., Jr. *Nueva Vizcaya: Heartland of the Spanish Frontier.* Albuquerque: University of New Mexico Press, 1988.

———. "Settlements and Settlers at La Junta de los Rios, 1759–1822." *Journal of Big Bend Studies* 3 (1991): 43–70.

Kelley, J. Charles. "Archaeological Notes on the Excavation of a Pithouse near Presidio, Texas." *El Palacio* 46, no 10 (October 1939): 221–34.

———. "Archaeological Notes on Two Excavated House Structures in Western Texas." *Bulletin of the Texas Archaeological and Paleontological Society* 20 (1949): 89–114.

———. "A Bravo Valley Aspect Component of the Lower Rio Conchos Valley, Chihuahua, Mexico." *American Antiquity* 17, no. 2 (1951): 114–19.

———. "Factors Involved in the Abandonment of Certain Peripheral Southwestern Settlements." *American Anthropologist* 54, no. 3 (July 1952): 356–87.

———. "The Historic Indian Pueblos of La Junta de los Rios." *New Mexico Historical Review* 27, no. 4 (October 1952): 256–95; 28, no. 1 (January

1953): 20–51. Facsimile reprint in David H. Snow, ed., *Native American II: Introduction to the Research*: 117–93.

———. "Juan Sabeata and Diffusion in Aboriginal Texas." *American Anthropologist* 57, no. 5 (1955): 981–95. Facsimile reprint in David H. Snow, ed., *Native American II: Introduction to the Research*: 195–209.

———. *Jumano and Patarabueye: Relations at La Junta de los Rios*. Anthropological Papers no. 77. Ann Arbor: Museum of Anthropology, University of Michigan, 1986.

———. "A Review of the Architectural Sequence at La Junta de los Rios." *Proceedings of the Third Jornada-Mogollon Conference*, edited by Michael S. Foster and Thomas C. O'Laughlin, *The Artifact* 23, nos. 1–2 (1985): 149–59.

———. "The Rio Conchos Drainage: History, Archaeology, Significance." *Journal of Big Bend Studies* 2 (1990): 29–41.

Kelley, J. Charles, and Ellen Abbott Kelley. "Presidio, Texas (Presidio County) Water Improvement Project: An Archaeological and Archival Survey and Appraisal." Fort Davis, TX: Blue Mountain Consultants, 1990.

Kenmotsu, Nancy Adele. "Helping Each Other Out: A Study of the Mutualistic Relations of Small Scale Foragers and Cultivators in La Junta de los Rios Region, Texas and Mexico." PhD diss., University of Texas at Austin, 1994.

———. "Jornada Connections: Viewing the Jornada from La Junta de los Rios." In *Late Prehistoric Hunter-Gatherers and Farmers of the Jornada Mogollon*, edited by Thomas R. Rocek and Nancy A. Kenmotsu, 177–203. Louisville: University Press of Colorado, 2018.

———. "Seeking Friends, Avoiding Enemies: The Jumano Response to Spanish Colonization, A.D. 1580–1750." *Bulletin of the Texas Archaelogical Society* 72 (2001): 23–43.

Kessell, John L. *Friars, Soldiers, and Reformers: Hispanic Arizona and the Sonora Mission Frontier, 1767–1856*. Tucson: University of Arizona Press, 1976.

———. *Kiva, Cross, and Crown: The Pecos Indians and New Mexico, 1540–1840*. Washington, DC: National Park Service, U.S. Department of the Interior, 1979.

———. *Mission of Sorrows: Jesuit Guevavi and the Pimas, 1691–1767*. Tucson: University of Arizona Press, 1970.

———. *The Missions of New Mexico since 1776*. Albuquerque: University of New Mexico Press for the Cultural Properties Review Committee, 1980.

———. *Pueblos, Spaniards, and the Kingdom of New Mexico*. Norman: University of Oklahoma Press, 2008.

———. *Spain in the Southwest: A Narrative History of Colonial New Mexico, Arizona, Texas, and California*. Albuquerque: University of New Mexico Press, 2002.

Kessell, John L., and Rick Hendricks, eds. *By Force of Arms: The Journals of Don Diego de Vargas, 1691–1693*. Albuquerque: University of New Mexico

Press, 1992.

Kinnaird, Lawrence. *The Frontiers of New Spain: Nicolás de la Fora's Description.* Berkeley: Quivira Society, 1958.

La Historia Eclesiástica y Civil de la Nueva Vizcaya, 1554–1831. Durango: Editorial de la Universidad Juárez del Estado de Durango, 2009.

Lehmer, Donald J. "The Jornada Branch of the Mogollon." *University of Arizona Bulletin* 19, no. 2 (April 1948).

Lister, Florence C., and Robert H. Lister. *Chihuahua: Storehouse of Storms.* Albuquerque: University of New Mexico Press, 1966.

Luján, Diego Pérez de. *Relación de la expedición de Antonio de Espejo a Nuevo México, 1582–1583.* Transcribed by Jerry R. Craddock, revised by Barbara De Marco. Berkeley: Cíbola Project, Research Center for Romance Studies, Institute of International Studies, University of California, 2013. http://escholarship.org/uc/item/5313v23h?query=espejo.

Maas, Otto, O.F.M., ed. *Misiones de Nuevo Méjico: Documentos del Archivo General de Indias (Sevilla).* Madrid: Imprenta Hijos de T. Minuesa de los Ríos, 1929.

———. *Las órdenes religiosas de España y la colonización de América en la segunda parte del siglo XVIII: estadísticas y otros documentos.* Vol. 2. Barcelona: A. G. Belart, 1929.

Madrid, Enrique Rede, trans. *Expedition to La Junta de los Ríos, 1747–1748: Captain Commander Joseph de Ydoiaga's Report to the Viceroy of New Spain.* Austin: Texas Historical Commission, 1992.

———. "The Lost Mission of El Polvo: Searching for the History of a State Archeological Landmark." *Journal of Big Bend Studies* 15 (2003): 55–68.

Mallouf, Robert J. "Comments on the Prehistory of Far Northeastern Chihuahua, the La Junta District, and the Cielo Complex." *Journal of Big Bend Studies* 11 (1999): 49–92.

———. "Late Archaic Foragers of Eastern Trans-Pecos Texas and the Big Bend." In *The Late Archaic across the Borderlands: From Foraging to Farming,* edited by Bradley J. Vierra, 219–46. Austin: University of Texas Press, 2005.

———. "A Synthesis of Eastern Trans-Pecos Prehistory." MA thesis, University of Texas at Austin, 1985.

Martin, Cheryl English. *Governance and Society in Colonial Mexico: Chihuahua in the Eighteenth Century.* Stanford: Stanford University Press, 1996.

McCarty, Kieran. *A Spanish Frontier in the Enlightened Age: Franciscan Beginnings in Sonora and Arizona, 1767–1770.* Washington, DC: Academy of American Franciscan History, 1981.

Mendoza Magallanes, Victor. *Riegos en la Nueva Vizcaya.* Chihuahua: Gobierno del Estado de Chihuahua, Comité de Planeación para el Desarrollo, y Asociación Agrícola Local de Camargo; [México, D.F.]: SEP, Programa Cultural de

Fronteras, 1989.

Merrill, William L. "Conversion and Colonialism in Northern Mexico: The Tarahumara Response to the Jesuit Mission Program, 1601–1767." In *Conversion to Christianity: Historical and Anthropological Perspectives on a Great Transformation*, edited by Robert W. Hefner, 129–63. Berkeley: University of California Press, 1993.

Miller, Myles R., and Nancy A. Kenmotsu. "Prehistory of the Jornada Mogollon and Eastern Trans-Pecos Regions of West Texas." In *The Prehistory of Texas*, edited by Timothy K. Pettula, 203–65. College Station: Texas A&M University Press, 2004.

Montgomery, Ross. "San Bernardo de Aguatubi, An Analytical Restoration." In *Franciscan Awatovi: The Excavation and Conjectural Reconstruction of a 17-Century Spanish Mission Establishment at a Hopi Indian Town in Northeastern Arizona*, by Ross Gordon Montgomery, Watson Smith, and John Otis Brew, 111–288. Papers of the Peabody Museum of American Archaeology and Ethnology, Harvard University, vol. XXXVI. Cambridge: Peabody Museum of American Archaeology and Ethnology, 1949.

Moorhead, Max L. *The Apache Frontier: Jacobo Ugarte and Spanish-Indian Relations in Northern New Spain, 1769–1791*. Norman: University of Oklahoma Press, 1968.

———. *The Presidio: Bastion of the Spanish Borderlands*. Norman: University of Oklahoma Press, 1975.

Morales, Francisco, O.F.M. *Inventario del Fondo Franciscano del Archivo Histórico de la Bibliotéca Nacional de Antropología e Historia*. Vol. 2. Washington, DC: Academy of American Franciscan History, 2008.

———. *Inventario del Fondo Franciscano del Museo de Antropología e Historia de México*. Vol. 1. Washington, DC: Academy of American Franciscan History, 1978.

Morales Natera, Francisco Javier. *Coyame Es Mi Pueblo*. Traducido por Janet Morales Arenivas. N.p.: Xlibris Corporation, 2012.

Moreno, Roberto. "Viajes de Fray Juan Agustín de Morfi." In *Anuario de Historia* (UNAM, Mexico), años VI–VII (1966–67): 171–98.

Morfi, Juan Agustín de. *History of Texas, 1673–1779*. Trans. and ed. Carlos Eduardo Castañeda. 2 vols. Albuquerque: The Quivira Society, 1935.

———. *Viaje de Indios y Diario del Nuevo México*. Edited by Vito Alessio Robles. México, D.F.: Manuel Porrúa, 1980.

Morgenthaler, Jefferson. *La Junta de los Rios: The Life, Death and Resurrection of an Ancient Desert Community in the Big Bend Region of Texas*. Boerne, TX: Mockingbird Books, 2007.

———. *The River Has Never Divided Us: A Border History of La Junta de los Rios*.

Austin: University of Texas Press, 2004.

Navarro García, Luis. *Don José de Gálvez y la Comandancia General de las Provincias Internas del Norte de Nueva España*. Sevilla: Consejo Superior de Investigaciones Científicas, 1964.

———. *Sonora y Sinaloa en el Siglo XVII*. México, D.F.: Siglo Veintiuno, 1992; 1st ed. Sevilla: Escuela de Estudios Hispano-Americanos, 1967, with different pagination.

Naylor, Thomas H., and Charles W. Polzer, eds. *Pedro de Rivera and the Military Regulations for Northern New Spain, 1724–1729*. Tucson: University of Arizona Press, 1988.

Newcomb, W. W., Jr. *The Indians of Texas: From Prehistoric to Modern Times*. Austin: University of Texas Press, 1961.

Norris, Jim. *After "The Year Eighty": The Demise of Franciscan Power in Spanish New Mexico*. Albuquerque: University of New Mexico Press in cooperation with the Academy of American Franciscan History, 2000.

Núñez Cabeza de Vaca, Álvar. *Naufragios y comentarios*. México: Editorial Porrúa, 1988.

Ocaranza, Fernando. *Crónica de las Provincias Internas de la Nueva España*. México: Polis, 1939.

———. *Establecimientos franciscanos en el misterioso Reino de Nuevo México*. México, D.F., 1934.

O'Crouley, Pedro Alonso. *A Description of the Kingdom of New Spain, 1774*. Translated and edited by Sean Galvin. N.p.: John Howell Books, 1972.

Officer, James E. *Hispanic Arizona, 1536–1856*. Tucson: University of Arizona Press, 1987.

Ortelli, Sara. *Trama de una guerra conveniente: Nueva Vizcaya y la sombra de los apaches (1748–1790)*. México, D.F.: Centro de Estudios Históricos, El Colegio de México, 2007.

Osante, Patricia. *Orígenes del Nuevo Santander (1748–1772)*. México, D.F.: Universidad Nacional Autónoma de Mexico / Universidad Autónoma de Tamaulipas, 1997.

Pacheco, Jaime, and Le Roy Anthony Reaza. "A Case of Mistaken Identity: The Forgotten Manuscript of Juan Antonio de Trasviña y Retes's Expedition into La Junta de los Rios and West Texas in 1715." *New Mexico Historical Review* 94, no. 2 (April 2019): 169–91.

Palladini, Eric Louis, Jr. "Making Fortunes on the Frontier of Enemies: The Agrarian Economy of San Felipe de Real de Chihuahua, 1709–1831." PhD diss., Tulane University, 2000.

Pennington, Campbell W. "Tarahumara." In *Southwest*, edited by Alfonso Ortiz, 276–89. *Handbook of North American Indians*, vol. 10. Washington, DC:

Smithsonian Institution, 1983.

Pérez de Ribas, Andrés, S.J. *Historia de los Triunfos de N.S. Fe entre gentes los más bárbaros y fieras del Nuevo orbe.* 3 vols. México, D.F.: Editorial Layac, 1944.

Porras Muñoz, Guillermo. *Iglesia y Estado en Nueva Vizcaya (1562–1821).* México: Universidad Nacional Autónoma de México, 1980.

Portillo, Esteban L. *Apuntes para la historia Antigua de Coahuila y Texas.* Saltillo: Biblioteca de la Universidad Autónoma de Coahuila, 1984.

Powell, Philip Wayne. *Soldiers, Indians, and Silver: The Northward Advance of New Spain, 1550–1600.* Berkeley: University of California Press, 1952.

Radding, Cynthia. "Colonial Spaces in the Fragmented Communities of Northern New Spain." In *Contested Spaces of Early America*, edited by Juliana Barr and Edward Countryman, 115–41. Philadelphia: University of Pennsylvania Press, 2014.

———. *Wandering Peoples: Colonialism, Ethnic Spaces, and Ecological Frontiers in Northwestern Mexico, 1700–1830.* Durham, NC: Duke University Press, 1997.

Reff, Daniel T. *Disease, Depopulation, and Culture Change in Northwestern New Spain, 1518–1764.* Salt Lake City: University of Utah Press, 1991.

Reindorp, Reginald C., trans. *The Founding of the Missions at La Junta de los Rios.* Austin: Texas Catholic Historical Society, 1938.

Reséndez, Andrés. *A Land So Strange: The Epic Journey of Cabeza de Vaca.* New York: Basic Books, 2007.

———. *The Other Slavery: The Uncovered Story of Indian Enslavement in America.* Boston/New York: Houghton Mifflin Harcourt, 2016.

Revilla Gigedo, Conde de. *Informe sobre las Misiones, 1793, e Instrucción Reservada al Marqués de Branciforte, 1794*, edited by José Bravo Ugarte. México: Editorial Jus, 1966.

Rock, Rosalind Z. "Nuestra Señora de Guadalupe Mission." *The New Handbook of Texas*, vol. 4, edited by Ron Tyler et al., 1065–66. Austin: Texas State Historical Association, 1996.

Rubio Mañé, J. Ignacio. *Introducción al Estudio de los Virreyes de Nueva España, 1535–1746*, III: *Expansión y Defensa*, 2 vols. México, D.F.: Universidad Nacional Autónoma de México, 1961.

Santiago, Mark. "'An Illustrious Victory': Hugo O'Conor's Battle with the Apaches in the Davis Mountains." *Journal of Big Bend Studies* 30 (2018): 103–19.

———. *The Red Captain: The Life of Hugo O'Conor, Commandant Inspector of the Interior Provinces of New Spain.* Museum Monograph No. 9. N.p.: The Arizona Historical Society, 1994.

Scholes, France V. *Church and State in New Mexico, 1610–1650.* Albuquerque: University of New Mexico Press, 1937.

———. *Troublous Times in New Mexico, 1659-1670.* Albuquerque: University of

New Mexico Press, 1942.

"Settler Colonialism in Early American History." *William and Mary Quarterly*, 3d ser., 76, no. 3 (July 2019).

Shackelford, William J. "Excavations at the Polvo Site in Western Texas." *American Antiquity* 20, no. 3 (1955): 256–62.

Sheridan, Cecilia. *Anónimos y desterrados: La contienda por el "sitio que llaman de Quauyla", siglos XVI–XVIII*. Mexico, D.F.: Centro de Investigaciones y Estudios Superiores en Antropología Social / Miguel Ángel Porrúa, 2000.

———. *El "yugo suave del evangelio": Las misiones franciscanas de Rio Grande en el periodo colonial*. Saltillo: Centro de Estudios Sociales y Humanísticos, 1999.

Sheridan, Thomas E., Stewart B. Koyiyumptewa, Anton Daughters, Dale S. Brenneman, T. J. Ferguson, Leigh Kumanwisiwma, and Lee Wayne Lomayestewa, eds. *Moquis and Kastiilam: Hopis, Spaniards, and the Trauma of History, Volume I, 1540–1679*. Tucson: University of Arizona Press, 2015.

Sheridan, Thomas E., and Thomas H. Naylor, eds. *Rarámuri: A Tarahumara Colonial Chronicle, 1607–1791*. Flagstaff, AZ: Northland Press, 1979.

Simmons, Marc. "History of Pueblo-Spanish Relations to 1821." In *Southwest*, edited by Alfonso Ortiz, *Handbook of North American Indians*, vol. 9, 178–93. Washington, DC: Smithsonian Institution, 1979.

———. *Spanish Government in New Mexico*. 2nd ed. Albuquerque: University of New Mexico Press, 1990.

Snow, David H., ed. *The Native American and Spanish Colonial Experience in the Greater Southwest. I: Introduction to the Documentary Records*. Spanish Borderlands Sourcebooks, vol. 10. New York: Garland Publishing, 1992.

———. ed. *The Native American and Spanish Colonial Experience in the Greater Southwest. II: Introduction to the Research*. Spanish Borderlands Sourcebooks, vol. 9. New York: Garland Publishing, 1992

———. "A Note on Encomienda Economics in Seventeenth-Century New Mexico." In *Hispanic Arts and Ethnohistory in the Southwest*, edited by Marta Weigle, Claudia Larcombe, and Samuel Larcombe, 347–57. Santa Fe: Ancient City Press, 1983. Facsimile reprint in David H. Snow, ed., *Native American II: Introduction to the Research*: 469–79.

Sonnichsen, C. L. *Pass of the North: Four Centuries on the Rio Grande*. El Paso: Texas Western Press, 1968.

Spicer, Edward H. *Cycles of Conquest: The Impact of Spain, Mexico, and the United States on the Indians of the Southwest, 1533–1960*. Tucson: University of Arizona Press, 1962.

———. *The Yaquis: A Cultural History*. Tucson: University of Arizona Press, 1980.

Stern, Peter. "Marginals and Acculturation in Frontier Society." In *New Views of Borderlands History*, edited by Robert H. Jackson, 157–88. Albuquerque:

University of New Mexico Press, 1998.

Tamarón y Romeral, Pedro. "Viajes pastorales y descripción de la Diócesis de Nueva Vizcaya," edited by Mario Hernández y Sánchez-Barba, in *Viajes por Norteamérica*, edited by Manuel Ballesteros Gaibrois, 947–1062. Madrid: Aguilar, 1958.

Thomas, Alfred Barnaby, trans. and ed. *Alonso de Posada Report, 1686: A Description of the Area of the Present Southern United States in the Late Seventeenth Century.* Vol. 4, Spanish Borderlands Series. Pensacola: Perdido Bay Press, 1982.

———. trans. and ed. *Forgotten Frontiers: A Study of the Spanish Indian Policy of Don Juan Bautista de Anza, Governor of New Mexico, 1777–1787.* Norman: University of Oklahoma Press, 1932.

———. trans. and ed. *Teodoro de Croix and the Northern Frontier of New Spain, 1776–1783.* Norman: University of Oklahoma Press, 1941.

Timmons, W. H. *El Paso: A Borderlands History.* El Paso: Texas Western Press, 1990.

Velázquez, María del Carmen. *El Marqués de Altamira y las provincias internas de Nueva España.* México, D.F.: Colegio de México, 1976.

Vetancurt, Agustín de. *Teatro Mexicano.* 2a ed. facsimilar. México: Editorial Porrúa, 1982.

Villaseñor y Sanchez, Joseph Antonio. *Theatro Americano: descripcion general de los Reynos y Provincias de la Nueva España y sus jurisdicciones.* 2 vols. Mexico: Imprenta de la Viuda de D. Joseph Bernardo de Hogal, 1746–1748.

Wade, Maria F. *The Native Americans of the Texas Edwards Plateau, 1582–1799.* Austin: University of Texas Press, 2003.

Walz, Vina. "History of the El Paso Area 1680–1692." PhD diss., University of New Mexico, 1951. https://digitalrepository.unm.edu/hist_etds/249.

Ware, John A. *A Pueblo Social History: Kinship, Sodality, and Community in the Northern Southwest.* Santa Fe: School for Advanced Research Press, 2014.

Weber, David J. *Bárbaros: Spaniards and Their Savages in the Age of Enlightenment.* New Haven: Yale University Press, 2005.

———. *The Spanish Frontier in North America.* New Haven: Yale University Press, 1992.

———. "Turner, the Boltonians, and the Borderlands." In *Myth and the History of the Hispanic Southwest*, 33–53. Albuquerque: University of New Mexico Press, 1988.

Weddle, Robert S. *Wilderness Manhunt: The Spanish Search for La Salle.* Austin: University of Texas Press, 1973.

West, Elizabeth Howard. "The Right of Asylum in New Mexico in the Seventeenth and Eighteenth Centuries." *New Mexico Historical Review* 41, no. 2 (April

1966): 115–53.

West, Robert C. *The Mining Community in Northern New Spain: The Parral Mining District*. Ibero-Americana 30. Berkeley: University of California Press, 1949.

———. *Sonora: Its Geographical Personality*. Austin: University of Texas Press, 1993.

Wheat, Carl I. *Mapping the Transmississippi West*, vol. 1: *The Spanish Entrada to the Louisiana Purchase, 1540–1804*. San Francisco: The Institute of Historical Cartography, 1957.

Worcester, Donald E. "The Beginnings of the Apache Menace of the Southwest." *New Mexico Historical Review* 16, no. 1 (January 1941): 1–14.

Wright, Robert E. "Latino American Religion: Catholics, Colonial Origins." In *Encyclopedia of Religion in America*, vol. 3, edited by Charles H. Lippy and Peter W. Williams, 1173–78. Washington, DC: CQ Press, 2010.

———. "The Native Mission Site at Polvo." *Journal of Big Bend Studies* 31 (2019): 167–77.

———. "The People of La Junta in 1750: A Census." *Journal of Big Bend Studies* 29 (2017): 21–38.

———. "Spanish Missions." In *The Handbook of Texas Online*, Texas State Historical Association, https://tshaonline.org/handbook/online/articles/its02, accessed 22 November 2018.

Index

Abadiano, Manuel Ysidoro (fray): biography, 295n37; in entry of Hidalgo detachment to La Junta, 175–80; he and Sanz de Lezáun left alone at La Junta, 177–78; flees to Chihuahua, 180; in Rubín de Celís entry attempt, 183; in expedition by Muñoz and Leizaola, 185, 187, 188; stationed at San Francisco, 189; contests the site of the presidio founding, 189–90; remains at La Junta until 1766, 198–200, 201, 209; meets with Bishop Tamarón and Zacatecan custos in Santa Ysabel, 204

Abriaches, language different from Otomoacos but they understand each other, 23. *See also* San Juan Evangelista; Santiago; Santo Tomás

Acevedo, Antonio (fray): biography, 51; and first mission at La Junta, 49, 51, 52–53, 54; flight from La Junta, 57, 251n36

Aguirre, Joseph de: Chihuahuan leader of rescue expedition to La Junta, 108–11; withdraws promise to support Hispanic settlement at La Junta, 112

Altamira, Juan Rodríguez de Albuerne, Marqués de: military advisor (auditor) to viceroy, 125; obtains approval for military inspection of frontier, 130; campaign for reduction of presidios, 125, 145, 152, 155, 168; advocates presidio near but not at La Junta, 155; list of missions, 276–77n1

Amesti (Amestigui), Joachin (fray): at Guadalupe in third founding of La Junta missions, 117–19, 121; injured and returns to Mexico City, 120

Anasazi-Mogollon culture, 110: La Junta as last outlier of, 12; religious gestures, 19

Anderson, Gary: history of La Junta, 228n5, 240n67; Native autonomy in northeastern Nueva Vizcaya, 241n5

Apaches: slaves in Nueva Vizcaya, 250n26; push into Edwards Plateau area, 32, 247n5; failed target of Domínguez expedition, 53; rare visitors at La Junta in 1715, 83; trading at La Junta, 84, 136–37, 140, 262n33; raiders in Nueva Vizcaya, 125; those raiding in Coahuila trading at La Junta, 137; Altamira orders that all be settled in towns or made captive, 155, 283n21; increased raiding in Nueva Vizcaya in 1750s–1760s, 145, 169, 172, 286n54; overtures of settlement at presidio with Julimeño assistance, 213

Alonzo Baptizado: resident at Púliques, 136; ally of Juntans opposing the presidio, 197

Don Pascual: frequent trader at La Junta, 136; compadre of Berroterán, 136, 143; his family baptized, 278n19; arrives to trade during Hidalgo detachment presence, 176; ally of Juntans opposing the presidio, 197

El Lijero: occasional trading at Púliques, 136; numbers, 278n17; obtains safe-conduct from Ydoiaga, 136; ally of Juntans opposing the presidio, 197

Lipanes, dominant in territory between Nueva Vizcaya and Coahuila in 1760s, 213

Mescaleros, dominant in territory between Nueva Vizcaya and Coahuila in 1760s, 213

Natagés: description, 136; traders at La Junta, 136; some allegedly from Julimes are briefly settled at San Yldefonso in Coahuila, 202; arrive to trade during Hidalgo detachment presence brandishing firearms, 176–77, 289nn10–11; ally of Juntans opposing the presidio, 197

present for patronal feast, 163, 164; camp of Hidalgo detachment in 1759, 175–77; several trading Apache nations unhappy at soldier presence (*see groups under* Apaches); people flee at entry of troops, 189; some conquered returnees but other families still fugitive, 203; abandoned in 1772, 212; Ojinaga today, 40

Hediondos, plot against friars at Púliques, 64
Hickerson, Nancy, on La Junta as a trade center, 231n10
Hidalgo, Juan, commander of detachment sent to La Junta in 1759, 175–78
Hinojosa, Joaquín de (fray): biography, 59, 254n47; at La Junta, 59–60, 64, 255n62; protected by Púliques, 64
Hispanics: definition, 228n6; non-missionary in La Junta valley, 6, 108, 138
Holy Gospel Province (Franciscan): history, 50; San Pablo Custody as regional unit, 50
Hopis, comparison with La Junta, 7, 222–23

Jones, Oakah, on presidio founding at La Junta, 288n6, 291n40
Joseph el Cíbolo: general allied with Juntan insurgents, 201; killed when refuses to surrender, 202
Juan Cantor (Juntan): slave captive, 17; interpreter for Chamuscado expedition, 17; intermediary at San Bernardino, 23
Juan Cíbolo (Síbula): plotter against La Junta missions, 103, 104; spy for belligerents in 1726 uprising, 110–11
Julimeños: term used by 1767 for principally Juntan Natives at Carrizo in Coahuila, 208, 294n34; scouts for Spanish military, 208, 215; Apaches' hope for Julimeño assistance to settle at La Junta, 213; viewed as enemies by higher officials, 214, 216; Morfi positive view in 1778, 214–15; positive description by missionary leader in 1786, 215. *See also* Carrizo, Vizarrón
Julimes (nation): location, 32, 37, 50; early history, 37; description, 38; joined 1645 uprising, 37–38; joined 1684 uprising,

57; noted as scouts by La Fora, 294n34; no Julimes at Julimes in 1778 but some at nearby San Pablo, 213, 297n54
Julimes (town), San Antonio de: history, 37–38, 206–8; alleged source of ladino deserters (Natagés and Cíbolos) at San Yldefonso in Coahuila, 202; Juntans moved to Julimes in 1766 soon fled, 211
Jumanos: distinguished from Juntans by Kelley, 29; physically like Patarabueyes, 26; above the Davis Mountains, 26; pressured by Apaches, 32; at La Junta, 50; and Domínguez expedition, 48, 53; in first Retana campaign with Cíbolos, 65, 67; Native religion, 233n20; recognition of Jumano Indian Nation of Texas, 256n67
Juntan nations, 56–57, 251n35. *See also* Abriaches, Cacalotes, Cíbolos, Cholomes, Conchos, Conejos, Mezquites, Oposmes, Otomoacos, Patarabueyes, Pescados, Pocsalmes, Polacmes, Púliques, Tapacolmes
Juntans (people). *See also* La Junta district towns; Norteños
autonomy: 75, 103, 122, 138, 181, 214; described by distant government officials after 1748 as hostility, 152–53, 155, 165, 167
and Catholicism: baptized and catechized, 51, 81, 85, 118; celebrate patronal feasts, 140, 162–63; described as Christians in name only by distant officials after 1748, 152, 165; hear Mass, 139; ignorance of Christian obligations, 92; lacking Christian life, 98, 103; married in the Church, 73, 81; a strong convert, 73
dispersal: to lower San Pedro river district, 101, 206; to Chihuahua district, 154, 157, 209; to Coahuila, 206, 208. *See also* Julimes (town); Julimeños; Vizarrón; Santa Cruz de Tapacolmes; Tapacolmes (Juntans)
at La Junta: kinship-based society, 13, 77, 91, 232n19, 259n16; Native governor as *gobernadorcillo*, 43, 189, 291n43; permanent residents, 3, 12–13, 18, 24; private landholding, 134; Spanish

174; entry of Hidalgo detachment in 1759, 175–77; entry attempt by Rubín de Celís, 183; entry by Muñoz and Leizaola, 185–89; founding of presidio, 189–90, 193–94, 291n42; presidio construction, 199–200, 293n16; attack on presidio, 201; population in 1762, 209; presidio and Juntans moved to Julimes in 1766, 210; woodwork all burned in abandoned site, 212; Julimes troops reinstalled at La Junta in 1773, 212; no Juntans in Presidio del Norte sacramental records, 296n53; later history, 296n51. See also Nuestra Señora de Bethlem; Presidio del Norte Nueva Vizcaya: Reglamento reduction of military forces and funds, 115, 271nn42–43; Altamira campaign for reduction of presidios (see Altamira); governor proposal to lessen presidios on eastern corridor, 152; 1751 elimination of the five eastern presidios, founding of one at Guajoquilla, "temporary" placing of troops destined for Pilares at Aguanueva, 168

Pueblito, San Antonio de: probably San Pedro site, 177, 289n12; Hidalgo detachment withdraws there, 177; mission with visita of Cuchillo Parado in 1759, 183. See also San Pedro (town)

Púliques (nation): resisted 1684 uprising, 56; protection of friars from Hediondos, 64

Púliques (town): Hediondos plot against friars, 64; Trasviña Retes expedition names San José, 82; population, 83, 133; also Cíbolo and Pescado residents in 1747, 133; called San Antonio in 1747, 134; people flee at entry of troops in 1759, 189; almost none return in 1760, 203; vacant in 1762, 209; abandoned in 1773, 212

Rábago y Terán, Pedro: governor of Coahuila, 136; inspection of La Junta, 136–37, 138–39

Ramírez, Andrés (Zacatecan friar): visits La Junta, 72–73; in founding of official missions at La Junta, 77, 79, 80, 81, 85

Rarámuri. See Tarahumaras

repartimiento. See under Native labor

Reséndez, Andrés, on Native labor as slavery, 242n18

Retana, Juan Fernández de: rescues missionaries, 57; campaigns along lower Río del Norte, 62, 66–67

Rio Conchos. See Conchos (river)

Rio del Norte: description, 3

Rio Grande: Rio del Norte in colonial period, 3; current border with Texas, 3

Rivera, Pedro de: military inspection tour of northern frontier, 112; advocates presidio at La Junta, 112; presidio founding at La Junta suspended, 112–13

Rodríguez, Agustín (fray), in Chamuscado expedition, 15, 18, 20

Rodríguez, Juan Mariano (fray), sent to La Junta in 1731, 117, 120

Rubí, Marqués de: comments on presidio move to Julimes, 210–11; recommendations for new line of presidios including return to La Junta, 211

Rubín de Celís, Alonso Victores: captain of El Paso presidio, 159; 1750 inspection tour of Rio del Norte, 159–64; finds multiethnic settlements in Coyame valley, 160; denigrates Juntans, 161, 162, 165; appointed captain to start presidio at Pilares, 168; attempts to found presidio at La Junta and removal as captain, 174–85 passim; blamed by Leizaola, 191

Saavedra, Lorenzo (fray): at San Francisco mission, 117–20, 124, 132; report on La Junta missions, 118–19; Inquisition commissioner for New Mexico, 123; memorandum on missionary conduct, 124; at times companionless at La Junta, 141; at La Junta during Ydoiaga visit, 131–32, 135, 139–42

Sabeata, Juan, Jumano leader: petition in El Paso, 48; ally in Domínguez expedition, 53, 250n27; leader of Cíbolos and Jumanos by 1688, 64; ally in Retana expedition, 65

Salaíces (Salaises), Juan de: same name as earlier hacienda owner, 54; rebels gather at

www.ingramcontent.com/pod-product-compliance
Lightning Source LLC
Chambersburg PA
CBHW020445100426
42812CB00036B/3463/J